Articles on
Russian and Soviet History
1500 – 1991

GENERAL EDITOR

Alexander Dallin
STANFORD UNIVERSITY

CONTRIBUTING EDITORS

Gary M. Hamburg
UNIVERSITY OF NOTRE DAME

Nancy Shields Kollmann
STANFORD UNIVERSITY

Gail W. Lapidus
UNIVERSITY OF CALIFORNIA AT BERKELEY

Daniel T. Orlovsky
SOUTHERN METHODIST UNIVERSITY

Bertrand M. Patenaude
KENNAN INSTITUTE

William Rosenberg
UNIVERSITY OF MICHIGAN AT ANN ARBOR

A Garland Series

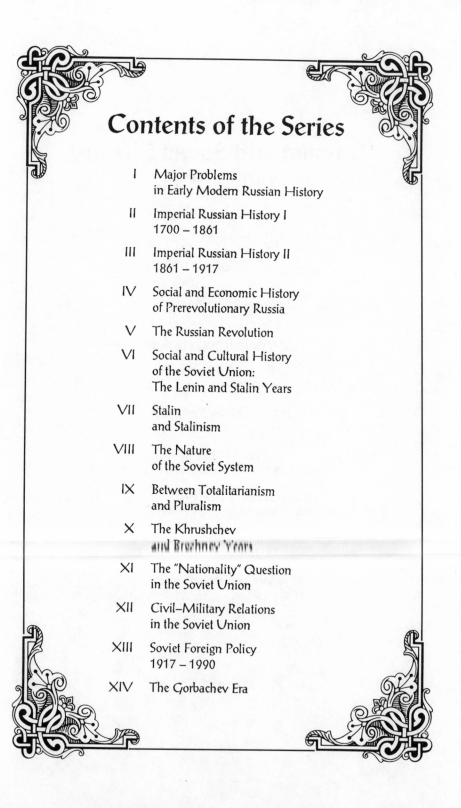

Contents of the Series

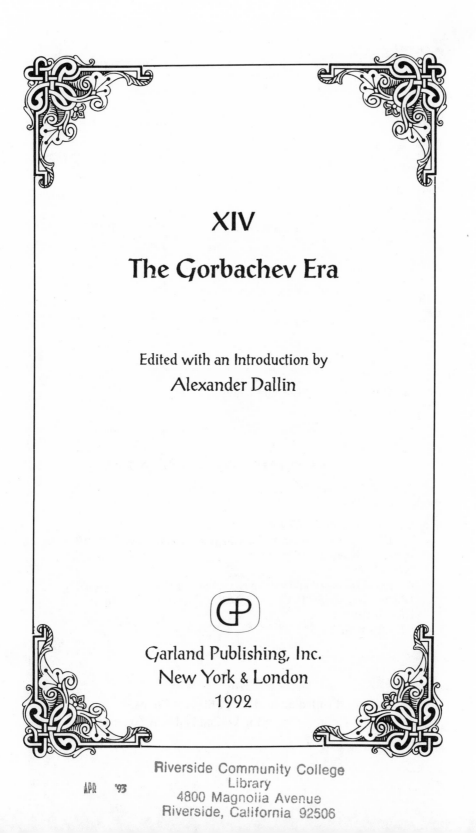

XIV

The Gorbachev Era

Edited with an Introduction by
Alexander Dallin

Garland Publishing, Inc.
New York & London
1992

Library of Congress Cataloging-in-Publication Data

The Gorbachev era / edited by Alexander Dallin.
        p.   cm.   (Articles on Russian and Soviet history, 1500-1991 ; v. 14)
Includes bibliographical references
ISBN 0-8153-0571-0
1. Soviet Union—Politics and government—1985–   2. Gorbachev,
Mikhail Sergeevich, 1931–   . I. Dallin, Alexander. II. Series.
DK288.G65   1992
947.085'4—dc20

                                                                    92-1190
                                                                    CIP

Printed on acid-free, 250-year-life paper
Manufactured in the United States of America

SERIES INTRODUCTION

The study of Russian (and Soviet) history has presented scholars, in and out of Russia, with multiple challenges. Some of these are among the problems that historians and social scientists share regardless of the area of their inquiry; the neglect, until recently, of social history and social problems, of attitudes and mindsets, as well as the relative scorn for regional, local, and interethnic history, is prominent among these commonalities.

Others stem more specifically from Russian and Soviet conditions. While there were a number of eminent Russian historians prior to the Revolutions of 1917, some aspects of the craft had lagged behind history as practiced in the West. But, far more significant, the Soviet era experienced the imposition of unprecedented controls, with disastrous consequences: stringent restrictions on access to primary source materials; rigorous management of politically acceptable and taboo topics and problem areas to investigate; a straightjacket of conformity with the dominant—indeed, the sole permissible—interpretation of events; and the training of generations of historians and social scientists in relative ignorance of certain earlier academic figures and their works and of intellectual developments abroad, and of course the impossibility of expressing any sympathy for their views. Certain subfields—for instance, intellectual history and comparative history other than along doctrinally prescribed lines—became virtually impossible to pursue. For the Soviet writer and reader, the historical landscape was littered with nonevents, nonideas, and nonpersons.[1]

Of course, in spite of all these constraints—beginning with the very existence of a mandatory official "general line"—the Soviet period witnessed a healthy growth of the number of professional historians and historical academic institutions (sociology and political science remained banned until recently, and the quality of works in economic history was a mixed bag at best) and of training in some politically "safe" subfields, such as paleography, as well as the organization of historical collections in parts of the Soviet Union where previously no archival depositories—especially in the indigenous languages and cultures—had existed.

And—such were the paradoxes of Soviet existence—in spite of all forms of censorship and prudential self-censorship, some scholars managed to publish occasional articles or chapters in which (usually after appropriate citations from the "classics of Marxism-Leninism") novel and unorthodox ideas or information were conveyed to the Soviet reader trained to read, as it were, between the lines.

It would be foolish to assert that this achievement negated the impact of Stalinist controls. Nor would it do to deny their diffuse impact on the study of Soviet history and society abroad. And the price for three generations of scholarship molded to fit the imperatives of doublethink and conformity, often in inevitable ignorance of alternative approaches, sources, and methodologies, will not soon be paid off.

To be sure, the situation has recently changed in fundamental ways. There is no more "party line." All topics, from the Norman theory of the origin of the Russian state to the alternatives—the "what might have been's"—to the October 1917 Revolution, from the problem of feudalism in Russia to the dynamics of legitimacy of the Soviet regime, are now openly and widely discussed. The spetskhrany—special library collections of presumably dangerous works that were not accessible to ordinary mortals—have been abolished. While it may take years to organize them and arrange access for interested scholars, Soviet archives (with some exceptions, one may assume) have been secured from destruction, and some day their holdings will presumably be available under normal conditions. Soviet scholars are increasingly interacting with colleagues abroad. And yet, assuming that such welcome and benign trends continue, even the optimists cannot expect the "situation on the historical front" to be soon or fully restored to normalcy, let alone transformed so as to produce a flourishing of original scholarship. Some fields—public opinion, attitudes and identities among non-Russian nationalities, the role of state security organs, or civil-military relations, for instance—remain difficult to investigate, particularly in a historical perspective.

Moreover, recent events have in turn added new analytical challenges: insofar as they do not fit into the Procrustean bed of previous interpretations (be it of inescapable totalitarianism, of the immutable impact of Muscovite political culture, or of the necessary translation of socioeconomic development into political dynamics), they demand serious and fundamental reconceptualizations.

Under these conditions, Western works on Russia and the Soviet Union, as well as studies published in fairly inaccessible or even obscure publications, assume relatively greater importance than they might otherwise. And yet, many students of Russian and Soviet history remain—through no fault of theirs—ignorant of some seminal works, some challenging intellectual controversies, and some valuable case studies. Many libraries in this country and abroad—let alone individual scholars—simply cannot acquire and maintain the sets of journals, the series of monographs, or the anthologies and conference volumes where such contributions have appeared.

It is with the hope of making available valuable articles and papers often neglected or forgotten that this series of volumes was conceived. The editors do not, of course, claim that the articles presented in these fourteen volumes adequately cover the totality of Russian and Soviet history; but it is our professional conviction that they supplement or modify in a significant way the sources and interpretations, the raw material, and the conceptualizations offered in standard book-length histories and texts.

In each instance the selections reproduced in this series are the choices of the individual volume editors, all of them leading American experts in their respective fields. In general, for reasons of convenience, we preferred to use English-language materials, though occasionally equally valid or valuable German or French contributions could have served. We were glad to include several articles by Soviet scholars, and it is our firm hope that over the next five or ten years their contributions will continue to increase in numbers as well as in quality.

I am delighted to thank the volume editors for their cheerful cooperation and for placing their superb knowledge at the service of this project. We are all grateful to Garland Publishing, Inc. and in particular to Carole Puccino for guiding this project over many shoals and barriers to successful completion. Among the Stanford graduate students in this field, Hillary Appel and Amy Weisman deserve particular appreciation for their research assistance.

Alexander Dallin

1. For some noteworthy discussions of the costs and conditions of Stalinist historical science, see Nancy Whittier Heer, Politics and History in the Soviet Union (MIT Press, 1971); Cyril E. Black, ed., Rewriting Russian History (2d ed., Viking, 1962); John Keep et al., Contemporary History in the Soviet Mirror (Praeger, 1964); Samuel Baron et al., Windows on the Russian Past: Essays on Soviet Historiography Since Stalin (AAASS, 1977); Hans Rogger, "Politics, Ideology and History in the USSR," Soviet Studies, January 1965; Lowell Tillett, The Great Friendship: Soviet Historians on the Non-Russian Nationalities (University of North Carolina Press, 1969); Konstantin Shteppa, Russian Historians and the Soviet State (Rutgers University Press, 1962); John Barber, Soviet Historians in Crisis, 1928–1932 (Macmillan Ltd., 1981); Donald Raleigh, ed., Soviet Historians and Perestroika (M. E. Sharpe, 1989).

INTRODUCTION

The years that followed Mikhail Gorbachev's accession to power witnessed fundamental, and generally unforeseen, changes in the Soviet system, in the structure and scope of the state itself, in the attitudes and behavior of the population, and in the policies pursued. The transition from the Brezhnev-era regime to the era of *perestroika* reached a major hiatus with the failed coup in August 1991 that provided the setting for the suspension of the Communist party and the disintegration of the Soviet Union itself. The years from 1985 to 1991 thus constitute a unit that merits scholarly attention and an effort to understand and explain the events in which they abounded.

One cluster of questions relates to the sources of change. In the selections reproduced in this volume, Moshe Lewin, Seweryn Bialer, and David Remnick deal with three different sets of factors that made possible the transitions. One deals with the transformation of Russia from a rural, semi-literate society to a predominantly urban one, with new values and aspirations. The second focuses on more direct, immediate political circumstances, economic constraints, and the "defense burden," as well as changes in technology and the international environment. Finally, the third seeks to identify some of the individuals whose ideas and insights made them "pioneers" of *perestroika*. Others may in the future wish to probe other causative variables, such as the impact of heightened interaction with the outside world in the preceding decade, and the role of corruption in the entire system. It will remain for future scholars to ponder how the structure of Stalinist controls could turn out to be so porous and the habits of obeisance so deceptively shallow as to permit as facile a disintegration as the country experienced in the Gorbachev years. Indeed, counterfactual history will no doubt explore whether other strategies of reform could have avoided the economic freefall or the ethnic explosion that ensued.

In their essays reproduced below, Thane Gustafson focuses on Gorbachev's political strategy in the early years, while Archie Brown carries the story of political change in the Soviet Union further in time, with Gorbachev and his cohort seemingly successful in skillfully disposing of one challenger after another. Thomas Remington deals with the issue of "pluralism of opinion," and Alexander Dallin examines the changes in the treatment of Soviet history in the same years—

in both instances, fundamental challenges to orthodox Stalinist theory and practice. No doubt, the combination of glasnost' and democratization, as they evolved in the late 1980s, made possible both the proliferation of authentic associations and the unraveling of institutions, authority, and controls.

If during the initial years most of the transformation was encouraging to the reformists, what deserved no less attention was the emergence of resistance to the process: Yitzhak Brudny discusses the opposition to *perestroika* among some prominent literary figures (and others as well). A comprehensive study of the multifaceted hostility to reform—on many grounds and expressed in various ways—remains to be produced. So is a study of the learning curve of Mikhail Gorbachev and his associates: at first remarkably fast, and in a few key areas disastrously slow.

Changes concerning the status of the federation and the nationalities, Soviet foreign policy, and civil-military relations are dealt with in other volumes of this series. Perhaps the most fascinating aspect of socio-political change occurred in the relations between state and society. S. Frederick Starr and Gail W. Lapidus analyze some of the trends that, they found, made for the emergence of a manner of civil society in the Soviet Union, a concept which, it is true, has generated considerable heat—in large part because of imprecise definitions. Victoria Bonnell and Vladimir Brovkin deal with the mushrooming of grassroots associations "from below": a remarkable and, in Russia, relatively novel phenomenon.

By early 1991 a stalemate appeared to have set in. Whether compelled or volunteered, Gorbachev's alliance with the "hardliners" resisting economic reforms, foreign policy "concessions" to the West, and a new "Union Treaty" led to the replacement of key reformers with mediocrities and obstructionists. The coalescence of "Democratic Russia" around Boris Yel'tsin as an alternative focus for both reformist and centrifugal sentiments offered a way out, and in April 1991 a new deal was struck between the Gorbachev and Yel'tsin forces. Abraham Brumberg analyzes the political maneuvering and the various camps directly before the attempted counterrevolution.

On August 18 came the quixotic but dangerous coup that momentarily united the vice-president, the prime minister, the ministers of defense and interior, and the head of the KGB, with the backing of key figures from the Communist party and the state economy, against Gorbachev and his program. Its remarkable failure paradoxically marked a serious blow to Gorbachev. The suspension of the Communist party and the seizure of its assets, offices, and records, and soon the declaration of independence of most of the Union republics effectively meant the end of the Soviet Union. Its successor states went their different ways, and it was by no means clear what form or scope their common ties would take in the future. In the excerpt reproduced below, George Kennan comments on the implications of the failed coup.

Finally, George Breslauer examines alternative futures that the Soviet Union faced. No one, in the Soviet Union or outside, could have fully foreseen the dramatic events that ushered in its end as a superpower, as a multinational empire, as the flagship of the communist world, and as the largest command economy in the world. To students of Russian history, some of what occurred was reminiscent of 1917, of the Civil War days, of the years of the New Economic Policy, of the Khrushchev era. But in equal measure the events of 1991 had no precedent or analog. For better or for worse, Russia and the other successor states were turning a giant new page.

Alexander Dallin

CONTENTS

3

Urban Society, a New Labor Force

In the history of Soviet cities, we may single out three large waves of growth: the recovery of the urban population in the 1920s to the prerevolutionary levels, the feverish development during the 1930s, and the postwar boom, especially the period after 1956, when the bulk of the nation became urban.

The social consequences of this transformation unfolded in fits and starts and, quite naturally, the emergence of an urban social structure also came in stages and, as it were, in patches. New urban groups and forms appeared, including those considered as the most advanced in any given historical period, but then they took quite a time to prevail over older, simpler, or more primitive forms to which majorities of the population still belonged. Characteristic of any such transition are situations in which modes of life expressing an earlier social setting coexist with new ones that are to become tomorrow's prevailing reality.

As is well known, in their earlier stage most Russian

1

cities were quite rural. During the 1920s, in the very heart of Moscow, observers found, with disbelief, authentic villages over big areas of the capital. A recent review of Walter Benjamin's *Moscow Diary*, a log of his travels in Russia in 1925–1927, quotes Benjamin as saying that in the streets of Moscow "the Russian village plays hide-and-seek" [74:28]. Smaller cities were even more deeply villagelike, with country-style courtyards, thatched roofs, and in-court wells. As I mentioned earlier, the *byt*, the rural way of life, permeated these fledgling cities. In brief, these cities corresponded to a preindustrial stage in the social history of the country.

The next stage may be called, though without any claim to precision, the early industrial period, characterized by the prevalence, in the composition of the labor force, of simple physical labor, with low skills and relatively little use of advanced machinery. Even if the rural dwellings and gardens disappeared, they were replaced only by drab and monotonous rows of overcrowded and poorly serviced dwellings that housed this rather unskilled or primarily semiskilled labor. Similar developments had marked the earlier history of Western industrial cities, but in Russia this stage of industrialization evolved and continued, in part, into the current period; it was particularly characteristic of the pre- and postwar decades. In 1939, for example, 82.5 percent of the Soviet labor force was engaged in primarily physical labor, the remaining 17.5 percent in primarily intellectual work. Astonishingly, and very significantly, by 1959 the relative sizes of these sectors changed only slightly, to 79.3 percent and 20.7 percent [35:130].

Certainly this small shift represented a considerable number of workers. Yet "intellectual labor" (*umstvennyi trud*) is much too pompous a label for the professional reality of the Khrushchev era. Even in the cities, where by 1959 an apparently impressive 29.4 percent of the workforce was employed in the "intellectual" sector (compared to 57 percent in physical labor), the majority of these employees were plain, low-key nonspecialists, as the sociologists call them; in other words, rather primitive paper shufflers [90:247]. Which is to say that less than half of the so-called intellectual urban workforce was engaged in professional endeavors. And of this group, only some had any professional education. Many others, lacking formal education, learned on the job to be engineers and managers. This class of praktiki will be of some interest to us. They, too, symbolize an era.

A similarly low level of skill pervaded the manual labor force during this phase of Soviet industrialization. In most of the cities the composition of the manual labor force reflected the national priority to industrialize. In 222 of the 304 cities whose populations exceeded 50,000, a high proportion of the labor force—between 50 and 70 percent—was engaged in industry, transportation, and construction. In addition to the predominantly industrial cities, a considerable number, some 134 of the 304, can be characterized as diversified administrative centers. Harris, who cites these figures, observes that "the overwhelming predominance of these two types— namely the administrative and the industrial—reflects the nature of Soviet economy as a command economy where the political administration focused its attention primarily on the industrial side of the economy" [29:61].

Thus by 1959 the peasantry had been slowly replaced by a working class. However, initially, one type of predominantly physical labor was merely replacing another, although the new jobs were located in different and crucially important sectors. The earlier stages of

3

this development deserve the epithet "extensive," as quantity and speed were the slogans of those years.

But during the next twenty years, we see the making of a more variegated and professionally differentiated national and urban social structure. Urbanization, industrial and scientifico-technical development, mass schooling and quality schooling, communications and arts, state policies and myriad spontaneous events changed the nation's overall social, professional, and cultural profile, and the social structure underwent a significant qualitative transformation. Workers in the national economy soared from about 24 million before the war, to almost 81 million in 1983; of these, the number engaged in industry jumped from 11 million to over 31 million. Transportation, construction, and communications also grew at a rapid pace; much more modest growth of employment was registered in different services. The role of the working class in the economy is underscored by the fact that it is now the prevailing group in society and in the cities: 61.5 percent of the population, almost twice their share in 1939. In comparison, the kolkhoz peasants, once over half of the population, are now barely 12.5 percent of the nation.

A second group, presented in Soviet statistics as "employees," increased from 11 million in 1941 to about 35 million in 1983, a rate of growth surpassing that of workers. To understand the importance of this group, we must turn to another way of classifying them.

"Specialists"—otherwise also called in the Soviet literature "intelligentsia"—show an even faster rate of growth than the category of "officials." Most notably, in 1941 only about 2.4 million of the 11 million employees had higher or specialized technical education; in 1960 only half of the 16 million employees were "specialists";

4

today, an overwhelming majority of officials accede to this category, thanks to considerably improved standards of professional education. Recent figures show over 31.5 million specialists, among them 13.5 million with higher education and over 18 million with specialized secondary training [70:397–99; 82:14].*

Before we turn to those officials qua "intelligentsia," let us survey the educational standards of the whole population. In 1939 the overwhelming majority of the workers and peasants had only an elementary education (four years of primary school). By 1959, little had changed: 91.3 percent of workers and 98.2 percent of kolkhoz peasants still achieved only elementary standards. But by 1984 no more than 18.5 percent of manual laborers had only an elementary education—and, one would assume, a majority of the least educated were from the older generation [99:18–19].

In the population at large the massive educational efforts yielded significant results. Forty-six million people received a "secondary incomplete" education (seven years of schooling). Fifty-eight million enjoyed a full secondary education, which is now legally obligatory for all children. Alumni of the "secondary specialized" establishments that train technicians of all denominations numbered 28 million. A full higher education was received by 18.5 million people, and another 3.6 million received an incomplete higher education.

Among university and high school graduates, the numbers of men and women are substantially equal. Women constitute 54 percent of university students, 58

---

*Since the major trends, and not the precise demographic statistics, are of most concern in this interpretive sketch, all the figures presented here have been rounded off. For the exact data, readers should consult the sources cited in the text.

percent of the enrollment in secondary specialized schools, and 60 percent of all specialists with both higher and secondary education. Further, though women constitute 51 percent of the labor force as a whole, they account for about 56 percent of educated specialists, and 40 percent of scientists and scholars [99:7]. This emancipation of women—for centuries the predominantly uneducated mass and the most neglected—is perhaps the most visible part of what can be called the Soviet "cultural revolution." (This term was improperly applied by official propaganda to the 1930s, when most citizens received barely three to four years of elementary education. Today, millions attend universities and high schools, and all children have access to at least a modicum of instruction. But by now, of course, "cultural revolution" acquires a new meaning again.)

Thus the development of professional and educational standards that began in the 1930s only to be interrupted by the ordeal of World War II, has come to fruition on a large scale during the last three decades. In particular, we must emphasize the making and remaking of the Soviet intelligentsia.*

The history of the intelligentsia is tortuous, even tortured, but it has now become, in fact, a mass of people, composed of all the professionals the modern world re-

*Soviet authors argue whether technicians with secondary special education should be included in the intelligentsia, a term that implies not only high professional skill but also an appropriate cultural background and the ability to use—if not create—concepts. Although this argument is of interest, it can be disregarded here. My primary point is that the creation of a layer of professionally and intellectually advanced people has long been at the center of Russian and Soviet theoretical and ideological debates. The Soviet leadership has always dreamed of producing a broad layer of such people, who would emerge from the popular classes and become committed to the new regime.

quires and of numerous groups, subgroups, and categories: technical, managerial-administrative, scientific, artistic, educational, and political. Even if we restrict ourselves to those with a higher education, their number reaches now about 15 million, a vast pool of "grey matter" and the fastest-growing part of the new social structure. While the employed population grew by 155 percent between 1960 and 1986, the number of specialists grew fourfold. Over 5 million students are attending institutions of higher education, taught by half a million professors [31:65].

An even slightly more rapid growth has occurred in the sector of scientific and technological research. Scientists and engineers working in research today number almost 1.5 million, flanked by a large cadre of auxiliary technicians—a serious and sizable "branch of the national economy," as a Soviet scholar termed it [87:110–11].

We will not at this point enter into the problems faced by these groups and classes—the imbalances, inefficiencies and general shortfalls that have resulted, notably, from their hectic formation. Whatever the problems, ailments, and even crises, they reflect a qualitatively different social structure than that of fifty years ago. In effect, in the past five decades the USSR has leaped into the twentieth century, although in the 1930s most of the nations of the territory still belonged to a far earlier age. The creation of the techno-scientific and intellectual class, accompanying the urbanization process, is thus a momentous development. The further advance of the economy and the survival of the political system are dependent on this layer, which has become a large, almost "popular" mass.

I will later explore the political sequels of these phenomena, but some implications are obvious already. The new intelligentsia, members of the different categories of this stratum, have moved beyond research institutes and universities. Numbers of them are government experts, medium- and top-level executives, participants and members of the highest administrative and political apparaty. And it is a sign of the new times in Russia that this amalgam is deepening and expanding. Studying this stratum, which supplies "cadres"—we may also say "elites"—for the system, will help us to understand the future of Russia and how it will meet the next century.

In the USSR today, the professional classes and the intellectuals direct all spheres of economic, political, and social life. (They did so even in conditions in which their own personal freedoms were denied to them.) Nevertheless, they are dependent on an important layer of less-qualified but vitally important "technicians," most of whom are trained in the system of "specialized secondary education." Without these technicians, the high-ranking specialists are incapacitated—as is quite well known to any student of the Soviet industrial and scientific establishments. Unfortunately, an impetuous cadres policy has pressed for ever more high-level specialists and neglected the formation of middle-rank technicians; the whole system was severely handicapped by the resulting imbalances. A similar situation developed in other sectors and lower layers in the productive and social ladder. Medium- and high-ranking specialists simply cannot operate efficiently unless they have enough skilled and motivated paraprofessionals and assistants.

It is obvious that the nation's entire workforce is an

interconnected system vulnerable to professional and social impairment if it is not continuously readjusted and re-equilibrated. Structural imbalances of different types have always plagued the Soviet economy, and this vexed problem is again on the agenda in a grand way.

The nationwide restructuring of the urban socio-professional profile described earlier in this chapter resulted from a historical process of readjustment that was only in part affected by policies. Short-term measures, after all, have little impact on massive social changes. Indeed, the government's day-to-day tinkering with the professional structure may even make things worse. Longer-term policies are indispensable at this stage, as they were during the upheavals in the 1930s, to provide coordinated measures in the educational and administrative areas, in labor and wage policies, and in the general realm of motivation and incentives.

As a result of the broad historical processes and direct interventions of policy, today's employed urban population falls into three groups: almost 60 percent are workers, about 40 percent are officials and specialists, and some 1 to 5 percent are kolkhoz peasants, most of whom live in the smaller towns and work in nearby kolkhozy.

Let us examine the first two groups more closely. Of the workers, 10–12 percent are unskilled or poorly skilled; 44–46 percent are skilled physical workers, the backbone of the industrial labor force; and 3–4 percent are highly skilled workers whose duties are deemed to require physical and intellectual aptitudes [92:23]. Much fuss was made by apologists who saw this highest layer as boding a future merger of intellectual and physical labor and the disappearance of all social inequality and classes. In fact, the thinness of this layer points to the rather poor state of the current industrial organization, still underequipped in advanced mechanisms and automation. Nevertheless, considering that youth now coming into the factories are rather well educated, they may be ready to learn high-level skills, if the new equipment does appear. Here is a faint hint of yet another important imbalance and social problem: too many well-educated people and not enough challenging, demanding jobs.

In the officials-cum-specialists group, 11–12 percent are poorly trained or untrained; 17–18 percent are in professional jobs demanding good training in secondary and specialized schools or in universities; 2.5–3 percent are in medium-rank managerial and professional positions that demand university schooling and additional training; and the top 2 percent perform highly skilled, largely intellectual functions in upper-rank leadership positions.

From these figures, it is quite easy to see the historical leap, in comparison with the NEP or any later stage, in the restructuring of the national labor force. But it is difficult to assess whether this is an adequate professional structure for the new age and what its dynamics are. A more fruitful approach has been proposed by two able Soviet sociologists, L. A. Gordon and V. V. Komarovskii [23:98–110]. In order to analyze the role of the professional structure in the development of the socioeconomic system, they studied three generations in the active working population: men born around 1910, who entered the labor force in the 1930s and reached their vocational peak in the 1950s; their sons, born in the 1930s, who entered the labor force in the 1950s and peaked in the 1970s; and their grandsons, born in the 1950s, who entered the labor force in the 1970s.

The vocational x-ray of these three generations, which now coexist and often work together, confirms and highlights the findings we have already reached from other sources and data on Soviet social development. Generation by generation, fewer people are working in agriculture and at physical labor; more people are employed in nonmanual jobs in industry, services, and information.* But this generational approach also vividly suggests the interactions and clashes that characterized the historical change of the guard.

The first generation carried the nation through the period of industrialization but was nevertheless predominantly employed in jobs that did not demand much if any schooling. These men were physical laborers of the traditional type, almost preindustrial in character, and many were still peasants. Even at the height of their careers, in the 1950s, 80 percent of them continued to do physical labor.

In the second generation, we see some results of the nation's industrialization. This generation was the first in which more workers were employed in industry than in agriculture; the first in which skilled labor predominated over unskilled physical labor; and the first in which the number of nonmanual workers equaled that of unskilled manual workers. But alongside the important shift from agriculture to industry and the lower ra-

---

*Gordon and Komarovskii have not yet published a complete set of data. Their preliminary analyses show that the percentage of the labor force employed in unskilled physical labor has decreased from 50 percent (cohort 1) to 29 percent (cohort 2) to 17 percent (cohort 3). Regarding field of employment: the percentage of workers involved in agriculture has dropped from 40 percent (cohort 1) to 22 percent (cohort 2) to 13 percent (cohort 3); the percentage employed in industry has increased from 38 percent (cohort 1) to 48 percent (cohort 2) to 50 percent (cohort 3).

tio of unskilled workers, this cohort's advance into the branches of information, services, and organization was modest.

In the third generation we see a substantial increase in the numbers engaged in the service and information professions, and a corresponding decrease in unskilled manual laborers and agriculturists. From the very start of their careers, twice as many of this cohort are entering the intellectual labor force as the physical labor force. Herein we see the industrial era yielding to the scientific-industrial-information era. Already this youngest generation lives in a different environment and faces different pressures.

Gordon and Komarovskii calculate that in contemporary society one-fourth of each generation moves up the socioprofessional ladder, and they predict that vocational mobility will probably accelerate. Unfortunately, these authors do not indicate whether this rate of intergenerational mobility is sufficient, nor do they cite the relevant Western figures for comparison. But, as they note, this rate is high enough to create tensions among the generations. The young quickly develop different styles of life, form new approaches to life and work, and often reject, we can safely add, the methods and culture of their predecessors.

Such tensions are unavoidable and not unexpected, and they are likely to increase in the coming decade as intragenerational changes accelerate. In the 1990s, Gordon and Komarovskii project, the proportion of crude agricultural and industrial labor will drop to barely 10 percent among the third generation, as it approaches its career peak, and close to 40 percent of this cohort will be employed in intellectual professions. And the researchers predict that 30–40 percent of the workforce will be involved in sociocultural and other services and in professions related to the creation and processing of information. These projections lag behind current Western professional profiles: In the West more people are already engaged in information and services, fewer in industry, and very few in agriculture. But the authors do not seem unduly worried, for the lag, they observe, can be addressed by informed government policies. (The researchers are probably quite sincere. The best of contemporary social science in the Soviet Union is no longer content to issue soothing and reassuring prognoses, as was expected of them by the older-style leaders. Today, a growing number of scholars seeks to expose the sharper and more menacing aspects of social life; they issue warnings and demand action.)

Yet Gordon and Komarovskii caution that this inter- and intragenerational thrust forward into modern intellectual and professional life portends social trouble of great magnitude if it is not matched by reforms in the prevailing economic mechanism and in the "relations of production" [23:108–10]. The different spheres of the socioeconomic system suffer from discordances (*rassoglasovanie*) that threaten the nation's entire professional and educational endeavor. The state cannot allow "a socioprofessional structure adequate to the needs of a scientific-industrial system to be straitjacketed into a production system that is still stuck in an earlier technical and technological age." In the absence of reform, not only will professionalization not improve the performance of the system, it could also create widespread social crises and even pressures to return to the old patterns.

The stern warning sounded by these researchers may seem overly alarmist, but it reflects recent developments well known to readers of Soviet sociology. The list is long: widespread job dissatisfaction among educated youth and highly trained professionals; low morale— poor "sociopsychological climate" is the Soviet term— in many workplaces; underutilized engineers and scientists who waste their time on menial jobs because of a shortage of technicians and auxiliary personnel; hordes of poorly trained people parading, easily, as engineers or scientists. These images of a wasted generation and a potentially disastrous backsliding for the whole country certainly hang over the heads of the nation's political and economic leadership.

"Caveant consules!" the scholars caution. But these days they seem to believe that the consuls, or some of them, are aware.

4

The Intelligentsia

Among the sociological and cultural changes of the post-Stalinist period, we earlier singled out the transformation of the professional layer of specialists into a mass phenomenon. The increasing number of professionals working in research and development, in communications, and in the arts signals the remaking and reemergence of stable, massive professional and cultural classes—a vast pool from which new leaders and elites are arising. Most importantly, the different approaches, outlooks, and ideologies that prevail among and within the generations are coexisting and competing without destroying each other.

This latter point is, of course, a novelty in Soviet history, where one destructive period followed another; repeatedly, the best cadres in the nation were decimated, and incumbent and potential leaders in politics, society, and culture were slaughtered. These chapters of Soviet history are well known, but it is worth recalling that the story of "elites" has been complicated from the moment the Russian Revolution occurred because of the paucity of adequate cadres or their unreliability, real or presumed, from the standpoint of the new regime's security and aims. The story of those groups that ruled the country is still to be written, but some stages can be sketched out briefly, both to intimate the problems and also to buttress my central interpretive arguments.

Indisputably, the revolution and the civil war inflicted considerable losses on the country's professional classes. Many died, others fled abroad, and many of the survivors who remained were either distrustful or distrusted. Nevertheless, pragmatism prevailed: the system could not function without these specialists. The politico-administrative elite, the groups in the upper echelons of government, came to be composed of a curious mélange of ex-professional revolutionaries, many poorly trained but politically reliable cadres from worker and peasant stock, and a crucial admixture of specialists called "bourgeois" because they were trained and privileged in the previous regime.

Mistrust and complicated love-hate relations were common in the government, and to some extent, although on different grounds, in the party. But it was the "bourgeois" group that constituted the class of experts who helped build the government machinery during the 1920s. (Some had already helped the Soviets earlier, notably in the Red Army.)

This explosive alliance was disturbed in the late twenties by the persecution of the ex-tsarist experts. These attacks subsided by 1932, but by then the institutions and the economy had so greatly expanded that the small numbers of the "ex-bourgeois" became a drop—though important because of their quality—in the sea of newcomers from the ranks and from the institutions of higher education.

All the institutions churning out the neophyte cadres were still in their infancy, but they hurried to produce the graduates badly needed by the expanding nonagricultural sector. From the midst of these newcomers, most of whom were from popular classes, were now selected in growing numbers the emerging elites. Concomitantly, the numbers of ex-revolutionaries (not just old Bolsheviks) and members of the prerevolutionary intelligentsia (several tens of thousands of "bourgeois" specialists at the end of the NEP) dwindled quite rapidly.

Among the newcomers, the category of praktiki was particularly numerous. Since the schools were not yet capable of satisfying the voracious demand for cadres, many people with no formal preparation received all their professional training on the job. Even those who benefitted from some preparation were most often inadequately trained. Such educational deficiencies were common in all walks of life, especially in the sphere of politics. Most of the political cadres had less education than other professions; they were trained or trained themselves on the job as best they could [62:38–41].

For a short time, some progress in schooling cadres was made. But the subsequent Stalinist purges severely obstructed the emergence and improvement of the professional and cultural classes. Countless up-and-coming professionals were murdered, and the asphyxiating atmosphere of the Stalinist counterrevolution stifled the flow of advanced and sophisticated ideas.

The damage to the nation's political and professional upper layers was enormous. The costly efforts of producing adequate leadership were wasted by a mass slaughter, notably of old Bolsheviks and of many Stalinists. The new replacements were often of lesser cultural and especially political standards and, of course, had less, if any, experience compared to those who had been purged. Further, this newest layer of elites was the third in a short period of time. A general deterioration of the country's political culture, including a decline in the top political echelons, ensued. By the end of Stalin's rule, and for some time thereafter, both the highest echelons and the political system at large were beset by an acute crisis of values and of leadership. A blind wall stood between the rulers and the ruled.

In the late 1950s and early 1960s, Khrushchev's efforts to open up and reform the system met with some success. But his initiatives were often frustrated by the growing complexity of problems, by the immense scale of social change, and by the limitations of a political system that provided for the handling of basic needs but did not promote any broader strategies for more substantive change. Still, the sum of small improvements—and a few spectacular ones—was far from negligible. The battered and much maligned bureaucracy had become more stable and potent, and it succeeded in imposing on the system a more acceptable and, from the bureaucracy's point of view, a far more secure and more professional method of ruling. More attention to the laws, better control of the police, elimination of the Stalinist concentration camps, the implementation of group or "collective" leadership: the list of improvements is impressive. For the first time, a consolidated ruling apparatus exercised control over the whole of the state machinery, and the stabilization and security thereby offered to functionaries resulted in many of the improvements that the citizens of the USSR experienced up through the late sixties.

But in the following two decades, the elite and the medium and lower layers in government began to lose momentum and to lose touch. The development of the country outraced the governing abilities of the networks in power. *Rassoglasovannost*, discordances and imbalances, spread throughout the system, widening the chasm between the mentality and professional abilities of top and medium-ranking cadres and the new realities of the day.

Was there during the 1970s and early 1980s enough renovation within the system to prepare a change of guard, whether the older generation wanted it or not? Was there some open or subterranean influx of new cadres in the bureaucracies and the networks close to them?

We know that changes were taking place on an intergenerational level in the working population at large. Something was going on in the party and state, too—though we have less material about them, except for data on the improved educational standards of most cadres. Too, it is unmistakably clear that the praktiki were disappearing. At the end of 1956, 57.2 percent of all industrial specialists of the USSR were still praktiki. Unbelievable as it may sound for a country that was already a superpower, 68.4 percent of factory directors, even 32.9 percent of all chief engineers and technical directors, belonged to this category. By the mid-sixties the proportions of praktiki had fallen substantially, and today the phenomenon is largely vestigial. Parallel developments have taken place in the political *apparaty*, with those at the very top being more resilient to the call of changing times than the layers just below them.

Further evidence of a partial modernization in the top cadres and their outlook comes from a study [61] of the efforts deployed by a group of leaders to reform the economy in the mid-sixties. An alliance of experts, managers, top government officials, and some party leaders fought tooth and nail for the preferred changes. Their main promoter was Prime Minister Kosygin, and with his support some battles were won. The reforms were launched, but were blocked by a coalition of conservatives and hardline ideologues. The infighting and internal struggles of those years seem to prefigure the even broader alliances that are battling it out today.

5

The Urban Microworlds and Their Power

One of the effects of massive urbanization was the increased visibility of problems that were once disregarded, swept under the carpet, because of the state's other preponderant interests. We have in mind, on the one hand, the intricate world and interests of the person or individual (*lichnost* in Soviet terminology) and, on the other, the multitude of small-scale, primary social forms that sustain individuals in their everyday life, that support their moral equilibrium and psychic health—or, as the case may be, undermine them.

The incredible social and psychological maze that is the city compelled scholars—in the footsteps of urban professionals who address everyday social problems (social workers, teachers, policemen, doctors)—to delve into the small-scale forms of everyday life. Previously, most of the political and hence also scholarly attention was focused on the macrodimensions—economic development, broadly defined social classes, national systems of education—and there was a tendency to believe that changes in the large-scale systems would force all the small-scale forms to follow suit.

There is not much left of this naive fascination with the primacy of the large-scale and massive dimensions of social life. Besides the inescapable countertrend that views the personal, intimate, and small-scale as the sole worthwhile dimension of life, Soviet scholars, leaders, and pedagogues have come to focus more closely on human relations, whatever their scale, and their interrelations and relatively independent momentums. In both the academic and political communities, the entire gamut of social forms of life has assumed a crucial importance for even the most broadly viewed objectives of national politics.

Hence a proliferation of discussions and research, and a broad preoccupation with subjects long familiar in the West but novel in the USSR. Moreover, these social analyses are now perceived as having deep implications for the political sphere. Themes like personality, individuality, and personal autonomy and issues of how to create an environment that enriches personal life have become important not just in scholarly circles, where such subjects have been debated in serious texts for more than a decade, but also in political discourse, which certainly borrowed from the scholarly literature. Undoubtedly, this emphasis on personal life is one of the results of Soviet urbanization. Freedom of movement, choice of profession, multiple choices in many walks of life—such rights are being demanded by the new waves of better-educated and more intellectual urban professionals.

That the city, more than any other environment, provokes critical faculties and intellectual freedom is, of course, a textbook truism. But despite the theoretical commonplaceness of it all, when an authoritarian social system begins to rediscover such terms and phenomena, we are witnessing an important event. For more than a decade at least one Soviet scholar, O. N. Ianitskii, has published articles on the theme that "the development of man as an individual and as a productive force becomes the center of gravity in the formation of modern cities" [34:38]. Over time, many others developed similar ideas until, finally, the party leader took it up as a key direction of policy. Such a turnabout is not just *in posse*; it must already be, to some extent, *in esse*. Ianitskii adds an example that will help us understand how urbanization manifests its social essence. As numerous studies of workers' preferences and behavior have shown, and Ianitskii cites some of the most important ones, most workers are equally sensitive to both the natural and social conditions of life: "Particularly substantive is the propensity to an integrative, syncretic understanding by people of their life conditions—they are not satisfied anymore with some set or other of specific conditions, they demand a new quality of the whole life environment." This is the type of issue confronting the politicians to whom the article is addressed.

The personal dimension also assumes a new importance in the contemporary techno-scientific revolution, which so intensifies the density of human communications in urban life. As Ianitskii puts it, "The advance of the scientific-technological revolution and of urbanization are intimately connected with the principle of autonomous activity of the person, of contacts between individuals as individuals" [32:74]. And here, again, he offers a directly political conclusion: such communications, which are the very condition of creativity, cannot exist in a coercive environment. Other Soviet scholars studying scientific activities have repeated the same the-

sis in different forms. Scholarship demands freedom of
the individual scholar, who is the best carrier of ideas
that fuel scientific advances. The role of free exchanges
is often illustrated by the importance of the "invisible
college," one type of informal group specific to the scholarly community.

This argument has implications that transcend the academic world. Demands concerning freedoms for scholars reverberate on a broader scale and are presented as
a universal need and right. The theme of *prava lichnosti*,
"the rights of the individual," has already attracted
quite a literature, and today it does not sound like just
another empty word. Scholars and political essayists are
quite categorical: the continuing denial of indispensable
rights will precipitate devastating results. Officials are
again duly forewarned that appeals for economic intensification and high productivity will only provoke another fiasco if the issues of rights are not addressed.

So much for personality and individuality per se. Before moving on to the welter of informal groups, we must
mention, however briefly, one small but rather formal
group: the family. Not surprisingly, the family has also
been studied as one of the roots of the autonomous individual. One scholar emphasizes that the modern urban family, whatever its problems, is characterized by a
higher degree of personal autonomy for all its members,
including women, youths, and even small children
[78:97]. Families promote the growing quest for and use
of individual autonomy and help spread it through the
population at large with an irresistible power, and this
process is autonomous, that is, spontaneous. Among 70
million Soviet families, one can be sure that many millions encourage an irresistible molecular pressure for
autonomy and, we should add, privacy. Although the lat-

ter concept is not yet used directly, it is implied in the demands for *prava lichnosti, uvelichenie lichnoi avtono-mii* ("rights and increased autonomy of individuals") and in the effort to strengthen the role of the family as a socializing force in society. Though some observers claim that in modern life the socializing role of the family has irretrievably yielded to large-scale forces like schooling, the media, and politics, most sociologists and other professionals involved propose the opposite conclusion. For them it is not the family that is an auxiliary of the state in socializing youth, but rather the other way around. Empirical studies show that when asked about the importance of different factors in their education, most respondents named the family as the most influential. The authors of one such study conclude that "social institutions and social organizations are only assisting the family, but cannot replace it" [92:87].

That the family is part of a system and adapts to changes in that system is a foregone conclusion. But the family has very specific functions and is endowed with its own impetus and an autonomy of sorts. Recognizing the dangers and futility of excessive regulation, contemporary Soviet legislation regulates the family only minimally, except to safeguard the rights of its members.

But the autonomous character of the family, its strengths and weaknesses, are also fashioned by heritage, tradition, and convention. For one group of authors "the most important regulator of human behavior in family life is a historically formed system of sociocultural and ethnocultural norms, which includes both norms formed in the past and those that emerge in contemporary conditions" [92:88]. This historical influence is best illustrated by regional or ethnic cultural and behavior patterns.

There are in the USSR, broadly, two patterns of "demographic conduct"—a problem of immense importance in view of the decline of birthrates in the cities. One pattern, which is widespread in the European part of the USSR, is based on individual decisions, relatively independent of any group norms, in questions concerning procreation; having children is a choice guided by very personal motivations and aims. The other pattern, which predominates in Central Asia, still follows the traditional norms, which disregard individual aims and instil a particular way of life [92:89].

A recent article by a noted student of the Soviet family, A. G. Kharchev [45], paints a very troubling picture of family problems, especially in the big cities: Youth are poorly prepared for marriage and their marital relations are relatively fragile; sexual exploitation, moral turpitude, and extramarital pregnancies seem to be on the rise; and too many children live in families without fathers. These problems are not unusual, of course, to observers of Western societies. Kharchev, however, raises one problem that is more common in the Soviet way of thinking than in the West. The education system, he claims, is busy spreading some forms of knowledge, but it does not educate the young, for knowledge in itself cannot establish an ethos or cultural values (*kulturnost*), and principles that guide people's behavior. The chasm in Soviet society between the standards of educational achievement and the more profound spiritual culture of society is exemplified by the disparity between "higher socialist values" and behavior in the sphere of marital relations [45:31].

These themes have direct repercussions in the realm of politics, as political discourse responds to the realization that social reality, notably its small forms, is a power not at all small. Despite the statist setting, social microforms have their own impetus and participate in creating and recreating the spiritual and moral world of the citizenry. These microforms can be gravely damaged by too crude an administrative interference. in the sphere of the personal and the familial, in neighborly relations, friendly groups, and other informal structures. Criminal behavior, of course, demands government intervention, but overzealousness in regulating the microforms in general may contribute to an increase in the less palatable phenomena.

It goes without saying that such theorems shatter the older stereotypes of bureaucratic thinking, which is premised on the primacy of state and politics in national life. Such a view of politics must be scrapped when events force politicians to learn about all kinds of informal structures—including those inside the bureaucracies (which they certainly knew about from experience but didn't want to acknowledge) and the invisible college of scholars—and their role in shaping the individual, his motivations and behavior. Should politicians fail to understand this lesson and in some way weaken urban microforms they will create for the authorities new nightmares. For it is only with the help of informal groups—friends at work and in school, fellow-villagers—that millions of migrants manage the difficult process of adaptation to city life.

But more: sociological surveys of young migrant textile workers "allow [us] to state with some assurance that in the majority of cases, the most basic [social] relations are formed with comrades at work and in schools" [48:194]. (We notice that it is not the Komsomol, the official youth organization, that is of any importance here; it is not mentioned in any of these studies.) On a similar line, scholars studying mass communications and their effect on public opinion are reporting on the crucial role of the small groups. It turns out that whatever people read in the press or see on television undergoes a considerable "working over" (*obrabotka*). The impact of the media is controlled by the sometimes even more powerful influence of interpersonal communications within informal and small groups. The same happens, certainly, in all the professions, notably in professional informal groups of *intelligenty*, whose influence may be even stronger than that of workers' groups.

One survey, conducted in a factory in Leningrad, concerned the relative influence of television programs and discussions with friends on workers' opinions of ideological questions. While 24.5 percent of the respondents said that watching television does not change their opinions (we do not know whether they agreed or disagreed with the program), 58 percent stated that their opinions do change after discussions with friends, colleagues, and relatives. Another survey in a number of Leningrad factories reports that 98 percent of the respondents obtain their information from the media, 90 percent of those discuss what they learn with friends and family, and 42 percent modify their views after such discussions. The reasons most often given for such changes of heart were: "The authority of my interlocutor influenced me"; "I accepted the opinion of the group"; "They simply made me change my mind"; and "I received additional information" [78:105].

Official views espoused by the media are, in effect, filtered twice: by the small group's leader and by the small group as a whole [77:48]. Thus interpersonal contacts, if they have a relatively stable character based on common interests, can be more powerful forums of self-expression than any other form of communications, even media of "the most intense and massive character" [77:49].

In conclusion, the microenvironment serves as a relay between the mass media and the individual [92:20]. The Soviet mass media cannot out-and-out brainwash people because interpersonal contacts—the maze of relatives, informal groups, and other broader social entities—serve as a shield against at least the cruder forms of indoctrination. No wonder the departments of agitation and propaganda repeatedly discover that their mass propaganda is often quite ineffective, sometimes even entirely a waste. The microcosms of urbanized society can prove stronger than the political macrocosm if "the group" feels that the official spokesman is "talking empty."

DOMESTIC AND INTERNATIONAL FACTORS IN THE FORMATION OF GORBACHEV'S REFORMS

by Seweryn Bialer

"Entia non multiplicanda praeter necessitatem"
-William Ockham

Mikhail Gorbachev is now nearing the end of his fourth year in office and the Soviet Union is in a state of creative turmoil. What is presently happening in the USSR can best be described as a gigantic experiment that in practical terms touches virtually all fields of endeavor. Intellectually, the very system of Russian and Soviet ideas and traditions is being called into question. This experiment is only beginning. The society and the political system within which the experiment is taking place still remain deeply Soviet in all of this term's negative Stalinist connotations. To make a significant difference, to take hold and to change the Soviet system, the new course initiated by the general secretary needs at least another decade.

What has already happened in the Soviet Union in many areas is very exciting and truly remarkable. Gorbachev hopes to attain the most significant breakthrough in the economic sphere. Indeed, the rationale of his entire policy agenda is subordinated to the goal of modernizing the Soviet Union. Yet the most startling developments of Gorbachev's tenure are not in the economy but in the political and cultural areas where radical action came as a surprise. Unless Gorbachev is forced to reverse them, these measures will profoundly change the nature of the system he inherited.

The changes that are taking place in the Soviet Union have deep sources. In Western writings on Gorbachev's domestic and foreign policies and reforms, there is very often a tendency to ascribe these changes primarily or even exclusively to domestic factors. There is no denying that the domestic factors are fundamental in explaining Gorbachev's reforms. Yet without taking into consideration the international factors that inform his actions, the explanations and analyses remain one-sided. Only by understanding the interaction of domestic and international factors can we begin to grasp the nature of Gorbachev's revolutionary course.

Domestic Sources of Soviet Reform

The domestic factors that promoted radical reforms by Gorbachev fall into three categories. They concern first, the domestic performance of the Soviet system during the Brezhnev era; second, the new and necessary conditions of

0022-197x/89/1314-0283$01.50/0

Soviet economic growth under contemporary circumstances; and third, the changed nature of Soviet society and the conditions of its stability. These factors explain the urgency of the actions undertaken by Gorbachev and the direction of his reform agenda. They also bring to light the obstacles that he is facing, and narrow the range of probable outcomes of his efforts.

Systemic Crisis

In the modern era, almost all programs of fundamental reform, let alone revolutionary transformations, have grown out of major crisis situations. The Soviet Union is no exception. The leaders who took power in the mid-1980s knew that they had inherited a country and a system in a state of material and spiritual crisis. A phrase used by the new general secretary at the June 1987 Plenum of the Central Committee sums up this assessment quite succinctly: The Brezhnev era, he said, was characterized by the appearance of "pre-crisis phenomena." The clear implication was that, due to the pattern of Brezhnev's leadership, without the urgent actions undertaken by his successors, the Soviet Union would have found itself at present in a crisis situation. The rector of Moscow State University in a speech published in *Pravda* in November 1987 described the situation more dramatically and more accurately: "We were sliding into the abyss and are only starting to stop the slide."

The speeches of the new leader and discussions in the Soviet press are extraordinarily frank. Their frankness stems from the seriousness of the Soviet predicament and can be explained by the need to shock the party and the masses into action, to mobilize the public for countervailing steps. The new leadership also makes it amply clear that the crisis conditions were, and are, not merely segmental, limited to a specific sphere, but were national in character and present in almost all fields of domestic endeavor. They were also, and are, systemic in character. They were not the outgrowth of any specific faulty policy but of the very nature and structure of the Soviet system as it existed over the last 20 years. To overcome the crisis, therefore, requires from the Soviet leaders not simply new and better policies, but a determination to change many basic characteristics of the Soviet system itself.

This national systemic crisis which confronted the new leadership as it took over the reins of power in the Soviet Union, could be defined as a crisis of effectiveness. The Soviet Union was running down. Its performance in almost every sphere but the military was below not only world standards, but the standards set by its own leadership. The official reports of how well it was doing were simply complete falsehoods. Without urgent and extensive actions undertaken by the new leadership the "crisis of effectiveness" could have been, and can still become, a "crisis of survival" in which the very existence of the system is put at risk.

By the end of the Brezhnev era, Soviet society was chronically ill according to the standards by which social diseases can be diagnosed. In the political arena, the most significant phenomenon was the alienation not only of the population at large, but also of the party—by definition the political public— from the rulers and from the regime. Political stability was achieved in one of the most politicized societies in the world through mass political apathy, the privatization of citizens' concerns and a lack of civic spirit cemented by coercion. The party-state administration became highly bureaucratized, penetrated through and through by a corporatist spirit, thoroughly corrupted in its particular segments by mafia-like informal associations.

As for culture, even the enforced mask of socialist realism, with its optimism at all costs, could no longer hide the sense of deep cultural pessimism permeating the educated strata. This cultural pessimism of the educated was mirrored by a feeling of hopelessness among the working strata. The Soviet Union was probably the only major country in the world where the youth neither rebelled nor channeled any youthful enthusiasm into creative public endeavors. The heroes of Soviet youth were their own "private" poets and balladeers (especially Vladimir Vysotskii), and their major public expression of satisfaction was associated with the meager artifacts of Western mass culture that were officially tolerated but not encouraged.

Economic Imperatives

With regard to the economy, in a speech given at the Plenum of the Central Committee in February 1988, Gorbachev summed up the state of affairs with a mind-boggling statement: In the 20 years previous to his accession to power, the Soviet national income, with the exception of production of alcohol, did not increase in real terms at all. The Stalinist model of the economy, which served the Soviets fairly well in the first phases of their industrial revolution when the development of heavy industry and military might took absolute precedence, was unfit to promote growth as priorities shifted. The new stage of economic development geared to better diet, mass production of durable consumer goods and high technology demanded a new approach. The functioning of the Stalinist model of the economy depended on administrative activity and regulation (it is therefore sometimes described as a command economy) and not on self-generating and self-enforcing economic forces. The Bolshevik fear of political spontaneity found its extreme economic expression in the Stalinist model; a model which stifled initiative and creativity, discouraged development, and with its expansion became more and more cumbersome and unmanageable. The Polish economist Oscar Lange aptly characterized this economic model as a war economy. One should note that this definition has found its way into Soviet economic discussions in the Gorbachev years.

The confining Stalinist model of the economy went hand in hand with the continuation, long after Stalin's death, of an extensive strategy of economic growth totally unsuited to the new Soviet circumstances. Using this model, Soviet leaders tried to achieve economic expansion by continually increasing inputs of labor, capital and land in the production and distribution process.

It was becoming clear by the early 1970s that the extensive model of growth had its absolute physical and economic limits and that its effectiveness was diminishing. The influx of new labor resources hit a steeply diminishing curve. Cheap sources of raw materials, so abundant in the past, were being exhausted, and costs began to increase exponentially when their extraction and production

33

moved from the easily accessible European parts of the country to the vast wastelands of Siberia. The expansion of land under cultivation was no longer possible, for this required very costly investments. The input of ever-expanding capital expenditures was becoming increasingly difficult. The declining ratio of capital formation to the size of GNP in turn strengthened the tendency towards stagnation. The monumental neglect of the economic infrastructure created extraordinary bottlenecks in the Soviet economy and accounted for an unbelievable waste of materials and labor. For example, more than 20 percent of the agricultural harvest and more than half of the vegetables and fruits do not reach the consumer due to lack of roads, storage facilities and sufficient railroad capacity.

The Soviet political leadership, to say nothing of Soviet economists, was aware of the unsustainability of the extensive strategy of growth for Soviet economic progress long before Gorbachev came to power. They knew, in a general sense, that the Soviet economy had to switch to an intensive strategy of growth, where the following elements necessarily would play a decisive role: (i) increased productivity of labor and capital through technological progress and better incentives; (ii) declining relative costs of production; (iii) conservation of raw materials and energy; and (iv) improved quality of products and a buildup of the infrastructure. Yet, even as they were making efforts to stress intensive factors of growth, they were determined, for reasons of inbred ideological and political conservatism, to do so without any serious changes in the Stalinist model of the economy. A complete dismantling was, under the circumstances, impossible. But so too was the achievement of intensive growth under the Stalinist economic model.

Even before taking power, the new leadership had already recognized elements of the unhappy economic reality hidden behind Brezhnev's bombastic phrases regarding "advanced socialism." After achieving political control, they recognized that they were faced with a fundamental economic crisis of major proportions. They soon reached the conclusion that what was required was a simultaneous change on both sides of the economic equation—a change in the strategy of growth from extensive to intensive, and a change in economic organization from the Stalinist-administrative model to an as yet undefined model where economic instruments and forces such as the market would play a much more determining role. They embarked on long-range solutions meant to synchronize the strategy of growth with the model of the economy.

Social Imperatives

The social sources of the Soviet systemic crisis can be defined very simply: In the post-Stalin period, Soviet society in all its segments and its aspirations has changed very significantly while the antiquated political order of a different era has remained largely unchanged. First, the Soviet social system of stratification that rewarded power and was indifferent to performance killed the work ethic of the population and was counterproductive to modernization. Second, official corruption and unfulfilled promises led to far-reaching political alienation of the society as a whole from the party and the regime. Third, in the post-

Stalin era the phenomenal growth of the Soviet middle class, and particularly its professional component, was not reflected in the official arena with power sharing and professional and political autonomy of any kind. Fourth, the expansion of the enormous Soviet welfare state combined its two worst possible characteristics—where it was necessary, its productivity was low and declining (e.g., the medical service), and where its existence in an efficient and well-functioning society would have been superfluous, it expanded beyond reason (e.g., subsidies of food prices).

International Sources of Soviet Reform

The political, cultural, economic and social phenomena that led to the crisis of the Soviet system, and made the new Soviet leadership opt for intervention instead of orthodoxy, were domestic in their origin and nature. It is my contention, however, that their virulence alone would not have been sufficient to cause the Soviet leadership to embark on the radical path of *perestroika* if they were not combined with two international factors of prime importance. The first factor, which is psychological in nature, concerns the Soviet leadership's deeply ingrained tendency to evaluate their domestic accomplishments and global standing against the background of economic and technological trends and developments in the capitalist world. The second and related international factor deals directly with structural limitations imposed by declining Soviet capabilities in the global arena.

Soviet Perceptions and the International Environment

The recognition of the virulence of the Soviet domestic crisis, and of the urgent need to counteract its harmful domestic consequences, was reinforced dramatically by the new Soviet leadership's perception of its negative correlation with developments outside the Soviet Union. For the Soviet leadership and political elite (as well as larger professional groups), the key measure of Soviet progress was, and continues to be, Soviet accomplishments as compared to that of industrially advanced capitalist countries. This relativism in judging Soviet progress is an internalized principle and a basic Soviet tradition. Starting with Lenin, but especially under Stalin and continuing in the post-Stalin era, the slogan of "catching up and surpassing," economically and technologically, the principal capitalist countries—in particular, the main Soviet adversary, the United States—was at the center of attention of the Soviet leadership and was a driving force behind Soviet policy formation. This "comparativist" attitude resulted primarily from ideological necessities, such as the proof of the superiority of the Soviet system, and from obvious security and foreign policy concerns.

The comparative perspective of Soviet economic standards and achievements is also of great importance to Soviet leaders because it serves as a reference point for their self-evaluation and self-esteem. Sputniks, space stations and intercontinental rockets help their self-esteem but the evaluation of relative progress must be decided on earth, on a much broader national scale, with respect not only to extraordinary, heroic deeds but also to everyday lifestyle standards and patterns.

It is significant and highly relevant, therefore, to pause for a moment and assess the changes that have occurred in the last two decades outside the Soviet Union. In the last 15 years, almost all capitalist countries entered the era of the Third Industrial Revolution. The enormous scope, the headlong (and still increasing) speed, and the deep effects of this revolution went far beyond even the most optimistic projections made in the late 1960s. At the core of the Third Industrial Revolution is the immensely expanded complex of communication systems and the enormous and previously unimaginable expansion of information collection, retrieval and exchange. Industrial and public services have broadened in scope and have increased drastically in productivity. There has been a qualitative change in durable consumer goods through their mesh with electronics and miniaturization, and a growing avalanche of new capital and consumer products entering the market. The fantastic speed with which the new production, managerial and leisure opportunities have permeated entire economies and societies has been made possible by the vastly increased role of science in the production and distribution process. The global nature of the market, and the economic and technological interdependence of all countries, based on the traditional principle of the international division of labor, has promoted the full participation, on a competitive basis, of a number of small and previously non-industrialized Asian countries that were able to grasp the advantages of relative backwardness.

The Soviet Union has yet to create many of the requisites for joining this revolution, from simple and reliable telephone networks to the much more complicated production of such primary electronic components as reliable and super-miniaturized microchips. By the end of the 1970s, parts of the Soviet political and professional classes were well aware of the revolution that was sweeping the West and the East, but the Soviet leadership apparently did not understand the nature of the challenge and did not contemplate a realistic Soviet response.

The combination of the trends of Soviet economic and technological stagnation with the explosive growth in the capitalist world was potentially, and in part actually, calamitous to the Soviet Union and to the domestic and international aspirations of its ruling circles. Excluding the Second World War, the 1970s to the mid-1980s was the first prolonged period in Soviet history when the Soviet Union was falling behind the major capitalist nations in key comparative economic indicators. Most important, the technological gap between the Soviet Union and advanced capitalist countries was widening sharply and with increased momentum.

These quantitative comparisons, however, do not tell the main story. The most important comparisons concern qualitative factors that can seldom be quantified. The major physical indicators of Soviet production, once the most visible signs of its accomplishment—and a matter of great pride to the Soviet leadership, political elite and people—now suddenly seemed either irrelevant or worse, an expression of backwardness.

The Soviet Union produces, for example, twice as much steel as the United States, with a GNP half the size of the United States, and still encounters chronic shortages of steel. The explanation for this anomaly is quite simple: The Soviet Union wastes steel by engaging in an unnecessary and unproductive enterprise. The amount of steel in Soviet capital and consumer goods is comparatively exorbitant. (This incidentally, is also true of lumber and other primary products, notably the wasteful consumption of electricity and oil.)

What counts economically in the contemporary world is not merely quantity. Rather, it is high labor and capital productivity in the production process; the modernity of the product mix; and the costs, quality and easy availability and serviceability of the products. In all these respects in the last two decades, the Soviet Union has regressed as compared to capitalist nations.

Soviet leaders are well aware of the state of affairs described above. They believe that they and their party's ideological sense of purpose are endangered. Their patriotic pride is hurt. The situation of Japan and the modernity of the newly industrial nations in Asia, which often defy imagination, must be a particularly bitter pill for the Soviets to swallow. More important, what they understand to be their patriotic destiny of international greatness has been called into question. Their sense of urgency in countering the economic-technological challenge is strongly reinforced by fears of its potential military consequences. They recognize that their international aspirations to greatness cannot be reconciled in the long term with their relative economic-technological weaknesses and the narrow range of their foreign policy resources. In the final analysis, it is this psychological motivation that is the deepest source of the present Soviet leaders' commitment to real change in the Soviet Union.

Soviet Capabilities and the International Environment

The second international source of the changes taking place in the Soviet Union is its deteriorating international position. At the end of the 1960s and during the early 1970s the Soviet international position was increasingly strong. To the Soviets it looked as if a qualitative change was taking place, the fulfillment of a dream for which generations had been sacrificed. It seemed to them that the "international correlation of forces," which describes not simply a momentary situation but a trend occurring over a large time segment, was moving solidly in their favor, perhaps irreversibly.

Soviet leaders expected major favorable political-international consequences from the American public recognition of a state of strategic parity with the Soviet Union. The *Ostpolitik* of the late 1960s, followed by détente in the early 1970s, was increasingly considered by Soviet leaders to be an offensive strategy. In their eyes, the United States entered the détente compact from a position of weakness brought on by Vietnam and magnified by the Watergate scandal— all of which paralyzed American political institutions and forced a public retreat from international activism. For the Soviets, in the final analysis, détente looked like a guarantee against dangerous confrontation with the United States. They believed that détente would be accompanied by the stabilization of the situation in Europe, including the recognition of Soviet domination of East Central Europe; the expansion of economic relations with the West, including large-scale technology transfer needed by the Soviets; and, at the same time, an almost free hand for the expansion of Soviet power and influence in the peripheral regions of Soviet-American competition.

By the late 1970s and the early 1980s, however, the Soviet international position had deteriorated significantly. While the invasion of Afghanistan in 1979 signified the end of Soviet-American détente, American defense policies in the late 1970s, and particularly in the early 1980s, ended the erosion of the strategic balance against America. The Soviets were faced with an intensive and costly new cycle of the unending arms race and Strategic Defense Initiative (SDI) that they feared could lead to an American technological breakout. The deployment of SS-20s in Europe, one of the most foolish acts of Soviet foreign and security policy, backfired by bringing the Atlantic alliance closer together. The Soviet campaign against intermediate-range nuclear forces (INF) was a textbook example of diplomatic clumsiness following a major military error.

While still weary of international military involvements, the United States largely left behind its nihilistic attitude toward international activism. It regained much of its past sense of confidence, increased significantly its military budget and started a qualitatively new stage in the modernization of its conventional forces.

At the same time, the Soviet Union found itself overextended in its international involvement. International commitments both strained Soviet resources and held no promise of near-term victories. As a case in point, the so-called national liberation movements that in the 1970s were a symbol of effective Soviet influence, became by the early 1980s an increasingly anti-Soviet force. The Soviet Union found itself with almost no major friends and with trouble in its empire. In Eastern Europe, the unprecedented events in Poland that began in 1980 brought together the working classes and the intelligentsia in a massive all-national movement against the communist regime. Luckily for the Soviet Union, these events were arrested without invasion by an internal security crackdown and martial law. But the problems that led to the creation of Solidarity were not resolved. In fact, Poland became the first non-communist country with an organized and nonviolent opposition.

During the leadership paralysis of the Brezhnev period, and the subsequent power vacuum of the Kremlin interregnum, Soviet supervision of Eastern Europe slackened, giving much greater leeway to the centrifugal tendencies of the native communist leaderships. The economic situation in Eastern Europe deteriorated, increasing the Soviet economic burden and creating potentially destabilizing conditions in the Soviet empire.

The Soviet Union's relative decline on the international scene, combined with its domestic crisis, created a situation that required an urgent reassessment of the strategic direction of Soviet security and foreign policies. It reinforced the previously described feeling among parts of the Soviet leadership, political elite and experts, of the inadequacy of Soviet foreign policy resources as related to Soviet global aspirations. The highly unimaginative Soviet leadership, frozen in old strategic concepts and traditional policies and tactically inflexible, could not even begin to address the situation. The obvious gravity of the existing condition in this respect provided an immensely forceful stimulant for deep change. As Gorbachev and his associates argue, with justification, the most important Soviet foreign and security policy statement consists of the program of domestic renewal and radical reform.

The Influence of Domestic Reform on Soviet Foreign Policy

These domestic and international factors explain why, in the early 1980s, a powerful pressure for change was building up in the Soviet Union. Yet the change now occurring in the USSR was not at all inevitable. The intense perception of the need for change had to combine with a catalyst. A conscious historical agent was needed to transform the pressures for change from a possibility into a reality. This catalyst emerged through the process of Soviet political succession, confirming once again the central role of leadership in human affairs.

The hope that we are presently witnessing changes that will affect the nature and long-term direction of Soviet foreign policy is based primarily on Gorbachev's effort to transform the Soviet Union domestically. The fiercest critics of the Soviet Union have repeatedly insisted that significant Soviet foreign and security policy changes could occur only if the domestic system itself will begin to change. The domestic changes that the United States hoped for have begun, and the Soviet Union is moving in a positive direction. One should not belittle what already is happening nor derogate the plausibility of further evaluation. However, a sober analysis of the potential impact on Soviet foreign policy must be based upon an understanding that this is only the beginning.

Long-term tendencies in Soviet foreign policy will depend primarily on three factors related to the process of domestic reform: (i) the complexity and timetable of Gorbachev's domestic reforms; (ii) the liberal direction of the reforms and their probable consequences; and (iii) the process of demilitarization of Soviet society (which is already becoming evident).

It is increasingly clear that Soviet foreign policy is becoming subordinated, more than at any time in the post-Stalin era, to exigencies at home and within the empire. Mikhail Gorbachev seems to be turning the gaze of Soviet leadership inward, toward galvanizing a moribund economy and mobilizing an apathetic public. The Soviet leadership wants to insulate the ongoing and extremely difficult process of implementation of a program of radical reforms from international challenges, obstacles and negative interventions.

The question is, however, how long will the process of giving priority to domestic concerns last, and how much of the country's collective energy will be expended primarily to achieve domestic goals? From what was said above we know how serious and multidimensional the crisis of the Soviet system is. We know how Gorbachev himself was gradually educated in office, identifying the mess he inherited in more and more ominous terms. Parallel to this, he has defined the measures necessary for a turnaround in increasingly radical terms. Again, Gorbachev himself uses the year 2000 as the benchmark when the results of his reforms will show clearly. Yet it is increasingly the opinion both of Western and Soviet analysts from every discipline (myself among them), that even in their least ambitious formulations, the economic, technological, social and political goals of Gorbachev's reforms will require more than a generation to become irreversible.

A top Soviet scientist at a meeting in summer 1988 with his American colleagues defined very succinctly what he considered to be a plausible outcome by the year 2000 of Gorbachev's goal of technological revolution: "Regardless [of] what we do, the gap between America and Russia in crucial areas of high technology, particularly computers, will dramatically *increase* at least until the year 1995. If by the year 2000 we can prevent the gap from further opening, it will be a miraculous success." The Soviets will probably be able to improve the standard of living as well as agricultural and industrial productivity within the next decade, but the program of a broad-based technological modernization of the Soviet economy, if possible at all, lies very far in the future.

Assuming that Gorbachev remains in power, one can say with certainty that even partial achievements of the pronounced goals of *perestroika* will require an entire lifetime of his leadership. If he does not preserve his power and is replaced by another reformer with a different program of modernization, the time needed even for a partial success will be longer still. From the point of view of our interests the conclusion is clear: The prolonged process of transformation will center the attention of the Soviets on domestic affairs for its duration. As Gorbachev noted in a conversation with an American, "Our country is very big, and our people do not take to new fashions (*novshestvo*) very easily. It will take us a long time to bring our country into motion. But when we achieve it things will move faster." The first part of his statement is certainly true; the second, however, remains to be proven. (Of course, if Gorbachev loses power and is not replaced by a reformer, the scenario would change substantially. But this subject is beyond our scope here.)

The Soviet Union is becoming a more liberal country. The new freedoms, however fragmentary and limited, have passed from the stage of implementation from above. They are now achieving a momentum of their own. The Yeltsin affair, the freedom from fear developing among the creative intelligentsia and the nationalistic disturbances in Kazakhstan, the Baltic republics and Transcaucasia have exposed the Soviet leadership to the perils of democracy, even if it is as yet only in its incipient stage. Elements of a civil society are developing in the Soviet Union. There is a freer flow of information, open debates, greater commitment of the media to the truth, greater autonomy of the professions and the creative stratum, and the existence (by the Soviets' own account) of about 30,000 voluntary clubs and associations which have come into being spontaneously. These elements, still highly vulnerable, are beginning to shape a new understanding of citizenship, of civic identity and of an incipient public opinion.

The emergence of a new Soviet civil society may have important foreign policy implications. If this process continues, it is certain to stimulate not only a greater knowledge about the outside world but also the intrusion of a new, non-manipulative public element in the formation of Soviet foreign policy and, perhaps most importantly, the growth of domestic public factors that will require greater accountability of the leadership for their foreign policy steps. Even today, at the initial stages of the democratization process, such taboo issues as the war in Afghanistan have become the subject of intense discussion. The debate itself probably caused the Soviet leadership to be even more eager to put an end to their calamitous adventure.

An integral part of Gorbachev's *perestroika* is a progressive demilitarization of Soviet society and polity. The Soviet Union under Gorbachev's predecessors was among the most militarized countries of the industrialized world. The militarization of Soviet society went beyond its military-industrial complex, taking on many forms in many dimensions, of which the following were of special importance.

First, a cult of the military was ingrained and promoted in the society. In public discourse it was a sacred cow that could not be criticized. It had the greatest degree of autonomy of any profession. The patriotic emphasis in Soviet education and everyday life kept the military constantly in the public eye where it was a major theme in cultural life. The officer corps was to a large extent a closed caste. The core of the High Command had major political influence.

Second, military considerations dominated decision-making in both domestic and foreign policy spheres. In the domestic area, it was assigned top economic priority. In the area of foreign policy, the importance of military power for achieving political goals, together with the Soviet leadership's view about the role of force in the international arena, kept the military factor at the very heart of Soviet decision-making.

Third, in deliberations over Soviet security policy, the High Command enjoyed a monopoly of expertise. The cult of secrecy and the compartmentalization of the Soviet economy and management was especially pronounced in the strict division between the military and the civilian establishments. Military evaluation, doctrine and the preparation of military options for the political leadership was almost entirely in the hands of the military.

Fourth, the priority assigned to military expenditures, and their great economic burden, was an important factor in the Soviet economic crisis. The apparent weight of Soviet military expenditures in the economy at large—Western estimates which vary from 12 to 20 percent of GNP, or two or three times higher relative to the United States—does not even begin to tell the story of the burden that military expenditures place on the Soviet economy with respect to the quality of human and material resources. The level of military expenditures has had an immense opportunity cost. Military spending has

41

drained civilian resources, stunted economic growth by limiting capital formation and even affected future military capabilities by lowering the technological
level of the economy as a whole.

What Gorbachev has already done, and will in all probability continue to do
in implementing *perestroika*, is to restrict the political role of the Soviet High
Command and eliminate the military's sacred cow status. He has imposed
perestroika on the military itself, criticized the fat that has accumulated in the
Soviet military establishment, and demanded accountability and cost-cutting from
the High Command. With regard to politics and policy-making, Gorbachev has
already broken the military's near monopoly of access to budgetary allocations,
thus showing a significant departure from the Brezhnev era, when the military
almost automatically got what it wanted.

The profile of the Soviet military in the political arena during the fourth
year of Gorbachev's rule is rather low. The decline of its prestige, due to its
inability to win the war in Afghanistan, is clear. Gorbachev's control over the
Soviet High Command is strong and seems to be growing. He began to purge
the upper echelon of the military from the second year of his rule. He used the
deep embarrassment caused by the Rust incident, when a young West German
landed his plane on Red Square, for a major replacement of field rank officers
(by our estimates about 200 officers of general rank). He appointed General
Dmitri Yazov, a man with few personal political ambitions and who is close to
the leader, as the new minister of defense, in the process jumping over two
dozen senior marshals and generals. He assigned a number of military intellectuals, whom he retired from active service, to the central party apparatus in
Moscow. In an effort to create an institution that would resemble an American
civilian think tank concerned with military affairs (e.g., the RAND Corporation
in California), he increased the access to and discussion of classified military
information within a civilian-staffed military department in one of the largest
institutes that study international relations. Competing civilian formulations of
Soviet defense policies, priorities and expenditures have already started to flow
to the new leadership. Gorbachev is clearly following the advice of Khrushchev
who in his memoirs wrote: "Who in our country is in a position to intimidate
the leadership? It is the military ... the military is prone to engage in irresponsible daydreaming and bragging. Given a chance, some elements within the
military might try to force a militarist policy on the Government. Therefore, the
Government must always keep a bit between the teeth of the military."

Gorbachev's *perestroika*, if it continues, will affect the long-range tendencies of Soviet foreign and security policies in two ways: directly, by changes in
Soviet concepts and perceptions of the international arena, and indirectly, by the
influence of several domestic factors on the foreign and security policy formation. We may be witnessing today a potentially revolutionary change in the
Soviet definition of domestic priorities and a parallel reassessment of Soviet
foreign policy and security goals. Soviet long-term aspirations in the international arena are still very high. Gorbachev and his generation of Soviet leaders
and political elite are highly ambitious and do not share the psychological

insecurities of the preceding generation. As adversaries in world diplomacy, they are much more intelligent and adaptable, and therefore more dangerous as opponents to American leadership.

Yet for now, and for the foreseeable future, their international aspirations will be tempered by domestic and international constraints. It is hoped in the United States that the changes in the Soviet Union will become permanent, and it should become a priority to explore the opportunities that have been created by Gorbachev's *perestroika* and new thinking for long lasting improvements in Soviet-American relations. What we should aim for are not only treaties in the field of arms control, but a Soviet-American dialogue that will fundamentally reassess the strategic political elements of our conflict. The current situation, not only in the Soviet Union but also in the United States, makes the chances of such a reassessment much better than ever before.

The American Side of the Equation

Changes that facilitate the improvement of Soviet-American relations, and particularly radical arms control agreements, are not limited to the Soviet Union. The conditions of the other superpower, the United States, are extremely relevant in assessing new trends in Soviet foreign policies, particularly in the area of arms control. They can clearly reinforce the influence of these Soviet domestic trends that are moving the USSR toward reversing the arms race, and thereby improve Soviet-American relations. It is probable that the decade from 1985 to 1995 will mark an end to the spiral of strategic rearmament that started after the Second World War and has continued unabated for more than 40 years. It seems likely that the domestic and international pressures on *both* superpowers will, for the first time, be strong enough to lead in this direction. It may be that, for once, Soviet and American thinking with regard to strategic weapons systems and to the question of national security is becoming increasingly synchronized.

The changes in the United States' approach to its relationship with the Soviet Union reflect two trends that are to a large extent externally induced and bear a similarity to the trends in the Soviet Union. First, whereas in the 1960s and 1970s the balance between economic and security interests clearly favored security, in the late 1980s and in the 1990s it is highly probable that economic interest will take precedence. Second, the United States is beginning to reassess its old international commitments that seem too burdensome given the new economic circumstances.

These changes in the United States with regard to national security goals are significant if they represent a trend, as they apparently do. The Reagan administration switched in its second term from its earlier position of "arm now, talk later" to a two-track policy that emphasized serious arms control negotiations with the Soviets. It is notable that the switch to the two-track policy occurred with a president who had deeply conservative instincts, an extraordinary mistrust of the Soviets, and a constituency that for the most part opposed *any* arms control agreements with the Soviet Union.

The agreement with the Soviets on the abolishment of all medium- and short-range nuclear weapons, while militarily of limited significance, was politically and psychologically of great importance and may herald a major future breakthrough. It demonstrated that radical arms control agreements can be successfully negotiated with the Soviets; that Soviet negotiating behavior can be both serious and flexible; and that the very complex and immensely sensitive political issue of verification through on-site inspection can be resolved to mutual satisfaction with regard to *mobile* weapons, even where the verification process is particularly difficult. The INF agreement, secured during the last year of the Reagan administration, now provides the needed impetus for carrying over arms control negotiations with the Soviets into the present Bush administration.

Toward a New Soviet-American Relationship

Public opinion polls and the visible mood in the Congress as a whole, and among the most respected congressmen and senators of the armed services committees in particular, indicate a change of attitude toward the unending arms race. It is becoming clear that the political public, the politicians, the media and the big business community are beginning to recognize that the Soviet-American arms race has reached an obvious dead end.

It certainly is not by chance that two such different leaders as President Reagan and General Secretary Gorbachev, who preside over diametrically different systems, arrived independently at a basically similar conclusion: The nuclear terror of an unending strategic arms race has to be brought to a stop. Their prescription for achieving that goal—the Strategic Defense Initiative in one case, and total nuclear disarmament in the other, are as different as their nations are. Yet the underlying basis for their prescription is identical—the recognition of the utmost irrationality of further build-ups of their respective bloated nuclear arsenals.

Economic circumstances in America, especially the enormous budget deficits and a national debt ceiling that has crossed the $3 trillion mark, create an increasing, possibly irresistible pressure for budget stabilization. Considering the cuts made by President Reagan in non-military budgetary expenditures, the very high proportion of non-cuttable entitlements in the budget, and the very large increases in military spending in the last nine years (beginning with President Carter in 1979), cuts in the military budget by the Bush administration and Congress are inevitable.

Moreover, SDI no longer appears to be such an insurmountable obstacle to radical strategic offensive arms reductions as it did only a year or two ago. Not only is its feasibility and cost questioned on the American side, but it seems probable that as long as a good chance exists for a major strategic deal with the Soviets, the anti-ballistic missile treaty will continue to be construed in its strict interpretation. On the Soviet side, after the foolish demand to prevent SDI research and all forms of component testing was abandoned, recognition is growing that no American Congress will trade a "bird in the hand"—a radical strategic arms agreement with the Soviet Union—for SDI, the "bird in the bush."

It also seems likely that observers of the American political scene, both here and abroad, may have exaggerated the extent, intensity and staying power of the popular and elite switch toward conservatism that brought Reagan into power and was reinforced by his policies. A movement toward the traditional center and moderation of American politics seems very likely during the tenure of the new administration and Congress. Most relevant to our analysis, it seems also that this trend is particularly noticeable with regard to American international relations, especially relations with the Soviet Union.

The Iran-contra affair and President Reagan's Persian Gulf policy demonstrated, in my opinion, that Congress and the public are not in an interventionist mood. With regard to relations with the Soviet Union, the public and elite interest in the Gorbachev experiment is higher than any time in the recent past. Gorbachev as a leader, and particularly his domestic reforms, have caught the imagination of American people of all classes. The general impression, reinforced by the media, is that the Soviet Union has embarked upon a path of great promise in a direction Americans like. This cannot but have an influence on American attitudes in dealing with the Soviets.

We are witnessing now, for the first time during the postwar era of the cold war, a significant measure of synchronization between Soviet and American interests and of policy predispositions and trends in both countries. The preoccupation with domestic and international economic concerns, the noninterventionist mood, and the movement in foreign and security policy formation towards the pragmatic center in both countries speaks optimistically for their relations in the remaining decade of the 20th century.

7

The Crisis of the Soviet System of Power and Mikhail Gorbachev's Political Strategy

Thane Gustafson

Mikhail Gorbachev's politics are a tough act to follow. When after one year in office he had not yet produced the millenium, Western reviewers were ready to dismiss him as a conservative and a technocrat. Then as he unveiled one radical measure after another over the next year-and-a-half, the critics called him naive and rash and began forecasting his fall. The latest reviews, following his dismissal of Moscow Party chief Boris Yeltsin in the fall of 1987, now bring us Gorbachev the Party opportunist, trimming to the conservative wind. Yet the man must have an underlying strategy. What is it?

When Gorbachev became General Secretary of the Central Committee of the CPSU in March 1985, he appeared to believe that the problems he faced were essentially economic. To the extent that they were political, this was because of Brezhnev's mistakes, not because of basic flaws in the political system. The key word of Gorbachev's first major policy speech in April, 1985, was "acceleration" ("*uskorenie*"), and the changes he proposed were confined mainly to the "economic mechanism."[1] But within a year Gorbachev had begun to speak of "restructuring," "radical reform," "revolution," and "democratization." By the first half of 1987 his diagnoses of the past, his initiatives for the present, and his proposals for the future raised fundamental political issues, many of which had not been touched since the 1920s.[2]

Naturally, in analyzing any politician's moves it is extremely difficult to separate the tactical from the strategic and the improvised from the premeditated. Was Gorbachev planning radical reforms from the start and only biding his time, or has his thinking evolved along the way? At this point we cannot say. But whatever his path, by the beginning of 1987 Gorbachev had concluded that the real crisis facing him was not only economic but political. His recent actions, therefore, should be seen not only as an attempt to revitalize the economy but also the political instruments and resources by which power and authority are generated and maintained.

It is logical, on reflection, that economic and political crisis should go together, because the political and economic systems created by Stalin were together the embodiment of a single development strategy.[3] What Gorbachev is now telling us is that as the strategy is outgrown, both its economic and its political sides are in crisis, and one cannot reform one without reforming the other. For Gorbachev, the "crisis of effectiveness" that Western scholars speak of is indeed a "crisis of survival."[4]

But is the political system any more reformable than the economic system is, short of wholesale systemic change? Just as there has been a treadmill of economic half-reforms since Stalin's death, has there not been a treadmill of political half-reforms as well? What, if anything, stands to make Gorbachev different from previous "reforming" General Secretaries?

Part I of this chapter describes the causes and consequences of the political crisis. Part II describes how Gorbachev's political strategy appears designed to respond to it. Part III evaluates the consistency of the strategy and its appropriateness as it has evolved so far.

The Crisis of the Soviet System of Power and Authority

On the surface, the Soviet system of power appears remarkably unchanged from what it was thirty years ago, after Khrushchev had gathered the reins back into the hands of the Party leadership. The power of the General Secretary and the collective power of the Politburo over the classic instruments of rule remain formally unopposed, unchallenged, and undivided. This small group of men still holds nominally total control over personnel, political agenda and economic priorities, organizational structures, official means of communication and sources of information, and instruments of coercion.

This point may have seemed in doubt under Brezhnev, especially in the first half of his reign. There was speculation in the West that patronage and clientelism were declining, that various interest groups were gaining power, that decision-making in Soviet politics was becoming incremental and consensual, and above all, that the powers of the General Secretary were in decline. But Brezhnev could move the traditional levers firmly enough when he chose to, as he showed by making sharp changes from time to time in investment shares (in agriculture, energy, and defense) or in personnel (as in Georgia and Azerbaijan). Indeed, under Brezhnev the office of the General Secretary became more of a formal institution than ever before. Since his death, the whirlwind of changes in personnel, institutions, and resource flows— all unleashed from the General Secretary's office—shows clearly that there is power in the old levers yet.

Neither has there been any deterioration in the Politburo's capacity to manage the politics of succession and power entirely within its own ranks, or to defend its prerogatives from potential encroachers. All three post-Brezhnev successions were handled within the closed club of the Politburo, and there is no sign that the Central Committee played any role other than the purely formal one of endorsing the choices of the Politburo. Even Iurii Andropov's care to have himself re-appointed a Party secretary in the spring of 1982 was a tacit acknowledgment on his part that the succession, as always, would be a matter of Party insiders choosing one of their own. The meager evidence available suggests that Gorbachev's election as General Secretary was no different.[5]

As for encroachment by other elite groups, Marshal Ogarkov's summary dismissal in the fall of 1984 showed that the Politburo, even under a feeble General Secretary, remained as able and determined as in the past to deal with high-ranking irritants. Despite talk in the Western media of the military as "king-makers" in the Andropov succession, the subsequent systematic humbling of the uniformed military under Gorbachev brings their apparent influence lower than it has been in decades.[6]

Thus the powers of the General Secretary and the Politburo remain awesome; yet, paradoxically, over the last generation they have also grown subtly weaker. Within the elite (which one might define very roughly as the top thousand positions in the system) political resources have broadened and the players—including the leaders themselves— have apparently accepted certain tacit rules. Among the former is an expansion of multilateral communication and information within the top elite, the emergence of "opinion" not controlled by the General Secretary, and the development of individual prestige attached to leading figures.[7] Among the latter is a greater freedom to discuss policy issues in public and to take dissenting positions without being accused of political disloyalty. These new features have not disappeared under Gorbachev; indeed, *glasnost'* favors them; and they undoubtedly help to explain Gorbachev's difficulties in dealing with resistance in the Central Committee, his deliberateness in personnel changes, or his care in dealing with the leadership of the KGB or the military-industrial ministries (and with the military hierarchy, for that matter, until the Rust affair), or with senior Brezhnev veterans such as Gromyko, Kapitonov, Ponomarev, and Baibakov, all of whom have been given prominent positions upstairs.

Such a subtle erosion of absolute power in elite politics one might call *le petit mal.* But alongside it there is a *grand mal,* which affects the leaders' control of the mass of officialdom and of the population at large. The leadership increasingly finds that its awesome power will not serve its goals; it is less and less able to carry out its political agenda; and the more it attempts to control events the more real control eludes it. As a result, the leaders' power fails to build authority, in the sense of enhancing their standing as problem-solvers or their credibility as spokesmen for society's values. The fundamental reason is not the character of General Secretaries or the dynamics of power at the top, but rather the evolution of Soviet society as a whole and the consequent changes in people's minds. These make the traditional levers less effective and their objects less responsive. This is the real source of political crisis; it is a crisis of power and authority.

Two Sources of the Decline
in the Leaders' Power and Authority

Before going on, let us pause briefly to look at what we mean by power. Power is not a physical force, although we often talk as though it were; it is a relationship between a subject and an object, and it always involves two aspects. If A wishes to move B, he must first transmit his will to B. The classic levers of transmission in Soviet politics are familiar: control of political organization, personnel, and agenda; education, indoctrination, and control of information; rewards, punishments, and threats, etc. But these are not the things that will actually move B; what actually moves B is what we call (aptly enough) *motives* — fear, faith, values, beliefs, habits, hope, greed, etc. These are inside B, which means that B must ultimately move himself for A to have power over him. Power, in all its varieties (coercion, influence, authority) thus always involves a lever acting at a distance on some resource in people's minds.

The reason for stressing this distinction is that the traditional Soviet system of power faces problems with both the levers and the motives: its traditional levers are too crude for the more delicate tasks they must now perform; they have increasingly harmful side-effects that act against the leaders' own goals,[8] and they are less and less able to manipulate the resources in people's minds—their motives, beliefs, habits, and perceptions—in the ways the leaders require. It is as though the leaders were trying to drive a tractor with reins and a whip.

The Leaders' Weakening Command of the Resources in People's Minds: Motives, Beliefs, and Habits

In the Soviet state in its third generation, mass terror has receded, social mobility has declined, and ideological elan has faded. Job security is taken for granted, and for a growing fraction of the population, privileges and amenities are as well. Therefore, what resources remain that will move either elite or population? Stalin's successors have gradually found themselves limited to a choice between faith and greed, and both pose growing problems.

The decline of ideological faith among the Soviet people is an old theme in Western sovietology. One may question how deep that faith was to begin with, but the long sclerosis of official thought has made ideology ineffective as a means of moving people. It would be hard to express the reasons for present-day apathy and cynicism more strikingly than Gorbachev himself did in his plenum speech in January 1987:

> The theoretical concepts of socialism remained to a large extent at the level of the 1930s–40s, when society was tackling entirely different tasks.
>
> The causes of the situation go far back into the past and are rooted in that specific historical situation in which, by virtue of well-known circumstances, vigorous debates and creative ideas disappeared from theory and social science, while authoritarian evaluations and opinions became unquestionable truths.
>
> There occurred a sort of absolutization of the forms of organization of society that had emerged in practice. Moreover, such ideas were essentially equated with the core characteristics of socialism, viewed as unchangeable and elevated as dogmas.

Gorbachev himself is manifestly a true believer in Marxism-Leninism, determined to revive faith and pride in a just, cleansed, and modernized socialism. But how many are there like him? Many Soviet citizens undoubtedly share his sense of shame over the country's stagnation and his disgust over the corruption and anomie of the 1970s, but those are emotions born of injured national pride and offended puritanism, not necessarily of faith in socialism. Gorbachev may be too late.

Indeed, one of the most remarkable recent developments in Soviet society is the rise of competing values that, potentially, pose strong obstacles to the leaders' efforts to appeal to ideology. Gail Lapidus sums them up in a recent essay:[9] (1) a growing preoccupation with universal moral concerns, which provide a broader basis for values than *partiinost'* and the moral categories of Marxism-Leninism; (2) a shift away from exclusive emphasis on collectivism toward increasing acceptance of diversity and individualism (including private and cooperative forms of property), as well as recognition of the legitimacy (and inevitability) of contending interests in society;[10] (3) an evolution away from insistence on single truths toward growing acceptance of the legitimacy of diverse opinions and of debate; (4) a weakening of the idea of human perfectibility and of the conviction that one can create a perfect society, free of human vice or failing. These changes appear to have two broad sources: first, the re-emergence of alternative values from private life into public view (and simultaneously, many people's increasingly open withdrawal from public life into private values);[11] and second, the alteration of people's beliefs and expectations as a result of their experiences over the last generation.

This evolution in public values and beliefs complicates immensely the task of the Soviet leaders, because it amounts to nothing less than a spontaneous reassertion of the norms of civil society, after two generations of absolute dominance by the state. By and large, the response of the state under Brezhnev was to accommodate itself, grudgingly and piece-meal, to society's evolving values, so long as they remained private, lashing out against them only when they became too public. The result was a tacit deal, which made it increasingly difficult for the leaders to mobilize people's energies by invoking official values. Gorbachev may find the intelligentsia of little help to him here, since it is precisely among them that the evolution of values has gone furthest.[12]

As a result, General Secretaries have gradually been thrown back on economic self-interest as the one popular resource on which they could really act, but that resource too has become more difficult to mobilize than in the past. As the sociologist Tat'iana Zaslavskaia argues, citizens' living standards have now risen so high that minor economic incentives will no longer force them to work hard at their jobs.[13] To get a bigger response, the leaders would have to increase both rewards and penalties, allowing some to get rich and others to lose their jobs. Both Khrushchev and Brezhnev shrank from the implications.

What about a return to mass coercion? The passing of mass terror has been more than simply a change in the style of coercion; a generation after Stalin's death, people's perceptions and expectations have gradually adjusted to a saner life. The results of surveys of recent Soviet emigrants are especially striking: they suggest that the habit of fear and the mistrust of others that still reach deep inside older people have largely faded among younger Soviet citizens.[14] The young see the pattern of KGB political repression as graduated and predictable rather than random; and provided one conforms outwardly the probability of trouble is perceived as low. More important, younger people do not fear to speak their minds to a wider circle of people than their immediate families. Along with mass terror, intimidation and atomization are fading as well.

As a result, while the state is still able to deter overt political nonconformity, it has lost the more general power over the population that mass insecurity once provided, and it is doubtful that that power could be recovered under any circumstances. People are losing the habit of doing the regime's bidding simply because they fear the consequences of not doing so, and as they lose their fear, they share their perceptions with one another, and the effect is multiplied. In short, while the regime's negative power to intimidate individuals or specific groups still remains, the threat of terror as a mobilizing force is gone.

In sum, the range of motives, habits, and beliefs on which the Soviet leadership can act has narrowed, while a number of competing ones, which they do not control, have reappeared. Bolshevik fervor has almost entirely disappeared as a motive force; acquiescence in the official values of the state is still widespread but largely passive. Fear can deter, but it can no longer mobilize. The leadership is driven to rely on economic self-interest, but they are deterred by their own ambivalence from making effective use of it. The result, at least under Brezhnev, was the slow emergence of a sort of tacit social contract that required the leaders to accept, without admitting it even to themselves, a decline in their active power over society.

It is possible to argue—and, as we shall see, Gorbachev does indeed argue—that what has changed is not people's motives but their circumstances, and therefore what is needed to move them is more vigorous and intelligent use of the levers. But here we come to the second cause of the deterioration of the leaders' traditional powers—the increasingly awkward side-effects of the traditional instruments of rule.

Declining Effectiveness of Traditional Levers

The traditional Soviet system operated with a surprisingly narrow array of political instruments,[15] of which the most important was the control of personnel, particularly within the Party organization. This was possible because the leadership confined itself to a narrow range of goals—essentially internal security, industrial growth, and military power—and concentrated its power on those.[16]

53

But since Stalin's death the list of objectives pursued by the leaders has broadened to include consumer welfare, agricultural modernization, and broad technological innovation, and simultaneously each of the main objectives has grown more complex than before. Consequently, side-effects that were once acceptable as the leaders sought to maximize a handful of objectives regardless of cost, have now become less tolerable to them.

1. The Personnel Weapon. Control of cadres remains the key to power in the Soviet system, but the weaknesses and drawbacks of the weapon of personnel have become more apparent in recent years. First, from the standpoint of the formation of power, General Secretaries since Stalin have learned that mere hiring and firing does not guarantee the loyalty or responsiveness of subordinates. Previous work associations produce the strongest bonds,[17] but simply appointing one's long-time proteges (assuming one has them) has disadvantages of its own, especially if one's cronies do not happen to be particularly competent. Second, the personnel weapon is a poor instrument for stimulating effective performance, because the wielder, particularly if located far away, is tempted simply to fire scapegoats instead of finding out the facts or looking for more precise remedies.

Third and most serious, the use of the personnel weapon leads to backlash. Since rank is the key to a whole system of graduated state perquisites that are taken for granted by the holders (such as deficit goods, travel, and access to information or "in" entertainment) efforts by all levels of leaders to use the broom as a routine instrument provoke bitter resentment and demoralization, lessen the cadres's experience and effectiveness, and make them less willing to speak out or keep their superiors accurately informed. This leads in turn to resistance from below; fired officials resurface in other high offices; ministry and party officials resist removal or transfer pointed articles appear in the local press on the need for trust in cadres and the harm done by excessive turnover. Such resistance is nothing new; the phenomenon of the "family circle" ("*krugovaia poruka*") of local officials conspiring to support one another against the center is more ancient than the Soviet regime. But as the decades go by the bureaucracy increasingly regards job security and orderly promotion as its prerogative.

As a result, those with political resources to trade use them to resist the personnel weapon. The most valuable and professional elements of the elite—the military, the scientists, the secret police—have sought and gained a measure of control over their own promotion systems. Under Brezhnev regional party leaders successfully bargained for job security for themselves—while retaining the personnel weapon for their own vigorous use. Far from declining in importance (as some Western observers thought at the time), patronage sank to the regional level, producing local satrapies, "zones beyond criticism," and family circles.

These the Gorbachev leadership is now struggling to undo; but having purged most of the Brezhnev-era appointees from the government and party apparatus, Gorbachev's men in the Secretariat are discovering that local patronage networks are re-forming around the new appointees. In the Party apparatus, in particular, few local officials are named from outside their own districts.[18] Thus the personnel weapon increasingly confronts the leaders with delicate problems of dosage: if you overuse it, it has toxic effects; but if you underuse it, others at middle levels will do so in your place. Appointing outsiders helps to produce loyal officials, but increases local resentment and resistance, and the outsiders' lack of familiarity with local conditions can make them less effective. There is no satisfactory balance, yet so long as cadres policy remains one of the principal powers of the party apparatus at all levels, the dilemma will remain.

2. Checkers and Watch-dogs. Another important traditional instrument is the use of multiple checkers and watchers and the practice of denunciation raised to a national art, the system that Merle Fainsod called the "institutionalization of mutual suspicion." This system engenders much the same toxic side-effects as the overuse of the personnel weapon, but in addition it is very labor-intensive. In a typical province there are thousands of paid local *revizory* and hundreds more who descend from Moscow, not to mention tens of thousands of volunteers nominally enrolled as People's Controllers.[19] It is not uncommon for half the personnel of a Soviet enterprise to belong to one or more of the innumerable bodies that exist to check up on one another.[20] Indeed, nearly every Soviet citizen ends up being involved in one way or another, since entire bureaucracies are deliberately set to check up on each other, not to mention the ubiquitous army of secret-police informers. As tasks throughout society grow more complex, the cost of the watch-dog system grows, because it absorbs vast numbers of people with scarce skills who are thus lost to production.[21]

From the beginning, the response of the watched has been to subvert the system, whether by co-opting the watchers on a grand scale,[22] or forming local "family circles" of mutual protection at the local level,[23] or watering down the control system by turning it over to the least qualified and poorest equipped, as with quality control in most civilian industry or enforcement of environmental-quality laws. Only the tasks of the highest priority—such as military production and political security—warrant elite snoopers;[24] the rest are distinctly lackadaisical.

The result is that the leadership gets the worst of both: the waste of time and energy produced by multiple meetings, reports, inspections, etc., and the corruption, misreporting, concealment, and resulting loss of control engendered by the family-circle response. The system produces negative criticism more than helpful advice, and it typically works best after it is too late, when all that remains is for the checkers to inform their superiors.[25]

Indeed, keeping higher-ups informed is the central purpose of the system in the first place. Unlike a conventional regulatory system, which is intended to encourage law-abiding behavior by providing clear rules, orderly adjudication, and fair punishment, the Soviet multiple-watchdog arrangement is part of a system in which the rules themselves are deliberately allowed to remain inconsistent and illegal behavior is tacitly recognized as necessary for the economic and administrative systems to function. The purpose of the checkers is to contain and inform more than to regulate, except during the relatively exceptional periods when the leaders mount a campaign or make examples. But as policy grows more complex and technical, an outside watchdog (particularly one such as the People's Control Commission), operating through periodic raids, is usually unable to report intelligently on what it has discovered or to recommend positive action. As an instrument of rule and a source of information, therefore, the traditional system is increasingly ineffective.

3. Controls Over Information. A third example of weakening levers with growing side-effects is the leadership's use of controls over the flow of information and discussion. By tightly limiting information from outside the country and managing it inside, the regime has tried to shape the population's perceptions and to ward off competing ideas. But information about the outside world is reaching the Soviet population in greater abundance, and above all in more convincing packaging, than ever before. Through videocassettes, attractive consumer goods, increased foreign travel, and even models passed on by the Soviet media themselves, Soviet citizens are now in daily contact with different ways of thinking and with standards of living far higher than their own. The models may not always be lofty ones (one sometimes sympathizes with Gorbachev's grumpings about "bourgeois mass culture"), but they are undeniably influential, and the old system is less able to control what the people see and think.

Yet graduated control over information is a central part of the regime's system of rationed privileges. "High-coercion systems are low-information systems," the political scientist David Apter once wrote, but he may not have foreseen that information itself would become a tool and a perquisite in the leaders' hands, so that once coercion declined the flow of information would not necessarily rise again in proportion. The consequences are increasingly apparent. By treating access to information and the freedom to discuss policy as political and institutional perquisites to be allocated according to individual rank or institutional prestige, the rulers have created a system of compartmentalized information which gives them poor protection against false data, little avail against professional monopolies of advice, and small opportunity, short of the very top, to debate the "big picture." Colleagues in neighboring ministries cannot get the information they need for policy, while hierarchical superiors are overloaded.

One result is policy mistakes. Official review commissions lack the detailed data necessary to resist bureaucratic pressures in favor of unsound projects, while whistle-blowers are prosecuted for exposing inside information.[26] Many laws and most of the innumerable agency regulations are unpublished and inaccessible, although many of them are obsolete or contain mistakes.[27] The lack of pertinent information as well as the lack of practice in using it to think about policy hinders learning and the formation of new consensus when old policies fail, and surely helps to account for the negative-mindedness, naivete, and impracticality of much of the Soviet literature of reform until recently. As a result, the leaders end up once again with the worst of both worlds—the side-effects of an overdeveloped control system, combined with a gradual loss of real control. Gorbachev has frequently noted that one result is a great deal of strain for the top leadership, and any reader of the weekly summaries of Politburo meetings will agree. But report after report, decision after decision, still fail to produce action. Not surprisingly, the Brezhnev leadership responded to this by calling for fewer and fewer reports, and the pattern spread to lower levels, contributing to the famous "zones beyond criticism."[28]

4. *Economic Incentives.* We noted earlier that because of the declining effectiveness of other motives, Stalin's successors have been forced to rely more heavily on economic incentives. Ironically, though, Stalin made more effective use of economic levers than they. Scorning egalitarianism with such withering phrases as "petty-bourgeois levelling," he created a steep scale of glittering rewards and chilling penalties, both tightly tied to performance. So extreme were the resulting inequalities that after his death his successors moved quickly to temper them.

But in the process they blunted their instrument. Under Brezhnev especially, the connection between performance and reward weakened and then virtually disappeared, as salary scales narrowed and the rules governing bonuses grew so cumbersome that in practice the same amounts ended up being given to all. Wages outstripped productivity, with the result that money in circulation grew faster than the goods to spend it on. Massive subsidies kept the prices of housing, basic services, and staple foods far below cost, further eroding the workers' sense that their supply was tied to their work; while subsidies to state enterprises (not only direct but indirect, as in the form of credits that were never repaid) had the same effect on managers.

Vast quantities of cash built up in bank accounts,[29] creating buying power that inevitably found an outlet "on the left," as the Russians say, while the authorities looked through their fingers (to use another Russian expression) at the moonlighting, mass theft, and bribery that grew up all around them. In addition to weakening the moral fabric of the system, the growth of the second economy undercut the state's own economic levers by creating powerful competitors to them.

In sum, all of the principal levers of the system—the personnel weapons, the checkers and watchers, the control of information, and economic incentives—have all weakened. Incidentally, it is not for lack of sophistication on the part of the wielders. The KGB's coercion of dissidents under Andropov, for example, was a sophisticated exercise in selective dosage. The careful rationing of official rewards (access to information and travel, allocation of professional status and participation in policy advice, and even the allocation of what one might call standing to official dissent) has become exceedingly refined. Even the Soviets' response to the information revolution shows creative thinking to fit the new opportunities with the old mechanisms.[30]

But the results remind one of Joseph Berliner's observation about Soviet economic reform: one eventually gets diminishing returns from tinkering with obsolete technologies. And like the command economy, the traditional system of levers is increasingly obsolete, because it gives the leaders forms of political power that are negative, blunt, or counterproductive, consisting mainly of the ability to prevent things from happening (if the leaders lean hard enough), or to secure the appearance of compliance and the absence of organized opposition. In political as in economic matters, the leaders are frequently deprived of timely, accurate information; they find themselves forced to resort to campaigns to overcome inertia; and they must reckon with the side-effects of their own actions. Despite their seemingly unlimited ability to hire and fire, to reward and to punish, to allocate, initiate, and block, Soviet leaders must increasingly be content with a limited degree of control over the everyday behavior of the mass of their citizens.

For Gorbachev, this paradox threatens crisis, because with such resources for power a General Secretary is virtually limited to caretaker government or possibly to some return to crude repression. Since Gorbachev intends neither, he cannot simply rely on firing people or

~~spying on them; he must give them a~~ stake in change. He cannot simply orate to passive crowds; he needs an active constituency. Therefore he has been attempting to draw on new resources in people's minds, to revive old levers and create new ones.

I. GORBACHEV'S APPARENT POLITICAL STRATEGY

Gorbachev's political strategy, as it has developed to date, combines old and new. On the one hand, as he must, he has vigorously grasped the classic levers: control of personnel, organizational structure, media, policy agenda, and allocation of resources. Turnover of personnel has been unprecedentedly high, and like his predecessors, Gorbachev uses mass public campaigns and political pressure applied through the party. Large parts of Gorbachev's economic and social program rely heavily on these traditional devices. The new quality-control program, *gospriemka*, for example, is operated by a new layer of checkers.[31] The law on individual economic activity, though it frees private enterprise with one hand, binds it with the other by promising two more bureaucracies, one to check individual incomes, the other to tax them. The reformed planning system adds a new horizontal layer, the regional "production-economic administrations," to the maze of vertical authorities that local managers must reckon with.[32] The anti-alcohol campaign, the war on corruption, the law on illegal incomes, and the drive to restore labor discipline, are all based on familiar coercive techniques. Gorbachev has redrawn organization charts and rejuggled performance indicators as enthusiastically as Khrushchev ever did; his speeches define the boundaries of official orthodoxy on history, culture, and dissent; and he is the vigilant guardian of party discipline. His rhetoric is filled with Bolshevik exhortation and familiar military metaphors. In short, in many ways Gorbachev is a very traditional Soviet politician.

But since his first days as General Secretary Gorbachev's political strategy has also contained strong elements of innovation, and these have become more prominent over time, especially after mid-1986. They fall into six general categories: (1) new ways of reaching the Soviet public; (2) measures to improve the availability and quality of information; (3) experimentation with various forms of voter power; (4) more systematic legislation and expanded legal guarantees; (5) a revival of economic levers; and (6) ideological innovation and the cautious beginnings of reflection on the roles of the party apparatus. Taken together, the innovative elements in Gorbachev's strategy appear designed to provide him with new ways of appealing to people's motives and influencing their perceptions. They also appear—and this is potentially far more daring—to be aimed at providing lower levels of the system with what one might call "delegated levers" of their own, to be used to bring pressure to bear on resistant middle-level officials and to provide protection to those who take risks on his behalf. Gorbachev's aim thus appears to be to build a mass constituency for his program, giving citizens not only economic but also political incentives to support his program, as well as providing them with information, protection, and even a measure of local power. In the process he is attempting to revitalize some classic levers, develop new ones, and use them to move people more powerfully than any Soviet politician has managed to do in a generation.

After discussing these six directions of change, we shall attempt in a later section to evaluate the Gorbachev strategy as a whole. As we shall see, it is still tentative, ambiguous, contradictory, and changeable. The biggest question is how the new is supposed to coexist with the old. Nevertheless, Gorbachev has already gone beyond previous General Secretaries in his ambitions as a political reformer, opening up issues, ideas, and options that have been closed since the 1920s.

Revitalizing Political Resources and Renewing Political Levers: Six Directions of Change

Improving Communication with the Public

Traditional Western thinking about Soviet politics has long emphasized the importance of "transmission belts" (although the phrase is actually Lenin's) as conveyors of the leaders' will to the people, but in the last couple of decades the transmission belts have become badly frayed. Soviet people discount the media as sources of information; they attend official meetings as a tiresome obligation; and the politicians find it difficult to reach them. It is here that the phenomenon of "exit," described in the chapter by Timothy Colton, has become most striking, and nowhere more so than among young people. As Gorbachev observed to a group of editors and writers in mid-1987:[33]

> When you and we painted life in pink colors, the people saw it all and lost interest in the press and in public activity. They felt humiliated and insulted when such phoney stuff was palmed off on them.

Therefore, Gorbachev has been trying to revitalize communications with the population. He has been tireless in making appearances throughout the country, bringing his message to every major city and

TABLE 1
The Spread of Television Since Khrushchev's Day

	1965	1985
TV sets per 100 families	24	97
urban	32	101
rural	15	90
TV sets per 1,000 population	68	293
urban	94	314
rural	37	255
Annual output of TV sets	3,655	9,371
of which color	0	4,024

Source: *Narodnoe khoziaistvo SSSR v 1985g*, pp. 169 and 446; *Narodnoe khoziaistvo SSSR 1922–82*, p. 448.

region. He is an outstanding orator, if not as earthy as Khrushchev (so far he has refrained from homilies about milkmaids or whistling shrimps), but clearly he is his own best ambassador.

The most striking aspect of Gorbachev's efforts to improve communications has been his aggressive, inventive, and abundant use of television. This reflects a basic change in Soviet life in the last generation: compared to Khrushchev's day, television has become a true mass medium which now reaches into nearly every Soviet home, reaching 97 percent of all families in 1985, compared to 24 percent in 1965. Annual output of television sets has nearly tripled since 1965, and nearly half of all TV's now produced in the Soviet Union are color sets. But what is most remarkable is their distribution: while in 1965 it was primarily the city-dwellers who owned TV sets, by 1985 rural families were rapidly drawing even (see Table 1). (In this respect as in others, the Brezhnev era prepared the way for Gorbachev.)

As a result, Gorbachev is the first Soviet TV politician and TV is one of the major tools of *perestroika*. Mass television opens the possibility of making a populist approach to authority-building work as it could not in Khrushchev's day.

But a populist politician is helpless if he cannot tell how his message is being received, and a necessary corollary of better communications downward is better communications upward. Khrushchev in his day had encouraged cautious experimentation with opinion research, but systematic surveys of public opinion are developing rapidly under Gorbachev. A new Center for the Study of Public Opinion is about to open and an Institute of Socio-Economic Problems is being formed. Soviet sociologists are being asked to supply the leadership with more abundant information about popular wages, incomes, health, consumption patterns, etc., as a basis for policy.[34]

To some extent, such information was being gathered before, by a variety of groups that had sprung up in the 1960s, including sociological teams inside the KGB, but the more significant findings were either classified or censored. The difference this time is that much more of what is being gathered now will be made public, giving the leadership an additional political lever. This brings us to the political significance of *glasnost'*.

Making Communication More Attractive and Credible: The Progress of Glasnost'

The most startling development of the last two years has been the extraordinary flowering of *glasnost'* in all the Soviet media. This is not a new device for Soviet leaders, of course; nothing could be more traditional in Soviet politics than the use of the media, the arts, and the social sciences to further the leaders' policies. *Glasnost'*, on one level, is no more than a selective relaxation of controls on public expression and information. But its real importance is that it marks a growing understanding of the roles of information in a modern society. Gorbachev has been trying to do three new things: first, to broaden access to existing information; second, to improve the quality and quantity of information; and third, to make better use of it to inform policy at all levels.

For the last two years journalists, artists, and scholars have been pushing back long-established barriers and asserting their right to explore previously forbidden zones. Few social issues are taboo any longer, and previously untouchable historical and ideological subjects are being opened up, often with a daring and frankness that would have sent their authors to prison only a few years ago. The next frontier is coverage of the military, space, foreign affairs, justice, and the environment, which have long been protected from criticism by special ministry-based systems of censorship.[35] The statistical system is being criticized as never before, and the range (if not always the reliability) of publicly available statistics is broadening.[36] The Party apparatus, up to the level of province committee or non-Russian Central Committee, is fair game for criticism,[37] and even the local offices of the KGB are no longer entirely immune.[38]

Natural and man-made disasters are now being reported promptly in the Soviet press. The nuclear disaster at Chernobyl' in the spring of 1986 was an important test of the *glasnost'* policy, which the leadership passed impressively, though after stone-walling at first. The media have reported on political incidents as well, including riots in Alma-Ata in December 1986, nationalist demonstrations in the Baltic Republics, Armenia, Azerbaijan, and elsewhere since 1986, the demands of the Crimean Tatars in July 1987, and the marches of Pamiat' and other groups.

The coverage of Chernobyl' illustrated the political payoff to be had from *glasnost'*: through its unprecedentedly frank coverage[39] the leadership was able to turn a catastrophe to some political advantage, especially since for once the Soviets' own coverage was more accurate than that of foreign radio services. Gorbachev skillfully used the Chernobyl' episode to bolster his case for arms control, discipline in the work place, and, of course, for *glasnost'* itself. Later in the year, he made similar use of the riots in Alma-Ata, when he told the Central Committee that national tensions only worsened when allowed to fester out of sight.

But so far *glasnost'* has spread unevenly. While it would be an exaggeration to say that it is confined to the Moscow intelligentsia or to the foreign community, one serious problem from Gorbachev's standpoint is that some Moscow editors are racing ahead, testing the limits of official tolerance with each new issue, while in the provinces the local press hangs back, frequently under pressure from local politicians. This is a new twist on a familiar Soviet story: in the traditional Soviet system of information, the circulation of ideas and news worsens as one moves from higher levels to lower, and the most striking expression of that is the dismal state of the local press. One of the aims of the *glasnost'* policy is to improve local reporting to keep local officials on their toes, but there is little on which to build. Long neglected and despised, local reporters are underpaid, undertrained, and easily intimidated. Defense of the local media has been a prominent theme in the central press and in Gorbachev's own speeches over the last two years, but there is little progress to show for it yet. At this point, citizens who wish to sound off about local issues still have little choice but to write a letter to the editor of a central newspaper.

Still, the improvement in the central media, particularly in Soviet television and in major dailies such as *Izvestiia*, has been so remarkable that Soviet citizens have begun paying much more attention to them. The circulation of *Izvestiia*, which had dropped off by 3 million during the Brezhnev era, by 1986 had recovered to over 7 million.[40] If one of the achievements of *glasnost'* is to get the people to listen to and contribute to the official media, then Gorbachev will have taken a long and essential first step toward reviving a political lever that has been losing power for half a century. But there is still a long way to go, beginning with the extension of *glasnost'* to publicity about decision-making within the central government itself. In this respect, Gorbachev still falls short of Khrushchev; despite rumors that Gorbachev wanted the proceedings of the January and June 1987 Central Committee meetings published, that has not yet happened; and the proceedings of the tumultuous session of October 21, 1987, which led to Boris Yel'tsin's downfall, will not soon be released.

Tampering with the Powers of Officialdom:
Gorbachev's Electoral Experiments

Accountability is a favorite word in Soviet political vocabulary, but in practice, of course, it has always meant accountability to higher authority, even when it was applied to officials theoretically elected from below. That is why the most startling measures Gorbachev has proposed to date are changes in elections and voting, possibly supplemented by fixed terms of office and new rules on compulsory retirements. If implemented fairly, these measures could indeed introduce a measure of accountability to voters below, giving citizens at all levels of the system quite new sorts of incentives.

Thus, multiple candidacies were introduced on an experimental basis in elections to the local Soviets.[41] Leadership positions in major enterprises, including the post of director, will also become elective under the new law on the socialist enterprise. But the most controversial idea advanced by Gorbachev is that secret ballots and multiple candidacies should be extended to positions in the Party apparatus itself, to levels as high as the first secretaries of republic central committees.[42]

Secret balloting is not an entirely new practice in Party organs, nor is it new as a reform proposal. The secretary of a local Party organ or large primary party organization (PPO) is typically elected by open ballot, but the bureau (or committee) of which he is a member is elected by the whole organization in a secret ballot "that usually seems to be truly secret."[43] Yet clearly the election of the secretary is what really matters, and in 1961 Frol Kozlov, then second secretary and heir apparent to Khrushchev, advocated secret ballots at the 22nd Party Congress. The idea is clearly controversial within the present Politburo. Thus Ligachev, writing in *Kommunist* in 1985, called for voting by show of hands as a more "democratic" procedure.[44]

Right behind the issue of electoral changes comes that of fixed terms of office and compulsory retirements. Gorbachev is thought to have attempted on at least two previous occasions to re-introduce fixed terms of office into the Party rules. The USSR Academy of Sciences has already adopted a rule requiring its members to surrender their administrative positions at 70, possibly a deliberate model for other officials.[45] Khrushchev's previous efforts in the same direction were praised by a former Gorbachev aide in *Pravda*,[46] and Gorbachev may intend to try again at the Party Conference planned for June 1988.[47]

A related theme introduced by Gorbachev in June 1987 is that of strengthening "elective" bodies over "executive" ones:

> An excessive growth of the role of executive bodies to the detriment of elective ones has occurred. At first glance everything proceeds as it should. Plenary meetings, sessions, and meetings of other elective bodies are regularly held. But their work is often overformalized. Secondary questions or even those decided in advance are brought up for discussion. (. . .) Let's face it, some comrades started to view elective bodies as a burden which brings only difficulties and hindrances.

Typically, of course, executives lightened the burden by not reporting to the electoral body at all; thus the Moscow *gorispolkom*, we are told, prior to spring of 1987 had not reported to a full session of the Moscow City Soviet in over 30 years.[48] Nothing surprising here, except that Gorbachev then went on to draw startling implications for the Central Committee itself:

> Let us say honestly: there were many crucial questions of concern to the Party and the people that remained outside plenum agendas for several years. Comrades will remember that plenums of the CC were brief and formal. Many members had no opportunity throughout their membership term to participate in debates or even to put forward proposals.

Gorbachev was careful to cover himself, though, by adding that the decisions of higher party committees would continue to be binding on lower ones.

At the January 1987 plenum Gorbachev justified the idea of multiple candidacies as a means of enabling the Soviets and the Party organs "better to know the mood and will of the population." The recent experience of East European countries suggests that such measures can be implemented without threatening the essence of the traditional distribution of power or the *nomenklatura* system.[49] Higher authorities will focus their efforts on controlling nominations instead of elections, assuming they do not rig the ballot box outright. But East European experience also suggests that secret ballots and multiple candidacies give the voters a weapon against the least-qualified candidates and introduce an element of uncertainty with which local officials must reckon, making them more responsive to the voters' wishes. This is democracy on the shortest of leashes, but from the leaders' point of view, it could rouse the citizens' interest in political participation and provide an added lever over middle-level officials, all at an acceptably small political risk.

More Systematic Legislation and Legal Guarantees:
Encouraging Countervailing Forces
and "Kontrol'" from Below

In the summer of 1986, the Supreme Soviet created a stir by announcing a five-year plan for new legislation.[50] Since then, a stream of new laws has appeared, more or less on schedule, providing an elaborate legal foundation for *perestroika*. Two aspects of this policy are of special interest. First, one of its apparent aims is to bring legislation into conformity with the 1977 Constitution, consistent with Gorbachev's avowed goal of closing the gap between public words and deeds. Thus a new law announced in July 1987, giving citizens the right to sue officials for illegal acts, was originally promised in Article 58. Another law published on the same date, which extends and codifies the practice of conducting national debates on proposed legislation, implements Article 114. It is noteworthy, however, that a law providing for national referenda, which was announced in the 1986 five-year program to implement the Constitution's Article 108, has not yet appeared, although it would not seem to pose a threat to the leadership.[51]

Second, the new legislation reflects a concern to give individual citizens and individual enterprises means of defense against arbitrary and illegal acts by middle-level bureaucracies. Thus the law permitting suits against officials, though it does not provide for recovery of damages, would if implemented bring the Soviet Union up to the level of most other countries except the United States. Similarly, the new law on the socialist enterprise, also enacted in July 1987, enables enterprises to go to court to appeal unjustified plan targets. Needless to say, for such laws to have any practical meaning, they must be applied by the courts, and in the past the courts have had no way of withstanding outside pressure brought against them, usually by local Party authorities.

The prominent role of legislation in *perestroika* presumably reflects the legal background of the new General Secretary and the progress of the law and the legal profession in Soviet life in recent decades. But it also appears to represent part of a larger strategy to strengthen countervailing forces at the local level and to bring them to bear against unresponsive or abusive officials. This strategy includes the courts, but other bodies as well, such as the local Soviets, the Komsomol, and the labor unions. Thus in February 1987, speaking to a congress of trade-union leaders, Gorbachev proposed legislation to give labor unions the power to stand up to management.[52] His suggestions come close to granting the unions veto power over managers' plans, over prices of major consumer goods and services—a startling change indeed for an institution that has spent most of the last sixty years "dancing the krakowiak" (as Gorbachev put it) with management.

One of Gorbachev's purposes here is clear enough. By giving local citizens and institutions protection and authority, he hopes to unburden the party apparatus and leadership from the load of *kontrol'* (i.e., checking and oversight) from above. Gorbachev frequently cites the endless meetings at the top, the burden of returning again and again to the same questions, the "literal avalanche of check-ups and inspections that descends on institutions, enterprises, and organizations." "For all the importance of *kontrol'* from above," he told the Central Committee in January 1987, "we must raise the level and effectiveness of *kontrol'* from below."

> If we achieve such *kontrol'* [from below], there can be no doubt that many causes for complaints and messages to higher authorities will disappear, and the majority of the questions raised in them will be decided at the local level.

But Gorbachev's thinking evidently goes beyond raising the efficiency of *kontrol'* and unburdening higher authority. A legislative framework, legal guarantees, and countervailing powers are logically an essential part of any coherent strategy to revive the political system, both to protect citizens against pressures and reprisals from local officials, and to introduce a measure of consistency and predictability, strengthening popular faith in the legitimacy of the system. That will require, of course, not only new and more public legislation, but a systematic effort to improve the administration of justice, particularly to strengthen independence of the judiciary against intervention by local authorities.[53]

'Raising the Authority of the Ruble': Strengthening Economic Levers

In one of the best-read classics of the Soviet period, *The Golden Calf* by Il'f and Petrov, the con-man hero, Astap Bender, has made a fortune through blackmail but is unable to find anything to spend it on. Under the classic command system, the market shrivelled up and money lost much of its importance; economic signals were displaced by administrative ones.

Gorbachev is now attempting to "raise the authority of the ruble," by increasing the role of economic signals and instruments throughout the system. Gorbachev's economic reforms are discussed elsewhere in this book, but what is important here is to point out the political implications: the new emphasis given to economic levers promises to add considerably to the regime's ability to move people. This has a positive side: citizens are being encouraged to form cooperatives and private businesses, farmers to sell up to one-third of their produce as they see fit, and managers to earn hard-currency abroad. But the "economization" policy also has a negative side: by raising the prospect that workers can be laid off or enterprises go bankrupt, the new leaders are reviving the potential for mass coercion, substituting the "icy water of economic calculation" for physical threats.

It isn't simply incompetent or undisciplined workers who stand to lose their jobs; once managers have to meet their own payrolls out of their own profits, they will have an incentive to move quickly—if allowed by the local party authorities—to cut back their overgrown workforces. So far, they have the blessing of the leadership. In one widely publicized experiment, begun under Andropov, the Belorussian railroads have released 13,000 railroad workers, with over 14,000 more to follow from the republic's metro, auto pools, and civil aviation.[54] Similar reports are becoming common throughout the country.

But there is more: if the center successfully unburdens itself by switching from administrative to economic methods, a large fraction of the 18 million people who work in bureaucratic and clerical jobs nationwide will become redundant,[55] particularly the 1.5 million who work in the supply system.[56] A vast slimming campaign is already under way: policemen, agricultural administrators, ministry officials, even the apparatus of the USSR Council of Ministers—all are in danger of losing their jobs. This has aroused understandable anxiety, and the leaders and their publicists have been at pains to reassure the citizenry that there will be no unemployment,[57] but the reports of mass layoffs continue.

Reinterpreting Basic Ideological Tenets

One definition of reform is that it is a reassertion of a political community's fundamental values and an attempt to bring political life back into conformity with them. The result is inevitably more like a reinterpretation, but it requires, to succeed, a common core of values on which most of the community's members and leaders can ultimately agree. In the case of the Soviet Union, if the political culture of the people has drifted so far from the state ideology that no such common core exists, then reform is impossible.

Therefore, at the base of Gorbachev's political strategy is, first, his belief that whatever the ossification of the system, whatever the decline in the Soviet people's faith in the leaders and their words, the people continue to embrace the fundamental values of socialism. Gorbachev professes that faith in every speech. Second, *perestroika*, while advertised as a restatement of those fundamentals, is necessarily a reinterpretation of them, an attempt to reconcile official values with the emerging culture (or more exactly, cultures) of Soviet society. Thus, one of the essential aspects of Gorbachev's reform strategy has been the beginnings of a review of basic ideological tenets.

Such a review necessarily begins with Lenin himself, since any reinterpretation must receive his posthumous blessing. The Lenin that has been emerging from the leaders' speeches and the literature of *perestroika* in the last two years is the Lenin of his last years,[58] the Lenin of the New Economic Policy,[59] the author of "On Cooperation," a Bukharinist Lenin of economic gradualism and political moderation. He is also the Lenin of the "Last Testament,"[60] a defender of legal rights, democracy, and national cultures to whom the crudeness and Great Russian chauvinism of a Stalin are foreign. The New Lenin is also a man of the market, a believer in money-commodity relations over administrative methods. Such a Lenin would have opposed forced collectivization, while supporting the use of various intermediate forms of cooperative economic activity for generations to come.[61] In short, Lenin is indeed *zhivee vsekh zhivykh* ("more alive than all the living"— a standard slogan over the decades) and as politically useful as ever.

Behind the official and semi-official re-imaging of Lenin is an attempt to rethink socialist property, the acceptable limits of social conflict and expressions of interest, the place of money and economic levers, the meaning of equality, and even, very cautiously, the roles of the Party itself. The first obstacle along this road, of course, is the utter novelty of it to most Soviet citizens, and especially to the keepers of ideology themselves. Addressing a meeting of social-science faculty department heads in the fall of 1986, Gorbachev criticized the dogmatism and scholasticism of most Soviet social science and called for an "activation of the theoretical front," buttressing his appeal, inevitably, with a quote from Lenin:[62]

> The first obligation of those who wish to seek "the paths to human happiness" is not to pull the wool over their own eyes, but to have the daring to acknowledge openly what is.

Accompanying Gorbachev's calls for doctrinal *aggiornamento* is the increasingly prominent theme that it is the people and their society who define "what is," which implies that the party and its theoreticians, if they are to justify their continued role as the leading elements of the system, must learn how to enlist the people's cooperation and support.

Yet at the same time Gorbachev is attempting to impose a personal vision of "what is," a vision that over time has grown more and more radical. In the fall of 1986 he began using the word, "revolutionary," to describe his program. But there is no revolution without contradictions to provoke it, and indeed the word, "contradiction," has recently become a prominent part of Gorbachev's vocabulary.[63] Gorbachev evidently takes these words most seriously; his portrayal of what is at stake in *perestroika* has grown more urgent. Thus his words in June 1987:

> History has not left us much time to resolve this task. . . . Depending on how *perestroika* goes, according to its results, the potential of socialism will be judged, what it gives to man, how socially effective a socialist society is. . . . There may be no "sweet tomorrows" if we don't work by the sweat of our brow today, changing our way of thinking, overcoming inertia, and mastering new approaches.

This vision is evidently sincere, but it is not clear how widely or strongly it is shared beyond a narrow circle of Gorbachev's followers. Hence one of the most serious potential contradictions in Gorbachev's own approach is between his instinct to look to the "mood and will of the people" (as he put it in January) and his conviction that he speaks from a higher consciousness. This point brings us to the next question: What are the aims of Gorbachev's political strategy and how likely is it to work?

II. IS GORBACHEV'S STRATEGY
AN EFFECTIVE RESPONSE TO CRISIS?

The first part of this essay described the crisis of the Soviet system of leadership as a weakening hold over the resources in citizens' minds and a deterioration of the traditional political levers, analogous to the crisis of the command economy, indeed, the political face of the same crisis. Is Gorbachev's political strategy an appropriate response? Can new or revived political instruments supplement and reinforce the old, or only conflict with them? Does Gorbachev's strategy presage a new "political contract" with a population that will share his goals, or is

70

he unleashing forces that he will be unable to control? It is clearly too early to do much more than raise these questions; but at least one can begin thinking how Gorbachev's latest moves fit with the traditional system of power, and how appropriate they are to the problems he faces.

The Possible Logic of Gorbachev's Political Strategy: Is It Really Anything New?

Gorbachev's political strategy appears designed to serve four objectives: (1) to strengthen Gorbachev's own hand by weakening that of his opponents; (2) to create a strong constituency for change; (3) to make his program irreversible; and (4) as an ultimate objective, to revive and strengthen the regime's legitimacy. Each of these, of course, serves the others, yielding an increase of power and authority for Gorbachev himself and for the political system as a whole. This last point is especially important: just as Gorbachev can argue that economic reform is a positive-sum game, because the resulting increase in wealth will benefit everyone, he might also justify political reform as a positive-sum game, because it will halt the dissipation of power and authority, the turning away of the people from the regime, that had reduced the latter years of the Brezhnev regime to the appearance of control, but with less and less of the reality of it.

It is clear, at any rate, that in Gorbachev's mind the traditional resources and levers are inadequate for his purposes. Consider for example the use of the personnel weapon. Despite the sweep of Gorbachev's "cold purge" since March 1985, it is striking to note that Gorbachev has been very careful not to challenge officials appointed since Brezhnev's death,[64] and he has shown some sensitivity lately to charges that cadres are being replaced too freely. Thus in August 1987 he suggested to a group of agricultural managers that in the future most of the personnel turnover would come through attrition:[65]

> If you ask me whether in order to carry out *perestroika* it is necessary to replace every one of our cadres, [I would answer] no. I think we must resolve the tasks of *perestroika* with the people and the cadres we have. . . . But in addition there is a natural process: there are those who have already come to the end of their working life, and that is understandable. Or some people simply don't have the strength to take on new tasks. That's understandable too, and there is no cause to dramatize the situation. . . . In principle we assume that basically the existing personnel will be able to handle these tasks. We do not intend to break our cadres.

71

The message is deliberately ambiguous, but its essence is clear: Gorbachev knows he must make do with the human material he has. Hence the key to his strategy is motivation. But Gorbachev is reluctant to rely on economic interest alone; on the contrary, one of his chief complaints about the Brezhnev era is that it tolerated the spread of consumerism, individualism, "private-property mentality," and materialism (which Gorbachev calls "thingism"). He appears to take some comfort, however, in the thought that consumer wants have also become more advanced, creating new demands that can be satisfied through collective and cooperative mechanisms.[66] And although he has condemned the tendency toward "levelling" (i.e., excessive egalitarianism in salaries and bonuses) that took place under Brezhnev and has begun increasing income differentials, Gorbachev, like Andropov before him, stressed that collectives, not individuals, should be the main beneficiaries to be rewarded in proportion to their work, and that the rewards themselves should be primarily collective as well (although more recently he has been fudging on this point, by treating families as acceptable "collectives"). Thus he apparently hopes to limit the destabilizing effects of economic inequalities and the moral corrosion of individualism.

Not only is economic self-interest an ideologically inadequate motive in Gorbachev's eyes, it is also politically insufficient, because it will not protect citizens who take initiative at the local level from being harassed by middle-level bureaucracy. This is one strong reason for Gorbachev's experimentation with *glasnost'*, improved legal guarantees, and democratization. Gorbachev does not use the term, "constituency," but beginning with the January 1987 plenum, he began talking about the need to guarantee that *perestroika* would be irreversible and that the mistakes of the past would not be repeated. There is ultimately only one way to do that, by recalling interests, political powers, not just economic ones, to the local levels, so as to weaken permanently the various apparatus on which the Stalinist system rested.

Is that really what Gorbachev intends? Until recently one could argue that Gorbachev's political strategy was not essentially different from that of his predecessors. Every General Secretary since Stalin, after all, has seen his power and authority erode relative to the man before him, and each one has fought back with a strategy of "reforms," described very well by George Breslauer.[67] They have always seen the middle of the bureaucracy as the main obstacle; they have invariably dwelt on the crucial importance of cadres; they have all manipulated history and have all invoked a "grandfather figure" against their immediate predecessor; and they have always started out sounding like populists—indeed, populism is a natural response in an authoritarian system. In the end, their political strategies have ended up much alike; as George Breslauer observes, "party activism, political intervention, and pressure are the constant winners in post-Stalin politics."[68] What makes Gorbachev different?

A comparison with Khrushchev yields some interesting answers. At first glance, their styles and techniques are similar in many ways. Gorbachev wields the broom as energetically as Khrushchev; he hectors the bureaucracy and exhorts the population in the best Khrushchevian manner, peppering his speech with proverbs and earthy examples; and Gorbachev has shown some of the same zest for raising the stakes when opposed. Both advertise themselves as reformers and men of the people, and both enjoy getting out of the office for a walkabout. Above all, Gorbachev is the same enthusiastic man of action, who would rather stir things up than sit safely by. Napoleon's "On s'engage et puis on voit" would do nicely as a motto for both.

Some differences, of course, are obvious too, particularly at the early stages of their careers as General Secretary. The Khrushchev of 1953–57 was an artful political tactician, who resembled the Stalin of the 1920s more than the Gorbachev of 1985–86. Khrushchev in those years staked out a conservative policy position against Malenkov's more liberal pro-consumer and pro-agricultural proposals, and this played a major part in his consolidation of power.[69] In contrast, in some respects he was far more vigorous in his early years than Gorbachev has been so far, firing a larger share of the obkom leadership of the Party and putting in his own proteges (of whom he had far larger numbers than Gorbachev, stemming from a longer and more varied political past). Khrushchev postponed announcing a reform program until he was fully in a position to challenge the old guard in the Politburo. In the process, he created a "constituency" in the Party elite. Gorbachev, facing less opposition in the Politburo and more of a consensus for change, has done the opposite, announcing a reform program before his constituency is fully consolidated.

The more one examines the two men, the more deeper differences appear. Khrushchev was a man of the years just after Stalin's death— "a quintessential Stalinist, if with a difference," Harry Rigby calls him.[70] He did not doubt that the Soviet economic system would catch up with the capitalists or that the political system could govern effectively. If he rejected mass terror, he had no compunctions about using coercion. Having restored the Party apparatus to the leading position in the Soviet political system, he pushed it deep into economic administration, and when that did not work he pushed it even deeper.[71] Khrushchev's "populism" was never more than half a policy, because no matter how much he might rouse people on the stump, he was

73

never willing to grant the local level real power; the people had no
meaningful political currency to contribute, other than their obedience.
His efforts to promote "public" bodies and "non-salaried" participants
were aimed strictly at increasing his mobilizational reach; and the
notion that labor unions, for example, might attempt to veto managers'
decisions would have horrified him.

Khrushchev invoked Leninist norms against Stalin's arbitrary law-
lessness, but his main intention was to reassure the Party apparatus
and the elite that henceforth it would be physically secure. His de-
Stalinization campaign drew a careful line at about 1934; the later
Stalin was dethroned, but the earlier one was not, and still less the
system he created. Gorbachev, in contrast, is not only challenging Stalin
as a leader but also the system he created; and this time it is Lenin
who is being divided in two, to support notions of socialist property
and economic policy that Khrushchev would not have approved of.

Khrushchev did not challenge the fundamentals he had inherited:
if he tried to revive agriculture, for example, it was largely through
administrative means, and not through investment at the expense of
heavy industry and defense. (Only in his last years, in 1962 and after,
did Khrushchev move toward the big-investment agricultural strategy
for agriculture that subsequently became the hallmark of Brezhnevian
policy.)[72] He did not doubt his authority to speak on all technical
subjects, whether agronomy or nuclear strategy, and to raise up or
humble technical experts as he pleased, largely according to whether
they supported his latest technological gimmick. Meeting frustration,
Khrushchev reacted by making ever more vigorous use of traditional
instruments of power—more hiring and firing, more reorganization,
more and more policy initiatives, and more administrative pressure.[73]

Gorbachev comes a generation later, after many a campaign and
many a "reform," and both he and his colleagues have long reflected
on the limits of the traditional system. (Indeed, the Gorbachev program
as it has evolved to the present must be seen not only as the result
of Gorbachev's learning on the job since 1985, but also of three decades
of collective learning—and unlearning—in Moscow and especially in
the provinces. The changes of the last two years would not have been
possible if the new leaders had truly been "naive reformers.")[74] Coercion
has its place in Gorbachev's panoply, but primarily to restore order
and discipline; he has no illusions about its power as an instrument
of change. Consistent with his stress on the importance of economic
levers over administrative ones, Gorbachev is ambivalent about the
role of the Party in economic management (more on that below).
Technology alone will not perform miracles; Gorbachev does not pre-
tend to know more than the experts, but neither does he expect them

to bring about the millenium within the existing structure. He is more than willing to question fundamental investment priorities; indeed, he states openly that the long imbalance in favor of military programs has been one of the main causes of today's troubles.

The most important difference, which drives all the rest, is the two men's differing assessments of the situation facing them: for Khrushchev the word "perfecting" (*sovershenstvovanie*) was truly the one that applied. Gorbachev questions the very viability of the system.

Consequently, one can make the case that Gorbachev's political strategy, especially since the beginning of 1987, does indeed go farther in challenging the fundamentals of the system and attempting to devise new political instruments than that of any Soviet politician since the 1920s. But does he stand a chance? In the next section we examine the coherence, consistency, and realism of Gorbachev's approach.

Contradictions and Dangers in Gorbachev's Strategy

Three Contradictions

A politician's strategy develops piece-meal, the product of improvisation, opportunity and tactics, good or bad advice, and insights that may be more intuition than logic. In the case of a Soviet politician, the process is further complicated by an extreme need for discretion. If Gorbachev's ideas on economic reform, we learn, began taking concrete shape after 1980 in informal discussions at country houses outside Moscow,[75] his thoughts on political reform must have evolved even more privately. Snapshots of Gorbachev and Andropov walking together in short sleeves through the woods, deep in conversation, suggest one source of his thinking, but how much of Gorbachev's early mullings would he have wished to discuss with his patron?[76]

At any rate, it is not surprising that Gorbachev's strategy, only two years after his accession, is full of inconsistencies. But three of them stand out as so fundamental that no mere process of thought can resolve them; as we shall see, they are inescapable constraints and basic political issues.

The first is that Gorbachev is forced to use the old to build the new, and consequently his program is in constant danger of being subverted, exhausted, or defeated. *Glasnost'*, for example, is being carried out by a media system that is more centralized than ever before, especially because of the prominence of TV. The printed essays and articles that are the most supportive of Gorbachev's program come almost entirely from Moscow journalists and media, causing Gorbachev to complain of "usurpation" and to wonder out loud, "Where is the rest of the country?"[77] But despite well-meaning phrases at the top about reinforcing the local media, it is clear that local journalism is so decrepit that it cannot possibly play a strong role for a long time to come. Assiduous protection from the center may ward off its enemies but will not make it competent or independent. Self-financing through advertising would be a long-term step in the right direction, but that is frequently opposed by the local Party apparatus;[78] and besides, money is the least of the resources which local journalists require.[79]

The weapon of *glasnost'* is being managed entirely from above, and no real measures have been taken so far to change the traditional structure of media control. Despite rumors in the summer of 1986 that the censorship agency, *Glavlit,* was about to be abolished, the fall brought instead an announcement of a new head. Discussion of censorship itself is still forbidden;[80] and to my knowledge there has been no public mention of the existence of the *Perechen',* the censors' list of forbidden facts and topics. The ministerial visa system, too, is still intact.

What is true of structures is also true of people. Despite the extraordinary turnover in personnel in recent years, Gorbachev can hardly avoid conducting *perestroika* with people who have long pasts in high places under Brezhnev. Undoubtedly largely by necessity, he has filled most of the top positions in the Party and government with people who are older than he, and with the exception of a handful who were clearly out of favor in the Brezhnev years (such as Politburo member Aleksandr Iakovlev and Gorbachev's new aide Ivan Frolov, *Ogonek*'s Vitalii Korotich, and *Novyi mir*'s Sergei Zalygin), most of them had to make their compromises before 1982. *Literaturnaia gazeta* is still in the hands of Aleksandr Chakovskii, an accomplished literary survivor; *Pravda* is in those of Viktor Afanas'ev, who held the same post under Brezhnev; cinema is under veteran Central Committee apparatus man Aleksandr Kamshalov; culture under Vasilii Zakharov, once in charge of ideological affairs under Romanov in Leningrad. There are many other examples. How dedicated to *glasnost'* would they be if the reforming energy at the top were to weaken? Gorbachev's real allies at the top are still few, yet reform still depends entirely on them and on their chief.

The second contradiction is that the *objectives* pursued by the new strategy must co-exist with the old—indeed, in most respects, they *are* the old objectives. *Glasnost'* is supposed to tell the "whole truth," but not, of course, if that truth tarnishes the 70th anniversary of the October Revolution. Local elections are supposed to reinforce the authority and responsiveness of local officials, but the program they must carry out is that of the center just the same. As one manager observed about the prospect that his post will become elective:[81]

> In any case we will be not be electing a program—especially since the program is assigned to us, it's the plan—but an individual capable of carrying it out. But let's say that a higher organ, the ministry or the *glavk*, keeps throwing new targets at us in the middle of the year, adds to our targets (which in fact happens all the time). Will that please the personnel? Hardly. What I am supposed to do then, resign?

The third contradiction flows from the second. It is that the reformers have barely begun to face up to the ambiguity that lurks in *perestroika*, namely, Who rules? Though he may talk about listening to the "mood and will" of the people, one may be sure that Gorbachev has no intention of dividing power; on the contrary, the main argument of this essay is that his aim is to regain the real control that his predecessors were losing. But Gorbachev is like the puppet-maker who dreams of giving life to his carvings: what will he do when they start to move on their own? He cannot go very far toward deconcentrating, delegating, and decentralizing, before he is obliged to reassert his hand. This is already clear in the case of elections. If enterprise directors are elected by their workers, who will choose the candidates? As a skeptical Moscow brigade leader commented in *Izvestiia*, after observing that all seven of his past directors had been "Varangians," that is, appointed from outside:

> This system is hardly likely to change after the new law is adopted. They may present us with a total unknown and say, "Here is your director, vote for him." Or, if we elect our own, he will in any case have to be approved higher up. One of two things is bound to become a formality: either the election or the approval [by higher authority]. It's not difficult to guess which one it will be.[82]

There is, in addition, a tactical reason why Gorbachev cannot "surrender control to regain control": if he fails to use the traditional instruments himself he will find that others will do so in his place—local Party leaders, in particular, who will rebuild the local patronage networks that Gorbachev is now having so much trouble dismantling. Control not exercised at the top will tend to be recaptured at middle levels, and the central leadership will need all its power to prevent that from happening.

Twin Dangers

As a result of these three contradictions Gorbachev's strategy faces two principal dangers. The first is that Gorbachev's reforming energy, in response to resistance from officialdom and passivity from the people, could degenerate into Khrushchevism, that is, an increasingly frantic use of the General Secretary's traditional powers over cadres and structure. Gorbachev is a willful man, and there is a hint of such a tendency in his words to an audience in Estonia in early 1987:

> I must tell you straight out: today we can still discuss these questions, exchange opinions, and seek approaches on how to bring to life the decisions of the January Plenum. Today perplexed questions are still in order, because we must think everything deeply through. But tomorrow those who remain stubborn and those who will not understand the demands of the present time, will simply have to get out of the way.[83]

By the time of his fall, Khrushchev had succeeded in alienating every major group in the political system, including the provincial party apparatus, which had saved him seven years before. So far, Gorbachev has been far more cautious and more skillful, not only in his dealings with the provincial party apparatus but also with the KGB. But from the summer of 1986 on he began hectoring and scolding officials at every level, and his attacks have escalated steadily since. The June 1987 plenum marks an even more aggressive phase, as Gorbachev attempts to use the build-up to the Party Conference of 1988 as a means of bulldozing opponents out of the way. Even now Gorbachev may be making more powerful enemies than friends.

We may be sure that as *perestroika* is implemented, it will face the classic problems of previous reforms, and the center will be forced to intervene, using the "administrative methods" that are now out of fashion. There will be "localism," the tendency of regions to look to their own priorities first. If managers produce what is profitable, awkward shortages and surpluses will result. If there is real price reform, there will be inflation; if real incentives, unforeseen inequalities. The experience of reforms in China, in particular, suggests how strong the pressure will be to intervene from the center, in effect returning to old ways.

The other danger is political disorder. To the extent that Gorbachev's strategy succeeds it will unleash forces that have been dormant in Soviet politics since the Revolution, breeding instability and disorder. A handful of essential conditions has kept the Soviet political system remarkably stable over the thirty-five years since Stalin's death.[84] The leaders have taken care to manage the population's expectations, partly through massive propaganda and the exclusion of competing ideas. But a program of reform that now aims at promoting new ideas is bound to cause popular expectations to soar; and indeed Gorbachev has already observed as much.[85] Another factor in stability has been the fact that formal organization from above has traditionally displaced social organization from below, and this has helped to keep the aspirations of different segments of the population from coalescing, preventing instabilities in one sector or region from spreading to the rest. But now the deliberate mobilization of local social forces may weaken the traditional bulkheads. Lastly, both the elite and population have traditionally been obsessed with maintaining order. Yet the Gorbachev policies are already threatening disorder and the signs of conservative backlash can already be seen.

What Becomes of the Functions of the Party Apparatus?

If even a fraction of the Gorbachev political strategy comes to pass, then what becomes of the functions and powers of the local Party apparatus? This is clearly the most crucial issue.

Statements by local Party officials during the last two years sound understandably confused. On the one hand, some are clearly attempting to rethink their traditional duties; others are clinging to their familiar roles.[86]

Beginning in January 1987, Gorbachev himself took up the issue. He sounded at first as though he envisioned the Party apparatus as a sort of ombudsman of *perestroika*. But in the same breath he denied that he had any intention of changing the apparatus's leading role in economic management;[87] indeed, in a subsequent speech he criticized those who might have misunderstood that the local apparatus should confine itself to "some sort of pure politics."[88] But under a reformed economic mechanism there should be no need for the Party apparatus to worry about contract fulfillment or supply bottlenecks; since the "economic organs" will be doing their job, they should get on with it without petty intervention by the Party:

> The raikom cannot act as the organ of economic management—that is what must be understood. That is not its function.[89]

The Party's chief instrument, as always, must be the selection and assignment of cadres and control over organization. In short, the Party's traditional basis for power remains intact and unchallenged. But needless to say, this ducks the real question, which is, Who is ultimately responsible for plan fulfillment? If it is ultimately the Party apparatus (as Gorbachev still insists it is), then the result will be the same merry-go-round of local hiring and firing as before. Just as Janos Kornai argues that in economic reform the ultimate question is whether the manager looks up to the planner or down to the customer for his orders, so also in political reform the final issue is whether local officials look upward to the Party for their jobs or downward to their voters. So far, Gorbachev's answer, for all its ambiguities, is clear enough on the basics.

Meanwhile, not surprisingly, the press reports that not much has actually changed in practice. In one recent article, a *Pravda* correspondent observes that in a group of *obkoms* (provincial committees) he surveyed, the branch departments of the *obkom* tend to be staffed by newly co-opted officials from the corresponding economic branches, who bring over with them their habits of mind unchanged: "My job as head of the construction department," they say, "is to oversee 'my' factories and meet 'my' plan." (This theme, of course, is not new; the new twist is that Salutskii asserts most instructors are brought in essentially "raw," and that such co-optation is the rule, not the exception.)[90] Another *Pravda* correspondent observes that the same point applies to many new *raikom* (district committee) first secretaries in rural areas: they are co-opted "specialists," as opposed to their predecessors, who were frequently generalists. One might have thought that Gorbachev's policies would call for precisely the opposite, but the Party's cadres departments probably had little choice: the "ossification" (*okostenenie*) that prevailed in cadres policy under Brezhnev meant that the new Party officials did not punch their career tickets in the time-honored sequence. Consequently, the Party is drawing on what is available, and that means economic specialists.[91]

With new personnel such as this, it is not surprising that the local Party apparatus may be moving in the opposite direction from what Gorbachev says he wants, that is, toward more *nadimēnī* and *pēlīy* tutelage, rather than less.

III. CONCLUSIONS AND SPECULATIONS

This essay has developed three themes: (1) The Soviet system faces not only an economic crisis but also a political one; indeed, they are two faces of the same problem, the exhaustion of the Stalinist strategy of development. (2) This is increasingly Gorbachev's own perception of the situation; accordingly, he has begun developing a strategy of political reform aimed at renewing the state's resources for reaching and moving its citizens. (3) Though he has already gone beyond previous general secretaries, Gorbachev has barely begun to confront the contradictions and dangers inherent in his approach. What are the chances that Gorbachev will manage these contradictions and dangers, keep himself in power, and forge ahead with *perestroika*?

Gorbachev is compared to the great reformers of Russian history. But Gorbachev must hope the analogy is false, because it assumes an enlightened ruler pushing a backward people into modernity. Instead, Gorbachev and allies have staked their chances for success on the opposite proposition: that the Soviet people have outgrown the Stalinist structures and beliefs; indeed, that the people have become more modern than the institutions. That is a positive way of saying that after three generations of the unique Stalinist mixture of repression, mobilization, nationalism, and social conservatism, there has somehow evolved a new society. It is not the society that Lenin or Stalin had in mind; and it is clear that today's leaders do not fully understand it or accept it even though they come from it. But Gorbachev's approach suggests a growing (if still tentative) understanding that this new society cannot be dominated by the state as it was in the past, and that politicians must come to new terms with it, using different instruments and policies.

To say that Gorbachev is prepared to come to new terms with Soviet society is not to say that he is prepared to let society dominate the state, despite his occasional references to the "will of the people." He still considers himself to be the source of initiative; and he still considers that the state will continue to shape the evolution of society.[92] If there is a formula from Russian history that Gorbachev himself might borrow, it is that of the "wager on the strong." But how optimistic Gorbachev is about this society's strengths and about its willingness to obey him! He is wagering that passivity and political apathy will give way to initiative and commitment—but that these will serve his purposes; that communal and cooperative values can co-exist with individualistic ones—and that neither will generate disruptive inequalities; that the population is "responsible" enough that democratization will not degenerate into disorder; that the intelligentsia will play a constructive role in *perestroika* instead of simply testing the limits of official tolerance; and finally that the rising consciousness of national groups will reinforce the Soviet community rather than the reverse. Does Soviet society really offer so solid a foundation on which to build? Can it really be so strong and yet so meek?

Probably not, at least not for years to come. Gorbachev is already being forced to strike out at excesses of *glasnost'*, to label some people dissidents and arrest them, to put down demonstrators, to limit enterprise autonomy, to limit private incomes. He is being driven, in

81

short, to define and enforce new boundaries between orthodoxy and heterodoxy, between approved participation and dissent, between autonomy and plan, and between popular wishes and the will of the state. *Perestroika* until recently has been at the stage when flowers bloom from rifle barrels and everything seems possible; but that stage is already over.

Does that mean that Gorbachev is fated to fail? Many economists, arguing that nothing short of wholesale systemic reform stands to make the Soviet economy efficient, tend to dismiss everything short of that as "tinkering." But tinkering is precisely what reformers do; it is what distinguishes them from revolutionaries; and Gorbachev, for all his rhetoric, is not a revolutionary. Whether his reform program can succeed, therefore, depends on where the new boundaries just named are ultimately drawn, and whether they produce a reconciliation of official and popular values, of "word and deed," or only disillusionment, cynicism, and continued "exit" by the population.

Notes

1. "O sozyve ocherednogo XXVII s"ezda KPSS i zadachakh, sviazannykh s ego podgotovkoi i provedeniem." Speech to the Plenary Meeting of the CPSU Central Committee, 23 April 1985, reprinted in M. S. Gorbachev, *Izbrannye rechi i stat'i* (Moscow: "Politizdat," 1985), pp. 7–23.

2. See in particular Gorbachev's speeches to the Central Committee in January and June 1987: "O perestroike i kadrovoi politike Partii," *Pravda,* January 28, 1987; and "O zadachakh partii po korennoi perestroike upravleniia ekonomikoi," *Pravda,* June 26, 1987.

3. This idea is ably developed by Peter Hauslohner in "Gorbachev's Social Contract," *Soviet Economy,* vol. 3, no. 1 (January-March 1987), pp. 54–89.

4. Gorbachev himself used the expression, "crisis phenomena" in his January 1987 speech to the Central Committee. Since then he has retreated to the formula, "pre-crisis," but he has grown ever blunter in his analysis of the symptoms.

5. Bohdan Nahajlo, "Mikhail Shatrov on the Treaty of Brest-Litovsk" (Radio Free Europe Bulletin, no. 14, April 8, 1987).

6. See Timothy J. Colton, *The Dilemma of Reform in the Soviet Union* (New York: Council on Foreign Relations, 1986), pp. 98–100.

7. Grey Hodnett, "The Pattern of Leadership Politics," in Seweryn Bialer, ed., *The Domestic Context of Soviet Foreign Policy* (Boulder, Colorado: Westview Press, 1981), pp. 92–93, 104.

8. This part of the argument is analogous to Charles Lindblom's metaphor of the "thumbs" of centrally planned economies. See his *Politics and Markets* (New York: Basic Books, 1977), pp. 65–75.

9. Gail W. Lapidus, "Gorbachev and the Reform of the Soviet System," *Daedalus,* vol. 116, no. 2 (Spring, 1987), pp. 8–9.

10. One of the most revealing changes is the growing use of the term, *interesy*. Initially, this was the property of liberal thinkers (see for example T. Zaslavskaia, "Chelovecheskii faktor rasvitiia ekonomiki i sotsial'naia spravedlivost'," *Kommunist*, no. 13 (September 1986), 63, 65–66), but more recently the word has been adopted by Gorbachev himself and has become widely used in Soviet publications.

11. Thus Zaslavskaia writes of the "alienation of a portion of the working, class from public goals and values." Zaslavskaia 1986, op. cit., p. 66.

12. In an excellent presentation at the AAASS annual meeting in New Orleans in 1986, Gordon Livermore of the *Current Digest of the Soviet Press* suggested that Gorbachev is likely to find today's intelligentsia more constructive-minded than Khrushchev did in his day, because the corruption and decay of the 1970s repelled intellectuals just as much as it did the Party reformers and technocrats, while the main disruptive issues of the 1950s, Stalinism and the camps, have largely been vented. Nevertheless, my argument suggests that behind the seeming congruence of aims there may lie a more fundamental potential divergence of values between Party reformers and intellectuals than ever before.

13. Zaslavskaia 1986, op. cit., pp. 62–63.

14. Donna Bahry and Brian D. Silver, "The Intimidation Factor in Soviet Politics: The Symbolic Uses of Terror," Soviet Interview Project Working Paper no. 31 (February 1987).

15. The clearest and best-known statement of this is Samuel Huntington and Zbigniew Brzezinski, *Political Power: USA/USSR* (New York: The Viking Press, 1963), pp. 194–195.

16. See the discussion of this point in Seweryn Bialer, *Stalin's Successors* (Cambridge: Cambridge University Press, 1980), p. 37.

17. T. H. Rigby, "The Soviet Regional Leadership: The Brezhnev Generation," *Slavic Review* (March, 1978), pp. 9ff.

18. For a discussion of this point, see Thane Gustafson and Dawn Mann, "Gorbachev's Next Gamble," *Problems of Communism*, vol. 36, no. 5 (September-October, 1987), pp. 1–20. Under Andropov and during Gorbachev's first year, several provincial party chiefs served a "tour" in the Central Committee before being re-appointed to their provinces. This pattern has faded, however, since the 27th Party Congress.

19. These estimates come from an article by-lined by Gennadii Kolbin shortly before he was reassigned to Kazakhstan from Ul'ianovsk ("Vyziskatel'nost'," *Pravda*, December 2, 1986). A recent estimate from Lithuania is that there are 90 different services with responsiblity for *kontrol'* ("Prostor initsiative," *Pravda*, August 8, 1987).

20. S. Maniakin, "Perestroika i kontrol'," *Pravda*, September 24, 1987.

21. This argument is developed by Tat'iana Zaslavskaia in "Chelovecheskii faktor . . . ," op. cit., pp. 61–62.

22. Thus throughout its history the Main Political Administration of the military has consistently failed the four basic tests of an effective watchdog agency, as Timothy Colton demonstrates in *Commissars, Commanders and*

Civilian Authority: The Structure of Soviet Military Politics (Cambridge, Mass.: Harvard University Press, 1979).

23. That this response was present from the earliest days of the command system is evident from the work based on the Harvard Project of the 1940s and 1950s. See in particular Joseph Berliner, *Factory and Manager in the USSR* (Cambridge, Mass.: Harvard University Press, 1957).

24. In a speech in Murmansk in the fall of 1987 Mikhail Gorbachev paid a rare public tribute to the system of "military representatives" posted in military-industrial plants: "Take defense," he said. "There we do not lag in any way. So we do know how to work. But there, I must tell you, the quality-control officers make it hot for everybody: for the workers, the designers, the engineers, and the managers. That is how *gospriemka* must work. ("Nemerknushchii podvig geroev Zapolar'ia," *Pravda,* October 2, 1987.)

25. Thus one of the lessons of the nuclear disaster at Chernobyl' in the spring of 1986 is that the presence at the site of representatives of all the major offices concerned with nuclear power (including safety officials) did not prevent the foolish experiments that caused the accident, but it guaranteed that news of it reached Kiev and Moscow very quickly, since no one wanted to be the last to report.

26. See for example an interview with Academician Boris Paton, "Bezopasnost' progressa," *Sotsialisticheskaia industriia,* October 10, 1986. An interesting recent case of whistle-blowing involves construction defects at the Minsk nuclear powerplant, caused by systematic neglect of design specifications. A Ivakhnov, "Nuzhny li stroikam Makaevy?" *Izvestiia,* October 24, 1986.

27. I. Kaz'min and A. Pigolkin, "Podzakonnyi akt," *Izvestiia,* October 17, 1986.

28. Thus, Ligachev observed in January 1987 that the Kazakh and Ukrainian Central Committees had not been summoned to report to the Politburo in twenty years.

29. Total savings in individual bank accounts grew 20-fold in a generation, from 10.9 billion rubles in 1960 to 220.8 in 1985. Revealingly, while the savings of the average city-dweller grew 5-fold during this period, those of the average rural resident grew nearly 9 times, reflecting both the improved earnings of peasants but also the scarcity of goods in the countryside. (Source: *Narodnoe khoziaistvo SSSR v 1985g* [Moscow: "Statistika," 1986], p. 448.)

30. The latest example is "Akademset'," the computer network of the Academy of Sciences, and similar experimental networks pioneered by INION. See O. L. Smirnov and Iu. A. Savostitskii, "Dialog cherez kontinenty," *Ekonomicheskaia gazeta,* no. 13 (March 1987), p. 9.

31. Implemented at the beginning of 1987 in a select number of enterprises drawn mostly from the machine-building sector, the *gospriemka* system differs from the traditional quality-control system in that it is operated by an independent watchdog agency subordinated to the State Committee for Standards, whereas this function was traditionally exercised by offices belonging to each producing enterprise.

32. The functions of the new regional administration are described in an interview with the chairman of the RSFSR Gosplan, N. N. Maslennikov,

"Perestroika upravleniia territoriei," *Pravda,* September 11, 1987. The new regional dimension added to the planning system is described in the 1987 planning decree, published in *O korennoi perestroike upravleniia ekonomikoi* (Moscow: Politizdat, 1987), pp. 76–80. The regions and republics, in particular, are to have extensive authority over the planning of all construction.

33. "Prakticheskimi delami uglubliat' perestroiku," *Pravda,* July 15, 1987.

34. Interview with I. I. Gladkii, chairman of the State Committee for Labor and Social Questions, "Po trudu, po spravedlivosti," *Pravda,* September 2, 1987.

35. At the Sixth Congress of Journalists in March 1987 *Pravda* chief editor V. G. Afanas'ev criticized the constraints on coverage of space and ecology, describing the "visas" required from the agencies concerned before anything negative can be published. Only direct support from a Central Committee secretary enabled *Pravda* to print material about the pollution of Lake Baikal or the need to review plans to divert northern rivers—and even then, Afanas'ev added, only with great difficulty. At the same Congress *Izvestiia* commentator Aleksandr Bovin criticized the restrictions under which foreign-affairs correspondents still work: "I envy my journalist colleagues who write on internal affairs," he said. Sure enough, *Pravda* did not publish his following words, which took the Ministry of Foreign Affairs to task. ("Na pul'se perestroiki," *Pravda,* March 14, 1987.) But foreign observers rubbed their eyes in disbelief over Bovin's public polemics with the General Staff over the deployment of the Soviet SS-20's, and his barbs at unnamed politicians who brought about the "relinkage" of Soviet arms-control positions at Reykjavik and after (*Moscow News,* no. 10, March 8, 1987), and over *Pravda*'s publication of numbers on the US-Soviet strategic balance on March 17. In early 1988, Soviet revelations related to the INF Treaty became more remarkable still.

36. For example, in the fall of 1986 the statistical annual *Narodnoe khoziaistvo SSSR,* for the first time in many years, published detailed figures on crop yields for 1985, and *Kommunist,* in a new statistical section that began in its first issue for 1987, revealed data on infantile mortality. On the other hand, in other respects the reliability of Soviet statistical reporting has actually declined, most notably the national-income statistics for 1986. See Jan Vanous, "The Dark Side of 'Glasnost'": Unbelievable National Income Statistics in the Gorbachev Era," *PlanEcon Report,* vol. III, no. 6.

37. Thus the Belorussian CP Central Committee and its apparatus were criticized in Pravda for slow implementation of perestroika, especially in light industry, for which the relevant secretary and department head were singled out by name. A. Simurov and A. Ulitenok, "S pozitsii trebovatel'nosti," *Pravda,* March 29, 1987. This clearly comes under the heading of "routine glasnost'" rather than Aesopian politics aimed at the Belorussian leadership, since the previous head of the Belorussian CP, Sliun'kov, had just been promoted to CPSU Central Committee secretary in Moscow and a new Belorussian first secretary, Ye. Sokolov, had just been installed a few months before.

38. On January 4, 1987 *Pravda* published an account of persecution of a local Ukrainian correspondent, V. B. Berkhin (M. Odinets and M. Poltoranin,

"Za poslednei chertoi"). On January 8 KGB Chairman Chebrikov signed a brief note in *Pravda*, announcing that the responsible officials, who turned out to belong to the Ukrainian KGB, had been punished.

39. See especially Jonathan Sanders, "The Soviets' First Living Room War: Soviet National Television's Coverage of the Chernobyl' Disaster" (Paper prepared for the Program on Global Disasters and International Information Flows: The Annenberg School of Communications, Washington D.C., October 8–10, 1986).

40. N. I. Efimov, first deputy editor of *Izvestiia*, in an interview in *La Repubblica*, June 21, 1986. In 1987 *Narodnoe khoziaistvo SSSR za 70 let* (Moscow: "Finansy i Statistika," 1987), pp. 582–584, published selected circulation figures of major periodicals. They do not quite bear out Efimov's claim, but they do show a sharp drop in circulation for both *Izvestiia* and *Ogonyёk*.

41. Not in the form of direct competition in single-member districts, evidently, but in the form of multiple-member lists in newly consolidated districts. With more candidates than seats available, seats will be awarded in the order of votes received.

42. Much has been made of the fact that the final resolution of the Central Committee plenum of January 1987 did not adopt this idea. But Gorbachev introduced it in strikingly tentative language, so that it appears not to have been a formal proposal. Recall his singularly crab-like formulas: "It appears advisable to take counsel about the refinement of the mechanism of forming leading Party bodies. Many different proposals have come in to the Central Committee in this connection. Allow me to report on the conclusions which have been drawn on the basis of the generalization of these proposals." And so forth in the same style. In short, the issue has not yet been joined. Gorbachev did not return to it at the June 1987 Central Committee meeting.

43. Jerry F. Hough, *The Soviet Prefects* (Cambridge, Mass.: Harvard University Press, 1969), p. 162.

44. Ye. Ligachev, "Sovetuias' s partiei, s narodom," *Kommunist*, no. 16 (1985), p. 63.

45. So far without much success, apparently. An interview with Academician Nikita Moiseev, one of the few to submit his resignation on time, reveals that most senior figures in the Academy have petitioned for extensions "on an exceptional basis." N. Il'inskaia, "Pochemu v otstavku?" *Pravda*, August 17, 1987.

46. G. Smirnov, "Revoliutsionnyi sut' obnovleniia," *Pravda*, March 13, 1987.

47. The device of a Party Conference is itself an innovation, or rather the revival of an institution long unused. None has been held since 1941 and its powers are naturally vague, but distant precedents suggest that a Party Conference can amend Party rules and remove members of the Central Committee, although not elect new ones. See Dawn Mann, "Party Conferences as Political Tools," *Sovset' News*, vol. 3, no. 3 (March 1987).

48. Iu. Kaz'min, "Litsom k cheloveku truda: zametki s sessii Moskovskogo gorodskogo Soveta narodnykh deputatov," *Pravda*, March 17, 1987. Kaz'min

adds: "Deputies had to make their way into the ispolkom as petitioners, not as the plenipotentiary elected representatives of the people—and they still do."

49. Werner Hahn, "Electoral Choice in the Soviet Bloc," *Problems of Communism*, vol. XXXVI, no. 2 (March-April 1987), pp. 29–39. The Polish experience is in many ways the most interesting. It is analyzed in greater detail in the same author's *Democracy in a Communist Party: Poland's Experience Since 1980* (New York: Columbia University Press, 1987).

50. *Vedomosti Verkhovnogo Soveta SSSR*, no. 37, 1986.

51. I am indebted to Professor Peter Maggs of the University of Illinois, whose analyses of recent legislation have been appearing regularly on *Sovset'*.

52. "Perestroika—krovnoe delo naroda," Speech by M. S. Gorbachev to the XVIIIth Congress of the Labor Unions of the USSR, *Pravda*, February 26, 1987.

53. Such "telephone justice" has been widely discussed in the Soviet press recently and has drawn many letters to the editor. See Peter H. Solomon, "Soviet Politicians and Criminal Prosecutions: the Logic of Party Intervention" (Soviet Interview Project, Working Paper no. 33, March 1987).

54. Interview with the First Secretary of the Belorussian CP, Ye. Ye. Sokolov, "Vremia uchit'sia," *Pravda*, September 3, 1987.

55. This figure comes from Gorbachev's speech in Murmansk in October 1987, "Nemerknushchii podvig," op. cit.

56. *Pravda*, August 21, 1987. This figure does not include employees of the ministry supply systems, the so-called "glavsnaby."

57. See for example the pair of articles by V. Kostakov, "Zaniatost': defitsit ili izbytok?" *Kommunist*, no. 2 (1987), pp. 78–89, and "Polnaia zaniatost'. Kak my ego ponimaem?" *Kommunist*, no. 14 (1987), pp. 16–25.

58. That this is the explicit intent of the new leadership can be seen from the guidelines issued to the new editorial board of the Central Committee's official theoretical journal, *Kommunist*, in August 1986. These specified that the journal should pay particular attention to the works of the last years of Lenin's life. (*Pravda*, August 22, 1986.)

59. See particularly Lev Voskresenskii, "Along the Road to the Socialist Market," *Moscow News*, no. 48 (November 30, 1986), p. 121. For background on the handling of the NEP theme, see Elizabeth Teague, "Symbolic Role Ascribed to the NEP," *Radio Liberty Research Bulletin*, RL 415/86 (November 3, 1986).

60. Egor' Iakovlev, "Farewell," *Moscow News*, no. 3 (January 18, 1987), p. 13.

61. Danilov, "Istoki i uroki," op. cit.

62. *Pravda*, October 2, 1986. The major speeches delivered at the meeting, together with summaries of participants' major points, will be found in *XXVII S"ezd KPSS i zadachi kafedr obshchestvennykh nauk* (Moscow: "Politizdat," 1987).

63. Thus in his speech to the Central Committee in June 1987, Gorbachev used the word "contradiction" again and again to describe the current situation in the country. For example, the "contradiction between the requirements of

renewal, creativity, and constructive initiative, on the one hand, and conservatism, inertia, and mercenary interests (*korystnye interesy*) on the other." (1/5) Gorbachev also referred to "contradictions between the interests of various groups of the population, collectives, agencies, and organizations," (1/5) and particularly to "the contradiction between the near-term, narrow-minded interests, even egotistical motivations of particular individuals and the interests of the whole society, the long-term interests of the working people." (1/5) Later on, he said, "We must learn the complex, dialectically contradictory art of perestroika." (3/4) In his analysis of the Stalinist system, he referred to its "ever-growing contradiction" with the requirements of economic growth today. (3/6) (The numbers in parentheses refer to page and column respectively of the *Pravda* version.)

64. For details on this point, see Gustafson and Mann, "Gorbachev's Next Challenge," op. cit.

65. Remarks to a meeting of managers of the "Ramenskii" Agro-Industrial Kombinat ("Perestroika izmeriaetsia delami," *Pravda*, August 6, 1987).

66. As Gorbachev observed in one of his earliest speeches, people are increasingly interested in good housing and amenities, leisure, and tourism. See "O sozyve ocherednogo XXVII s"ezda . . . ," op. cit., p. 15. Since then he has given steadily stronger emphasis to social programs, health care, and housing, all of which are amenable to collective and cooperative approaches.

67. George W. Breslauer, *Khrushchev and Brezhnev as Leaders: Building Authority in Soviet Politics* (London: George Allen and Unwin, 1982).

68. Breslauer 1982, op. cit., p. 278.

69. See Rigby, op. cit., and Breslauer, op. cit.

70. Rigby, op. cit.

71. See Barbara A. Chotiner's summing up of the lessons of the 1962 bifurcation of the Party in her *Khrushchev's Party Reforms: Coalition Building and Institutional Innovation* (Westport, Conn.: Greenwood Press, 1984), pp. 273–290.

72. George Breslauer argues this point convincingly in *Khrushchev and Brezhnev as Leaders*, pp. 61ff. Khrushchev's evolution toward what became the Brezhnevian agricultural policy is described in my *Reform in Soviet Politics* (Cambridge: Cambridge University Press, 1981), pp. 16–25.

73. See especially Michel Tatu's description of Khrushchev's reaction to frustration in his *Power in the Kremlin* (New York: Viking Press, 1970).

74. For a discussion of the process of learning and innovation in Soviet policy-making, see "Bringing New Ideas into Soviet Politics" in my *Reform in Soviet Politics*, op. cit., Chapter 6.

75. From Philip Taubman's interview with Abel Aganbegian, "Architect of Soviet Change," *New York Times*, July 8, 1987, p. D1.

76. One such photo, seemingly from an amateur's camera, is reproduced in Dusko Doder, *Shadows and Whispers* (New York: Random House, 1986).

77. "Prakticheskimi delami uglubliat' perestroiku," *Pravda*, July 15, 1987.

78. V. Fedotov, "Kogda razgovor ser'eznyi," *Pravda*, October 26, 1986. Fedotov's account describes local press in the province of Lipetsk, which has been repeatedly featured as a showcase for *perestroika*.

79. One of the more potent threats is to deny new housing to the staff of a troublesome local newspaper. For a good description of the dynamics of intimidation of the local press, see N. Shabanov, "Za chto sulili gazetu?" *Pravda,* August 6, 1986.

80. *Pravda* chief editor V. G. Afanas'ev came as close as anyone I have seen when he referred at the 6th Congress of Journalists to the widespread practice of "self-censorship." (*Pravda,* March 14, 1987, op. cit.)

81. M. Berger, "Predpriiatie i perestroika: obsuzhdaem proekt Zakona SSSR," *Izvestiia,* March 4, 1987.

82. Berger, op. cit.

83. "Rech' M. S. Gorbacheva na vstreche s partiinym, sovetskim i khoziaistvennym aktivom Estonskoi SSR," *Pravda,* February 22, 1987.

84. See Seweryn Bialer's discussion of the conditions of stability in Bialer 1980, op. cit., pp. 145–182.

85. As Gorbachev commented to the XVIII Congress of Labor Unions, "The high goals set by the Party, the growing changes in the economy and in the social and political spheres have led to what one might call a 'revolution of expectations.'" ("Rech' M. S. Gorbacheva na XVIII s"ezde profsoiuzov SSSR," *Pravda,* February 26, 1987, p. 1.

86. See in particular the remarkable fictional conversation between Shirokov and Streshnev in Fedor Burlatskii, "Conversation Without Equivocation," *Literaturnaia gazeta,* October 1, 1986, p. 10. (Trans. in FBIS, *Daily Report/ USSR,* October 8, 1986, p. R6.)

87. "I want to emphasize that no one can relieve the Party committees of their concern and responsibility for the state of affairs in the economic field."

88. Tallinn speech, op. cit., February 21, 1987.

89. Ibid.

90. Anatolii Salutskii, "Svoi i chuzhie," *Pravda,* December 21, 1986.

91. Iu. Makhrin, "Obnovlenie," *Pravda,* January 14, 1987.

92. One recalls here Seweryn Bialer's words at the end of the 1970s: "One can agree that the post-Stalin era witnessed a decline in the role of the political, a decrease in the extent of its relative autonomy from the social environment. At the same time, however, the political factor continues to affect the evolution of Soviet society to a greater extent than it does other industrial societies on a similar level of industrial development. The shaping of the political factor by social influences continues to be low in comparison to the shaping of the social environment by the active, mobilizing, and directing influence of the political factor." (Bialer 1980, op. cit., pp. 124–125.)

The Russian Review, vol. 48, 1989, pp. 271–304

A Socialist Pluralism of Opinions: Glasnost and Policy-Making under Gorbachev

THOMAS REMINGTON

Alexander Herzen, attempting to explain the sensation occasioned by the publication of Peter Chaadaev's famous "Philosophical Letter" in 1836, characterized it as a "shot that rang out in the dark night." The scandal, he records in his memoirs, testified to the power of the word in a country, shaped by Nicholas I's policies of "official nationality," that had grown disaccustomed to open, independent speech. The essay appeared after a decade in which many of Russia's boldest intellectual spirits had been exiled, a time when "to speak was dangerous—and there was nothing to say anyway."[1]

Glasnost' has demonstrated the continuing power of the word in Russia. From the leadership's standpoint, *glasnost'* is a principal fulcrum in a massive effort at social engineering directed as much at reconstructing Soviet political culture as at reforming the structures of power. As its architects have formulated the matter, *glasnost'* is narrowing the "gap between words and deeds"—a formula widely used in the late 1970s and early 1980s by both reformist and orthodox wings of the political elite to deplore the disparity between commonly accepted norms of public and private behavior, and the pieties of party-mindedness and collectivism to which everyone was expected to pay obeisance. Alluding to Orwell's famous concept of double-think, the venerable Soviet scholar Igor' Kon analyzed this gap as a problem of social psychology. Double-think he regards as a condition in which "a different meaning is imputed to the same words; and the same person, depending on the situation (for example, at a meeting or at home) with equal sincerity affirms diametrically opposing things."[2]

This discrepancy was in fact less between "words and deeds," or, in social-scientific terms, culture and behavior, than between two interdependent but opposed codes of language *and* behavior: one for the realm of the unsanctioned-private, whether collective (such as dissident activity, religion, small-scale graft and illicit enterprise, and large-scale organized crime), or individualistic (including various forms of private rebellion and

[1] A. I. Gertsen, *Byloe i dumy* (Moscow: Detskaia literatura, 1968), pp. 440–41.
[2] I. Kon, "Psikhologiia sotsial'noi inertsii," *Kommunist*, no. 1, 1988, p. 70.

withdrawal and the other for the realm of the official—the *"kazennoe"*—including ceremonial occasions, the mass media, and official acts—for which an entirely distinct set of verbal symbols was employed. "Words" also referred to expression in the realm of ideas, social theory, art, and philosophy. "Deeds" in contrast applied to the field of observable behavior, of results rather than means, the real rather than the ideal. The gap between words and deeds also implied a contempt for the irreality of words, their inability to signify the inner truth of social life; it was also a tacit acknowledgment that the populace generally held the ritualized world of public life in private contempt.[3] As one wit put it, when there is no *glasnost'*, there is *ustnost'*; that is, when that which people know or believe or want to know about is kept out of the public record, face-to-face verbal communication takes the place of the mass media.

As the public realm, corrupted by the constant demand for gestures of fealty to the state and its ruling party, drifted further away from the world of private convictions and association, the sector of independent associational activity and opinion referred to as the civic or public realm (expressed in the Russian term *obshchestvennost'*) atrophied. Although doctrine paid lip service to the *concept* of *obshchestvennost'*, the freely expressed voice of social interests, in fact virtually every political undertaking outside the state sooner or later reverted to the norm for all large-scale Soviet organizations—a hierarchical, monopolistic, incorporated pyramid, its territorial councils built upon local cells, managed and controlled by an *apparat* inextricably intertwined with the party-state administrative elite at all levels. The Rodina Society, dedicated to the preservation of historic sites, is a characteristic example: formed in 1965, by the early 1980s its central *apparat* boasted some sixty-five subdivisions; it had hundreds of local full-time secretaries, and was spending more money on personnel than on preserving cultural monuments. Understandably, rank-and-file participation in public organizations acquired roughly the same negligible significance as trade union membership.[4] Although certain loose opinion and discussion groups formed in

---

[3] The classic version of this gap was a short story, "Levers," by Alexander Iashin, published over thirty years ago, in the period of political thaw. Four communists on a collective farm grumble bitterly about the incompetence and ignorance of local district officials on their problems, the unrealistic plans they are assigned, and so on, as they wait to convene a party meeting. The fifth member of the party organization, a schoolteacher, arrives, complaining about how she will obtain firewood for the school. The others interrupt her, "We'll talk about business later, now we need to hold the meeting." And the meeting proceeds with all verbiage of self-congratulation and self-exhortation on over-fulfillment. This scene is recounted by Alexander Iakovlev, Gorbachev's chief advisor for ideology, in an important address to the social sciences section of the Presidium of the Academy of Social Sciences on April 17, 1987. "Dostizhenie kachestvennogo novogo sostoianiia sovetskogo obshchestva i obshchestvennye nauki," *Vestnik akademii nauk*, no. 6, 1987, pp. 51–80.

[4] On the swelling of staffs in voluntary societies, see Anatolii Agranovskii's last, and posthumously, published article in *Izvestiia*, May 13, 1984, "Sokrashchenie apparata." A letter to *Pravda*

the late 1970s and early 1980s without becoming dissident in regime eyes, these rarely coalesced to the point of developing a formal internal organization. In turn the incapacity of the media and existing state and public organizations to articulate or mediate social impulses allowed the swelling of the reservoir of unrepresented, potentially mobilizable social needs and interests to approach a critical threshold.

If the silences and absences, the sterility and banality, of public life contributed to what Robert Tucker has called a "crisis of belief,"[5] still more dangerous from the center's standpoint was the decay of the crucial steering function the media are called upon to perform in the Soviet polity, as well as the feedback of information to superior authorities to allow them to evaluate actual performance in the light of policy goals. Reinforcing the media's role as an instrument for celebrating the status quo—what Alexander Iakovlev termed the "universal exultation" characteristic of the media in the Brezhnev era—was the weakness of "criticism and self-criticism." Given the insignificance of the targets singled out for public censure, most criticism amounted to praise through faint damnation. Poor performance left the media equally incapable of assisting either central policy direction or social reconnaissance.

Glasnost' is intended to reverse this resulting drift of the Soviet system toward crisis or even breakdown[6] with painful, frequently radical self-examination intended to build popular pressure for deep reform—to enable a new liveliness and credibility of "words" to serve the goal of reform in the area of "deeds" by activating personal initiative and material

---

about Pamyat' and other groups points out that the recognized public organizations such as the Rodina Society, DOSAAF, the Temperance Society, and so on have become bureaucratized and top-heavy, losing contact with their volunteer base. Their immobility, according to the letter, stimulates the formation of the new informal groups. "O pamiati mnimoi i nastoiashchei," *Pravda*, March 18, 1988.

[5] See Thomas F. Remington, "Gorbachev and the Strategy of *Glasnost'*," chap. 4 of idem, ed., *Politics and the Soviet System: Essays in Honour of Frederick C. Barghoorn* (London: Macmillan Press, 1989); Robert Tucker, "Swollen State, Spent Society: Stalin's Legacy to Brezhnev's Russia," in Tucker, *Political Culture and Leadership in Soviet Russia* (New York: Norton, 1987), p. 126.

[6] The formula "pre-crisis situation" was employed by Gorbachev in his January 1987 Plenum address and it represented a deepening and radicalization of the official interpretation of the severity of the current state of affairs. (According to a *samizdat* report of the plenum, Gorbachev, in fact, went further, and claimed that the Soviet Union was at the crisis stage, but that, in contrast to other socialist systems which had reached crisis—such as Poland, Hungary, and Czechoslovakia—there was no one who could extend help to the Soviet Union in solving its problems. See "Plenum TsK KPSS," *Strana i mir*, no. 4 (40), 1987, p. 38. Gorbachev cited some eleven crises in socialist countries to date, including those in Hungary, Czechoslovakia, China, and Albania; and no fewer than five in Poland. The veteran journalist Vasilii Seliunin and the economist Girsh Khanin have gone considerably further in their assessment of the current economic situation in the USSR, and in articles and seminars, they have repeatedly and publicly forecast that without radical economic change, the Soviet economy will reach the point of crisis and collapse by the mid-1990's. See Vasilii Seliunin, "Istoki," *Novyi Mir*, no. 5, 1988, p. 170; also Richard E. Ericson, "The Soviet Statistical Debate: Khanin vs. TsSU," *Harriman Institute Occasional Papers*, no. 1 (May 1988), p. 35.

self-interest in the state and public spheres. *Glasnost'* entails both a loosening and a reprogramming of the ideological content of public expression; as Gorbachev put it in December 1984:

> Broad, timely and frank information is testimony to trust in people, respect for their intelligence and feelings, their ability themselves to interpret various events. It raises the activeness of the toilers. *Glasnost'* in the work of party and state organs is an effective means of struggle against bureaucratic distortions and it obliges them more thoughtfully to approach the adoption of decisions and the organization of *kontrol'* over their fulfillment and the eradication of deficiencies and omissions. And in fact on this to a large extent depends the persuasiveness of propaganda, the effectiveness of upbringing, the ensurance of the unity of word and deed.[7]

Even before he became party leader, Gorbachev linked *glasnost'* with stiffer enforcement of bureaucratic accountability and higher effectiveness of party ideological work.

The problem is that the instrumental objective of making party ideological work more credible by tolerating freer criticism is at cross-purposes with the ideological pluralization actually resulting from the expansion of freedom for interest articulation and representation. The policy drive of "democratization," especially marked since January 1987, has accorded ideological legitimation to such liberal values as free speech and free association. These ideals, partly realized through *glasnost'*, have been valued not just instrumentally, but in themselves by democratically minded sections of the intelligentsia, although the conservative elements of the political elite undoubtedly interpret them as merely a measured extension of the familiar practice of criticizing the mistakes of the preceding leadership period.[8] The instrumental aspect of *glasnost'* works by reprogramming ideological controls over public life: it is aimed at improving the steering capacity of the center by reducing the opacity and resistance of the lower reaches of the bureaucracy to supervisory control from above and by generating national public discussion and support for policy decisions that have already been adopted. The bitter struggle over

---

[7] M. S. Gorbachev, *Zhivoe tvorchestvo naroda* (Moscow, 1984), p. 30.

[8] A typical example of the "instrumental" view was the comment by the newly appointed first secretary of the Rostov provincial party organization, Boris Volodin, who observed that in the past, the lack of openness protected incompetence and irresponsibility. Allowing more criticism "raises the accountability of party officials for their assigned tasks" and will provide "a graphic example to all the toilers that we treat the acts of communists, regardless of the position they hold, with the party by-laws which are the same for all communists." Furthermore: "It goes without saying that all our work in expanding *glasnost'* is not an end in itself" but should "contribute to the fulfillment of tasks set by the Twenty-seventh Party Congress, the June 1986 Central Committee Plenum, and develop the initiative of labor collectives, rousing in people the aspiration to achieve higher results." (B. Volodin, "Rasshirenie glasnosti—vopros politicheskii," *Partiinaia zhizn'*, no. 17, 1986, pp. 23, 24, 27).

glasnost', therefore, is a dispute over the political consequences of ideological liberalization.

This article is intended as a preliminary effort at stocktaking after three years of *glasnost'* and addresses above all the impact of *glasnost'* on changing patterns of articulation and mediation of political interests. It will argue that the leadership strategy of employing *glasnost'*—that is, encouragement of more open expression in public communication in order to mobilize support for the reform program—has resulted in stimulating still more radical, and ultimately unincorporable political expression generated by Soviet society's deeper unresolved cleavages.

–1–

Prompted by a significant shift in policy at the center, *glasnost'* alters authority relations throughout the political system. Above all it makes it considerably harder for well-organized bureaucratic interests to appropriate the party's ideological control over political expression for parochial political needs. Formerly so many social issues were closed off to critical comment at meetings, in the media, in the arts, and in other arenas of public life that the realm of problems that were acceptable topics for deliberation narrowed to the point of irreality. In the early 1980s, matters had reached the point that only the lowliest and weakest agencies and territorial organizations' bodies were unable to fend off routine criticism. *Glasnost'*, then, has reduced though not eliminated the power that many party and government offices exercised in demanding that public comment on matters falling under their territorial or departmental purview first be "cleared" with them.

Because of the difficulties this trend posed for central control over bureaucratic performance, the initial and generally accepted premise of *glasnost'* as a strategy was expressed in the formula, first offered by Egor Ligachev at the 27th Party Congress, and subsequently repeated by many others, that there are no zones off-limits to criticism. The party encouraged criticism in the interests of enforcing high and uniform standards of performance throughout the political system. Particularly following the January 1987 plenum, however, which laid particular emphasis on the principle of "democratization," *glasnost'* allowed radical statements challenging established doctrines, such as Nikolai Shmelev's essay on the bankruptcy of central planning in the June 1987 number of *Novyi mir*, the rapid growth of pressure for the rehabilitation of Stalin's Old Bolshevik victims, and the profusion of harsh attacks on water projects in many publications, including *Ogonek*, *Novyi mir*, and *Kommunist*. Indeed, since early 1987, *glasnost'* has opened to public discussion virtually every theoretical postulate formerly regarded as essential to Marxism, including the nature of property under socialism, collectivized agriculture, central planning versus markets, the party's monopoly on policy-making and cadre appointments, social equality, the doctrine of world class struggle, collectivism, and the primacy of military force in protecting national security. Although by the end of 1988 restrictions on reporting remained—the Ministry of Health, for example, sought to prevent reporting of the fact that DDT continues to be manufactured and used, and the space program remained shrouded in secrecy—most of those restrictions that survived stemmed from administrative rather than ideological considerations. That is, they reflected powerful agencies' preferences for operational autonomy as opposed to the party's need to maintain a monopoly on socialist doctrines.[9]

Moreover, through law and decree no less than through *glasnost'*, Gorbachev has swept away decades of homage to collectivism, seeking to unleash personal interest as a motive force in production and trade, and to improve quality and performance through competitive pressure both in economic and political spheres. According to the reformists, indifference to the public weal, the attitude that the realm of the state is not the common property of the whole people but is rather "no one's," has created a dangerous vacuum of moral integrity, a breakdown in the normative fabric that keeps personal amorality in check and thus preserves social peace; it has nurtured as well a habitual indifference to economic productivity.[10] Thus Nikolai Shmelev, an economist who has been one of the boldest spirits in the new literature of liberal reform, has flatly pronounced that "whatever is efficient is moral and whatever is moral is efficient."[11] The problems of economic reform have prompted sharp and searching debates over the essential nature of justice under Soviet socialism: the permissible degree of social inequality, the legitimacy of personal interest, the creation of "safety nets" to protect the economically deprived, and the trade-offs between efficiency and equality.[12]

[9] On the DDT story, see the remarks by Kazakh poet M. Shakhanov at the plenum of the USSR Writers' Union as published in *Literaturnaia gazeta*, January 25, 1989. On the continuing secrecy surrounding space and defense installations, see A. Pokrovskii, "A chto v 'iashchike'?" *Pravda*, August 6, 1988.

[10] Professor Butenko cites numerous cases of a worker and a peasant accused of theft of state property. The worker responded to the charges as follows: "Does what you call social property really belong to society? Not at all! Here property, as they used to say in the old days, is God's, that is, nobody's. No one has any use for it, so therefore I took the box with the tool so it wouldn't go ownerless (*bezkhoznym*). If I hadn't taken it, someone else would have!"The peasant charged with stealing a bag of grain from a collective farm testified: "If this grain had truly been ours, the peasants', would it really have been lying around (*valialos' by*)? . . . when it's locked up, then it is someone else's, you can't touch it. I took the bag because I sowed and reaped grain, and took it since it was not someone else's but nobody's!" A. P. Butenko, "O kharaktere sobstvennosti v usloviiakh real'nogo sotsializma," *EKO*, no. 2, 1988, pp. 15–16.

[11] Nikolai Shmelev, "Avansi i dolgi," *Novyi mir*, no. 6, 1987, p. 158; idem, "Novye trevogi," *Novyi mir*, no. 4, 1988, p. 175; idem, "The Rouble and Perestroika," *Moscow News*, no. 6 (February 14–21), 1988.

[12] For the views of two conservative social scientists who conclude that the dispute over the

A new concern with individualism has also entered the debate over political reform. A recent letter to *Kommunist* argues that decades of propaganda have persuaded people that the balance between state and individual interests must always favor the state: we must instead recover, writes the author, head of the chair in state and law at Kaliningrad University, the ancient tradition of the fundamental worth and dignity of the individual citizen. The citizen is hgher than the state: he forms it, and should not be brought up in blind obedience to it. The authority of the citizen, the letter concludes, must become the point of departure for all political and legal reform.[13] In both the political and economic reform debates, values associated with liberal individualism are gaining strength as the only intellectually defensible alternative to the threadbare formulations which had served as rationalizations for the post-Stalinist system.

In turn, the breathtaking assault on long-established and often deeply cherished ideological tenets has resulted in an intense backlash and perhaps even a direct challenge to Gorbachev's power in the Andreeva affair.[14] The sensation and fear the Andreeva article provoked among the intelligentsia and the outpouring of attacks that appeared once *Pravda* published an authoritative rebuttal centered less on the defense of Stalinism and the chauvinistic and anti-Semitic views Andreeva propounded than on the harsh, authoritarian tone in which the article was written, which created the impression, according to *Pravda*, that it was expressing an ideological platform, "a manifesto of the anti-perestroika forces."[15] Yet for all her own reactionary views, "Andreeva" is indeed justified in interpreting *glasnost'* as a challenge to socialist ideology both in form and content.

This is true both because the revision of doctrine has granted a variety of political forces access to public attention that could not have

---

relative priority of individualist and collectivist conceptions of social justice lies at the root of many other values, such as subsidies to poor families, the proper level of the inheritance tax, and the degree of freedom to be allowed private enterprise, see N. F. Naumova and V. Z. Rogov;n, "Zadacha na spravedlivost'" in *Sotsiologicheskie issledovaniia*, no. 3 (May/June) 1987, pp. 12–23. Another review acknowledges that the majority opinion regards the accumulation of individual wealth as illegitimate and incompatible with the norms of socialism, as indicated by the many letters in the press supporting restrictions on the incomes and activities of individual entrepreneurs under the new laws authorizing individual labor activity. The author considers this indifference to the problem of productivity as having been nurtured under the system of statism prevalent from the Stalin era to the present. (G. S. Batygin, " 'Dobrodetel' protiv interesa," *Sotsiologicheskie issledovaniia*, no. 3 (May/June) 1987, pp. 24–36.)

13 V. Prokop'ev, "Demokratiia i chelovecheskoe dostoinstvo," *Kommunist*, no. 8, 1988, pp. 43–45.

14 Nina Andreeva, "Ne mogu postupat'sia printsipami," *Sovetskaia Rossiia*, March 13, 1988.

15 "Printsipy perestroiki—revoliutsionnost' myshleniia i deistvii," *Pravda*, April 5, 1988. Other refutations followed, including Nikolai Bodnaruk, "Sluchai i iavleniie," *Izvestiia*, April 10, 1988, which employed much the same phraseology as *Pravda's* unsigned comment; I Nastavshev, "Prikosnis' k istochniku," *Kommunist*, no. 6, 1988, pp. 109–15.

gained a hearing in the past; and, still more importantly, because the mechanisms of ideological direction and control over society have been drastically reduced. This is turn has permitted an extraordinary flourishing of independent associational activity, much of it aimed at influencing policy decisions.

–2–

Since July 1987, Gorbachev has repeatedly used the novel term, "socialist pluralism of opinions," to describe the vigorous public debate of social problems and their possible solutions. Since the phrase, with its ideologically provocative hint of bourgeois liberalism, had not been used before, even in so qualified a way, and since Gorbachev has taken care almost always to apply pluralism to opinion (that is, words) rather than power, property, or interests, it is clear that he is using the term deliberately and conservatively.[16] Through it, Gorbachev distinguishes between the legitimate diversity of interests and opinions consistent with socialism and unacceptable efforts to institute multiparty competition or restore private ownership of capital.

Gorbachev first employed the term "socialist pluralism" in his address to media executives shortly after the June 1987 Central Committee plenum, where major economic reforms were adopted. Urging that editors not allow newspapers and magazines to be creatures of narrow group interests, he demanded that the media present the voices of the whole society, so that "the whole, so to speak, socialist pluralism is present in every publication."[17] Assumed is the inner, unifying truth that transcends the limited and partial visions of the many. In September 1987, just after his extended summer leave, Gorbachev referred to socialist pluralism again in a response to a question posed by a member of a group of French public figures, but did not elaborate on the idea; he did not confine it to the sphere of opinion, distinguishing only "socialism pluralism" from its counterpart under capitalism.[18]

These comments might have seemed casual and off-handed had Gorbachev not returned to the concept of pluralism repeatedly in early 1988, now qualifying it with the "of opinions" phrase. In his address to the February 1988 plenum, devoted to basic ideological thery, he observed that: "For the first time in many decades we are really experiencing a socialist pluralism of opinions" and in the same speech he introduced another theme that also harkened back to the Eastern European humanist

[16]For example, pluralism was not mentioned by Alexander Iakovlev in his highly revisionist address to the social science section of the Academy of Sciences Presidium in April 1987 (Iakovlev, "Dostizhenie," *Vestnik akademii nauk*, no. 6, 1987).

[17]"Prakticheskimi delami uglubliat' perestroiku," *Pravda*, July 15, 1987.

[18]*Pravda*, September 30, 1987.

Marxists of the 1960s, the applicability of Marx's category of "alienation" to socialist society. In Poland, Yugoslavia, Czechoslovakia, and other socialist countries the view that man could be alienated from the means of production, his labor, and from spiritual values even under socialism had been seriously discussed by theorists in the post-Stalin reform period, but the debate was received coldly in Moscow, especially after 1968. Now Gorbachev was reinstating two of the most resonant concepts of the Eastern European Marxist humanists, alienation and pluralism.[19]

Again in May 1988, meeting with media executives, Gorbachev referred to pluralism and insisted that, notwithstanding the icy blast of Stalinism released by the Andreeva letter in *Sovetskaia Rossiia*, the party was not retreating from its commitment to democratizing socialism. Criticism must be in the interests of socialism and against conservatism; there must be "freedom of expression of opinions and choice," but all within the socialist order. A truly Leninist socialism made room for "pluralism of opinions, interests and needs."[20] Pluralism, qualified both as socialist and as "pluralism of opinions" then became a frequently repeated totem of liberal critics of Andreeva's broadside. She had challenged the Gorbachev leadership with an accusation that socialist ideology itself was in jeopardy because of the loss of sharp frontiers between socialism and bourgeois liberalism. She accused these forces of "disseminating an extra-socialist pluralism" and politicizing the newly born independent organizations "on the basis not at all of socialist pluralism."[21] *Pravda*'s response reaffirmed the current diversity of expressed opinion, which it called a sign of "the real, currently existing socialist pluralism of opinions."[22] The "Theses" issued by the Central Committee a month before the June Party Conference went so far as to drop the "socialist" qualifier from the phrase, but Gorbachev in his address to the conference itself reverted to the standard wording, "socialist pluralism of opinions," although associating it with a newly emphasized concept of "competition" (*sostiazanie* and *sostiazatel'nost*).[23] Again, in his rather critical address to the media in September 1988, with its unmistakable tone of urgency (as in the reminder that the working class is growing impatient with mere "conversations"—that is, words), Gorbachev reaffirmed his previous position: "Publish everything. There should be a pluralism of opinions. But with such directedness that the line of perestroika, the cause of socialism, are defended and strengthened."[24]

[19] *Moskovskaia pravda*, February 19, 1988.

[20] "Cherez demokratizatsiiu—k novomu obliku sotsializma," *Pravda*, May 11, 1988.

[21] Andreeva, "Ne mogu," *Sovetskaia Rossiia*, March 13, 1988.

[22] "Printsipy perestroiki—revoliutsionnost' myshleniia i deistvii," *Pravda*, April 5, 1988.

[23] "Tezisy Tsentral'nogo Komiteta KPSS k XIX Vsesoiuznoi partiinoi konferentsii," *Pravda*, May 27, 1988; Gorbachev address, Central Television Program One, June 28, 1988.

[24] "Na novom etape perestroiki," *Pravda*, September 25, 1988.

Addressing a select audience of leading intellectuals in early January 1989, Gorbachev restated his carefully delimited doctrine of socialist pluralism, welcoming differences of opinion so long as they contributed constructively to perestroika, but rejecting open competition for power. His position, as before, relegated pluralism to the realm of opinions and treated debate as "truth-seeking" aimed at "a synthesis of different opinions, on the basis of which we get nearer to the truth."[25] He begs the question, therefore, of whether there is, in the end, a single truth in politics, and simply reformulates the traditional "choral" or "orchestral" view under which the diversity of opinions in society (albeit now linked to diversity of social interests) are "synthesized" or harmonized into consensus. Moreover, he did not mention, let alone defend, the theory of socialist pluralism when he addressed a group of workers at the Central Committee the next month, where instead he expatiated contemptuously on the "nonsensical" idea of a multiparty system.[26]

On the other hand, liberal intellectuals could not long remain content with an interpretation of pluralism that confined it solely to the expression of opinion. Stimulated by the official refutation of the Andreeva letter in early April 1988 and the preparations for the June party conference, reformists began elaborating a broader conception linking pluralism to wider participation and competition in the political system. Expressing gratification at the legitimation of a concept the very mention of which, as one writer put it, "we awaited with hope, never in our wildest dreams expecting to get it," they pressed for liberalizing and democratizing change. Nonmembers of the party, even non-Marxists and religious believers, should be able to take part in political life and "check" the party; they should be allowed to rise to executive positions and be chosen for membership on the boards of public bodies. Unofficial organizations should be free to form, compete for members, and run candidates for deputies to soviets.[27] Some called for the creation of an all-union "Patriotic Front," an umbrella organization which would in some sense counterbalance the power of the CPSU.[28] For the most part, the liberals

[25] British Broadcasting Corporation, Summary of World Broadcasts, Soviet Union (hereafter SWB SU) 0353, C/1–14, January 9, 1989.

[26] SWB SU/0389, C/1–18, February 20, 1989.

[27] O. Smolin, " 'Zashchitnye mekhanizmy' sotsialisticheskoi demokratii," in "Demokratizatsiia partii—demokratizatsiia obshchestva," *Kommunist*, no. 6, 1988, pp. 28–32; and L. Shevtsova, "Garantii narodovlastiia," *Literaturnaia gazeta*, April 27, 1988.

[28] This suggestion was advanced along with a series of other democratic reforms in a letter to *Kommunist*'s series on party reform. It has been backed by Tatiana Zaslavskaia, Boris Kurashvili, and other reformers. Its proponents envision it as a Soviet equivalent to the united fronts which have maintained a shadowy parliamentary existence in the people's democracies since the establishment of communist rule in the late 1940s. At the party conference, Gorbachev himself stopped short of endorsing the idea, calling simply for more discussion of the appropriate forms for the "patriotic movement" of Soviet youth, women, believers, and other strata which was forming in support of

sought to reconcile institutions associated with liberal democracy, such as parliamentarism, a constitutional court, a directly elected head of state, contested elections of party and government officials, and real local government, with one-party rule and state ownership of the basic means of production.[29] But by the end of 1988, the linkage between private property as a defense against the power of the state and political pluralism in the sense of freely competing interest groups and parties was being explored in the press.[30]

–3–

Although Gorbachev's provocative albeit qualified use of the term "pluralism" accepts a substantial loosening of ideological controls over political expression, it is a good deal less satisfactory as a description of the development of central press discussion even since 1987. To a much greater extent than is commonly recognized, public debate has followed the pattern of sponsored "discussion campaigns," which are a standard feature of party ideological work. Discussion campaigns are devices to

perestroika. Much like the Czechoslovak reform movement in 1968, the proposals preserve the communist party's leading role while allowing the "patriotic front" to expand political participation. See A. Krechetnikov, "Nazrevshie izmeneniia," *Kommunist*, no. 8, 1988, p. 43; Bill Keller, "A Gorbachev Adviser Urges a Political Alternative to the Communist Party," *New York Times*, May 24, 1988; Gorbachev, Soviet TV, June 28, 1988.

[29] Consider the effort by Boris Kurashvili, a leading reformer and a senior associate of the Institute of State and Law of the Academy of Sciences, to reconcile single-party rule with both separation of powers and a system of checks and balances: "In the conditions of a one-party system that took historical form in the USSR, the pluralization of public life, the determination of a course of development for the country, the resolution of disagreements and contradictions linked with the advancement and selection of alternatives, can readily occur within the framework of a single ruling party, by means of a mechanism of intra-party democracy more developed than at present. That classical form of pluralism known as "the separation of powers" (legislative, executive, and judicial) is another matter. "Separation of powers" does not mean the absence of unity of power, as though each of the three aforementioned powers addressed society independently of the others with its decisions. In its dealing with society the state power acts as a united whole. United, but having its own internal structure. In the framework of this structure and by the interaction of the different, sometimes mutually opposed, subsystems, the governmental impacts of a unified system of power on society are worked out. And here society, its collective and individual members, can "send back" an illegal or inappropriate governmental decision to the system of power and in this way bring into motion the "separation of powers," here understood as a mechanism for complementing and balancing the powers of one state organ (which has taken a decision) with the powers of another organ, in order to achieve the adoption of a more well-founded decision, its annulment or correction." (B. Kurashvili, "K polnovlastiiu sovetov," *Kommunist*, no. 8, 1988, pp. 31–32.

[30] An article in *Sovetskaia Litva* in February 1989 suggested that private, or at least nonstate, property helped protect society against the power of the state bureaucracy and called for a multiparty system. The fearless Boris Kurashvili, in a roundtable discussion on the question of pluralism, was quite willing to contemplate the possibility that a "socialist bourgeoisie" might strive peacefully to protect and advance its property interests. See E. Proshechkin, "On State Ownership and Pluralism," in Foreign Broadcast Information Service, USSR, Daily Report (hereafter FBIS-SOV) 89–026, February 9, 1989, pp. 51–52; For Kurashvili's cited comments see "Sotsialisticheskii pliuralizm," *Sotsiologicheskie issledovaniia*, no. 5, 1988, p. 18.

illuminate policy goals of the leadership over a defined period, a period culminating in the adoption of a document or final draft of a document, such as a law of resolution. The campaign is intended to build public support and awareness for important enactments by creating a public atmosphere of mass participation in the policy's elaboration. The forms of discussion campaigns have been extensively described both in the Soviet and Western literature, and need not be detailed here.[31] Suffice it to say that mass discussion as a form of ideological campaign has a long history (for example, the discussion of the 1936 Constitution lasted five months, during which time *Pravda* published numerous critical letters from around the country, and over thirteen thousand suggestions were examined by the Central Executive Committee)[32] and that it has remained a standard feature of ideological work through the Khrushchev, Brezhnev, and post-Brezhnev eras, contributing in no small measure to the tendency for public ceremonial to grow increasingly detached from social realities. Upon assuming the party leadership, Gorbachev inherited some ideological campaigns, redirected others, and initiated still others in his effort to mobilize public support for his ambitious program of social reconstruction. Among the campaigns he inherited in 1985 was the observance of the fortieth anniversary of victory in World War II, a campaign which, as the first modern Soviet leader not to have participated in the war, Gorbachev could do little to redirect for his own ideological goals.[33] Another was the fiftieth anniversary of the Stakhanov movement, marked by a media campaign tying Stakhanovism to the goals of accelerating social modernization, raising labor productivity and discipline, and putting en-

[31] Robert Sharlet analyzes the discussion campaign leading to the adoption of the final draft of the 1977 Constitution in his book *The New Soviet Constitution of 1977: Analysis and Text* (Brunswick, OH: King's Court Communications, 1978); see also Thomas Remington, "Policy Innovation and Soviet Media Campaigns," *Journal of Politics*, vol. 45, no. 1 (February 1983), pp. 220–27, which illustrates the standard media campaigns of the late Brezhnev era on the basis of a comparison of two 1979 media campaigns; further detail may be found in Thomas F. Remington, *The Truth of Authority: Ideology and Communication in the Soviet Union* (Pittsburgh: University of Pittsburgh Press, 1988). Iasen Zasurskii, dean of the journalism faculty of Moscow University, writes in a book published as recently as 1987 that the mass media have done much to popularize and publicize current party policies and to shape public opinion about them; strangely indifferent to the current near-universal contempt for the hollow, ritualistic press campaigns of the Brezhnev era, he cites the public discussions of the 1977 Constitution, the discussion of the new Law on the Labor Collective in 1983, and the reform of the general and vocational education system in 1984 as positive examples of recent press discussions. See Ia. N. Zasurskii, ed., *Zhurnalistika i politika* (Moscow: 1987), p. 17.

[32] V. P. Smirnov, "Iz istorii massovykh obsuzhdenii v partiinoi pechati," *Voprosy istorii KPSS*, no. 5, 1986, p. 23.

[33] Nevertheless, there were hints of a new ideological line prior to the fortieth anniversary. See, for example, the *Pravda* editorial for March 23, 1985, entitled "Vospitanie istorii." While not explicitly revising any shibboleths, it suggested that there was much to be learned from a sober study of the facts of Soviet history that would benefit future generations. It represented the first suggestion that ideological work should shift from an emphasis on celebrating anniversaries of the mythologized past to a new objectivity designed to improve progress in the future.

terprises on a footing of economic accountability.[34] Still others were the seventieth anniversary of the October Revolution and the 800th anniversary of the campaign against the Polovetsians recounted in the epic *Lay of Igor's Host.* An ideological campaign which Gorbachev initiated in May 1985, shortly after his installation as general secretary, was the temperance campaign, an aspect of which has been discussion in the press of the social pathologies caused by alcohol abuse.[35] Another was the campaign organized around the theme of "scientific-technical acceleration."

Perhaps of greatest significance from the standpoint of the development of *glasnost'* was the reorientation of the most important ideological campaign Gorbachev inherited, the preparations for the 27th Party Congress, and specifically the drafting of a new version of the party program. Decisions on the scale and themes of the campaign preceding the 27th Party Congress were adopted at the October 1985 Central Committee plenum, and evidently presupposed a campaign structure basically similar to the discussion campaigns surrounding the 1977 Constitution, the 1983 labor collective law, and the 1984 education reform.[36] It was, to be sure, the October Plenum which approved the drafts of the new edition of the party program, the revisions in the party statute, and the guidelines for economic development through 2000, and directed that they be published as a basis of discussion before the impending party congress.[37] However, the October plenum was only reorienting a campaign already in progress. Apart from the resolutions to be adopted at the congress, upon which a new general secretary would have needed to set the stamp of his own policy program, preparation of the new edition of the party program had long been underway, and it was important for Gorbachev to strip the current draft of as many of the theoretical conceptions associated with the Brezhnev-Chernenko forces as possible, and to turn it into a reference source for ideas associated with his leadership. A case in point, one on which Gorbachev himself commented at the congress, is the progressive delegitimation of the Brezhnev-era formula of "developed socialism," now regarded simply as a rationalization of conservatism and decay.[38]

The October 1985 plenum illustrates Gorbachev's skillful use of party meetings—plenums, conferences, and consultations—to conclude

---

[34] See Gorbachev's speech, "The Unfading Traditions of a Labor Exploit," *Pravda* and *Izvestiia,* September 21, 1985, excerpted and translated in *Current Digest of the Soviet Press* (hereafter *CDSP*), vol. 37, no. 38 (October 16, 1985), pp. 10–11.

[35] For early articles providing factual information and background material for conducting the media temperance campaign including results of sociological surveys of drinking, see Boris Levin, "Issledovanie pokazalo," *Zhurnalist,* no. 7, 1985, p. 44.

[36] E. A. Blazhnov, "Partiinaia pechat' v ideologicheskom obespechenii preds'ezdovskoi kampanii," *Vestnik moskovskogo universiteta,* ser. 10 Zhurnalistika, no. 2, 1986.

[37] See *Pravda,* October 16, 1985.

[38] This issue is discussed in Remington, *The Truth of Authority,* chap. 1.

press discussions which, in the scope and radicalism of permitted expression, go far beyond the changes envisioned in the policy statements which launch them. For example, the pre-congress discussion of changes in the party statute and program raised two topics which ultimately proved too sensitive for the congress to deal with, yet which by virtue of being addressed were added to the latent political agenda.[39] One was the question of the privileges enjoyed by the political elite, and the other was the need to limit the terms of office-holders. In both cases, guidelines to editors on the scope of permissible criticism were ambiguous, creating the circumstances which led the normally cautious editors of *Pravda* to publish T. Samolis' famous review of reader mail on the subject of the privilege enjoyed by political officials, "Ochishchenie" ("Cleansing"), in February 1986, for which *Pravda* was rebuked by name at the congress.[40] These themes were not so much ideologically unacceptable as premature. Both returned as major foci of discussion in the run-up to the 19th party conference in 1988. Samolis herself, for example, whose article had stirred up the scandal, published a second congratulatory article in *Pravda* in June 1988. Not only had she not been fired from her job for her earlier article as many had expected, she wrote, but her position had been vindicated by the tide of subsequent reader mail.[41] Although the theme of illegitimate privilege was evidently now acceptable for discussion, it was not the object of any policy decisions at the party conference (although earlier in 1988 a decision was taken to restructure the system of closed coupon stores for privileged Soviet shoppers); on the other hand, ways of limiting the term of government and party officials became a major running theme of discussions leading up to and at the party conference, having been focussed by the proposal in the Central Committee Theses to limit party and government officials to two, and under exceptional cir-

[39] In their study of agenda-formation, Cobb and Elder distinguish the "governmental" agenda, consisting of issues before policy-makers for decision, from the "systemic" agenda, referring to issues that elements of the citizenry believe require public attention. See Roger W. Cobb and Charles D. Elder, *Participation in American Politics: The Dynamics of Agenda-Building*, 2nd ed. (Baltimore: Johns Hopkins Press, 1983), pp. 85–86.

[40] T. Samolis, "Ochishchenie," *Pravda*, February 13, 1986. *Pravda* must have been immediately called to task for this article, because its February 15 issue carried a rebuttal. Although individual party members might exist who fail to meet the party's high standards, it was wrong, according to a reader whom *Pravda* quoted by way of recantation, to generalize from them to the existence of an entire "party-administrative stratum" resisting the loss of its perquisites. On articles calling for ways to induce the voluntary retirement of aging officials, see V. Vasinsky and A. Ezhelev, "Application for Retirement," *Izvestiia*, December 1, 1985 (trans. in *CDSP*, vol. 37, no. 46 [November 15, 1985], p. 12); also see the round-up of articles about the renewal of members of leading party posts by means of mandatory rotation, and on the problem of getting rid of unwanted older leaders in *CDSP*, vol. 38, no. 6 (March 12, 1986), pp. 4–6.

[41] T. Samolis, "Ochishchenie pravdoi," *Pravda*, June 7, 1988. The title is nicely ambiguous, since it suggests that she had been vindicated both by *pravda*, truth and *Pravda* the newspaper.

cumstances, three, five-year terms. Once again, discussion seemed to follow the familiar contours of an organized media campaign: a leader signals his interest in a press discussion of a particular idea in order to generate a consensus around a preferred policy, and then, once the policy has been enacted, a press discussion is held to publicize it and demand its implementation.

Because of the enormous sensitivity surrounding Stalin and Stalinism, the campaign marking the seventieth anniversary of the October Revolution became the occasion for multiple and competing high-level statements of guidance to the mass media. In March 1987, Ligachev addressed a meeting at the State Radio and Television Committee to outline the media's tasks in preparations for the October anniversary; he advised them to emphasize "propaganda of the achievements of Soviet power," avoiding the temptation to portray "our history as a chain of constant mistakes and disappointments."[42] In July 1987, following the June plenum on economic reform, Gorbachev met with editors and other officials in the ideological sphere to discuss media coverage of the results of the plenum as well as media work more generally. His comments about the treatment of history urged balance of negative with positive material. While the repressions of 1937–38, he stated, can never be forgiven or justified, by the same token the media must also reflect positive light on the great accomplishments of the people in constructing a socialist state that succeeded in withstanding and defeating Naziism.[43] Just two months later, during Gorbachev's extended leave from work during August and September 1987, Egor Ligachev again met with editors to offer authoritative advice on coverage of the anniversary theme, where he again warned against an excessively negative slant in treating Soviet history.[44] Gorbachev's comments on the Stalin period in his seventieth anniversary address, taken as ideological signals, represented a compromise between radical calls for the rehabilitation of Bukharin and other other Bolsheviks repressed by Stalin and tributes to Stalin's wise leadership.[45] But at the same time that the speech concluded one "discussion," it initiated a new and more radical review of history that resulted in Bukharin's full rehabilitation, and a blanket rehabilitation of all victims of Stalinist mass repression.

One of the most important discussion campaigns preparatory to a major political event was the debate leading up to the general party con-

[42]"Navstrechu 70-letiiu Velikogo Oktiabria," *Pravda*, March 24, 1987.

[43]"Prakticheskimi delami uglubliat' perestroiku," *Pravda*, July 15, 1987.

[44]"Soveshchanie v TsK KPSS," *Pravda*, September 17, 1987.

[45]M. S. Gorbachev, "Oktiabr' i perestroika: revoliutsiia prodolzhaetsia," *Pravda*, November 3, 1987.

ference held in June-July 1988. Both before and after the publication in early May of the Central Committee's "Theses," designed to specify the agenda for the conference as well as to formulate proposals for adoption in conference resolutions, the Soviet press was brimming with diverse, frequently extraordinary proposals for political and economic reform. The debate gave reformers an opportunity to advance ideas more radical than any ever published in the Soviet media. As in previous discussion campaigns, Gorbachev skillfully allowed the range of published views in effect to "bracket" his own position, chosen from the middle ground between the most radical and the most conservative viewpoints set forth in the debate. Gorbachev's proposals for change stopped well short of the most sweeping proposals that had been advanced in the press: he failed to endorse the "patriotic front," the separation of powers principle, or the constitutional court. In each case, however, he proposed a reform meeting the liberals part way. With respect to the constitutional court and the power of judicial review, he proposed a vague, compromise form, a "committee of constitutional supervision" to oversee lower government bodies, a cross between the people's control committees and the procuracy. Instead of a patriotic front he offered a "congress of people's deputies" to be made up in equal numbers of delegates elected from territorial constituencies, national constituencies, and recognized public organizations. Instead of fully endorsing a separation of powers he proposed a radical expansion of the powers of territorial soviets vis-à-vis both central branch bureaucracies and territorial party committees. These proposals, all subsequently enacted in conference resolutions and later in constitutional amendments which were hastily adopted only one month after they were published in draft form, represented potentially significant steps toward the activation of the soviets and democratization of electoral procedures. Time and again, the final outcome of a discussion campaign is a policy decision envisioning change which is substantial but less sweeping in its intended impact than some of the proposals which have been offered in the course of the campaign. The final decision represents a policy outcome which has been initiated by the central leadership, defended and fleshed out in public debate, and finally specified and enacted by the central leadership.

No less significant than discussion campaigns in anticipation of a major decision or event are the campaigns following them, which also invite authoritative guidance to the media on appropriate treatment. More than past leaders, in fact, Gorbachev has made it a practice to meet with editors and other executives in the ideological establishment both before and after high-level political forums to advise them on the appropriate balance in their coverage of the themes associated with the policies adopted at the meeting. After the 27th Party Congress, Gorbachev met with media executives to explain the tasks devolving to them from the congress.[46] Two weeks after the January 1987 Central Committee plenum, Gorbachev held a six-hour-long meeting with media executives, reviewing the significance of the plenum and indicating the ways the media should aid in implementing its decisions.[47] Again, after the June 1987 Central Committee plenum, Gorbachev addressed a conference of media representatives at the Central Committee to explain the objectives of the *perestroika* program and the ways the media should contribute to its fulfillment.[48] He held a fourth meeting with the media in early January 1988, a meeting which lasted seven hours.[49] He held another, in anticipation of the June party conference, on 7 May 1988.[50] Again, following the summer of 1988, with its clear indications of a struggle over the general line in foreign and ideological policy, Gorbachev met with the media; this occurred shortly after the Politburo adopted a major plan on Central Committee restructuring but before the sudden plenum of September 30, and Gorbachev used the occasion to heighten the sense of national urgency about *perestroika*.[51] Both Ligachev and Iakovlev have also addressed gatherings of editors and ideological officials, but far less frequently than has Gorbachev.[52]

No better example might be cited, in fact, of the responsiveness of

---

[46]"Vstrecha v TsK KPSS," *Pravda*, March 15, 1986.

[47]"Ubezhdennost'—opora perestroiki," *Kommunist*, no. 4, 1987, pp. 20–27.

[48]"Prakticheskimi delami uglubliat' perestroiku," *Pravda*, July 15, 1987.

[49]"Demokratizatsiia—sut' perestroiki, sut' sotsializma," *Pravda*, January 13, 1988; Yegor Yakovlev, "Checking Our Watches," *Moscow News*, no. 3 (January 24–31), 1988, p. 4.

[50]"Cherez demokratizatsiu—k novomu obliku sotsializma," *Pravda*, May 11, 1988.

[51]"Na novom etape perestroiki," *Pravda*, September 25, 1988.

[52]Besides the occasions already noted, Ligachev met with the staff of the State Radio and Television Committee in November 1985, expressing serious dissatisfaction with its work, and admonishing broadcast workers to ensure that "our television and radio must be entirely and fully political television and political radio." Recognizing one needs political slogans in every broadcast, he nevertheless insisted that "television and radio programs must be subordinate to one goal—propaganda, exposition and implementation of party policy." *New York Times*, November 21, 1985, citing *Pravda*, November 21, 1985. More recently, and after Iakovlev had reportedly replaced Ligachev as the senior secretary charged with ideological policy, Ligachev met with the staff of the newspaper *Sovetskaia kul'tura*. Here he complained that *glasnost'* had allowed "scum and garbage" to rise to the surface; he assaulted the flood of cheap and primitive mass culture which had saturated the media; he warned against always making party and government officials into targets of criticism and urged instead that they be given greater opportunity to have their say in the press. "Broaden the Framework of Activity, Encompass All Sectors of Cultural Construction," *Sovetskaia kul'tura*, July 7, 1987 (trans. in *CDSP*, vol. 39, no. 34, [September 23], 1987). After the nineteenth party conference, Ligachev addressed a conference of media officials in Gorkii on the subject of current media policy. (See "Povyshat' sozidatel'nuiu rol' pressy," *Zhurnalist*, no. 9, September, 1988, pp. 1–9). Iakovlev has addressed conferences of social scientists on theoretical and ideological issues, but has less often been featured as a speaker at meetings with media executives. One such meeting, however, was a Central Committee conference for executives from the media, science, and culture on December 1, 1987. Another was after the February 1988 Central Committee plenum. See *Sovetskaia kul'tura*, December 5, 1987; *Pravda*, February 27, 1988. Iakovlev also briefed the media on the significance of the June 1988 party conference. "Brat'sia za delo bez promedleniia," *Pravda*, July 14, 1988.

media and party organizations to political "signals" from the center than the Andreeva affair, although of course ideologically it represented a volte-face. The scandal of the Andreeva affair was less the publication of the original article than the minor cascade of sympathetic reprintings, party meetings, and organized "discussions" that the article set off. Immediately after its publication in *Sovetskaia Rossiia* on March 13, Ligachev reportedly met twice with media editors to praise the article. Within days, the article was reprinted in a number of provincial newspapers, even after TASS instructed local newspapers to obtain clearance from local party authorities before republishing it. Leningrad television broadcast a sympathetic discussion of the article. According to the historian Iurii Afanas'ev, some thirty obkoms immediately took the article as a directive (*ukazanie*). (However, *Pravda*, publishing his article, accompanied this assertion with a disclaimer stating that they could not confirm the accuracy of his claim.) Some lower party committees held discussions of the article; some scholarly institutions held meetings devoted to supporting it. Photocopies of the article began circulating. At a time of tension and uncertainty in the political atmosphere, and with Ligachev apparently throwing his own authority behind the article, many party leaders took the publication as a sign of a significant shift in the general line, and hastened to get into step.[53]

It would be a serious error, therefore, to imagine that the attack on the orthodoxies of the past under *glasnost'* represents an attempt to weaken the fabric of party authority over the ideological sphere per se, although it has that effect because of the inescapably antiauthoritarian consequences of liberating political expression from party control. Rather, Gorbachev has used *glasnost'* to liberalize social theory, relying on the liberal intelligentsia to supply the intellectual content supporting his policies, and thus to employ the central media to popularize and publicize the general contours of the reform program. Indeed, probably no Soviet leader since Lenin has devoted as much personal attention to ideology and the mass media as Gorbachev, who in speeches since before he became general secretary has repeatedly explicated the ideas at the core of his program of reconstruction.[54] So far as the central media sys-

---

[53] On the affair, see Peter Reddaway, "Resisting Gorbachev," *New York Review of Books*, August 18, 1988, pp. 36–41, and the articles by Paul Quinn-Judge in the *Christian Science Monitor*, April 27, 1988, and October 6, 1988. Soviet sources providing information about the mini-campaign following the article's appearance include: Nikolai Bodnaruk, "Sluchai i iavlenie," *Izvestiia*, April 10, 1988; Iurii Afanas'ev, "Otvety istorika," *Pravda*, July 26, 1988; and Pavel Demidov, "Ne nado zabluzhdat'sia," *Zhurnalist*, no. 5 (May), 1988, pp. 20–21; and the interview by P. Demidov with V. Seliunin, " 'Nam tak nuzhna tverdost'!" *Zhurnalist*, no. 8 (August), 1988, pp. 38–41.

[54] Two examples are the address he delivered to a general conference on ideology in December 1984, and his statement about the "ideology of renewal" at the February 1988 Central Committee plenum. See M. S. Gorbachev, *Zhivoe tvorchestvo naroda* (Moscow: Politizdat, 1984) and *Revoliutsionnoi perestroike—ideologiiu obnovleniia* (Moscow: Politizdat, 1988).

tem is concerned, therefore, Gorbachev has set the agenda of public discussion through the party's powers of ideological guidance and control. Over 1986–87, roughly through the June 1987 plenum, debate centered on the problems of economic liberalization: proposals concerned ways to strengthen enterprise autonomy, to improve performance measures, to raise competitiveness, productivity, initiative, and responsibility on the part of enterprises, and to reduce the role of planning, price-setting, supply-allocating, credit, and other levers of central control over enterprises. Other market-oriented ideas were also discussed and enacted, in particular the legalization of private and cooperative enterprise.

Over 1987–88, the debate shifted, again in response to cues set at the center, to liberalization in the political sphere. From January 1987's Central Committee plenum to Gorbachev's address at the February 1988 plenum, and then, much more intensively in the month preceding the June 1988 party conference, media debate centered upon ideas for curtailing the power of the state administrative bureaucracy to subvert central policy direction. Reformers called for expanding the power of local government over the vertically organized state agencies, encouraging meaningful local political participation, increasing the accountability of party and government officials for their performance, enforcing and extending the primacy of law, and reducing administrative interference in scholarship and culture. To be sure, neither the economic decisions of 1987 nor the political reforms of 1988 enacted change as radical as some of the more far-reaching proposals published in the press. But the discussion in each case responded to an agenda set at the center, generally supported the direction of the proposed reform, and bracketed the decisions that were eventually adopted. Remarkable as many of the proposals have been when contrasted to the Brezhnev era's aversion to reform, it is impossible to escape the conclusion that for the most part, as academician Paton complained of pre–1986 press coverage of the northern river diversion project, "all this could not be called a discussion—so much did the 'exchange' of opinions move in a single direction."[55]

–4–

On the other hand, the explosion of associational activity that has developed in territories and sectors of subcentral rank has strongly pluralistic effects. "In countries governed by authoritarian regimes," Robert Dahl observes, "pressures for organizational autonomy are like coiled springs precariously restrained by the counterforce of the state and ready

[55] B. Paton, "The Safety of Progress," *Literaturnaia gazeta*, October 29, 1986 (trans. in *CDSP*, vol. 38, no. 48 [December 31, 1986], pp. 1–4).

to unwind whenever the system is jolted."[56] Unquestionably the general rise of material well-being, growth of city populations, educational attainments, and other factors commonly cited as the social background to the Gorbachev reforms have been contributing factors to the dramatic spread of interest representation by new political associations, as in the Western Europe of a century ago which saw a similar burst of organized political activity; but they cannot entirely explain it.[57] To draw direct parallels, as is frequently done with theories of a "new Soviet middle class" or a "civil society," is to overlook the pronounced differences between the rise of the industrial and commercial bourgeoisie in the late nineteenth century in Western Europe as the dominant class in society and the evolution of postwar Soviet society, where neither private property nor liberal polity have been available to generate class cohesiveness.[58] The embourgeoisement of the political elite is not the same as the rise of a Soviet bourgeoisie.

Rather, the present wave of political activity derives from the failure of the incorporation strategy employed by the political elite in its relations with the rapidly growing professional and managerial elites through the 1950s, 1960s, and 1970s. The share occupied by the middle technical and managerial echelons in the labor force has grown more rapidly since the war than has that of any other occupational stratum. Despite a general slowing in the growth of the industrial labor force by the late 1970s, engineering-technical personnel (ITRs) were the fastest-growing segment in it, rising from 8.3 percent in 1950 to 14 percent in 1982. While total employment in the state sector of the economy grew less than three and one-half times between 1941 and 1983, the number of specialists in the economy grew around thirteen times over the same period and the increase of the ITR stratum was over eighteen-fold.[59] At the same time, the economy was incapable of integrating this influx of professionally trained cadres, leading to a depreciation of the very social status which secondary

---

[56] Robert A. Dahl, *Dilemmas of Pluralist Democracy: Autonomy vs. Control* (New Haven: Yale University Press, 1982), p. 3.

[57] Cf. Philippe C. Schmitter, "Interest Intermediation and Regime Governability in Contemporary Western Europe and North America," in Suzanne Berger, ed., *Organizing Interests in Western Europe: Pluralism, Corporatism, and the Transformation of Politics* (Cambridge: Cambridge University Press, 1981), p. 289.

[58] Seweryn Bialer describes Soviet society as one "socially dominated by a large new middle class, which may be politically fragmented and powerless but which sets the lifestyle for the society at large." ("Gorbachev's Program of Change: Sources, Significance, Prospects," in Seweryn Bialer and Michael Mandelbaum, eds., *Gorbachev's Russia and American Foreign Policy* (Boulder and London: Westview Press, 1988), p. 236). Gail Lapidus argues that the past decades have brought about an "embryonic civil society" increasingly capable of self-regulation, and have transformed Russia into a society "with a highly differentiated social structure and an increasingly articulate and assertive middle class." ("State and Society: Toward the Emergence of Civil Society in the Soviet Union," in Seweryn Bialer, ed., *Politics, Society and Nationality inside Gorbachev's Russia* [Boulder: Westview, 1989], pp. 124, 125–26).

[59] Remington, *The Truth of Authority*, pp. 58–59.

and tertiary education promised. As a result, a growing number of graduate engineers perform jobs well below their level of qualification; one study of several enterprises found that less than half of the actual working time spent by engineering personnel consisted of operations requiring an engineer's qualifications.[60] Igor' Bestuzhev-Lada observes that of the country's six million graduate engineers, one million have fled to become taxi drivers, sales clerks, loaders, and so on, and several million more are working at jobs where their skills are not needed.[61] Contributing to the devaluation of professional status was the drift toward convergence of relative pay levels between ITR and manual occupations.[62] As the main body of the specialist stratum—what official literature terms the "intelligentsia"—sank into a social status increasingly indistinguishable from that of the working class, the gap widened between it and the small segment of it (perhaps one-fifth) which entered *nomenklatura* careers (that is, political and administrative appointments controlled by the Party).[63]

In turn, conscious of the potential social influence of these groups, the pre-Gorbachev Party made them the target of a concerted campaign of political cooptation. The regime sought to enlist them en masse into political work and a doctrinal training program, particularly after a Central Committee adopted a resolution on the point in 1971.[64] The apparent success of this recruitment effort was reflected in extremely high rates of nominal participation in the many channels of formal, ceremonial activism on which Soviet sources dutifully reported, such as numbers enrolled in party education, numbers carrying out mass political work, numbers discharging spare-time social assignments, and the like: these are the "behavioral" attributes of political culture which Stephen White analyzed in his 1979 book. With the benefit of hindsight it is evident that the crisis of disbelief was far stronger than White or most Western observers suspected.[65] Brian Silver's conclusions about the dissatisfaction of the

---

[60] L. S. Seniavskii et al., eds., *Aktual'nye problemy istorii razvitogo sotsializma v SSSR* (Moscow: Mysl', 1984), p. 188.

[61] Cited in A. N. Kochetov, "Novye tendentsii v sovershenstvovanii sotsial'noi struktury sovetskogo obshchestva (1980-e gody)," *Istorii SSSR*, no. 6 (December), 1988, pp. 9–10. Kochetov observes that one can quibble with the figures, but the point is accurate.

[62] On this point, see F. R. Filippov et al., eds., *Formirovanie sotsial'noi odnorodnosti sotsialisticheskogo obshchestva* (Moscow: Nauka, 1981), pp. 93–94; Kochetov, "Novye tendentsii," p. 15; and V. S. Semenov, *Dialektika razvitia sotsial'noi struktury sovetskogo obshchestva* (Moscow: Mysl', 1977), p. 177.

[63] Kochetov, "Novye tendentsii," p. 11.

[64] "Ob uchastii rukovodiashchikh i inzhenerno-tekhnicheskikh rabotnikov cherepovetskogo metallurgicheskogo zavoda v ideino-politicheskom vospitanii chlenov kollektivov," in *Kommunisticheskaia Partiia Sovetskogo Soiuza v rezoliutsiiakh i resheniiakh s"ezdov, konferentsii i plenumov TsK*, vol. 12, 1971–75 (Moscow: Izdatel'stvo politicheskoi literatury, 1986), pp. 164–69.

[65] Professor Paul Roth of the Universitat der Bundeswehr, Munich, indicates that a Soviet scholar confirmed to him that unpublished Soviet survey data indicating the seriousness of the ideological crisis in Soviet society led to Brezhnev's sharp criticism of the state of ideological work at the

"middle class," based on the Soviet Interview Project, were nearer to the mark.[66] It is now clear that during the late 1970s and early 1980s a near-universal reaction against the bankruptcy of official propaganda set in among most groups in Soviet society. As we have seen, Gorbachev has deployed this consensus to legitimate his own program of liberal reform. But the contempt shared by both reformists and conservatives for the former atmosphere of corruption, slack discipline, sterile and ritualized ideological work, and declining productivity is not the same as the emergence of a new liberal-minded middle class, such as is characteristic of Korea, Taiwan, Argentina, Brazil, and the other authoritarian systems which have begun transitions to democracy. Indeed, the failure of an ideologically based alliance between "power elites" and "prestige elites" has allowed the most deeply rooted sources of social solidarity to exert the greatest influence on the new political movements, above all primordial sentiments of ethnic, national, and religious community, generational and occupational interests, and the newly potent movement against environmental degradation.

The Gorbachev leadership adopted a two-front strategy toward the scientific and cultural intelligentsia, improving their position as "consumers" of state benefits, and, more significantly, appealing to them to provide the intellectual and moral leadership necessary to lift the country out of its torpor. The leaders resurrected the prerevolutionary definition of the intelligentsia—an identity sharply contrasted with a materialistic middle-class "*meshchanstvo*" and defining itself as embodying the national mind and conscience—and encouraged the Soviet intelligentsia to elaborate a similar vision of a humane and democratic socialism.[67] This has given the intelligentsia a significant share of influence over both the reform pro-

---

November 1978 Central Committee plenum, and the subsequent preparation of a major campaign to improve the quality and effectiveness of propaganda. See his "Propaganda as an Instrument of Power," in Hans-Joachim Veen, ed., *From Brezhnev to Gorbachev: Domestic Affairs and Soviet Foreign Policy* (New York: St. Martin's Press, 1987), p. 228.

[66] Stephen White remarks that "the middle class is typically more active and better informed than the mass of industrial workers" and links to this feature of social stratification the relative success the authorities have enjoyed in activating at least nominal participation in public life. (*Political Culture and Soviet Politics* [London: Macmillan Press, 1979], p. 64). On the other hand, Brian D. Silver, analyzing the results of the Soviet Interview Project, suggests the reason for leadership concern is in the "apparent disaffection of the educated class as a whole." He concludes: "This is the middle class for whom the Big Deal was arranged. This class is growing in size and importance to the Soviet economy, but with its increasing political sophistication comes increasing disaffection." (Political Beliefs of the Soviet Citizen," in James R. Millar, ed., *Politics, Work, and Daily Life in the USSR* [Cambridge: Cambridge University Press, 1987], p. 127).

[67] A striking expression of the favorable view of the self-definition of the intelligentsia as a critical, self-aware unincorporated group, inclined toward dissent and assuming moral and intellectual responsibility for the fate of the country, was an article by an associate of the chair of scientific communism of the Academy of Social Sciences of the CPSU Central Committee, L. Smoliakov, "Ob intelligentsii i intelligentnosti (razmyshleniia filosofa)," *Kommunist*, no. 16, 1988, pp. 67–75.

gram and its own corporate status, and has put it in a mediating position between the proliferating social movements that have sprung up "from below" and the state. The uneasy coexistence of the guided liberalization of expression under *glasnost'* and the decompression of society is complicated further by the divisions within the intelligentsia, particularly the antiliberal forces identified with the "Russian party."

Of the principal social cleavages which have formed the basis for the new public movements under *glasnost'*, the most well-known is that of the nationalities. But in fact several different kinds of nationality-related issues need to be distinguished. In the case of the Armenians living as a minority in Azerbaijan, both the Armenian populace of Karabakh and the Armenian segments of the population of towns such as Sumgait, Baku, and Nakhichevan, the nationality issue arises from the situation of an encapsulated minority, that is, an oppressed minority population living among a larger population who are themselves another minority; similar enclaves of Slavic settler populations are to be found in the Baltic republics analogous to English enclaves in Quebec and Catholic Irish in Northern Ireland. A second issue is the more familiar variant of the search for national autonomy from central and Russian dominance in virtually every union republic. A third is the growth of certain aspects of Russian national self-assertiveness, particularly themes of martyrdom and messianism. Common to most of the national movements has been alarm over the despoiling of the natural environment through industrial development and the deterioration and destruction of many cherished cultural monuments. But because of the dominant place of Russians at the all-union level of power, the *Russian* nationalist movement has strong roots within the *Soviet* establishment, while nationalism on the periphery, although supported by a national intelligentsia, is largely a movement for autonomy *from* the center. A second source of social tension has been the growth of inequality over the 1970s and 1980s, especially through illicit forms of income redistribution, despite official policy in favor of equality. Here again we are only beginning to learn the true extent of the corruption and decay of the ancien régime. Three trends seem to have coincided: the economy declined to a flat or negative rate of national income growth; inflation and shortages worsened the absolute economic position of some groups; and corruption or political status enabled other groups to increase their level of material privilege.[68] The impact on social consciousness was complex, judging from the intense press discussions of equality and priv-

---

[68] A. G. Aganbegian, "Programma korennoi perestroiki," *EKO*, no. 11, 1987, p. 7; Gregory Grossman, "Roots of Gorbachev's Problems: Private Income and Outlay in the Late 1970s," in Joint Economic Committee, Congress of the United States, *Gorbachev's Economic Plans*, vol. 1 (Washington, DC: USGPO, November 23, 1987), p. 227; Batygin "Dobrodetel'," p. 28; Zaslavskaia interview in *Argumenty i fakty*, March 21–27, 1987 (trans. in *CDSP*, May 20, 1987, vol. 39, no. 16).

ilege: the widening of social differentials through corruption and semi-licit, "left" enterprise exacerbated a strong existing strain of resentment at privilege, one reinforced by decades of official suspicion of those whose activity brings material reward; on the other hand, some groups whose relative social position stagnated or declined, such as engineers and other scientific and technical personnel, resented the loss of status, while many individuals from the same social layers sought opportunities to engage in private enterprise,[69] and liberal social scientists deplored the combination of official leveling policies in wages with the actual gaping inequalities that were developing through corruption. The reformists therefore have sought to mobilize popular resentment against bureaucratic obstruction of the market-oriented pursuit of legitimate personal interest and against illegitimate forms of elitism and personal gain and to direct it toward support for the new legislation on individual and cooperative enterprise, while conservatives have sought to channel the same instincts against the manifestations of social inequality, personal interest, and market enterprise.

Concomitant with the growth of illegitimate inequality has been the relative decline in the status of many occupational and professional groups, a number of which have recently reasserted their corporate status interests. Teachers, scientific-technical employees, lawyers (*advokaty*), industrial designers, and theatrical workers have all formed professional associations or unions. Both the association of sociologists and the union of journalists have sought to enhance public and self-esteem by adopting codes of professional ethics, and scientists in a number of research institutes under the Academy of Sciences have revolted against the deadening influence of their appointed directors.[70] Similar movements for higher professional status and autonomy have been evident in the film industry, theater, and literature. Not the least disgruntled are party professionals, who are complaining about low pay (the average salary of party workers

[69] A striking figure presented at the January 1987 Central Committee plenum was that some 40 percent of those polled expressed a wish to take advantage of the new law on individual enterprise. "Ianvarskii (1987 g.) Plenum TsK KPSS," *Strana i mir*, no. 4, 1987, pp. 38–40.

[70] On the sociologists' "code" adopted at the conference of the Soviet Sociological Association in March 1987, see the appendix, "Professional'nyi kodeks sotsiologa," to V. A. Iadov, *Sotsiologicheskoe issledovanie: metodologiia, programma, metody*, 2nd ed. (Moscow: Nauka, 1987). Also see Boris Firsov, "I Have the Honour . . ." *Moscow News*, no. 13 (April 3–10, 1988), p. 11. On the journalists, see "The Journalist's Ethics," *Pravda*, February 11, 1988 (trans. in *CDSP*, vol. 40, no. 6 [March 9, 1988], pp. 23–24); on the revolt in science, see such representative articles as Roald Sagdeyev, "USSR Academy of Sciences at a Turning Point," *Moscow News*, no. 1 (10–17 January), 1988, p. 12; Arkady Popov, "Curtains of Secrecy Can't Always Conceal," *Moscow News*, no. 30 (August 2–9), 1987, p. 12; open letter to President G. I. Marchuk of the Academy of Science, "Tak chto zhe 'nachal'stvu vidnee'?" *Literaturnaia gazeta*, July 8, 1987; B. Kurashvili and A. Obolonskii, "Demokratiia po-akademicheski," *Literaturnaia gazeta*, May 20, 1987; E. Mishustin, "Demokratiia v zhizni nauchnogo kollektiva," *Kommunist*, no. 12, 1987, p. 55.

places them twenty-sixth among the professions, writes one; another comments that they are being paid less than the managers and engineers they supervise), long hours, and constant abuse in the press. They resent being called upon to solve a number of problems that are properly the responsibility of government and which turn them into mere "dispatchers and technologists." Lower party staff positions, such as *raikom* instructor jobs and paid secretaryships of enterprise committees, are increasingly attracting only women and raw youth.[71]

A third fault line is generational. As a professor of the journalism faculty of Moscow University quipped, it used to be said that the youth were a "lost generation," whose depoliticization and passion for the material consumer culture of the West left them largely indifferent to socialist construction; but now the youth are actively engaged in social and political life, while it is the older generation, the generation that fought the war, industrialized and reconstructed the country, that is alienated and defensive toward the current reforms.[72] Certainly among the older generation a romantic myth of the thirties and forties has a strong following[73] and it is disproportionately represented among the large although minority body of opinion defending Stalinism.[74] The party has been sufficiently concerned about the disaffection of the older generation to authorize the inception of a new weekly supplement to *Trud*, called *Veteran*, published under the auspices of the All-Union Organization of Veterans of War and Labor.[75]

On the other hand, this is not the only generational group whose awakening consciousness concerns the political authorities. According to a *samizdat* account of the January 1987 plenum, youth between the ages of fifteen and thirty are regarded as a lost generation.[76] A specialist on youth movements employed by the Ministry of Internal Affairs as a professor at the Moscow Higher School of the Militia explains the rebellious-

[71] V. Bobkov, "Partiinye komitety: struktura i funktsii," *Kommunist*, no. 4, 1988, pp. 86–88; V. Anoshkin et al., "Bez formalizma," *Kommunist*, no. 3, 1988, pp. 38–39; S. Karnaukhov, "About Privileges and Openness," *Pravda*, August 1, 1988 (trans. in *CDSP*, [August 31, 1988], vol. 40, no. 31, p. 19).

[72] Personal communication to author.

[73] See the review of reader mail in L. Kurin, "The People Will Tell the Truth," *Pravda*, July 23, 1987 (trans in *CDSP*, vol. 39, no. 29 [August 19, 1987], p. 7). One reader wrote to say, for example, that under Stalin, people were inspired by a great idea: "It was a time when fairy tales really did come true."

[74] Vera Tolz and Julia Wishnevsky, "Materials Defending Stalin in the Soviet Press," *Radio Liberty Research Bulletin*, no. 4, 1988 (December 21, 1987). Tolz and Wishnevsky cite a comment by Rybakov that roughly a tenth of the mail he received after the publication of *Deti Arbata* was Stalinist. A rather higher proportion of the letters received by *Ogonek* on law reform attacked liberalization and advocated instead returning to the draconian legislation of the Stalin era, including expanded use of the death penalty and labor camps for anti-Soviet activity or for infractions of labor discipline.

[75] "Popolnenie v kruge chteniia," *Pravda*, January 1, 1988.

[76] "Ianvarskii Plenum TsK KPSS."

ness of the present youthful subculture as a reaction to the "dualism of behavior" prevalent in the 1970s and the ritualism and meaninglessness of Komsomol activity.[77] All sources agree on the considerable amount of overlap between youth and membership in the new informal organizations which have sprung up in recent years: by one count, over half of the membership of the informal organizations are also Komsomol members; according to another, 30–35 percent of seventh- through tenth-grade pupils in Moscow secondary schools consider themselves members of various informal groups.[78] The youth subculture includes groups and movements with primarily social and political interests, others indifferent to politics, and some which embrace both cultural and vaguely political values. Among the first are groups devoted to political study, environmental protection, and cultural preservation; among the second are the sports fan clubs, the body-building and martial arts clubs, and an assortment of break-dancers, rockers, heavy metallists, punkers, and others. In between are groups such as "the system," religious and mystical groups, and pacifists. Altogether the usual number cited in the Soviet press of such informal groups and organizations is 30,000.[79]

Since we are concerned here with political expression, we shall not further explore the movements of withdrawal into self-narcotizing narcissism. Rather, in an effort to trace the ideological bases of the new social movements, we shall concentrate on those whose demands are political.

–5–

First, it is important to point out that the emergence of the informal groups must be dated to the late Brezhnev period. In a poll of groups' members taken no later than 1987, 40 percent of the engineering and technical personnel who were members had belonged to them for five years or more; so had 25 percent of the working-class group members.[80] According to an account in *Pravda*, Pamiat', by far the best known of the new groups, coalesced in the early 1980s from among engineers, students, historians, workers, and others at the Ministry of the Aviation Industry. Concerned about the destruction and deterioration of Moscow's

[77] I. Iu. Sundiev, "Neformal'nye molodezhnye ob"edineniia: otpy ekspozitsii," *Sotsiologicheskie issledovaniia*, no. 5, 1987, pp. 56–58.

[78] "A Scholar Approaches Unofficial Groups," Interview by A. Afanas'ev with Evgenii Levanov, *Komsomol'skaia pravda*, December 11, 1987 (trans. in *CDSP*, vol. 39, no. 51, [January 20, 1988], p. 24); Sundiev, "Neformal'nye," p. 61.

[79] In addition to the sources cited in the two previous footnotes, see also the round-up of press coverage of groups in *CDSP*, "Limits Prescribed for Political Initiative," vol. 39, no. 51, January 20, 1988; V. Iakovlev, "Proshchanie s Bazarovym," *Ogonek*, no. 36 (September 5–12), 1987, pp. 4–5; "Demokratiia i initsiativa," editorial leader in *Pravda*, December 27, 1987.

[80] Levanov, "A Scholar Approaches Unofficial Groups."

architectural heritage, they organized to preserve old buildings from dem-
olition, sending numerous collective petitions and protests. With time,
and under the stimulus of *glasnost'*, their horizons broadened and they
began to take interest in problems of the Russian North, the depopulation
of the countryside, worsening alcoholism, and declining birthrates.[81] Preoccupied with alarm at the loss and destruction of the cultural heritage of
Russia, they were susceptible to paranoid and conspiratorial thinking. A
comparable group in Leningrad, *Spasenie*, has not taken the same route
into proto-fascism, reportedly because of the moderating influence of
academician Likhachev. The motifs of reactionary nationalism—spon-
soring the theory, for example, that the Russian Revolution was actually
the product of a Masonic or Masonic-Jewish conspiracy—have been,
however, "in the air" through the 1970s and 1980s; and they have, of
course, a far longer history in Russia.[82] Anti-Semitism has recently taken
a novel but apparently widely shared form of resentment against emigrants who abandoned the homeland for the West only to return to it after
their inevitable disillusionment; it is felt they have been getting more favorable publicity now than those whose loyalty had never flagged.[83] By
widening official tolerance of unofficial social activity, *glasnost'* spurred
the precipitation of a variety of existing currents of public opinion, particularly where grounded in primary-level ties such as friendship and ethnic-
ity, into organized political associations.

In the hands of such writers as Sergei Zalygin, editor of *Novyi mir*,
Valentin Rasputin,[84] Iurii Bondarev, and many others, the cause of environmental protection has become the most important vehicle for the
expression of Russian nationalism. In their concern for environmental
protection and their intense opposition to "bureaucratism," the nationalists are useful publicists for current central policy. Their outrage and fury
at the development agencies (such as Minvodkhoz, the Ministry for Water
Resources and Land Reclamation, and Minenergo, the Ministry for Energy) have prompted extraordinarily ferocious polemics. Andrei Nuikin,

[81] Vladimir Petrov, "'Pamiat'" i drugie," *Pravda*, February 1, 1988. This article has the tone of a
police warning to Pamiat' and two other groups named.

[82] On the popularity of the "Masonic" theory and its links to an extreme form of Russian chauvinism, see Andrei Cherkizov, "Demokratiia—ne raspushchennost'," *Sovetskaia kul'tura*, March 31,
1987. The myth of the international Judeo-Masonic conspiracy was given circulation in the "Proto-
cols of the Elders of Zion," which were concocted in prerevolutionary Russia.

[83] See both the article by Vera Tkachenko, "'Rodina dana nam odin raz i do samoi smerti',"
Pravda, August 21, 1987, and the follow-up article published in *Pravda* on September 7, which
excerpted a number of readers' letters, several of which took similar sentiments still further. In its
tone and themes, the Tkachenko article was a forerunner of the Nina Andreeva article in March
1988.

[84] Rasputin is increasingly considered, however, to have aligned himself with Pamiat'. See *Izvestiia*, February 27, 1988.

for example, described the now-suspended northern river diversion project as "a nightmarish ecological Auschwitz of planetary scale."[85] Rasputin compares the attitude of technocrats in the water, timber, energy and other ministries, who promote development heedless of spiritual values, to AIDS.[86] Iurii Bondarev's address at the 8th Writers' Congress in 1986 cited disasters such as Chernobyl' and the river diversion project as evidence that science in the hands of vain and crafty bureaucrats is a murderous force.[87] Soulless, destructive bureaucratism is counterposed to ethical values, above all truth,[88] and to a renewed vision of organic unity. Rasputin, for example, laments the "fractionated," differentiated condition of the people today, in which the main goals are superseded by secondary ones; he is rather ambivalent toward the new informal groups, despite having affiliated himself with the environmental and cultural preservation movements, because for the most part they pursue "egoistic" goals, feeding parasitically on society.[89]

Other distinctive themes sounded by the nationalists are disdain for mass culture, with its imported Western tastes and consumerist predilections;[90] a concern with the decline of the Russian countryside, particularly in the North (the "non-black earth zone"); and a defensiveness about injured Russian national pride. A reader who wrote in to *Pravda* to defend *Pamyat'* asserted that many articles are published in the press honoring Armenian, Ukrainian, Georgian, and other national cultures, but that as soon as someone defends Russia, it is called chauvinism and nationalism.[91] The writer Maia Ganina, in an address to the board of the Writers' Union, felt compelled to protest that the Russian people must not be held responsible for the crimes and mistakes of the Georgians Stalin and Beria, or the Jew Kaganovich, or the Russians Khrushchev and Brezhnev.[92]

It is also characteristic of the new Slavophilism to appeal to the old myth of an essential Russian national spirit in condemining liberal principles of competitive self-interest. As a writer in the journal *Nash sovre-*

---

[85] Andrei Nuikin, "Idealy ili interesy?" part 2. *Novyi mir*, no. 2, 1988, p. 215.

[86] "Esli po sovesti," interview with Rasputin by E. Shugaeva, *Literaturnaia gazeta*, January 1, 1988, p. 10.

[87] *Literaturnaia gazeta*, July 2, 1986.

[88] Maia Ganina deplores the prevalent atmosphere of lies, which until recently formed the basis of the entire culture, and hopes that through the new "culture of cleansing" a new social self-consciousness is being born." ("Bez obol'shchenii prezhnikh dnei," *Literaturnaia gazeta*, January 13, 1988, p. 11).

[89] "Esli po sovesti."

[90] In his chat with the staff of *Sovetskaia kul'tura* in the summer of 1987, Egor Ligachev cited a recent conversation he had had with Rasputin, where they had agreed on the deleterious influence of the recent flood of cheap, hack, mass popular culture. See "Broaden the Framework," *CDSP*, vol. 39, no. 34, September 23, 1987.

[91] "O pamiati mnimoi i nastoiashchei," *Pravda*, March 18, 1988.

[92] *Literaturnaia gazeta*, March 9, 1988 (trans. in *CDSP*, vol. 40, no. 11 [April 13, 1988], p. 7).

mennik put it, "the genius of Russian culture" since ancient times has preferred things of the spirit to material wealth: "the Russian inclination of mind" scorned the spirit of commerce in the doctrines of political economy, developing instead a deep sense of love and attachment to the soil.[93] Generally, according to one review of this notorious journal, the writers for *Nash sovremennik* see themselves engaged in endless battle against conspiracies and enemies such as antipatriots, cosmopolitans, Zionists, emigrés and particularly emigrés who subsequently return to the homeland.[94]

Probably the most vivid expression of most of these ideas is presented in the Nina Andreeva article.[95] Andreeva distinguishes two ideological streams in contemporary Soviet culture: "left liberalism" and "traditionalism." She adeptly caricatures each in order to place her own position squarely in the middle. Nevertheless her malicious polemic usefully conveys the antipathy felt by the conservative nationalists for liberal ideas. The "left liberals," according to Andreeva, believe in a pure, classfree, humanist individualism, and tend to dismiss the entire socialist experience of the Soviet Union as a mistake, dwelling on the negative rather than positive chapters of Soviet history. They take the concept of rights to ridiculous extremes, going so far as to defend the legal rights of animals. They would adopt forms of democracy native to contemporary capitalism. They believe that for the first time, they are allied with the regime, but in fact they renounce socialism itself despite having received an education paid for by the whole country. It is difficult to convey the full flavor of the combination of the text's antiliberalism, antiintellectualism, anti-Semitism, and national *ressentiment*, which produced, like Chaadaev's famous Philosophical Letter, a sensation like a shot ringing out on a dark night. If Russian self-assertiveness has allied itself with the traditions of illiberal, sometimes reactionary, organic nationalism, as well as with the more recent demand for environmental protection, national movements on the periphery are more diverse politically. Generally such groups as the now-illegal Karabakh Committee in Armenia and the Popular Fronts springing up in nearly all national republics and in a number of cities in the RSFSR have identified themselves with support for *perestroika*, particularly the democratic and decentralizing elements of the reforms. At the same time they have often advanced demands considered unacceptably radical by local and all-union leaders. Despite the moderating influence of respected representatives of the national intelligentsia, the rapid rise in these movements' influence has se-

---

[93] Cited from M. Antonov, "Uskorenie: vozmozhnosti i pregrady," *Nash sovremennik*, no. 7, 1986, by Nuikin, "Idealy ili interesy," p. 214.

[94] Elene Gessen, "Bitvy 'Nashego sovremennika'," *Vremia i my*, no. 99, 1987.

[95] Andreeva, "Ne mogu."

riously strained the party's tolerance of their activity even in the Baltic republics, where the local party adopted a nonconfrontational posture toward them.[96]

–6–

So far we have discussed the liberal platform of the reformers sympathetic with Gorbachev's policy program; and we have identified an antiliberal, organic nationalism in the recent manifestations of Russian nationalism. It remains to discuss one more social movement, one which, until a better term suggests itself, might be termed "green." By the term green I wish to call attention to two features of this incipient and still rather apolitical movement in which it resembles its German counterpart: its birth in local citizen initiative groups, and its hostility to the destructive effects of industrialism.

In cities such as Irkutsk, Volgograd, Kirishi, Ufa, and Krasnodar in Russia, Daugavpils in Latvia, Erevan in Armenia, Odessa and Nikolaev in the Ukraine, Minsk in Belorussia, sizable public movements have protested environmental destruction. In Irkutsk a petition signed by over seventy thousand people objected to the plan to build a pipeline to carry away effluents from the pulp plant on Lake Baikal; the campaign was sponsored by an initiative group formed at a meeting with academician Logachev, chairman of the Eastern-Siberian Branch of the Siberian Division of the Academy of Sciences.[97] In Volgograd a group of over one thousand signed a letter to *Kommunist* protesting plans to start production of a highly toxic pesticide; a government commission investigating the issue sided with the public and decided to halt further construction of the plant.[98] Another initiative group in Volgograd has spent years fighting plans to build a new canal linking the Volga and Don Rivers and an immense irrigation network with it, the group has sent out some seventy mailings, each with hundreds of pages of documentation, demonstrating the harm that the project will cause. They wrote the Central Committee on seventeen occasions, only to have their case referred to the authorities whose actions they were protesting.[99] In Krasnodar the public protested

[96] An indication of what is likely to become a trend toward polarization between the autonomous national movements and the party leadership, itself faced with strong pressure from Moscow, was Lithuanian First Secretary Brazauskas' sharp warning to the Popular Front at the Lithuanian party Central Committee plenum, February 22, 1989. See SWB SU/0392 i, February 23, 1989. Brazauskas bluntly warned Lithuanians that their republic was reaching the point at which it, like Nagorno-Karabakh, might be placed under special direct rule from Moscow.

[97] "Esli po sovesti," *Literaturnaia gazeta*, January 1, 1988.

[98] A. Gaidar and V. Iaroshenko, "Nulevoi tsikl: k analizu mekhanizma vedomstvennoi ekspansii," *Kommunist*, no. 8, 1988, p. 85.

[99] See the letter entitled "V otvete pered potomkami" included in the review of reader response

plans to build an atomic power plant in an active earthquake zone; prompted by Chernobyl', the Council of Ministers of the USSR overruled the Ministry of Energy and halted construction.[100]

In the town of Kirishi, on the Volkhov River, a postman has spearheaded a protest movement against a local plant manufacturing a protein-vitamin concentrate, emissions from which are causing the population serious medical problems. Twelve thousand residents of the town—20 percent of the inhabitants—attended a rally organized to protest the plant. The postman registered his action group as a section of the town nature conservation society. The authorities have responded by harassing the postman, annulling, for example, his residence permit. But he has not been arrested, and the strongly sympathetic article that appeared about the case in *Komsomol'skaia pravda* is likely to have some impact.[101]

In Nikolaev, located near the mouth of the Dnepr on the Black Sea, 25,700 people signed a petition protesting plans to build a canal linking the Dnepr with the Danube, and sent it to *Kommunist*. Among the signatories were high-ranking officials and enterprise managers.[102] The hydroelectric station at Daugavpils in Latvia, which will take valuable farmland and require the resettlement of the affected population, was protested with petitions signed by 30,000 people; the Latvian Council of Ministers eventually declared itself opposed.[103]

Environmental protest in the national republics has joined with nationalist and frequently anti-Russian sentiments. In Estonia, speakers at a Komsomol meeting at the University of Tartu referred to a mining project in the republic as "typical colonialist economic thinking" and a letter signed by 350 Armenian intellectuals in the summer of 1987 protesting the dangerous condition of the environment in Erevan and other regions referred to the "biological genocide" of the Armenian people.[104] Without question, the mobilization of public opinion in Erevan over environmental issues in 1986–87 was a precipitating factor in the far wider movement of protest this year over the Karabakh issue. At a plenary meeting of the board of the USSR Writers' Union in January 1989 devoted to ecological themes, Central Asian writers bitterly denounced the region's dependence on cotton monoculture, which they blamed for the poisoning of the soil,

---

under the title, "Kak sovershaetsia povorot," edited by Sergei Zalygin, *Novy mir*, no. 7, 1987, pp. 211–16.

100 K. Aksenov, "Tishina nad Perepravoi," *Pravda*, January 21, 1988.

101 S. Razin, "Postman Vasil'ev's 'Bomb'—When the Latest Commissioner Left Empty-handed He Put the Documents in His Briefcase and Headed for Moscow," *Komsomol'skaia pravda* (trans. in SWB SU/0108. March 24, 1988).

102 Gaidar and Iaroshenko, "Nulevoi tsikl," p. 85.

103 "Komu sluzhit stroika?" *Kommunist*, no. 9, 1987, p. 40.

104 Aaran Trehub, "The USSR State Committee for Environmental Protection," *RL*, no. 27/88, January 21, 1988.

the shortage of water, the drying up of the Aral Sea, the prevalence of child labor, skyrocketing infant mortality, and corruption. An Uzbek poet, Muhammad Solikh, called the results of monoculture "a national tragedy."[105]

In the Ukraine and Belorussia, above all under the influence of Chernobyl', nuclear power has become a national issue. Public protests have reportedly resulted in decisions to halt construction work of nuclear power stations near Minsk and Odessa and a heat and power station outside Kiev.[106] Since Chernobyl', the prominent Ukrainian poet Boris Oliinik has publicly and repeatedly questioned the logic of expanding nuclear power in a small republic with a dense population, which already has a quarter of the country's nuclear power stations.[107] The lingering effects of the Chernobyl' disaster are termed "a time-bomb affecting the gene pool of an entire people" by Belorussian writer V. Iakovenko, while Ales' Adamovich compares the damage from Chernobyl' to the Nazi decimation of the republic.[108] Similarly, the Armenian writer Silva Kaputikian said of the nuclear power plant outside Erevan, finally to be shut down, that "it had threatened to destroy the very genotype of the Armenian nation."[109] If in Russia, the Ukraine, Belorussia, Moldavia, the Baltic, the Transcaucasus, and Central Asia, alarm over the state of environmental degradation has fueled movements of national self-consciousness and self-assertion, it has also stimulated the emergence of new forms of social action. Youth form the basis of dozens of new initiative groups under names such as "Eko," "the Greens," "Flora," and so on.[110] And like their counterparts in Western Europe in the 1970s, who united local initiative groups in a national movement, student environmental organizations from thirty-six cities met in March 1988 and formed the basis for a larger network of action.[111] In December 1988, a new all-union organization, called the "social-ecological union," formed as an umbrella group over some 100 ecological and relation associations.[112] One of the new body's first acts was to declare February 12, 1989, a "day of protest" against the construction of the Volga-Chograi Canal.[113]

---

[105] "Zemlia, ekologiia, perestroika," *Literaturnaia gazeta*, January 25, 1989.

[106] Sergei Voronitsyn, "Plans for Nuclear Power Stations Dropped?" *RL*, no. 96/88, March 7, 1988.

[107] E.g., Boris Oliinik, "S istinoi ne mozhet byt' torga," *Literaturnaia gazeta*, July 1, 1987, p. 13.

[108] Iakovenko's comments are in the above-cited transcript of the Writers' Union meeting, *Literaturnaia gazeta*, January 25, 1989; Adamovich's are in his article "Chestnoe slovo, bol'she ne vzorvetsia," *Novyi mir*, September 9, 1988, pp. 164–79.

[109] *Literaturnaia gazeta*, January 25, 1989.

[110] Sundiev, "Neformal'nye," p. 61.

[111] Gaidar and Iaroshenko, "Nulevoi tsikl," p. 84.

[112] See SWB SU/0352 C/1, January 7, 1989; FBIS-SOV 88–249, December 28, 1988.

[113] Sergei Zalygin, *Literaturnaia gazeta*, January 25, 1989.

The new "green" and national movements have realized the collective power of *obshchestvennost'*, that is, the concept of the public acting for itself outside the framework of the state, a concept until recently honored in the breach. The status and rights of the independent organizations continue to be negotiated and there is extremely wide variation across regions and republics in the degree to which their activity is tolerated. As a matter of principle, the central political authorities have drawn the line on two crucial elements of political participation and competition: independent movements may not constitute themselves as political parties, and they may not found independent publishing houses. In practice, however, in those areas, primarily in the Baltic republics, where they have widest freedom in practice, the independent movements publish their own newspapers and run candidates in elections to the Congress of People's Deputies. Their autonomy derives from the very substantial sympathy for their aims shared among the national political elites and intelligentsias in the Baltic republics as well as from Moscow's evident interest in fostering greater economic self-sufficiency on the part of the republics.

–7–

I have outlined a pattern of bifurcated or segmented political representation and expression. At the top, the leadership has used rather traditional forms of ideological control over the central media system to encourage searching discussions of economic and political liberalization that work in support of the policies Gorbachev has proposed and enacted. At the same time, the retraction of ideological controls has resulted in the formation of politically active social associations of every stripe, which reflect grievances and cleavages long left unresolved. To a large extent the new movements of civic activism have gained access to public consciousness through the support of established organizations of creative intellectuals, especially the writers' unions, universities, and republic Academies of Science.

Clearly attempting to incorporate as much of the new associational activity into support for the restructuring program as possible, Gorbachev appears to be gradually moving the institutional framework of the state toward a multi-tiered system of representation and policy-making through his proposals for a corporatist "congress of popular deputies" to which public organizations elect representatives and which will form a newly enfranchised federal parliament, and for a more powerful position for himself as both party leader and head of state. The party's leading role is to be enhanced by pulling it out of the operational management of government and the economy, its general ideological function insulated from the opening up of capital markets and pluralistic politics "below," where such questions will be resolved on the basis of a competition among opinion and pressure groups empowered to seek public approval and influence. Ideally, these would cut across the divisive existing cleavages of nationality and generation, tending to unify groups across the entire system; in one's most utopian moments one might imagine a labor party and a liberal-individualist party, for example, competing for representation in a lower chamber of the all-union parliament. Above, ideology, defense and foreign policy, long-term development strategy, and the central nomenklatura system would continue to be controlled by the CPSU's central organs. Such a hybrid system might combine elements of France's two years cohabitation between a socialist president and conservative premier, of the slow opening the PRI has given the opposition parties in Mexico, or the skillful management of the transition from Francoism under a democratically minded monarch in Spain, in all of which a "higher" sphere of the system delegated certain governmental powers to opposition elements. But such a regime would have to reconcile the pluralistic features of a parliamentary democracy with the monocratic rule of a single party, a combination which defies the imagination, since it is difficult to accept that the partitions between "high" and "local" politics will long remain unchallenged. The contest for influence among the newly active political movements will surely only stimulate new efforts to question the party's permanent monopoly on ultimate control of the government. Nationality movements have become closely identified with movements for economic decentralization and environmental protection, bringing about a tendency for social cleavages to cumulate and reinforce one another rather than to cut across and balance one another out. In view of the raising of popular expectations that the well-advertised policy of "democratization" has brought about, if the resources for *actual* participation and contestation are denied to the new peripheral-nationality and "green" movements pressing from below, the old gap between words and deeds will reappear, threatening the reform strategy and Gorbachev's own power. Gorbachev has used the party's ideological levers to introduce significant political and economic reforms. The debate opened under *glasnost'* has in turn enabled a variety of social movements to acquire political voice and to demand greater influence over policy. The question is whether a "socialist pluralism of opinions" can become a socialist pluralism of power without overturning communist rule.

POLITICAL CHANGE IN THE SOVIET UNION
Archie Brown

A new Soviet political system is being created from day to day. At the moment, the new sits uneasily alongside the old, and the old is not giving way without a fight. The changes call into question a great deal that has been taken for granted throughout much of Soviet history, and it has become more difficult than ever before to predict what the system will look like a decade from now. But even those who as recently as 1987 were arguing—wrongly—that nothing of consequence had changed in the Soviet Union must now recognize that dramatic and fundamentally important change is taking place.[1]

Political reform is, of course, proceeding much faster and more successfully than economic reform. So long as material shortages get worse rather than better and there is no improvement in the standard of living of the average Soviet citizen, the continuation of political reform cannot be taken for granted. But many Western commentators, even once they belatedly accepted that Gorbachev was serious about radical reform, have underestimated his staying power and the prospects for *perestroika* moving forward. It has been argued, for example, that the opposition of the party and state apparatus represents an insurmountable obstacle, or that conservative forces are able to draw strength from popular grievances and disappointed expectations.[2]

The combination of freedom to criticize and lack of economic progress is undoubtedly an important factor in the Soviet political equation. But so far, while it has reduced Gorbachev's *popularity* at home as compared with the early days of his leadership in 1985, it has not undermined his *power*.[3] On the contrary, Gorbachev has skillfully used both old and new institutions—on the one hand, the powers of the party general secretary-

Archie Brown is a fellow of St. Antony's College, Oxford and (from October 1989) professor of politics at Oxford University. His latest book, as editor and co-author, is Political Leadership in the Soviet Union *(Bloomington, IN: Indiana University Press, 1989).*

ship and, on the other, the outcome of the elections to the Congress of People's Deputies and the first meeting of that legislative body—to reduce the numerical weight and political influence of conservative Communists in the highest echelons of the party and state apparatus.

The energetic part being played by radically reformist journalists, social scientists, and writers has helped to create a political climate in which it is far from easy for conservative party and state bureaucrats to exploit domestic economic and social problems to their advantage. There are many differences between the present period of Soviet history and Khrushchev's time of attempted reform. One, of course, is the greater political insight and subtlety of Gorbachev, but no less important is the far greater sophistication of the political analyses appearing now in many (though not all) Soviet journals and newspapers and on some radio and television programs. There has been a dramatic increase in the circulation of the most liberal and forward-looking weeklies and monthlies, and the enhanced political education of their readers is now a factor to be reckoned with. (The most spectacular example of this trend is the weekly *Ogonek* which, since Vitaly Korotich became its editor in 1986, has increased its circulation from a few hundred thousand to almost three-and-a-half million. The monthly journal *Znamya*, now under the editorial direction of Georgy Baklanov and Vladimir Lakshin, has a circulation of 980,000 copies today as compared with 175,000 in 1985; and *Novy Mir* currently has a print run of 1,573,000 copies monthly as compared with approximately 496,000 as recently as late 1987. *Novy Mir's* announcement that it would serialize George Orwell's *Nineteen Eighty-Four* in 1989—which it has, indeed, now published—was one reason for the substantial rise in the number of subscriptions taken out for the present year.)

New ways of thinking and speaking about Soviet politics as well as new ways of behaving have emerged in Gorbachev's Soviet Union, especially since 1987. In an article written for this journal at the end of 1986, I emphasized the significance of the political developments already under way but described the change (in itself far from insignificant) in the postwar Soviet Union as one "from quasi-totalitarianism to authoritarianism to the beginnings of a more enlightened authoritarian regime."[4] In the past two-and-a-half years, the Soviet system has developed beyond that. It is now indeed a more enlightened authoritarian regime and one, furthermore, that already contains some significant elements of political pluralism and of democratization.

In this article, after first putting these changes in context, I focus on two interconnected aspects of Soviet political developments—conceptual change and institutional change. Some attention will be paid also to the resistance that is manifesting itself both to the new thinking and to the institutional developments. This resistance takes many forms and, although (or perhaps because) the Gorbachev era has thus far been one of unprecedented progress on the part of Soviet reformers, there is still an intense political struggle taking place. On the one hand, new actors have emerged on the political stage who have adopted positions more radical than that of Gorbachev. On the other hand, Gorbachev remains significantly more of a political reformer than a majority of the party Central Committee. This remains the case even after his spectacular success, in late April, in engineering the removal of more veteran members of the Central Committee than had ever before left that body between the quinquennial party congresses.[5]

Models of Socialism

So far as *political* change is concerned, what is happening now in the Soviet Union is the most comprehensive reform effort since the Bolshevik Revolution, not excluding Lenin's New Economic Policy launched in 1921. One of the most important elements of that change is in the realm of language and ideas. Given the explicit role accorded to theory and ideology in Communist states, and the vast resources traditionally devoted in the Soviet Union to bolstering the position of a specific political doctrine, here, even more than elsewhere, "conceptual change must be understood politically, and political change conceptually."[6]

Some of the new ideas that are now being proclaimed in the Soviet Union were cautiously anticipated in Brezhnev's time, but as one of the most innovative thinkers then and now, Evgeny Ambartsumov, has put it, in those days — so far as the social sciences at least were concerned — "creative search and bold scientific endeavor were reprehensible and even risky."[7] As Ambartsumov notes:

The tone was set by hallelujah-singers who eulogized the status quo, by dogmatists and scholastics who studied speculative, far-fetched, unrepresentative categories and properties and not real processes. Given the atmosphere of ostentation and social apologetics, this was an intellectually fruitless, but paying occupation. That is why many young and some mature scientists took the line of least resistance, adjusting themselves to the situation. Even if they dared to pose a burning question, they tended to mask it with verbosity, seeking safety behind platitudes and commonplace statements.[8]

127

In contrast with Brezhnev's time, when it was firmly held that though there could be different *roads* to socialism, there were not different *models* of it (socialism was what was to be found in the Soviet Union and in other orthodox Communist states at any given time), there is now a cautious espousal by the top party leadership — and a more wholehearted embracing by many party intellectuals — of the idea that different models of socialism can and do exist. There is, in addition, a much greater willingness to learn from the experience of others.[9]

Developments in Communist countries as diverse as China, Hungary, Poland, East Germany, Czechoslovakia, and Yugoslavia have been closely scrutinized, with different Soviet leaders drawing upon different models. Thus, aspects of the Hungarian and Chinese economic reforms, especially in agriculture, appeal to those of more radical reformist orientation, while Egor Ligachev, the overlord of Soviet agriculture within the Central Committee Secretariat, prefers to look to the more conservative Communist states of East Germany and Czechoslovakia to justify his faith in the essentials of the state and collective farm structure.

Of course, attention is being paid to the negative as well as the positive aspects of the experience of other Communist countries. In the case of China, with which the Soviet Union has reestablished interparty as well as interstate relations following Gorbachev's visit in May (itself an important event, although overshadowed by the collapse in the authority of the Chinese leadership that was, coincidentally, taking place), it has for some time been agreed by social scientists in the Soviet Union and China with knowledge of the other country that while Deng Xiaoping's China was ahead of the Soviet Union in the radicalism of its economic reform, the Soviet Union was well ahead of China in political reform and in relative freedom of expression.[10]

The mass student protests of May and early June and the eventual brutal military suppression of peaceful and popular demonstrations in Beijing are doubtless being interpreted in very different ways by different opinion groupings within the Soviet Communist Party. For some, it is confirmation of the dangers of allowing spontaneous political movements to get out of hand and of the need for an early restoration of firmer "discipline" within the Soviet Union itself. For reformers, however, it is one more proof of the correctness of creating political institutions (the freest Soviet elections in 70 years and the nearest thing to a parliament the Soviet Union has ever had) that provide a mechanism for a higher degree than hitherto of accountability on the part of political officeholders as well as a forum for criticism and debate. The present period of remarkable ferment and innovation in a significant part of the Communist world (notably, in Hungary and Poland as well as the Soviet Union and China) is one in which events in one country can have a dramatic impact on another, and not always in predictable ways.

It is not only, however, what is happening in other Communist states that is now influencing the top Soviet leadership. The sources of learning have been extended to include certain aspects of the political systems of "bourgeois democratic" countries and not merely, as in the past, technical or managerial features of their economic systems. Both Gorbachev and Vadim Medvedev, a Politburo member and the secretary of the Central Committee with responsibility for ideology, have stressed the necessity of learning from the nonsocialist world as well as from other socialist countries.[11] Medvedev has appeared to call for a reinterpretation of the achievements of European social democracy, a shift of which there have been numerous other signs in Soviet publications (and on Soviet television), including sympathetic discussion of Sweden and other Scandinavian countries.[12] Indeed, on the reform wing of the Soviet Communist Party the long-standing barrier between communism, on the one hand, and social democracy or democratic socialism, on the other, is crumbling. In a dramatic break with the past, it is not uncommon now to hear prominent Soviet party intellectuals and some of the more enlightened officials say that they regard Sweden not only as an example of socialism but as the best model currently on view.

At the inaugural meeting of the Congress of People's Deputies, held at the end of May and beginning of June, the prominent Soviet writer Chingiz Aitmatov went further. Aitmatov made two major speeches to the congress. In the first, it was he who proposed Mikhail Gorbachev for the post of chairman of the Supreme Soviet.[13] The very fact that Aitmatov was preselected to do this by the overwhelming majority of deputies who are members of the Communist Party and that he was, furthermore, one of the 100 deputies chosen by the party to represent it at the congress is evidence enough that he is in good standing with the party leadership and in the mainstream of reformist thinking rather than on its radical fringes. Yet Aitmatov, in the second of his speeches to the congress, stretched the meaning of socialism in ways unimaginable a few years ago. His address was a long way from traditional socialist theory, in almost any of its variants, but a good example of the importance of understanding the changing meanings of concepts politically and not merely from a theoretical or doctrinal standpoint.

Instead, said Aitmatov, of making an idol of socialism as "the holy of holies of our theoretical doctrine," and instead of laying down the law on what did and what did not constitute socialism, it was necessary to reach an understanding whereby it was judged by its fruits—that is, by its contribution to people's creativity and prosperity. He suggested that the Soviet Union could learn from other countries for whom the Soviet example had performed the service of demonstrating how *not* to go about constructing socialism:

I have in mind the flourishing law-governed societies of Sweden, Austria, Finland, Norway, the Netherlands, Spain and, finally, Canada across the ocean. About Switzerland I don't even speak—it's a model. The working person in those countries earns on average four to five times more than our workers. The social protection and the level of welfare of those societies are something we can only dream about. This is real and, if you like, worker trade-union socialism, although these countries do not call themselves socialist, but are none the worse for that.[14]

The comparisons important Soviet reformers now make both with the Soviet past and with Western countries are remarkable. Aleksandr Yakovlev, Gorbachev's closest ally on the Politburo, said in response to the questions of a Soviet television journalist on May 27, "For the first time in the history of our country we have a platform of conscience, a platform of morality."[15] When he was asked whether the Congress of People's Deputies could be compared with parliaments abroad, Yakovlev did not argue for the superiority of the new Soviet legislature, though until very recently Soviet officials routinely suggested that even the unreformed Supreme Soviet was vastly more democratic than Western parliaments. Instead, he emphasized the comparative underdevelopment of Soviet parliamentary theory and practice:

Parliaments in other countries have existed for decades and they have entirely different traditions. They have written many volumes about procedural matters there. We do not have that. Of course, we must learn professionalism in the economy and politics; above all we must learn democratic professionalism. We must learn democracy, tolerance of others' opinions and thoughts. That's not easy. I believe that the work of the Soviet parliament will demonstrate where we are right and where we are wrong; what we must continue and what must be corrected.[16]

New Concepts

As James Farr has noted in a recent essay, "Where there are different concepts, there are different beliefs, and so different actions and practices,"

130

even though political practice is only partly constituted by concepts.[17] But while acting politically "for strategic and partisan purposes," people do so "in and through language" and "language is an arena of political action." Accordingly, "political change and conceptual change must be understood as one complex and interrelated process."[18]

In the Soviet context, three new concepts in particular deserve special emphasis, for they help to open up space for new political activity and provide a theoretical underpinning for some of the concrete reforms that the more radical interpreters of *perestroika* are attempting to implement. It is worth noting that within a period of 18 months—between the summer of 1987 and the end of 1988—all three received the endorsement of Gorbachev.

The first of these concepts is that of "socialist pluralism," and its adoption represents a radical break with past Soviet doctrine. It is of interest that whereas many reformist concepts are to be encountered first in the writings of scholarly specialists and only later in the speeches of party leaders, in this instance it was Gorbachev who took the bold step of embracing the concept of "pluralism" in public before anyone else had done so.[19] Indeed, the notion of pluralism had been the subject of so many attacks by Soviet leaders and ideologists since it was adopted by "Prague Spring" intellectuals in the late 1960s and by "Eurocommunists" in the 1970s that it would have been difficult for anyone other than the top leader to break the taboo on endorsing it.

But Gorbachev took the lead on this because he was persuaded that to continue to attack "pluralism" was to play into the hands of those in the Soviet Union who wished to stifle debate and innovative thought, and to assist the enemies, rather than the proponents, of *perestroika*. Only one year separated Gorbachev's first use of the term "socialist pluralism," in the limited context of opening up the columns of Soviet newspapers to a wider range of writers in order that "the whole of socialist pluralism, so to speak, is present,"[20] to his use of the concept in a broader sense, and the endorsement of that use in a most authoritative party forum, the 19th Conference of the Soviet Communist Party in the summer of 1988.[21]

Thus, what had seemed to some to be no more than a throwaway remark when first used by Gorbachev in conversation with Soviet writers in July 1987 had a year later been elevated into new party doctrine, the traditional "monist" theory of the Soviet state and oft-repeated claim of the "monolithic unity" of the party and the people notwithstanding. Gorbachev's adoption of the concept of "socialist pluralism" and the positive reference made to a "socialist pluralism of opinions" in the resolution on

131

glasnost adopted by the party conference represented a considerable boost for the more radical Soviet political reformers. These endorsements provided a legitimacy previously lacking for political debate and diversity of opinion on political and social issues in Soviet publications, even though the fact that "pluralism" was qualified by the adjective "socialist" indicated that there were still limits on what was deemed fit to print.

Whereas in Poland and Hungary, following fierce struggles, the top party leaderships now speak approvingly of "political pluralism" (though there remains room for argument concerning its scope in practice), Gorbachev and even the reform wing of the Soviet leadership continue to make a distinction between "socialist pluralism"— desirable — and "political pluralism"— still suspect because of its free-for-all connotations and implication that under such a banner the "leading role" of the Communist Party might cease to be guaranteed. In practice, a "socialist pluralism of opinion" makes ample room for publications by Roy Medvedev, previously regarded as a dissident but now a member of the new Supreme Soviet and also readmitted to the Communist Party, but has not so far accommodated an Aleksandr Solzhenitsyn, who made increasingly clear after the publication of his works in Russia ceased in the mid-1960s that his rejection of the Soviet system was a root-and-branch one that embraced Lenin and Leninism as well as Stalin and Stalinism. (Even in Solzhenitsyn's case, however, some recent movement has taken place. TASS, the Soviet news service, reported on June 6 that the publishing house Sovetskaya Rossiya would be bringing out Solzhenitsyn's *Cancer Ward*, written in the Soviet Union but never published there, as well as *One Day in the Life of Ivan Denisovich* and *Matryona's Home*.)[22]

The boundaries of "socialist pluralism" are not fixed. On the one hand, many Soviet commentators now use the term "pluralism" positively— and with reference to political, cultural, and intellectual life in the mass media, without finding it necessary to qualify it either with "socialist" or "political." On the other hand, all this is being accompanied by a debate on, and constant redefinition of, socialism itself. If that process continues, the shackles imposed by the word "socialist" may be far removed from the constraints it implied in the Soviet past.[23]

The second concept adopted in recent times that is of great importance for the advancement of the cause of political and legal reform is that of the *pravovoe gosudarstvo*, or the state based upon the rule of law. While there is nothing new about an emphasis on "socialist legality," the idea of the *pravovoe gosudarstvo* goes beyond that. The "socialist legality" introduced under Khrushchev meant an end to the excesses and extremes of arbitrariness of Stalin's time, but lawyers and the legal system remained firmly subordinated to the party leadership. The aim of the serious proponents of the *pravovoe gosudarstvo* is a system in which all institutions and individuals are subordinate to the law as administered by impartial and independent courts. What is more, while it is generally assumed in Soviet writings that a "socialist legality" has prevailed in the Soviet Union throughout the post-Stalin era, the state based upon the rule of law is seen as a goal to which Soviet society should aspire, rather than as one that has already been attained.

The idea of the law-governed state is part of a much more profound analysis of arbitrary rule and the abuse of power than took place in Khrushchev's time. It reflects a consciousness of the extent to which powerful individuals and institutions have been able to bend the law to their own purposes, as well as a concern with the inadequacy of the rights of attorneys and of the independence of judges in cases where the interests and views of well-connected officials are involved. A prominent Soviet scholar of notably reformist disposition, Mikhail Piskotin, who was from 1978 until 1987 chief editor of the major legal journal, *Sovetskoe gosudarstvo i pravo*, and who now heads the Center of Political Science Research established in Moscow in the summer of 1988, has written in the newspaper *Sovetskaya kul'tura* that even today "it is far from possible to regard our state as one fully based on the rule of law," adding that the attainment of the *pravovoe gosudarstvo* requires reform of the political system.[24]

The concept of the state based upon the rule of law has not only been embraced by Gorbachev but was also included in the resolution on legal reform adopted by the 19th party conference in early July 1988.[25] It leaves open many questions, including, not least, the issue of whether in practice courts will have any independence vis-à-vis the very highest party and state authorities, as distinct from the competence to check abuses of power at local levels. As with other innovative concepts that have been accepted by the Soviet leadership, different leaders and theorists can interpret the idea of the law-governed state in different ways. But adoption of the concept marks a considerable step forward in the advancement of the *role* of law—even if there does not yet exist in practice a full-fledged *rule* of law—in Soviet society.

The third concept that is quite new in the Soviet context is that of "checks and balances." Its adoption is a remarkable departure from previous patterns of Soviet thought and it, too, is part of the breakthrough in thinking about the Soviet political system that took place in 1987 and 1988. In the past, the notion of checks and balances, insofar as it was referred to at all, was viewed as part of the deceptive screen behind which the ruling class exercised untrammeled power in bourgeois states. But the more serious Soviet study of foreign political systems in recent years, as well as the contemplation of some of the horrendous results of unchecked power within the Soviet Union (especially in the Stalin period), have led to a reevaluation of the theory and practice of checks and balances. The idea that the concept might have something to offer reformers of the Soviet political system was first broached in print in Moscow as short a time ago as July 1987,[26] and it was adopted by Gorbachev even more recently—at the end of November 1988, in his speech commending the first phase of political reform to the Supreme Soviet.[27]

This is one instance where the influence on Gorbachev's thinking can be traced with some confidence. It was at a meeting of the Soviet Association of Political Sciences presided over by Georgy Shakhnazarov in February 1987 (reported in the monthly journal *Sovetskoe gosudarstvo i pravo* in July of that year) that the call for the development of a "socialist theory of checks and balances" was first heard.[28] To assist in the elaboration of this, it was advocated that the development of bourgeois states should be studied from the standpoint of the creation within them of checks and balances and that relevant Western theoretical writings should also be examined. All this was linked to the necessity of "preventing the concentration in the hands of one organ (or individual) of all political power."[29]

Shakhnazarov was already at that time—while still first deputy head of the Socialist Countries Department of the Central Committee—an informal adviser of Gorbachev, but in early 1988 he became one of his four *pomoshchniki*, or full-time personal assistants. He is now an influential figure whose judgment Gorbachev clearly respects. Accordingly, when Gorbachev concluded a discussion of the proposed Committee for Supervision of the Constitution by commenting, "Thus, one may say, comrades, that our own socialist system of 'checks and balances' is taking shape in this country, designed to protect society against any violation of socialist legality at the highest state level,"[30] it was not difficult to detect the influence of Shakhnazarov and of scholars in the reform-minded Soviet Association of Political Sciences, whose presidency Shakhnazarov still combines with his senior political advisory functions. For the leader of the Soviet Communist Party and head of the Soviet state to accept the need for checks and balances, albeit *socialist* checks and balances, is a significant illustration of the "new thinking" that has emerged on Soviet political institutions as well as on foreign policy.

The Process of Institutional Change

The most important point about reform of the Soviet political system is that it is not an event but a *process* and, in all probability, a *long-term* process if the reform wing of the Communist Party continues to prevail, as it has increasingly done since Gorbachev became general secretary (and especially since 1987). Gorbachev himself has emphasized that the reforms adopted by the old Supreme Soviet at the end of November 1988 represent only the first phase of reform of the political system. It is impossible to say where they will end, for Soviet reformers themselves do not know. There was much less serious thinking about reform of the political system than about reform of the economy (inadequate though that was) prior to *perestroika*, and ideas on institutional change are being elaborated all the time. It is entirely possible that reform of the Soviet political system will go very much further than it has already if the balance of influence continues to shift in favor of "new thinkers," as it has over the past few years.

The institutional change that has already taken place is far from inconsequential. On the one hand, some major existing institutions are functioning in a significantly different way from before. This is true of the Communist Party as a whole and of some of its constituent institutions. On the other hand, a number of essentially new political institutions have been created. Thus, for example, Soviet elections in 1989 were so different from what were called "elections" in the Soviet Union in the past that they have little in common except the name. Similarly, the new Supreme Soviet is likely to be a much more serious legislature than the body that carried that name previously, and it has been elected by a novel (and already important) institution, the Congress of People's Deputies. There is a new-style presidency, and there is to be a Committee for Supervision of the Constitution. Though it is not possible to provide here an exhaustive survey of the changes in Soviet political institutions, three aspects of this process particularly merit closer examination: electoral reform, the evolving legislature, and the changing structure and role of the party.

Elections. As early as 1987, by way of "experiment," Soviet voters were offered a choice of candidates in elections to local soviets in approximately 5 percent of the constituencies.[31] But the big breakthrough in the Soviet electoral system came with the elections to the new Congress of People's Deputies in late March of this year. Of the 2,250 members of the congress, 1,500 are drawn from territorial constituencies, with 750 seats distributed among the various parts of the country on the basis of population density and 750 divided equally among the national-territorial units from union republics to autonomous regions (thus giving disproportionate representation to the smaller nationalities, since tiny Estonia and the enormous Russian republic return the same number of deputies on this "nationality slate"). Approximately three-quarters of the territorial elections to the congress were competitive ones,[32] but even running in a single-candidate district was no guarantee against defeat, as a number of party officials discovered to their dismay when they failed to secure 50 percent support from those who voted.

A negative vote could be cast by crossing out the names of the candidate or candidates a voter wished to reject. However, all voters had to mark their ballots, even if they wished to support the prospective deputy in a single-candidate election. This was an important change from previous Soviet electoral practice, whereby voters were not obliged to enter the voting booth at all. To drop an unmarked ballot in the ballot box counted as support for the candidate and was the normal way of voting. To make any mark at all on the ballot was, up until the most recent elections, to draw attention to oneself as a probable negative voter. Thus, the 1989 national elections were the first in Soviet history to combine universal adult suffrage with secrecy of the ballot and the competitive principle in at least a majority of seats.

The electoral process varied widely from one part of the country to another and had many imperfections. The party apparatus was, for example, much more successful in Soviet Central Asia than in the major European cities in getting its favored candidates elected. But elsewhere the attempt of party officials to foist themselves or their nominees on the electorate provoked, in many cases, an effective backlash. Thus, with the entire Moscow party apparatus opposed to the election of the maverick populist Boris Yeltsin and putting its resources behind his factory manager opponent, Yeltsin won a landslide victory with approximately 90 percent of the votes in a constituency comprising the entire city of Moscow. In fact, the three major Soviet cities—Moscow, Leningrad, and Kiev—all returned deputies who were chosen by the electorate in defiance of their city party bureaucracies. In Moscow, they included not only Roy Medvedev but also the radically reformist director of the Moscow Historical-Archival Institute, Yuri Afanasev, who was elected in a working-class district of Moscow where the overt hostility to him of the local party machine evidently counted in his favor with the electorate. In Moscow, Leningrad, and Kiev there was an easily detectable "anti-apparatus" vote, of which the most highly placed victim was Yuri Solovev, the first secretary of the Leningrad regional party organization and a candidate member of the Politburo.

Not surprisingly, the election results (even though they included a comfortable majority of successful candidates who could be relied upon to follow the lead of the top party leadership at the Congress of People's Deputies) sent shock waves of alarm and anger through the party apparatus. At a Central Committee plenary session held on April 25, many of the regional party secretaries who spoke blamed shortages, the mass media, insufficient party unity, and the central party leadership for their lack of electoral success. The first secretary of the Krasnodar regional party committee, Ivan Polozkov, said it was getting harder to answer people's questions as to why there was no butter, children's shoes, baby carriages, or bicycles for sale. He added sarcastically: "They listen, but they do not understand very well. And as for the absence of soap, they do not wish even to listen."[33] Aleksandr Melnikov, a former Central Committee department head and now a regional party secretary, complained that ordinary people had been led astray by "a massive onslaught from the mass media."[34]

The defeated Leningrad party chief, Yuri Solovev, noted that "not one of the six leaders of the party and soviet in Leningrad and its region assembled the necessary number of votes."[35] This, as he pointed out, was not unique to Leningrad, and the only pattern he detected in such votes against the local official establishments was that they had been cast in "major industrial, scientific and cultural centers."[36] That was hardly an encouraging postmortem for the Central Committee.

The 750 deputies who were chosen by public organizations—ranging in size and political weight from the Communist Party itself to the Soviet Culture Foundation and the Soviet Peace Foundation, and including such important bodies as the Academy of Sciences, the Komsomol, and the creative unions (writers, artists, etc.)—produced a still clearer majority of people who could be relied upon not to rock the boat too much.[37] At the same time, though, these organizations provided a minority who were among the most radical people to attend the inaugural session of the Congress of People's Deputies. This was especially true of the Academy of Sciences, whose Presidium produced a list of only 23 candidates, out of which the membership was to choose 20 representatives—and left off the list some of the country's most talented and politically outspoken scientists and scholars, including Academician Andrei Sakharov, who had been nominated by some 60 scientific institutes. In response, the Academy voters struck out 15 of the names presented to them, giving the required 50 percent support to only eight of the candidates. These results necessitated a second round of voting, this time for a list that included the names of some of the Soviet Union's most prominent reformers (the Presidium had learned its lesson). In the end, practically every deputy elected from the Academy was close to the liberal or radical reformist end of the Soviet political spectrum. In the second round, Sakharov was elected comfortably and one of the boldest of economic reformers, Nikolai Shmelev, topped the poll.[38]

The move from elections without choice, in which the social composition as well as the political conformity of the deputies could be determined in advance, to competitive elections and opportunities for citizens to nominate candidates from below (though still within the framework of a one-party system) had a number of consequences probably unintended by the top party leadership. One was that in certain republics, especially the Baltic ones, only those candidates—whether party or nonparty—who were prepared to take a strongly national line and defend the interests of the titular nationality of their republic could hope to be elected. Another was the radical shift in the occupational and class composition of the Congress of People's Deputies as compared with that of its predecessor, the unreformed Supreme Soviet "elected" in 1984. The proportion of industrial and farm workers, for example, went down from 49.5 to 23.1 percent. The representation of employees with higher education and of intellectuals went up. Heads of higher educational institutions, who were entirely unrepresented in the 1984 Supreme Soviet, made up 4.1 percent (83 deputies) of the 1989 Congress of People's Deputies. The representation of senior KGB officials went down between 1984 and 1989 from 1.1 percent to 0.5 percent, while entirely new categories of occupations to be represented in the list of deputies included those of scientific workers (61 deputies; 3 percent), journalists (28 deputies; 1.4 percent), attorneys (two deputies; 0.1 percent) and clergymen (five deputies; 0.2 percent).[39]

In practice, these changes meant a strengthened representation of highly articulate deputies; not surprisingly, though, the decline in worker representation was strongly attacked by opponents of reform. The growing importance of initiative from below, as opposed to control from above, also led to a sharp fall in the proportion of women deputies as compared with the old Supreme Soviet. This may be a backhanded tribute to the vastly greater significance of the new legislature, given the generally weak position of women in Soviet political life; there has for many years been an inverse relationship between the power of an institution in the Soviet political system and the percentage of women to be found in that body.

Taking the elections as a whole, they must be seen as a remarkable landmark in the process of the democratization of the Soviet political system. The fact that they were still held within the framework of a one-party system did not, as many Soviet citizens feared, mean that there was nothing to choose from among different candidates in terms of their policies and principles. The political reality that the Soviet Communist Party itself (a 20 million–strong body comprising approximately 10 percent of adult citizens) is a coalition of very diverse viewpoints and interests became clearer than ever. In a number of the major cities, there was a lively clash of opinions in the course of the election campaign. This was notwithstanding the fact that 85.3 percent of candidates nominated and 87.6 percent of those actually elected to the Congress of People's Deputies were party members.[40] Short of a "counterrevolutionary" reversal of the entire process of *perestroika*, it is difficult to see any return to the sham elections of the past. In view of the evident dissatisfaction of many of the electorates presented with only a single candidate in the 1989 elections, it is much more likely that movement will be in the direction of electoral choice in *all* constituencies.

One issue that remains unresolved thus far is whether party first secretaries who were defeated in the elections for the Congress of People's Deputies should resign their party office (or be forced to resign by their party committee). There have been hints from Gorbachev that this should indeed happen; the line taken by the top party leadership as a whole has been that a case-by-case approach to this question should be adopted by the various party committees concerned. It would be even more difficult for first secretaries at the republican, regional, city, and district level to keep their party posts if they were defeated in elections to soviets at those levels (as distinct from the all-union Congress of People's Deputies). This is no doubt one reason (though the need to improve the electoral law is given as the main one) why local elections have been postponed from late 1989 to the spring of 1990.

Given that the breakthrough toward heterodox voting has already been made, and given the decline in the authority of the party apparatus that was acknowledged both at the April plenary session of the Central Committee and at the Congress of People's Deputies, defeat for many local party bosses in the elections for local soviets is a real possibility. In such cases, the party, if it wishes to retain authority at the local level, will come under pressure from its rank-and-file membership (and probably from Gorbachev and the reformers now consolidating their ascendancy at the top of the party hierarchy) to elect a new first secretary for the locality. This will then constitute an important and unforeseen element in the democratization of the Soviet political system. It will, in effect, give the nonparty majority of the local electorate a veto over the party's choice for first secretary in their locality (a choice that in the past often owed more to the preferences of the apparatus one rung higher in the party hierarchy than to the local party committee itself). While that change would still occur within the confines of a single-party system, it would be a dramatic departure from what the "leading role" of the Communist Party has meant hitherto. Indeed, the party would be following rather than leading.

This electoral dilemma should be seen in a broader context. A revitalized and politicized Soviet society—no longer "the most silent majority in the world"[41] —poses entirely new challenges to the party. No one recognizes this more clearly than Gorbachev. In his closing address to the First Congress of People's Deputies on June 9, he argued that Soviet society still needed a vanguard party, but added that if it is going to be such a vanguard, then "the party must reconstruct itself faster than society."[42]

The New Legislature. Just one of many unique features of the First Congress of People's Deputies was that no one (not even Gorbachev) knew how long it was going to last. As originally conceived, it appeared that the main task of the 2,250 deputies was to elect the inner body, the bicameral, 542-member Supreme Soviet. It is the Supreme Soviet that is to be the more or less permanently functioning part of parliament, meeting for more than half of the year (unlike the old Supreme Soviet, which met for only a few days annually). But the First Congress of People's Deputies itself was in session for far longer than was the pattern with the unreformed Supreme Soviet; it began its deliberations on May 25, and ended them on June 9. If the elections that brought the deputies to the Palace of Congresses in Moscow were a milestone on the road to a form of democracy in the Soviet Union, the congress itself broke new frontiers in public freedom of speech. And it was quite a public. What made the impassioned debate and the breaking of one taboo after another of far greater political consequence than would otherwise have been the case was the live broadcasting on Soviet television and radio of the congress proceedings. The speeches were heard by an estimated audience of between 90 and 100 million people.[43] Some of the addresses, if they had been distributed even in 90 or 100 copies five years ago, would undoubtedly have earned their authors a spell in a labor camp.

A public opinion poll conducted on the eve of the convening of the Congress of People's Deputies showed that there were relatively high hopes for the congress, as well as a new popular willingness to distinguish between the role to be played by the hierarchy of elected soviets and the activity of the party.[44] Asked with which institutions people linked their hopes for an improvement in the state of affairs in the country, respondents mentioned the Congress of People's Deputies more often than any other institution. The soviets at all levels came next, and the general secretary, as a source of hope, was in third place (but, significantly, enjoying a higher level of support than all other party institutions, such as the Politburo, the Central Committee, and party congresses).[45]

The atmosphere at the First Congress of People's Deputies was characterized by one Soviet commentator, Vitaly Tretyakov, as "*glasnost* galore." Even more important, the congress had, in Tretyakov's words, "reduced to a minimum the distance between the canonized *glasnost* and freedom of speech."[46] And this was, said the same author, a "selfless *glasnost*" because "as is very well known, the legal and political guarantees of any *glasnost* are pretty weak in our country still."[47]

One speaker Tretyakov probably had in mind was Yuri Vlasov, a writer and former champion weightlifter who devoted most of his speech (carried, like the others, live on Soviet television and radio) to an attack on the KGB. Vlasov described that organization as "not a service, but a real underground empire" that was "subordinate only to the apparatus" and not "under the control of the people". He called for the KGB to be moved out of its Dzerzhinsky Square headquarters in central Moscow to "a modest building in the suburbs" and insisted that it must be held accountable for its activities to the new Supreme Soviet.[48] Vlasov's speech, *Izvestia* noted, was greeted with "prolonged applause."[49]

One of the most important outcomes of the First Congress of People's Deputies and of the initial sessions of the new Supreme Soviet was the setting up of a whole series of commissions (both permanent and ad hoc) and committees, which include a new permanent committee of the Supreme Soviet on defense and state security.[50] It seems likely that at least a minority of deputies on that committee and in the Supreme Soviet as a whole will be prepared to ask awkward questions and to demand that steps be taken toward making the defense establishment and the state security organs accountable to the legislature. Previously, the military and the KGB were politically accountable only to the party leadership, but if the Congress of People's Deputies and the Supreme Soviet continue as they have begun, these bodies may be subjected to a more detailed scrutiny than that to which they have become accustomed.

The Committee on Defense and State Security is just one of 15 committees set up by the Supreme Soviet as a whole. In addition, each of the two chambers of the Supreme Soviet (the Soviet of the Union and the Soviet of Nationalities) has set up standing commissions of its own. Thus, for example, the Soviet of Nationalities has set up a commission on national policy and interethnic relations within the Soviet Union.[51]

141

The Congress of People's Deputies, in response to pressure from many of the deputies who addressed it, has also set up commissions of its own to investigate particularly sensitive issues. These include a commission "to investigate the circumstances connected with events in Tbilisi on 9th April 1989"[52] (the killing and wounding of a number of Georgian demonstrators by soldiers, an event that outraged public opinion in Georgia and became a major bone of contention at the Congress, with deputies from the Baltic republics and from Moscow giving support to their Georgian colleagues), and a commission to make a "political and legal appraisal of the Soviet-German non-aggression pact of 1939."[53] The latter commission was formed after deputies from the three Baltic republics had insistently brought up the issue of a secret protocol to the Molotov-Ribbentrop pact sanctioning the forcible incorporation of Estonia, Latvia, and Lithuania into the Soviet Union.

It is noteworthy that the composition of the various commissions was the subject of discussion both in front of the cameras and behind the scenes, and that enough deputies of independent mind and, in some cases, of radically libertarian views were included to give the commissions authority in the eyes of the aggrieved parties. Thus, for example, the 23-person commission on the events in Tbilisi includes the greatly respected literary scholar, Academician Dmitri Likhachev; the equally respected scientist and outspoken reformer, Academician Roald Sagdeev; the radical young Moscow deputy and historian, Sergei Stankevich; and the prominent and liberal specialist on criminal law at the Institute of State and Law in Moscow, Aleksandr Yakovlev—not to be confused with his Politburo namesake.[54]

The Politburo's Aleksandr Yakovlev (himself very much on the "new-thinking" wing of the Politburo) was named chairman of the 26-member commission on the Soviet-German pact. The Baltic republics themselves are strongly represented on the commission, which also includes such liberal or radical non-Balts as the historian, Yuri Afanasev; the Armenian sociologist, Lyudmila Arutyunyan; and the editor of *Ogonek*, Vitaly Korotich. Other members include the writer, Chingiz Aitmatov; the director of the Institute of the USA and Canada, Georgy Arbatov; and the head of the International Department of the party Central Committee, Valentin Falin.[55]

A particularly important body created by the Congress of People's Deputies toward the end of its deliberations is the Constitutional Commission. (This is a different body from the Committee for Supervision of the Constitution that has yet to be set up and that will provide quasi-judicial review of the consitutionality of governmental acts.) It has now been decided that the Soviet Union needs a new constitution to replace the current one, which was adopted in 1977 under Brezhnev, and the main task of the Constitutional Commission is to draft that new fundamental law.[56] This provides opportunities to develop further the reform of the Soviet political system and to institutionalize and solidify some of the changes for the better—such as the great strides toward freedom of expression—that have already manifested themselves, but that are still excessively dependent on the enlightened intervention or benign non-intervention of Gorbachev and the reform wing of the party leadership.

The chairman of the Constitutional Commission is Gorbachev, who was duly elected to the new-style state presidency at the beginning of the First Congress of People's Deputies. Its deputy chairman is his close colleague Anatoly Lukyanov, who was elected to the vice-presidency of the Supreme Soviet at the congress. Lukyanov, a fellow student of Gorbachev's at the law faculty of Moscow University in the early 1950s, has maintained particularly close links with academic lawyers, especially at Moscow's Institute of State and Law. Lawyers are in fact well represented on the 107-person commission, and they include quite a wide spectrum of opinion from within their professional ranks—from, for example, the relatively conservative Dzhangir Kerimov through the cautiously reformist Vladimir Kudryavtsev (the former director of the Institute of State and Law, now vice-president of the Academy of Sciences with responsibility for law and the social sciences) to the long-standing proponent of electoral reform and reform of the soviets, Moscow University law professor Georgy Barabashev.[57]

While *radical* reformers may not—and that is hardly surprising—constitute a majority of the members, the Constitutional Commission includes enough people who both fit that description and possess intellectual weight for them to exercise a more than proportionate influence on the elaboration of a new constitution. The most remarkable name on the list, in the context of recent Soviet history, is that of Andrei Sakharov. Such bold reformers as Oleg Bogomolov, Gavril Popov, and Tatyana Zaslavskaya are also members of the commission, as is the radicalized and unpredictable Boris Yeltsin. Two members likely to be important are Fedor Burlatsky and Georgy Shakhnazarov. Both of them have long records as significant within-system reformers whose whole lives have, in a sense, been a preparation for the opportunities open to them now. Burlatsky—now a member of the Supreme Soviet as well as political commentator for the Writers' Union newspaper, *Literaturnaya gazeta*—has never been short of ideas for political reform, and Shakhnazarov—one of Gorbachev's full-time aides and, therefore, especially well placed to make an impact

143

on the content of the new constitution — has, like Burlatsky, been in the forefront of "new thinking" on both foreign and domestic policy.

The tone of the Congress of People's Deputies was set on the first day, shortly after Gorbachev was proposed as chairman of the Supreme Soviet (the new and more powerful state presidency). One of the very first speakers to be called to the rostrum by Gorbachev was Sakharov, who protested against the fact that only Gorbachev was being nominated for the presidency and argued for the necessity of a competitive election. Sakharov said that he did "not see anyone else who could lead our country," but he stressed that his support for Gorbachev was "of a conditional nature."[58] Though many conservative voices were heard as well at the Congress of People's Deputies, and the speeches embraced a very wide spectrum of political opinion, the radicals from Moscow (who were soon being dubbed the "Moscow group" or even the "Moscow faction"), the Baltic republics, and elsewhere were given a greater share of time to speak than their minority representation within the total body of deputies strictly merited. This was partly a tribute to their determination and articulateness, but it could not have happened without Gorbachev's guidance and support and his uphill struggle to create a spirit of tolerance in an atmosphere that was often highly charged.

In the event, Gorbachev did have a challenger in the election for the presidency — a self-proposed, previously unknown but nevertheless impressive 46-year-old engineer/designer from the Leningrad region, Aleksandr Obolensky. A non-party member, Obolensky attacked the privileges attached to the *nomenklatura*, which, he said, corrupted its beneficiaries by giving them a material interest in the maintenance of the existing system and also provided a convenient lever for controlling them.[59] Obolensky who, like Sakharov, was concerned to establish a precedent of competition for all high political offices, was able to make his case at length, but in a vote as to whether his name should appear on the ballot, a majority of deputies — 1,415 — voted against, though a very sizable minority — 689 (there were 33 abstentions) — voted in favor. In the secret ballot for or against Gorbachev that followed, the general secretary was supported by 95.6 percent of those who voted, with 87 votes cast against him.[60]

One of the most controversial, as well as important, parts of the work of the Congress of People's Deputies was its election of the Supreme Soviet. After the election had taken place, Yuri Afanasev made a combative speech in which he accused the deputies of having chosen an inner body that was no better than the Supreme Soviet of Stalin's and Brezhnev's time.[61] That was a considerable exaggeration. Many of the republics and regions put forward no more candidates than was their entitlement for the Soviet of the Union and the Soviet of Nationalities, and so the conservative majority in the Congress of People's Deputies had no choice but to endorse them. This ensured that a significant minority of outspoken critics — from, for example, the Baltic republics, Georgia, and Armenia — made their way into the Supreme Soviet. The cause of the dissatisfaction of Afanasev and that of other radicals was the fate of the Moscow slate of candidates. Endorsing the principle of competitive elections, the Moscow group of deputies put up 55 candidates for its allotted 29 places in the Soviet of the Union and 12 candidates for 11 places in the Soviet of Nationalities. This gave the regional party secretaries and their like-minded colleagues who formed a majority in the Congress an opportunity to take their revenge on the most outspoken Moscow intellectuals and cross out the names of Popov, Stankevich, Zaslavskaya, and others from the list. Even so, Roy Medvedev and Fedor Burlatsky were among the 29 from Moscow who made their way into the Soviet of the Union.

The cause of greatest outrage was Boris Yeltsin's 12th-place finish in the election for the Soviet of Nationalities, so that he became the *only* Moscow nominee for that body to fail to be elected, notwithstanding the fact that he had been supported in the elections to the Congress of People's Deputies by more Muscovites than anyone else. For Gorbachev and the reformers within the leadership, this was an embarrassment, even though Yeltsin has become one of their critics (while saving his harshest remarks for Egor Ligachev). When another elected deputy resigned to make way for Yeltsin, Gorbachev lost little time in guiding the congress to accept that proposal.[62] Yeltsin is likely to be a thorn in the flesh of the leadership from within the Supreme Soviet, but he would be of more danger to them — and, in particular, to the authority of the new legislature — if he were excluded from that body, given the level of popular support he commands. It may well be that helping to make the Supreme Soviet a critic of the executive and holding ministers and party leaders to account will be the most useful function Yeltsin can perform. Every parliament needs its Yeltsins, whereas it would be an illusion to think that he could lead the Communist Party or head the Soviet state with the imagination and skill of a Gorbachev.

Intraparty Change. The Communist Party is undergoing significant change as a result of the reform of its internal structure, the personnel changes that have reduced the decision-making power of conservative Communists, and the creation of new state institutions. In particular, the introduction of competitive elections and the formation of a new legislative assembly have helped to bring to life dormant political forces within the Soviet Union and have compelled the party to become more responsive to that society as a whole, if it is to retain authority and, perhaps, even its power.

In a memorandum to the Politburo dated August 24, 1988 (but published in a new Soviet journal only in 1989),[63] Gorbachev put forward concrete proposals for the restructuring of the Central Committee apparatus. By authorizing its subsequent publication, he revealed publicly for the first time the precise size of that body immediately prior to its radical reorganization, which was implemented in October. "Today," Gorbachev wrote in the memorandum, "the apparatus of the Central Committee numbers 1,940 responsible workers and 1,275 technical staff."[64] Western estimates of the number of officials working in the Central Committee apparatus have generally varied between 1,000 and 1,500, whereas the actual figure was close to 2,000, excluding support staff. By the beginning of 1989, the numbers were closer to what Western observers had imagined they were before. Gorbachev was aiming at a 50 percent cut in the size of the central apparatus, and by the end of 1988 approximately 40 percent of Central Committee officials had moved either into retirement or to other posts.

The most important feature of this party restructuring was the reduction of the number of Central Committee departments from 20 to nine[65] and the creation of six new Central Committee commissions, the latter giving senior party members outside the apparatus a greater opportunity to exercise influence on policy. The commissions, approved at the Central Committee plenary session at the end of September 1988, concern party construction and cadres policy (chaired by Georgy Razumovsky), ideology (headed by Vadim Medvedev), social and economic policy (chaired by Nikolai Slyunkov), agriculture (headed by Egor Ligachev), international policy (chaired by Aleksandr Yakovlev), and legal policy (chaired by Viktor Chebrikov).[66] Three of the six commission chairmen—Razumovsky, Yakovlev, and Medvedev—are close to Gorbachev (especially the first two) and can be regarded as serious reformers. Ligachev and Chebrikov are on the more conservative wing of the Politburo, while Slyunkov stands somewhere in between. Taken in conjunction with the leadership changes at the same September plenum of the Central Committee—the retirement of Andrei Gromyko and Mikhail Solomentsev from full membership of the Politburo, and the removal of three candidate members (Vladimir Dolgikh, Petr Demichev, and Anatoly Dobrynin, of whom the first two were far from enthusiastic about the Soviet Union's dramatic turn toward reform) — the creation of the new commissions represented a considerable strengthening of Gorbachev's personal position and of the commitment to *perestroika* within the leadership.[67]

It involved, however, some compromises on Gorbachev's part. The price he paid for moving Chebrikov out of the chairmanship of the KGB was, in effect, to promote him, for Chebrikov became a secretary of the Central Committee alongside the full membership of the Politburo he already enjoyed. Moreover, his 21 years in a senior position in the KGB did not make him the most obvious person to head a commission with responsibility for advancing the cause of the state based on the rule of law. Similarly, by cutting back on Ligachev's supervisory responsibilities within the Secretariat — which had previously included agriculture, but also much more — and confining him to agriculture, Gorbachev forced Ligachev to concentrate his attention on an area crucial to the success of reform, and one that might have benefited from being in the hands of someone less suspicious of marketization. Given, however, Gorbachev's knowledge of and personal interest in agriculture and his degree of commitment to the introduction of a leasehold system granting greater autonomy to groups of farmers (including family groups), Ligachev's new post gave him fewer possibilities to apply a brake to the process of reform than he had previously enjoyed.

Gorbachev's skill and determination in using both his authority and power to the full to advance the cause of reform were shown again in April, when the first Central Committee plenum after the elections for the Congress of People's Deputies took place. While many of the current members of the Central Committee took the opportunity to voice their discontent about the new insecurity of their positions generated by the elections and the changed political climate, the plenum accepted the resignation of 74 full members of the Central Committee, 24 candidate members, and 12 members of the Central Auditing Commission.[68] At the same time, it promoted 24 candidate members of the Central Committee to full membership. Taking into account both the resignations and the promotions, the number of voting Central Committee members was reduced from 303 to 251.[69]

This was an unprecedented degree of turnover to occur between party congresses. Since it is only at these congresses, held every five years, that regular elections for the Central Committee take place, Gorbachev's chances of achieving a Central Committee more attuned to the spirit of the times (that of 1989 rather than 1986, when the present Central Committee was elected) seemed slim. But by *persuading* those Central Committee members who had lost the jobs that justified their membership in that body in the first place (a fact that itself made them a disgruntled and potentially dangerous group within the Central Committee) that they should resign in April rather than wait to be removed at the next regular elections (at the 28th Party Congress due to be held in early 1991), Gorbachev was able at a stroke to reduce substantially the conservative deadweight within that important party institution. Those who departed included such former members of the top leadership team as Gromyko, Nikolai Tikhonov, Dolgikh, and Boris Ponomarov, as well as Petr Fedoseev—the man who, in his capacity as vice-president of the Academy of Sciences with special responsibility for the social sciences, bore a good deal of personal responsibility for the sorry state of those disciplines in Brezhnev's time.[70]

As general secretary, Gorbachev has played a major role in the radicalization of the political reform agenda, but at every stage he has had to carry his Politburo colleagues with him. He began as the most radical member of the Politburo he inherited and, quite apart from the extent to which some of his own views have developed, could not have proposed to that body in 1985 some of the things he advocated in 1987, 1988, and 1989. With the emergence of *glasnost*, competitive elections, and a legislature in which radicals have been given a forum for public protest, Gorbachev and the progress of *perestroika* now have liberal as well as conservative critics. While in some ways this makes life even tougher for the Soviet leader, on balance it is to his political advantage. He can play the role of a centrist, albeit one clearly leaning to the liberal side of center, while taking on board more of the policies of the liberal critics than of their conservative counterparts. The conservatives, in any event, suffer from their lack of a viable alternative policy or program. There are those who would wish to turn the clock back only 15 years and others who would be happier turning it back 40 years, but none of them has a vision remotely relevant to the 21st century. Gorbachev, by contrast, has in mind a Soviet Union that in the year 2000 will be far more democratic and markedly more efficient economically than ever before. His problem is getting from here to there, for the problems of the transition period are horrendously difficult.

The Challenges Ahead

The transition to a political system that is qualitatively different from the one that has prevailed in the Soviet Union for so long is well under way. It has made remarkable progress within the space of four years. However, the transition from a centrally administered command economy to one in which market forces play a major role has brought the Soviet Union still closer to economic crisis than did the unreformed economic system Gorbachev inherited. Though some mistakes in economic strategy have been made, the present alarming situation is in no small measure due to the intrinsic difficulties of moving from one type of economic system to another without serious dislocation. The problems of the Soviet leadership have been exacerbated by the drop in the country's foreign earnings as a result of the fall in oil prices, as well as by expensive man-made and natural disasters, including the Chernobyl nuclear accident in 1986 and the Armenian earthquake in 1988.

Money incomes have risen much faster than the supply of goods, so that shortages of foodstuffs and consumer goods are worse in 1989 than they were in 1985. A major contribution to a dangerously high budget deficit has been made by the cutbacks introduced early in the Gorbachev era in the manufacture of vodka, sales of which have in the past enabled the Soviet state to come much closer to balancing its budget.

Whereas a halfway house of political reform has had mainly beneficial results — raising levels of political consciousness, introducing political accountability, opening up new opportunities for meaningful popular participation in the political process, and pushing back the limits on freedom of expression and debate — a halfway house of economic reform has made things worse. The old economic institutions have lost some of their powers and much of their authority, but the intermediate institutions of a market-oriented system — such as commercial banks and wholesale trading operations — do not yet exist.

The observer of the Soviet scene can quickly move from optimism to pessimism simply by focusing on the economy rather than the polity. Yet there is ultimately, of course, a strong interlinkage between political and economic reform. Some organizations, such as certain departments of the party Central Committee and many of the ministries, are simultaneously important political and economic institutions. They have, moreover, become an arena of recent change. In the reorganization of the Central Committee apparatus that took place in October 1988, the largest single category of department to be abolished was that of the branch economic departments. In the process of bringing the total number of departments down from 20 to nine, such departments as those responsible for heavy industry and energy, machine-building, the chemical industry, the military industry, and light industry and consumer goods were abolished completely.[71] The sole branch economic department existing today at the Central Committee level is the Agriculture Department. The only other economic department of any description, the Social and Economic Department, has more general oversight responsibilities.[72] So long as there were numerous Central Committee branch economic departments, whose structure corresponded broadly to that of Gosplan (the State Planning Committee), the leadership's protestations that it wished to withdraw the party from detailed economic tutelage rang hollow. The abolition of departments whose raison d'être was to supervise economic ministries and to intervene in economic decision-making is evidence of a new degree of seriousness of that intent.

In June 1989, Nikolai Ryzkhov, after being nominated by Gorbachev to continue in office as chairman of the Council of Ministers and being confirmed in that post by the Congress of People's Deputies, introduced the most drastic restructuring of the ministerial system to have been undertaken in the era of *perestroika*. He announced a reduction in the number of branch industrial ministries from 50 to 32 and, in answer to a deputy of the Supreme Soviet's question about what this would mean in terms of reduction in the size of the administrative apparatus, Ryzhkov said that ministerial staffs should be cut by at least 30 percent.[73] Moreover, the personnel changes among the ministers themselves were dramatic. As Ryzkhov put it to the Supreme Soviet: "I want to inform you that, of the government which was formed in 1984 and numbered 100 people without counting the chairmen of the union republican councils of ministers . . . only 10 people remain in the composition which is being proposed today."[74] More than half of the members of the Council of Ministers holding office at the beginning of June 1989 were relieved of their offices, and there was a considerable infusion of new blood.

A potentially important appointment was that of one of the Soviet Union's leading academic economists, Leonid Abalkin, hitherto the director of the Institute of Economics of the Academy of Sciences, to head a new state commission for economic reform with the rank of deputy chairman of the Council of Ministers. One of the difficulties with the introduction of Soviet economic reform has been the lack of an overseer of the reforms with a conceptual grasp of what is required and responsibility for avoiding contradictions and ambiguities. The task is greater than Gorbachev or Ryzhkov—with their multifarious other duties—are able to perform, and the appointment of Abalkin and the creation of the new state commission constitute grounds for hope that the strategy for economic reform will acquire greater coherence.

How long the Soviet population will give credence to a leadership that does not produce concrete economic results remains a moot point. The relevance of political reform in this context is that it provides institutional forums for pressure, criticism, and debate and enough freedom of information and expression to make it hard for conservative Communists to sustain the argument that the problems could be solved by returning to the status quo ante. Gorbachev's consolidation of his power at the top of party and state hierarchy, together with the process of institutional change, have probably secured for the reformers in the Soviet leadership several more years in which to make some improvements in living standards to accompany and reinforce political progress. There are many people, both in the Soviet Union and the West, who would regard that view as overly optimistic and hold that instant improvement is required if a counterreformation is to be avoided.[75] Since instant enhancement of living standards is impossible, that is a counsel of despair. It underestimates the primacy of politics in the Soviet system (even though developments in the 1980s have been described as "the revenge of the base on the superstructure") and the new institutions and political climate that would make a Kremlin coup of the kind that overthrew Nikita Khrushchev in October 1964 much more difficult to implement.

Clearly, of course, there exist powerful people who feel that their institutional and individual interests have been undermined. As the April plenum of the Central Committee made clear, such people are to be found in the party apparatus. It is quite evident that they must also exist in the ministerial apparatus, as well as in the military and the KGB, though opinion in these bodies is divided. That there is considerable diversity of view even within the army emerged from the line taken by different military candidates in the 1989 elections for the Congress of People's Deputies.

The ethnic unrest in the contemporary Soviet Union cannot go unmentioned. An unintended consequence of *perestroika* but, at a more profound level, a product of decades of pre-*perestroika* insensitivity to national feelings and aspirations, ethnic unrest constitutes, along with the critical economic situation, the main danger to the further progress of reform and one of the potential justifications that might be offered for intervention by a potential "national savior" offering to restore "order." In reality, strong-arm tactics would, of course, be a disaster. The present path, characterized by the Soviet leadership's increasing responsiveness to national grievances and its apparent determination to move toward a full-fledged federalism, offers the best hope of dealing with an almost intractable "national question." Even a genuine federalism, however, would by no means solve all the problems, for some of the most bitter conflicts are not between the center and periphery but between one neighboring republic and another (above all, the dispute between Armenians and Azeris over Nagorno-Karabakh) or between the titular nationality of a republic and a minority ethnic group within its boundaries (as the case of the Uzbek assault on the Meskhetians in the summer of 1989 starkly illustrated). It is clear that there is a legitimate role for the army or police in protecting one national group from another—especially the minority from the majority in a number of areas—but that any attempt to "solve" the national question by means of coercion would be doomed to failure.

A combination of severe economic and nationality problems, together with a reduction in the budget of the military and—as must follow if political reform continues—of the KGB, could provoke individuals in those organizations to take action against the reformist leadership. It may be worth noting the high public profile that has been sought by Gen. Boris Gromov, the 45-year-old former commander of the Soviet armed forces in Afghanistan. Gromov vigorously defended the Soviet military and its role in Afghanistan in his speech at the 19th Party Conference in 1988,[76] later ostentatiously announced that he would be the last Soviet soldier to leave Afghanistan, and was subsequently duly filmed crossing the border. Having been elected to the Congress of People's Deputies, he withdrew his candidacy for the Supreme Soviet, since election to that body would have forced him to relinquish his military command, and he deemed it "inexpedient" to leave his post as commander of the Kiev Military District.[77]

However, the traditionally rather effective Soviet political control over the military has acquired new bases of support. A combination of economic hardship and the release of far more information than hitherto about the view of the military burden on the Soviet economy has led a majority of Soviet citizens to support reductions in military expenditure equal to, or even greater than, the 14 percent announced by Gorbachev at the First Congress of People's Deputies. In an opinion poll published on the front page of *Izvestiya* on June 4, less than 10 percent of respondents in each of the six Soviet cities of Moscow, Leningrad, Kiev, Tallin, Tbilisi, and Alma-Ata opposed reductions in military spending.[78] Those against such cuts ranged from 9 percent in Moscow to 1 percent in Tbilisi.[79] Despite a significant number of "don't knows," the total number of respondents who either agreed with a 14 percent reduction or favored even larger cuts in military spending ranged from a low of 62 percent in Leningrad (a city with a substantial military industry) to a high of 82 percent in the Estonian capital of Tallin (among whom 66 percent thought that the cuts should have been greater). In Moscow, 75 percent of respondents were for cuts equal to or greater than the ones announced by Gorbachev, with a third of the population of the capital regarding the 14 percent reduction as insufficient.[80] While the publication of such figures may be unwelcome to the military, they both reveal and reinforce popular support for the Gorbachev leadership's "new thinking." Public opinion constraints may not totally rule out an intervention at some point against democratization and the new thinking by an alliance of conservative Communists and the military (as has happened in China), but it is not the most probable outcome. With the balance of power and influence in the higher echelons of the party moving in favor of the reformers, and with the development of electoral and legislative checks on the holders of executive power, it has become much more difficult to put this process into reverse.

The entire Communist world is in a period of unprecedented volatility. The Chinese gerontocracy has taken fright at the very prospect of political dialogue with its own citizenry, a dialogue that is already an encouraging reality in the Soviet Union. Hungary and Poland have carried political change significantly beyond the stage reached by the Dubček leadership in Czechoslovakia in 1968, which was at that time sufficient to provoke Soviet military intervention. (The point is rapidly approaching when it will no longer be meaningful to regard Hungary and Poland as Communist systems.) But the most important change—for better or worse—in terms of its impact on global politics is that occurring in the Soviet Union. The politics and economics of the transition period are imposing almost intolerable burdens on and challenges to Gorbachev and committed Soviet reformers. In the political sphere, these reformers have already changed more than even the optimists predicted four years ago, and the skeptics, who doubted the seriousness of their intentions, have been totally confounded. If the Soviet reformers succeed, it will be as great a victory in peace as the Soviet Union just 44 years ago attained in war. And unlike the latter victory—with its postwar imposition of a Stalinist order on Eastern Europe—it will be possible to welcome it in retrospect as much as the Soviet contribution to the defeat of Nazism was welcomed at the time.

Notes

[1] I have, from the outset of Mikhail Gorbachev's general secretaryship, suggested that he was a reformer by disposition and that he would be an agent of significant change. See, for example, my articles, "Gorbachev: New Man in the Kremlin," *Problems of Com-*

munism, Vol. 34, No. 3 (May-June 1985); and "Can Gorbachev Make a Difference?" *Detente*, No. 3 (May 1985). By 1987, change—especially in the political climate and reform agenda—was proceeding faster than anyone had foretold, though it has gone still further in the two years since the June Central Committee plenum of that year. Yet in 1987 there was still a blinkered inability on the part of many observers to understand what was happening in the Soviet Union. A review article of mine on Soviet politics, "Change and Challenge," published in the *Times Literary Supplement* (March 27, 1987) that should, with the benefit of hindsight, have been criticized for its excess of caution, was vehemently attacked for its excessive optimism in a series of readers' letters published between May 15 and July 10. One of the letter-writers (and by no means the most virulent), Françoise Thom, was the co-author with Alain Besançon of a rather extreme contribution to a symposium entitled "What's Happening in Moscow?" published in *The National Interest*, No. 8 (Summer 1987). The symposium embraced a wide spectrum of views, including my own, but in their almost total misunderstanding of Soviet developments, Besançon and Thom were in a class apart. Gorbachev's policy, these authors tell us, "consists of an all-out attack on civil society" (p. 27), and the Soviet Union remains "a uniform, atomized and voiceless society" (p. 29).

² In the above-mentioned symposium in *The National Interest*, Peter Reddaway did not make the mistake of thinking that Soviet change was merely cosmetic, but he was pessimistic about the prospects for Gorbachev and for *glasnost*: "If Gorbachev is trying to square the circle by embarking on the democratization of the Soviet system, as he shows every sign of doing, then, in my view, he is unlikely to remain in power for many more years. Sooner or later, the *nomenklatura* will surely remove him. And in that case *glasnost* would be bound to suffer in the inevitable conservative reaction," (p. 26).

³ I have discussed Gorbachev's consolidation of his power at some length in my contributions to Archie Brown, ed., *Political Leadership in the Soviet Union* (Bloomington, IN: Indiana University Press, 1989). See also Seweryn Bialer, ed., *Politics, Society and Nationality Inside Gorbachev's Russia* (Boulder, CO: Westview Press, 1989), especially Bialer's final chapter; the symposium, "Gorbachev and Gorbachevism," in *The Journal of Communist Studies*, Vol. 4, No. 4 (December 1988), especially the contributions of Ronald J. Hill, Alex Pravda, and Stephen White; and Patrick Cockburn, "Gorbachev and Soviet Conservatism," *World Policy Journal*, Vol. 6, No. 1 (Winter 1988–89).

⁴ Archie Brown, "Soviet Political Developments and Prospects," *World Policy Journal*, Vol. 4, No. 1 (Winter 1986–87).

⁵ *Pravda*, April 26, 1989, p. 1.

⁶ Terence Ball, James Farr, and Russell L. Hanson, eds., *Political Innovation and Conceptual Change* (Cambridge: Cambridge University Press, 1989), p. x.

⁷ Foreword by E.A. Ambartsumov to A.N. Yakovlev et al., *Soviet Society: Philosophy and Development* (Moscow: Progress, 1988), p. 6.

⁸ *Ibid.*, p. 7.

⁹ See, for instance, Vadim Medvedev in *Pravda*, October 5, 1988, p. 4; Georgy Shakhnazarov, *Pravda*, September 26, 1988, p. 6; the press conference given by Oleg Bogomolov, reported in BBC Summary of World Broadcasts, SU/0381 C2/3-C2/4, February 10, 1989; and Evgeny Ambartsumov in A.N. Yakovlev et al., *Soviet Society* (fn. 7), p. 9.

¹⁰ On a study visit to China in September 1988, I encountered massive support among Chinese social scientists, including those with expert knowledge of the Soviet Union, for the political reform process under way and for the great expansion in cultural freedom and of the possibilities of the mass media in the Soviet Union. One of their main hopes was that the reestablishment of harmonious relations with the Soviet Union would be

a stimulus to political reform in China. Gorbachev was held in enormously high esteem and there was a yearning (and, as later events were to show, with good reason) for a "Chinese Gorbachev."

[11] Gorbachev's speech to the United Nations in December 1988 was notable for its insistence that the time of "closed societies" was over. See *Pravda*, December 8, 1988, pp. 1–2. See also Vadim Medvedev, *Pravda*, October 5, 1988, p. 4.

[12] Medvedev (fn. 11). For a variety of interesting views on the contemporary meaning of socialism, including some that do away with the distinction between socialism of a "Marxist-Leninist" type and "democratic socialism," see the symposium on the concept of socialism in *Voprosy filosofii*, No. 11 (November 1988).

[13] *Pravda*, May 26, 1989, p. 3.

[14] *Izvestiya*, June 4, 1989, p. 2. In the most recent issue of this journal, the director of the Institute of Economics of the World Socialist System, Oleg Bogomolov, is quoted, in answer to a question about what he hoped the Soviet Union would look like 20 years from now, as replying, "Sweden . . . Sweden or perhaps Austria." See Richard Parker, "Assessing Perestroika," *World Policy Journal*, Vol. 6, No. 2 (Spring 1989), p. 294.

[15] BBC Summary of World Broadcasts, SU/0473 C/1, June 3, 1989.

[16] *Ibid.*

[17] James Farr, "Understanding Conceptual Change Politically," in Ball, Farr, and Hanson (fn. 6), p. 29.

[18] *Ibid.*, pp. 30 and 32.

[19] On Gorbachev's expanding use of the notion of "socialist pluralism," see also Archie Brown, "The Soviet Leadership and the Struggle for Political Reform," *The Harriman Institute Forum*, Vol. 1, No. 4 (April 1988).

[20] *Pravda*, July 15, 1987, p. 2.

[21] *Pravda*, July 5, 1988, p. 3.

[22] BBC Summary of World Broadcasts, SU/0480 i, June 12, 1989.

[23] For Soviet discussions of "socialist pluralism," see "Sotsialisticheskiy plyuralizm" (the proceedings of a round table), *Sotsiologicheskie issledovaniya*, No. 5 (September-October 1988); and N.N. Deev and N.F. Sharafetdinov, "Sotsialisticheskiy plyuralizm v politike," *Sovetskoe gosudarstvo i pravo*, No. 4 (April 1989).

[24] *Sovetskaya kul'tura*, July 14, 1988, p. 3.

[25] *Pravda*, July 5, 1988.

[26] S.E. Deytsev and I.G. Shablinsky, "Rol' politicheskikh institutov v uskorenii sotsial'no-ekonomicheskogo razvitiya," *Sovetskoe gosudarstvo i pravo*, No. 17 (July 1987), p. 120.

[27] *Pravda*, November 30, 1988, p. 2.

[28] Deytsev and Shablinsky (fn. 26), pp. 118–120.

[29] *Ibid.*, p. 120.

[30] *Pravda*, November 30, 1988, p. 2.

[31] For an interesting account of these elections and of some of the surrounding discussion, see Jeffrey Hahn, "An Experiment in Competition: The 1987 Elections to the Local Soviet," *Slavic Review*, Vol. 47, No. 2 (Fall 1988).

[32] See G. Barabashev and V. Vasilev, "Etapy reformy," *Pravda*, May 7, 1989, p. 3.

[33] *Pravda*, April 27, 1989, p. 5.

[34] *Ibid.*, p. 6.

[35] *Ibid.*, p. 4.

[36] *Ibid.*

[37] For a list of the public organizations designated to elect deputies, their quota of representatives, and the number of candidates who competed to represent each organization in the elections to the Congress of People's Deputies (and for a useful brief discussion

of the elections themselves), see Dawn Mann, "Elections to the Congress of People's Deputies Nearly Over," *Radio Liberty Report on the USSR*, Vol. 1, No. 15 (April 14, 1989).

[38] *Izvestiya*, April 21, 1989, p. 3.

[39] *Izvestiya*, May 6, 1989, p. 7.

[40] *Ibid.*

[41] The phrase is that of Alexander Kabakov. In context, it reads: "For decades we have been the most silent majority in the world. Really interesting points were discussed only in kitchens, with the closest friends, in the compartments of trains, and with unknown people who do not know your name and address and, therefore, are safe. Today we are probably the most vocal nation. Everything left unsaid accumulated over a long time, and it is impossible to talk about all points at the same time." See *Moscow News*, No. 24 (June 11, 1989), p. 14.

[42] *Pravda*, June 10, 1989, p. 14.

[43] Telephone polls of respondents in major Soviet cities suggested that, in fact, the overwhelming majority of these urban dwellers were watching or listening to the congress proceedings all or most of the time, whether at home or at work. Thus, for example, a poll conducted on May 29 found 81 percent of Muscovites following the proceedings constantly or almost constantly, a figure that had dropped only to 78 percent by early June. The other cities included in these polls were Leningrad, Kiev, Tallin, Tbilisi, and Alma-Ata, and other questions put to the respondents brought out wide differences in the reaction of the inhabitants to some of the major issues discussed at the congress. See *Izvestiya*, May 31, 1989, p. 7; and *Izvestiya*, June 4, 1989, p. 1.

[44] *Izvestiya*, May 24, 1989, p. 6.

[45] *Ibid.*

[46] Vitaly Tretyakov, "Congress of People's Deputies: Whose Hopes will it Justify?" *Moscow News*, No. 24 (June 11, 1989), p. 7.

[47] *Ibid.*

[48] *Izvestiya*, June 2, 1989, pp. 4–5.

[49] *Ibid.*, p. 5.

[50] *Izvestiya*, June 8, 1989, p. 1.

[51] *Ibid.*

[52] *Pravda*, June 1, 1989, p. 1.

[53] *Pravda*, June 3, 1989, p. 6.

[54] *Pravda*, June 1, 1989, p. 1.

[55] *Pravda*, June 1, 1989, p. 1.

[56] For a list of members of the Constitutional Commission, see *Pravda*, June 10, 1989, pp. 1–2.

[57] *Ibid.*

[58] *Izvestiya*, May 26, 1989, p. 4.

[59] *Izvestiya*, May 27, 1989, p. 4.

[60] *Ibid.*

[61] *Izvestiya*, May 29, 1989, p. 1.

[62] Soviet television, May 29, 1989, as reported in BBC Summary of World Broadcasts, SU/0475 C/3-C/6, June 6, 1989.

[63] *Izvestiya TsK KPSS*, Vol. 1, No. 1 (January 1989), pp. 81–86.

[64] *Ibid.*, p. 85.

[65] For a list of the new departments and their heads, see *ibid.*, p. 86.

[66] *Kommunist*, No. 15 (October 1988), p. 4.

[67] For a full list of the leadership personnel changes made at the September 30, 1988 plenary session of the Central Committee, see *ibid.*, p. 3.

[68] *Izvestiya TsK KPSS*, Vol. 1, No. 5 (May 1989), pp. 45–46.

[69] *Ibid.*, p. 47.

[70] Fedoseev's valedictory speech damned "socialist pluralism" with faint praise and called for the ideological unity of the party. See *Pravda*, April 27, 1989, p. 4.

[71] *Izvestiya TsK KPSS*, No. 1 (January 1989), p. 86.

[72] *Ibid.*

[73] Soviet television, speech of June 10, 1989, as reported in BBC Summary of World Broadcasts, SU/0483 C/2–6/7, June 15, 1989.

[74] *Ibid.*

[75] The Soviet researcher Viktor Belkin, speaking in mid-June 1989, said that "the economic situation is worse than we can ever have imagined," adding: "Sometimes I wonder if we can survive until the autumn." Even the newly appointed deputy chairman of the Council of Ministers in charge of economic reform, Leonid Abalkin, gives the Soviet economy only another one-and-a-half to two years to show some signs of improvement if society is not to be "destabilized" and if "a rightward swing" of unpredictable form is to be avoided. The leading specialist on agriculture in the Soviet Union, Vladimir Tikhonov, has said that he expects famine "in the very near future" if peasant farmers are not soon given full control over the land, and Boris Yeltsin has warned that "a revolutionary situation" will develop in the Soviet Union unless living standards are raised rapidly. These dire warnings from prominent figures in Soviet life appear in a Reuters report published in *The Guardian* (London), June 17, 1989, p. 24.

[76] *XIX Vsesoyuznaya konferentsiya kommunisticheskoy partii Sovetskogo Soyuza, 28 Iyuniya–1 Iyulya 1988 goda: Stenograficheskiy otchet*, Vol. 2 (Moscow: Politizdat, 1988), pp. 23–27.

[77] BBC Summary of World Broadcasts, SU/0470 c/7, May 31, 1989.

[78] A telephone poll (by a random sample of telephone numbers) of between 250 and 300 people in each of those cities was conducted during the Congress of People's Deputies. See *Izvestiya*, June 4, 1989, p. 1.

[79] The popularity of the military in Georgia has been at a particularly low ebb since a Soviet army unit killed a number of young demonstrators in Tbilisi on April 9, 1989, an event that is now the subject—as noted in the text of this article—of a commission of inquiry.

[80] *Izvestiya*, June 4, 1989, p. 1.

BY WRIGHT FOR THE PALM BEACH POST, FLA

The Pioneers Of Perestroika

Back to the intellectual roots of Soviet reforms

By David Remnick
Washington Post Foreign Service

MOSCOW—Fifteen years ago, at a remote academic institute in central Siberia, a young economist named Abel Agenbegyan began his evening meals with a toast: "We shall outlive them!" At times, when he was even less sure that the Kremlin's aged leaders would ever step aside, he lifted his glass and said to his liberal young colleagues, "Comrades! To our noble and hopeless work!"

Agenbegyan, a rotund scholar whose bookshelves bulge with the works of Vladimir Lenin and Milton Friedman, is representative of the generation of intellectuals and party reformers who were inspired by the brief liberalizing "thaw" of the Nikita Khrushchev era of the late 1950s. They are now the leaders of both the intelligentsia and the liberal, reformist wing of the Communist Party—the "*perestroika* army."

Suddenly, the dreams of Agenbegyan and the small core of progressives within the Communist Party are taking shape. The party, led by Mikhail Gorbachev, took its most dramatic step last month, abandoning its monopoly on power in hopes of restoring its own credibility in an increasingly pluralistic political system.

Gorbachev's decision was the result of outside pressure—the start of multi-party systems in Eastern Europe, the rise of popular independent political groups in the Soviet Union—and the evolution and evident triumph of the liberal wing of the party.

The intellectual roots of last month's drama go back decades. Scholars such as Agenbegyan and party officials such as Gorbachev survived the post-Khrushchev era of "stagnation" under Leonid Brezhnev in the 1970s and early '80s by leading double lives, working quietly on their plans and dreams, always hoping that a period of reform would come.

Couching some of their best ideas in the vague language of Aesop fables and leaving other ideas for another day, they never took the risks of dissidents. Some compromised themselves completely and, according to journalist Len Karpinsky, "lost their souls forever."

Gorbachev, who spent nearly a quarter-century as a party official in the provincial city of Stavropol, was one of the few party officials who were intellectually and morally receptive to ideas that contradicted the dogmas of Stalinism.

"Mikhail Sergeyevich did not just drop out of the sky. There are historical, intellectual reasons that he is who he is," says Oleg Bogomolov, a liberal economist who once worked in a reformist circle of advisers under future Soviet leader Yuri Andropov in the Central Committee apparatus in the 1960s.

"The current of reform never ran completely dry."

This is the the story of those years of double lives, and of the way Gorbachev pulled together his generation of reformers to provide himself with both an education and a supporting structure of reform intellectuals and politicians.

The world knows a great deal about the brave Soviet dissidents, prophetic figures such as Andrei Sakharov, who insisted on essential human rights and values in the 1960s and '70s despite the unimaginable pressures of the KGB and the party apparatus. Few others had the moral courage to put themselves, their jobs and their families at such risk.

"We all led double lives, not only scholars but a few progressive-minded politicians like Gorbachev. Except for Sakharov, maybe, there was not a single one among us who could say we never made a single compromise," says Tatyana Zaslavskaya, one of Agenbegyan's colleagues in Novosibirsk and now one of Gorbachev's favorite intellectuals.

The bitterness of such double lives, the need to advance and then retreat, forever holding a finger to the political wind, is evident not only in the published works of the intellectuals who surround Gorbachev, but in Gorbachev himself.

In May 1978, the year he was brought to Moscow by the Kremlin, it was easy to see the duality of the man.

That month, at an ideological conference in Stavropol, Gorbachev extolled Brezhnev's "talent for leadership of the Leninist type"—the supreme compliment. He even praised Brezhnev's torpid, ghost-written memoir, "The Little Land," as a work of "great philosophical penetration" and "spiritual and moral strength." The speech was a required act of subservience.

And yet that same May, Gorbachev wrote an astonishingly open report on agriculture for the Central Committee in Moscow. The report made its argument on economic rather than ideological grounds, proposing faster agricultural development, new pricing mechanisms, the return of peasants to their own land.

Those notions are now the basics of perestroika, or restructuring, but 12 years ago, when Gorbachev was summoned to Moscow to serve on the Central Committee, such ideas were close to heresy.

The crucial formative event for Gorbachev's generation was Khrushchev's denunciation of Joseph Stalin's "cult of personality" at the 20th Party Congress in 1956. "It was like a rocket across the sky," says Karpinsky, a columnist at the weekly Moscow News. Bogomolov says Khrushchev's speech was "the official start of perestroika."

In those first years of "The Thaw," as novelist Ilya Ehrenburg called it, Gorbachev's generation saw a world of possibilities. That sense of hope and breakthrough was captured in the literature of the time: Vladimir Voinovich's "I Want to be Honest," Alexander Solzhenitsyn's "One Day in the Life of Ivan Denisovich," Yevgeny Yevtushenko's "The Heirs of Stalin" and Vladimir Dudintsev's "Not by Bread Alone." The literary journal Novy Mir, under Alexander Tvardovsky, was the closest thing the country had to an opposition press.

But in the later years of Khrushchev's tenure, the climate hardened. And following the overthrow of Khrushchev in 1964, Brezhnev began an era of retrenchment. The currents of reform were forced underground. The dissident movement stirred.

For the rest, an era of double lives had begun.

Yuri Andropov, who one day would lead the country and groom Gorbachev as his successor, was the Central Committee secretary in the 1960s charged with relations with Communist-ruled countries. He was a careful man, steeped

in the orthodoxies of the time, but he was more intelligent than most of his colleagues in the Kremlin leadership.

In the early '60s he acquired a young circle of advisers, party intellectuals who were brighter and more progressive than the rest of the party apparatus on Staraya Square. Many of those young Andropov advisers are now key figures in the "perestroika army": political commentator Alexander Bovin, Foreign Ministry spokesman Gennadi Gerasimov, economist Oleg Bogomolov, journalist and legislator Fyodor Burlatsky, Central Committee adviser Nikolai Shishlin and Gorbachev's personal aide and adviser, Georgi Shakhnazarov.

"In the other offices there were just little Marxes and Engelses, only with less hair," says Bovin, now the main foreign policy voice of the government newspaper Izvestia. "Our group was a bunch of white crows, strange birds, in the Central Committee. I was just 33, a kid, walking around the halls of the Central Committee in my flannel shirt without a necktie."

Says Bogomolov, "Andropov is being idealized now. If he had lived, he probably would have changed things some, but he would not have touched the underlying structures of society. He was careful, conservative, maybe a bit like [Politburo member Yegor] Ligachev.

"But Andropov in the days we worked for him was distinguished from the rest. He spoke well and he had a flexible mind."

Andropov kept his distance from his more liberal young aides and never promoted them. When they crossed the street to a local cafeteria to gossip about Kremlin politics and argue policy, Andropov never joined them. But at the office he listened carefully to his young aides, and, through them, was connected firmly to the generation of Gorbachev.

Under Khrushchev, Andropov and his staff were capable of small victories. When Khrushchev had the notion in 1962 of creating a "super-international planning ministry" controlling economies throughout the socialist world, the Andropov circle saw it as just another layer of control and bureaucracy, a potential disaster. They managed to dissuade the leadership from including it in a major address.

The latter years of Khrushchev's rule were marked by inconsistency. At first, Andropov thought that Khrushchev's downfall might lead to a resumption of the thaw. "Now we are going to be more persistent in following the course of the 20th Party Congress," Andropov told his staff triumphantly, according to both Burlatsky and Bogomolov.

Just days after Khrushchev's downfall, Andropov and his staff began writing the domestic policy section of the leadership's traditional speech for the anniversary of the Bolshevik Revolution. Brezhnev would deliver the speech, but his ide-

PAGE 9

ology chief, Mikhail Suslov, known in Andropov's office as "The Gray Cardinal," had full power over its contents.

"When our draft came back from Suslov, everything about 'peaceful coexistence' and 'democratization' had been slashed," Bogomolov says. "It was a great leap backward, and we were crushed."

In the coming years, Andropov's circle fought other Kremlin factions over the rehabilitation of Stalin. "I think

159

we accomplished another small victory and kept it from becoming an open, full-blown rehabilitation," Bovin says.

Andropov tried to bring more liberal opinions to Brezhnev and even took steps to set up a meeting between Brezhnev and Sakharov, who was beginning to publish his dissident essays in 1967 and 1968. But Suslov and adviser Sergei Trapeznikov, the keepers of the neo-Stalinist orthodoxies, vetoed any such plans.

Although Andropov tried to subtly expand

Abel Agenbegyan

the limits of the possible, he also was content to retreat and play politics. Bovin recalls a night at Brezhnev's dacha in the Moscow suburb of Zavidovo when, after dinner and wine, Brezhnev, Andropov and a few others sang songs.

"Yuri, you sing so well, maybe you ought to be a soloist," Brezhnev said.

"No," Andropov answered, "I've always preferred to sing in the chorus."

That exchange, Bovin says, "reflected something more than just musical preferences."

A few days later, Bovin sat on a bench outside the Bolshoi Theater and read a copy of the party newspaper Pravda. To his horror he read the announcement: Andropov had been put in charge of the KGB. The young circle of advisers was shocked, and they saw Suslov's imprint. "Obviously they wanted Andropov moved over, because our tradition was that once you are KGB chief you can't go any higher," Bogomolov says. "Of course, it didn't quite work out that way."

The final blow for the small group of reformers in the Central Committee apparatus was the decision to invade Czechoslovakia in 1968. Bovin was one of the few aides to write a memo advising against intervention.

"We had even been preparing a Central Committee plenum at the time on—believe it or not— democratization. Not like what we are seeing today, but a step forward," Bovin says. "Then came the reforms in Czechoslovakia and everyone around Brezhnev

Oleg Bogomolov

started telling him, 'Look, Leonid Ilyich! Look at Czechoslovakia, is that the road we want to take? Uncontrolled freedom of the press? Everything, including the party, being criticized?' And so it all came tumbling down."

Bovin did not resign. "I had to go along. There was party discipline to observe," he says. "I thought about leaving but then I thought if I do, someone worse will just come and take my chair. If I could have explained my views to Pravda, then that might have made an impact, but that was not possible."

The decision hardly mattered. The "Andropov Circle" was shattered. The young aides went to institutes and newspapers, all waiting for another day.

A decade later Andropov, despite all his ugly work as KGB chairman, would contribute to reforms once more and bring Mikhail Gorbachev to Moscow.

Len Karpinsky was a Communist golden boy. His father, Vyacheslav, was a revolutionary and a friend of Lenin. The Karpinsky family lived in the most elite apartment building in Moscow, "the house on the embankment." Len went to privileged schools, ate the finest foods, summered at the best dachas. Some of Karpinsky's relatives disappeared in Stalin's purges but his Communist faith was restored and emboldened by Khrushchev's reforms.

By the early '60s, he was one of the national leaders of the Communist Party's youth branch, the Komsomol. He got to know powerful people such as KGB chief Vladimir Semichastny and men who would one day serve in Gorbachev's Politburo, including Alexander Yakovlev, Boris Pugo and Eduard Shevardnadze.

At one meeting, Suslov turned to the young star and said, "Keep up the good work. We have high hopes for you."

Karpinsky was drafted to write for Pravda––a job that transcended mere journalism in the party's eyes—and he aligned himself quickly with the paper's few liberal writers. In 1967, however, Karpinsky lost his job for writing for the youth paper Komsomolskaya Pravda an article that was ostensibly on theater but was really an attack on censorship and the cultural bureaucracy. That was a key moment for Karpinsky, who began to realize he could no longer guard himself, that he could no longer live in privileged privacy.

"Many people had become convinced that we were destined to live in this awful way for centuries, and they retreated into family life, their salaries and jobs that were somehow apart from politics," Karpinsky says. "I was among the people who thought that change was inevitable. The question was when.

"My friends and I, many of whom you see now in the legislature and the Moscow intelligentsia, had a dream that was both pragmatic and romantic. We could not create too much, but we did want to prepare certain intellectual currents and keep them alive."

Only a few heroic figures could abide by Solzhenitsyn's credo, "Live Not by Lies." Karpinsky's circle took a less exalted route but tried to maintain a part of their souls and minds, tried to speak the truth when they could. To go the "complete dissident route," Karpinsky says, meant living the life of a saint and putting yourself and your family, perhaps, at risk.

"I used vague language and paragraphs of orthodoxy and then tried to make certain progressive hints," he says, describing the balance of the "double life" in a "countersociety" of liberal intellectuals who did not join the dissidents. "I concluded that one could adapt to certain conditions and, at the same time, resist them."

Tatyana Zaslavskaya

Working now apart from the party and Pravda, Karpinsky became even more daring. He became what he calls "a half-dissident." Under the pseudonym "L. Okunev," he wrote in 1969 a manifesto,

"Wor ls Are Also Deeds," that anticipated the "inevitability" of *glasnost*—openness—and the intellectual revolution of perestroika a decade in advance.

Karpinsky's thesis was that Khrushchev had set in motion an "irreversible" attack on Stalinism and that the Brezhnev regime and its apparatus were engaged in a futile attempt to battle ideas, technology, democracy and "our future."

The dissident historian Roy Medvedev published Karpinsky's essay in his underground journal, Political Diary. During a KGB search of Medvedev's apartment, agents discovered the manuscript.

In 1975, Karpinsky, Suslov's golden boy, was expelled from the party. His ideas had been arrested. But only temporarily. Under Gorbachev, Karpinsky was readmitted to the party and made a prominent columnist at the liberal Moscow News.

About a half hour's drive from the industrial city of Novosibirsk is Akademgorodok, or Academic City, an ivory tower on the Siberian plains.

In the 1960s and '70s, when the Communist Party kept a tight grip on the major institutes in Moscow, Abel Agenbegyan, at age 33, assembled a team of young, liberal economists and sociologists to do in Siberia the work that could not be done in Moscow.

"We could work more easily there," Agenbegyan says. "We were a bunch of like-minded people and we had nothing else to do there but work. It was perfect." Zaslavskaya says

she left her job in Moscow for two reasons: In Siberia, she and her family got a larger apartment, and "finally I could stop writing books that did nothing but summarize the statistics in 12 other books. The intellectual freedom in Novosibirsk was like a miracle. I felt 10 years younger there."

Agenbegyan, Zaslavskaya and the Siberians were relatively protected from the compromises of Moscow politics. But they could not always express themselves the

Alexander Bovin

way they wished. And when they refused to do the Kremlin's hack work, they suffered. Both Zaslavskaya and Agenbegyan were called upon by Brezhnev's science secretary, Sergei Trapeznikov, to "update" his book on collectivization, which extolled a policy that had led to the starvation and death of millions.

"I refused and Tatyana begged off, saying she was ill," Agenbegyan recalls. "We switched off the telephone for a while after that, but they got their revenge. We received our reprimand."

The main goal of the economists in Siberia was to see the economy plain, to ignore the lies of the official statisticians and the orthodoxies of the ideologists, and to examine what worked and what did not. Like Gorbachev years later, they investigated periods of reform in Russian and Soviet history

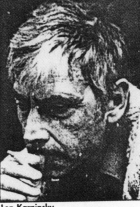

Len Karpinsky

for clues to the Soviet future. In their unpublished reports they toyed with heresies such as "the market" and "pluralist forms of property."

"Economic perestroika did not start on a completely fallow field," says Agenbegyan, adding that these reforms have their roots in Lenin's New Economic Policy of the early 1920s. "When the program actually started ideas began to crystallize and with time they grew more and more radical."

In 1983, with Andropov now general secretary, the world discovered Novosibirsk. Zaslavskaya and her colleagues held a seminar on the conflicting interests of classes and social groups in the economy. The "Novosibirsk Report," as it was known after it was leaked to the Western press, was essentially a sociological framework for what would one day be known as perestroika.

But the regional committee of the Communist Party condemned the group for "disclosing government documents." Two years later, Agenbegyan and Zaslavskaya would play a major role in the political education of the man who would lead the Second Russian Revolution. ∎

SOVIET UNION:
A CIVIL SOCIETY

by S. Frederick Starr

What better way is there to initiate a program of reforms than to persuade the public that life stagnated under a predecessor's policies? There is no better evidence of Soviet leader Mikhail Gorbachev's political prowess than the thoroughness with which he has accomplished this discrediting. In his view, the vitality of the post-Stalin thaw gave way to a period of turgid bureaucratism during which not only the Soviet government and economy but also the society at large succumbed to a profound malaise.

Successful political slogans must contain at least a grain of truth, and the notion of general stagnation under the late Soviet leader Leonid Brezhnev meets this test. Long before the economy went flat about 1978, the regime had become petrified and oligarchic, thereby repressing the very forces that might have stimulated economic renewal. Where Gorbachev is seriously wrong—and where many Americans err in accepting his view—is in his claim that the manifest stagnation in the Communist party and bureaucracy pervaded Soviet society as well.

Much of what happened in Soviet society under Brezhnev was bound to strike a provincial bureaucrat like the young Gorbachev as decadent, but this says as much about the mentality of officialdom as about the social dynamic itself. For while the official economy lagged, an entrepreneurial "second economy" burgeoned. In unprecedented numbers young Soviets became contributing participants in the global youth culture, forcing the government to accept what it could not alter. Individual citizens in countless fields plunged into innovative work, blithely ignoring official taboos and following wherever their interests led them. Torpor may have reigned in the official world, but Soviet society in Brezhnev's time experienced great ferment. To be sure, cor-

S. FREDERICK STARR *is president of Oberlin College and founding secretary of the Kennan Institute for Advanced Russian Studies at the Woodrow Wilson International Center for Scholars.*

26.

ruption abounded. But the rise of corruption must be laid directly to the regime's failure to open legitimate channels for the new energies rather than to some cancerous venality that had entered the body politic. Indeed, the social energies that were marginalized or suppressed under Brezhnev provide much of the impetus to today's economic and political reforms.

Gorbachev may be excused for playing down the dynamic element in Soviet sociey. To accept it he would be acknowledging that much of the initiative for change has shifted from the Communist party to society. Gorbachev then would appear not as the revolutionary leader calling a somnolent nation to action but as a conservative reformer trying to save a system facing pressures beyond his control.

Western analysts cannot so easily be excused for their narrow concern with Kremlin politics to the neglect of the social realities underlying them. To their credit, American researchers first identified the impact of alcoholism on the life expectancy of Russian men, as well as the demographic trends creating a labor shortage in European Russia and a baby boom in Soviet central Asia. But most have dismissed the broader changes occurring in Soviet society as not germane to explaining Moscow's actions to U.S. television viewers and members of Congress.

Gorbachev's June 1986 statement to Moscow writers that "Soviet society is ripe for change" exemplifies his sleight of hand and reveals the source of westerners' analytic errors. For Soviet society was already in the process of change; what is "ripe for change," but until recently unaffected by it, is the governmental apparatus. Economic stagnation, like its kin, corruption, occurred because the system failed to adjust to the emerging values of the populace, especially its best educated and technically most competent elements. Today Gorbachev is not creating change so much as uncorking it. The measure of his reform program is whether it adapts the party and government to the dynamic elements in Soviet society.

Fundamental shifts in Soviet society are going forward, and these increasingly define the national agenda. Since most recent analyses minimize this factor, a fuller review of the causes and character of the social transformations is in order.

27.

Among the causes, none is more fundamental than the rapid urbanization of the past 30 years. A rural society at Joseph Stalin's death in 1953, the Soviet Union today is only about 10 per cent less urban than the United States and about as urban as Italy. This change occurred in spite of official policy rather than because of it. Boldly defying severe residency laws and internal passport controls, peasants flooded into the cities.

This great migration marked the waning of peasant Russia and the passing of a controversial national archetype. Long-suffering Russian peasants are a fixture of both Russian and Western writing. For centuries they seemed to epitomize all that made their country different and distinctive—they bowed to authority, engaged in elemental and anarchistic rebellion, were natural communists in their village communes, and strove desperately to escape the extended family's despotic might. In the eyes of Slavophiles they were noble savages, and to westerners, a barrier to Russia's integration into the community of modern countries. Today, fewer than one in four Soviets is a peasant, and the number continues to plummet.

City air may not have made all rural migrants free, but it has emancipated their offspring. Sons and daughters of Russia's collectivized peasantry have plunged into urban life with a vengeance, pulling strings to get their children into the right schools, hustling for better apartments, and cutting deals for everything from seaside vacations to birth-control pills. In the process, the new urbanites have grown more independent than their forebears. Those who have gained access to the best goods and services can give credit as much to their own initiative as to the largess of the system. As their expectations rose they grew more critical. Dissatisfaction is more common in the city than in the poorer countryside and is greater in large and more affluent metropolises than in smaller centers, where the peasant mentality still holds sway. Responding to their new environment, Soviet urbanites assert their individual rights in the face of what officialdom sees as their collective duties. As this happens they cross, albeit unconsciously, the ideological fault line running in Western political theory between the writings of Thomas Hobbes, who stressed the

28.

164

individual's need for security, and those of John
Locke, who stressed the right to liberty.

Rapid economic development spurred this shift
in outlook. Notwithstanding its recent stagnation, the Soviet economy remains the world's second largest and has grown faster than the U.S.
economy through the postwar years. Millions of
new jobs have been created, many requiring great
expertise and sophistication. Important responsibilities have been entrusted to tens of thousands
of people far outside the narrow circles of party,
bureaucracy, and military that controlled national life in the Stalin era. No longer does the
Communist party enjoy the relative monopoly on
skills it had when the economy was smaller and
simpler. Today's professional elite is for the most
part staunchly loyal but far less beholden to the
party and state bureaucracy than was its Stalinist
predecessor. Brezhnev, by withholding from
technocrats and intellectuals the rewards he extended to labor, hastened the growing autonomy
of these elements.

Much of the initiative for change has shifted from the Communist party to society.

The Soviet Union still lags behind the United
States on many key educational indicators, but
progress in this area, too, has been significant.
Advances in education have fostered the individuation and sense of autonomy unleashed by urbanization and economic growth. In 1987, 245
million people, or 89 per cent of the Soviet population, had at least a 10th-grade education. The
comparable figure in 1939 was 10 per cent; in
1959 it was 32 per cent. As the number of those
able to read has expanded, so has the number of
those capable of reading between the lines. Millions are now acquiring and assessing critically
information that their grandparents would have
found utterly inaccessible, the object of fear or
awe. Not surprisingly, the rising levels of education have been accompanied by a proportionate
erosion of faith in the state's ability to organize
and micromanage such diverse functions as med-
icine, specialized manufacturing, and the provision of services.

Paradoxically, the recent economic slump has

29.

165

fostered the sense of individual autonomy that prosperity generated. As the sociologist Vladimir Shlapentokh showed in a 1986 study, applicants to Soviet universities now have less than one-half as good a chance of gaining admission as they did 20 years ago, and graduates have access to fewer positions in the ranks of bosses and managers. As the escalator of social mobility has slowed, especially at the upper floors, the young, educated, and ambitious increasingly have been thrown on their own resources.

The exercise of personal choice was once a privilege offered by urban life. Today it is a necessity. The State Planning Agency (Gosplan) may still bear formal responsibility for formulating comprehensive plans embracing all of the country's material and human resources, but in today's organizationally more complex environment it has lost the ability to carry out this task effectively. As a result, life decisions formerly made by the state—such as the selection of a career, employer, and place of residence—are either subject to personal influence or left fully to individual choice. The Soviet system of planning remains distinguished for its coerciveness and paternalism when compared with even the most socialized advanced industrial countries elsewhere. Compared with its own past, however, the Soviet system today devolves far more decisions to individual initiative.

All inhabitants of the peasant village knew where their neighbors were and what they were doing. But in the modern metropolis millions of urbanites rush about like unplottable electrons in an atom. Such circumstances have lowered the level of regimentation and surveillance the regime can expect to maintain. True, the Soviet Union remains a police state. Most of the laws and institutions created under Stalin are still in place. Now, however, the KGB has no choice but to focus its surveillance on a few individuals and groups. Many recent articles on criminality prove that police tactics often fail. That draft dodging could reach unprecedented proportions during the war in Afghanistan attests to the difficulty of operating a police state when the inhabitants are determined and resourceful in pursuing their own interests. The decline of fear as an instrument of control is both a cause and an effect of this situation.

30.

166

Some future revisionist historian will remind the world how much Brezhnev and former Prime Minister Aleksei Kosygin did to reward the laboring men and women of the USSR. Whether from a sense of social justice or from concern that Soviet workers might follow the example of their Polish counterparts, they increased salaries steadily throughout their term in office. However, they failed to bring about commensurate growth in the supply of consumer goods, with the result that individual Soviet citizens had no choice but to salt away billions in savings accounts. Although total savings in 1960 equaled only 50 rubles for each Soviet citizen, by the 1980s this figure had risen to more than 600 rubles, equal to nearly three-fourths of the country's entire annual outlay for salaries.

This development, too, has advanced the process of individuation. For half a century Soviet workers were encouraged to identify with the progress of a command economy in which the state was the sole producer. Now workers with bank accounts of unspendable rubles have a personal stake in prodding the economy toward responding to their own demands as consumers. Of course, the government would be foolish to alienate the owners of so significant a source of investment capital.

When the regime has failed to produce desired goods and services, citizens have not hesitated to create them. Thus enters the twilight second economy, which is estimated to account for one-seventh of the USSR's nonagricultural output. Whether semilegal or fully underground, this privatized economy has come of age. Pioneered by young people 30 years ago, it now touches every segment of the population. Hence when Gorbachev talks of expanding the small private sector he really means extending legal legitimacy—and taxability—to areas of the gray or black markets. After all, as a former general administrator, he scarcely can be ignorant of the fact that industrial firms and communes throughout the Soviet provinces rely on the services of semilegal *sabashniki*, free-lance teams of builders and laborers who outperform their official counterparts in spite of bureaucratic harassment.

During the Brezhnev regime Soviet society moved steadily in the direction of individuation, decentralization of initiative, and privatization. A

31.

virtual revolution in personal communications in that supposedly stagnant era dramatically strengthened these processes of change. V. I. Lenin and Stalin both labored to establish "top-down" vertical systems of communication. They nationalized and imposed strict political controls over such technologies as radio, film, sound recording, and modern postal services. More important, they limited or suppressed such horizontal technologies as the private telephone and the intercity telegraph. Their successors did the same with xerographic machines and desk-top computers. In the 1970s the USSR was the only country moving toward advanced industrialization that successfully braked the spread of private automobiles. All forms of international communication—radio, travel, mail, and telephone— were restricted or muzzled. As a result, society was left unable to communicate with itself. It was atomized and, in theory at least, rendered passive.

Extensive controls on the dissemination of information remain in effect today, yet millions of Soviet citizens routinely evade them. Over many years they have been astonishingly resourceful in their efforts to gain access to whatever information they desire. In the process they have taken advantage of such officially sanctioned major technologies as intercity telephones, whose number has increased rapidly but which are still in short supply. Equally important, they have skillfully exploited such seemingly innocuous "small technologies" as the cassette-tape recorder, the personal camera, the videocassette recorder (VCR), and the ham radio. In each case the state tried to suppress or strictly curb access to the new information technology. Outwitted by the public, it then sought a face-saving avenue of retreat. In the 1960s it had to reckon with a wave of illegally imported cassette-tape recorders that transformed their owners into publishers. The state then fell back on producing and selling its own. In the 1980s the process was repeated with imported VCRs. Eventually the Soviet government began producing its own VCRs in the hope that it at least could influence the use of a technology it no longer could prohibit.

By such steps the Soviet state lost its monopoly on information. A privatized system embracing large segments of the population now exists alongside the controlled official system of com-

32.

munications. What one Soviet writer, Vladimir Simonov, called "technotronic *glasnost*" was a fact long before Gorbachev took up the latter word for his own purposes. Thanks to this *glasnost*, or "openness," instituted by the public itself, members of Soviet society have gained the ability to communicate with one another and, increasingly, with the outside world. With or without official *glasnost*, few events in the USSR or abroad long escape notice. Even the darkest corners of Soviet history eventually will be illuminated by the more resourceful members of society, whatever the party and state may desire.

Improved communications have made possible a degree of "networking" among Soviet citizens that would have been inconceivable a generation ago. Controls over the freedom of assembly are still in place and enforced sometimes with extreme severity. Yet persons with common interests throughout the Soviet Union can readily locate one another and enter into communication by means of the legal and semilegal technologies available to them. Whether model-airplane enthusiasts, rock music fans, Hare Krishnas, Afghanistan war veterans, or ecologists, interest groups of like-minded people form with relative ease and establish regular channels of communication among their devotees.

By the early 1980s the initiative for ideas had shifted from state to society in a process of de facto democratization.

What began in the 1950s with networks of underground jazz fans spread in the 1970s to the sphere of public affairs. The Communist party newspaper *Pravda* acknowledges the existence of more than 30,000 *neformaly*, grass-roots voluntary associations dedicated to various types of civic improvement. What Western political scientists call "interest group articulation" reached a record high in August 1987, when a conference of some 600 politically oriented clubs and associations—in this case, all nominally socialist in their program—convened in Moscow under the aegis of the city's party boss at the time, Boris Yeltsin.

The existence of such entities testifies to the ability of the Soviet people to generate ideas in-

33.

dependently on virtually any topic and to air
them broadly. It also confirms that the state's
powers to form and inculcate social values from
above are strictly limited. This sea change took
place in the arts more than a generation ago and
in recent years has occurred in many other areas
of endeavor. Although manifestations of official
ideology remain ubiquitous, by the early 1980s
the initiative for ideas had shifted from state to
society in a process of de facto democratization.
In the sphere of ideology, this democratization
has been accompanied by a de facto seculariza-
tion, in which revolutionary myths retain their
status and even some of their evocative power but
have yielded much of their day-to-day relevance
to that yeasty body of ideas being generated by,
and circulated among, the public at large.

The void left by a waning ideology is filled by
an ever more assertive and potent public opinion.
The growing importance of public opinion can be
gauged by the progress of efforts to measure it.
Tentative contact with American public-opinion
research firms was made as early as the 1960s.
The legitimation of sociology as a field of research was achieved in the 1970s, by which time
Soviet newspapers and official organs had begun
analyzing public opinion to seek feedback.

The ability of Soviet public opinion to influence decision making is exemplified in the field of
ecology. The conquest of nature has been a sacred ideal of Russian communism since before
the revolution. Yet when government agencies
proposed over the past decade to divert water
from Siberian rivers to water the arid steppes of
central Asia, aroused public opinion succeeded
in killing the project. In 1987 a water-control
scheme for the Kamchatka Peninsula was
thwarted in the planning stage by local activists,
many of them blue-collar workers.

As public opinion gained in strength it grew in
diversity. The public's increased facility at networking has brought to the fore a bewildering
range of views on virtually every issue of the day.
That some virulent forms of Russian nationalism,
extreme by any standard, are among them is not
surprising, since the USSR lacks the regularized
public forums at which advocates of maximalist
positions might moderate them through inter-
change with people representing other views. But
even the most extreme manifestations of public

34.

170

opinion are important because they attest to the living diversity and pluralism beneath the surface of the "unbreakable unity of Party and people" today in the USSR.

Becoming a "Civil Society"

These, then, are some of the fundamental changes that took place during the otherwise stagnant Brezhnev era. Together they constitute part of the social reality that the Gorbachev administration will ignore only at its peril.

Clearly the new tendencies in Soviet life will soften many features of the social system forged by Lenin and Stalin. The old society's tendency was for everything outside the party and state apparatus to be turned into an amorphous mass, the whole country becoming "as if déclassé," in the words of the historian Moshe Lewin.[1] The emerging society, by contrast, includes large numbers of autonomous and assertive personalities among both the rulers and the ruled. The sense of duty that the late anthropologist Margaret Mead found so characteristic of the Soviet public under Stalin is being balanced by millions of individuals actively trying to affirm their rights under law. People who formerly viewed themselves as subjects are taking on the mentality of citizens.

Gorbachev has declared his goal to be the democratization of society. But Soviet society already has moved far in this direction thanks to developments fostered or tolerated by his predecessors. The key question is whether the party and state will follow suit. To the extent they do, the Soviet Union will move toward becoming a radically different type of society than it has been for 70 years—namely, a "civil society."

This concept has a rich history in Western political thought, most notably in the writings of Locke, Alexis de Tocqueville, and John Stuart Mill. It is grounded in ideals of citizenship under law; in freedom of speech, of the press, of assembly, and of worship; and in the protection of minority rights under majority rule. Above all, it holds that society is distinct from government and that government is but one of several institutions coexisting in a pluralistic social fabric.

So greatly do these ideals differ from the cur-

---

[1]*Moshe Lewin*, The Making of the Soviet System *(New York: Pantheon, 1985)*, 265.

35.

171

rent situation in the Soviet Union that it might be tempting to dismiss as utopian all talk of civil society there. The Communist party still exercises a degree of control over the citizenry that is antithetical to notions of civil society. Whatever melioration has taken place in recent years has occurred de facto and not de jure.

It might also be objected that the very idea of civil society is too narrowly Western in origin to be applied appropriately beyond Western Europe and North America. Clearly civil society in the Soviet Union will be shaped by Russian traditions, just as those in Great Britain and France bear the very different mark of their national heritages. Starkly different structures, however, can fulfill similar functions. To acknowledge the differentness of Russia's political heritage does not disqualify it from experiencing evolutionary change. For someone in 16th-century England, 18th-century France, or 19th-century Japan to have claimed that those countries would someday become civil societies would have seemed no less outrageous than for someone to make a similar claim today for the USSR.

Russians themselves have drawn attention to the signs of a national shift toward a civil society. Writing in the twilight of the Brezhnev era, the late dissident author Yevgeny Gnedin observed, at the very time the party and state apparatus were growing more sclerotic, that

> society gradually comes to life and grows pluralistic. One can observe the beginnings of a not-yet-mature political pluralism . . . a diversity of outlooks. This ferment in society, proceeding without *glasnost*, does not mean that there is no philistine inertia, no inertia of obedience to the powers-that-be. Yet, this intellectual and spiritual diversity . . . is the sign of a search for a way out of the labyrinth.[2]

Many recent statements by one of Gorbachev's advisers, the sociologist Tatiana Zaslavskaya, and by the influential publicist and political scientist Fyodor Burlatsky, more fully develop these same ideas. The latter has declared that "not so long ago we were afraid of [pluralism]. It seemed to us that it had an exclusively bourgeois flavor. But the development of pluralism in our country is a real fact. Glasnost itself . . . is a manifestation of pluralism."

---

[2]*Yevgeny Gnedin*, Vykhod iz labirinta *(New York: Chalidze, 1982), 117.*

36.

172

Arguably the most astonishing utterance from any member of Gorbachev's inner circle was Aleksandr Yakovlev's declaration last year, that the Soviet Union "should operate more by the common law principle that everything not explicitly forbidden by law is permitted." As if acting on the general secretary's advice, Soviet courts in the first half of 1987 sent back more cases for further investigation, handed down more acquittals, and threw out more suits than in any previous 6-month period in Soviet history. Such words and deeds would seem to reflect an understanding of civil society at the highest levels in the Kremlin.

Yet the suspicion remains that Gorbachev's démarche toward the new social realities is merely a tactic. What will happen when *glasnost* is directed not against the Brezhnev legacy but against Gorbachev's own record? How quickly will his administration pull back when the extension of openness to non-Russian peoples in the Soviet Union unleashes centrifugal forces incompatible with Great Russian pretensions? And how sharply will Gorbachev shift directions when the cycle of reform is played out, as must inevitably happen?

Such questions are intriguing but premature. Most of the announced reforms, particularly in the crucial area of law, are still being prepared. Until the first drafts emerge it will be impossible to determine how much substantive wheat is mixed with the rhetorical chaff. But there are serious grounds for doubting that legislation embodying principles of a civil society will get very far. First, Gorbachev has declared his commitment to maintaining all the inherited prerogatives of the Communist party. Second, he fully shares the traditional Marxist opposition to private property. Indeed, his limited acceptance of a private sector seems designed more to co-opt the unruly second economy than to affirm the right to property that Locke posited as the basis of citizenship in a civil society.

Third, and most important, Gorbachev's highest priority is not to introduce liberal reforms but to revive the bedraggled Soviet economy. That administrative decentralization and sharp staff cutbacks in planning organs spell disaster for thousands of bureaucrats is well known. Less often noted is the way the economic reforms might

37.

173

hurt the interests of labor. To put it bluntly, Gorbachev's economic program contains many facets that, if crudely imposed on the Soviet public, would sour the atmosphere for reform in other areas. How, after all, is a Soviet worker to view proposals calling for deregulation, the suspension of wage and price controls, the expansion of the powers of local managers, compulsory job reassignments for millions of blue-collar laborers, and the stretching out of salary scales for the purpose of rewarding diligence and punishing sloth? The economy may desperately need such measures, but to the Soviet worker they can only appear as a speedup.

Any other reforms put forward when such controversial measures are being implemented will be tarred with an antilabor brush. If the economy fails to respond to Gorbachev's stimuli—and 1987's results give little reason for optimism—then many common Russians will pine for the good old days when labor was not punished for the country's economic malaise. That serious problems with poverty and unemployment in the USSR are only waiting to be discovered by the public simply adds to the risks. It will be all too easy to draw the conclusion that the inevitable price of political freedom and civil rights is an unacceptable level of economic inequality. If embittered bureaucrats forge ties with alienated labor, the reform program will face formidable opposition that will test Gorbachev's powers as a political broker.

Reviewing such arguments, some Western observers have begun penning Gorbachev's political obituary and have written off the prospects for basic change in the civic sphere. In rushing to the latter conclusion, if not the former as well, they reveal the analytic bias discussed earlier. Such factors as the erosion of planning, the progress of decentralization, the spread of privatization in the service sector, the information revolution leading to openness, and the overall individuation of society—what Gorbachev calls the "human factor"—all call for a different perspective, one emphasizing change from below rather than from above. At issue is not whether such fundamental developments will be erased or thwarted, but when, to what degree, and by what political processes the ruling party and government will make their peace with them.

38.

It might be argued that it is not too late for these changes to be reversed and for the political superstructure thereby to escape their effects. This scenario is possible, but its cost rises daily. Citizens in a civil society are less malleable and less subject to manipulation by the state than subjects under an authoritarian regime. And as society becomes less malleable, society and the state grow more interdependent, each gaining the power to limit and influence the other. Since the state has long wielded broad power over Soviet society, the focus of change today is for society to gain reciprocal powers over the Soviet state—that is, to reach a condition in which "every branch of [the] civil policy supports and is supported, regulates and is regulated, by the rest," as the 18th-century English jurist Sir William Blackstone wrote in his *Commentaries*. In July 1986 Gorbachev himself decried those "who try to put the Party and society at loggerheads." If he is to avoid this, Gorbachev must take steps to accommodate the system to the new social reality.

The thesis presented here holds that profound changes have taken place in Soviet society and that these changes eventually will exert an influence upon both the traditional institutions of government and what George Kennan, in his "Mr. X" article in *Foreign Affairs* in July 1947, called "the mental world of the Soviet leaders." Only time will tell how deeply these new conditions will alter the political superstructure. But to the extent that Soviet leaders resonate to the new social forces, they are bound to behave differently from their predecessors in the international arena, particularly in the U.S.-Soviet relationship.

This is not to suggest that a complete transformation looms on the horizon. Just as certain continuities persisted from czarism to communism, some features from the eras of Lenin and Stalin undoubtedly will carry over into future U.S.-Soviet dealings, especially after the current "breathing spell" has passed. Indeed, as Gorbachev has noted, the tactic of a breathing spell is itself an inheritance from Lenin's thought.

Soviet leaders will continue to view their country as a superpower and to claim the prerogatives of that status. As other major powers emerge, the price tag for maintaining this lofty self-image will rise. Yet the Soviet government will surely continue to assert itself globally in behalf of friendly

39.

175

governments. Gorbachev's stated desire to turn inward has nothing to do with the rise of civil society as such. Many of the last century's great colonial powers were among the most developed civil societies of their time.

Gorbachev frequently has asserted his belief in the priority of domestic over foreign affairs. This may be a convenient way to present the rival claims of guns and butter, but it oversimplifies the nature of foreign policy under civil societies. The academician Yevgeny Primakov's reference to the "organic link" between domestic and foreign affairs, cited in the July 9, 1987, issue of *Pravda*, states the relationship more accurately. He might have added that, as Karl Marx predicted of bourgeois states, the relevant domestic issues are the country's economic interests.

To succeed politically within the new social context, the Kremlin's foreign policy must be seen by the Soviet public as serving its interests and not just those of the Communist party. Foreign-policy initiatives must pass muster with domestic public opinion, including the opinions held by both the cosmopolitan and the more chauvinistic sectors of society. And while Kremlin leaders will feel the impact of public opinion on their foreign policy, they will have fewer ways of influencing such opinion than in the past.

At the negotiating table, therefore, Soviet leaders will have less freedom of action than before. Kennan also observed in his Mr. X article, written in Stalin's day, that the Kremlin's diplomats are "under the compulsion of no timetable." The activation of civil society already has begun to change this situation, as Gorbachev's impatience for progress in arms control talks over the last year and a half demonstrates. Short-term diplomatic triumphs and defeats gain more meaning in civil societies than in closely controlled societies. Soviet negotiators in the era of the strategic arms limitation talks expressed frustration over what they considered the mercurial nature of American politics. As they are compelled to become more closely attuned to their domestic pulsebeat, Soviet policymakers probably will also be less relentlessly consistent in their actions, more preoccupied with tactics, and thereby more concerned with the art of the poker player than that of the chess master.

At various times both America's hard-liners

40.

176

and its soft-liners have found it convenient to argue that the United States can exert little influence on Soviet international behavior. However, America's impact on Soviet life will grow with the emergence of civil society there, since the decline of the USSR's economic autarky is accompanied by the waning of its cultural and psychological autarky as well. Americans—both elected leaders and the public—will be able to appeal directly to Soviet public opinion, just as Soviet leaders have done so frequently in the United States. The element of uncertainty in the U.S.-Soviet relationship will therefore expand and place a premium on the ability to manage tensions as they arise.

These potentially destabilizing factors will be offset to the extent that Soviet leaders, compelled to respond to their own domestic constituency, are better able to appreciate the constraints under which their American counterparts labor. Approaching America with the benefit of their mounting acquaintance with civil society, Soviet leaders will be less inclined to seek the sources of American behavior in the machinations of Wall Street and more disposed to appreciate the presence in modern societies of what de Tocqueville called "a kind of intellectual atmosphere in which both governed and governors exist and from which they draw the principles of their conduct."[3] During the Stalin era Western diplomats often noted with dismay that Soviet leaders understood long-accepted concepts of international relations quite differently from Western leaders, thus impeding communications at the most basic level. To the extent that the USSR evolves in the direction of a civil society, words may regain some of their common meanings. This in itself does not guarantee U.S.-Soviet accord, but it is essential for maintaining purposeful dialogue between the two governments.

---

[3]*Alexis de Tocqueville*, Oeuvres complètes *(Paris, 1864–66), vol. 9, 123.*

41.

4

State and Society:
Toward the Emergence
of Civil Society in the Soviet Union

Gail W. Lapidus

There is a difference between reform and quasi-reform. If quasi-reform is a reorganization at the top, purely a reorganization of the apparatus, reform is a more serious matter. Reform vitally changes the organizational relationships between the state apparatus and members of the society, collectively and individually, and this is what its main substance lies in.[1]

—B. P. Kurashvili

Western analyses of the contemporary Soviet scene frequently portray Mikhail Gorbachev as but the latest in a long line of reforming tsar-autocrats, from Peter the Great to Iosif Stalin, who have sought to impose radical and coercive programs of modernization on a passive, backward, and recalcitrant society. Although this analogy is not entirely off the mark, it fails to capture the extent to which the process of reform now under way in the Soviet Union is also a long-delayed response by the leadership to fundamental social changes that are altering the relationship of state and society. The current attempt at reform is only in part a renewed effort at mobilization from above; this process of reform is also a far-reaching and highly controversial effort to adapt a set of anachronistic economic and political arrangements to the needs of an increasingly complex modern society.

The Roots of Gorbachev's Reforms

Gorbachev's initial reform strategy was animated by the need for serious and comprehensive economic reform to arrest the deterioration of Soviet economic performance that jeopardized both domestic stability

121

and international power. But Gorbachev and his associates increasingly came to recognize that economic stagnation had its roots in deeper social and political problems and that far-reaching changes were necessary if these problems were to be successfully addressed. Gorbachev's sweeping attack, made at the January 1987 Plenum of the Communist Party's Central Committee, on the cumulative effects of economic stagnation, social corrosion, political conservatism and inertia, the spread of apathy and cynicism, and the absence of legal and political accountability (an analysis remarkably similar to that of many Western Sovietologists in the late 1970s and early 1980s) demonstrated a clear recognition that sociopolitical change was a prerequisite for successful economic reform. His remarks expressed a realization that in the environment of the 1980s the "human factor" had become decisive.[2]

This growing recognition of the social sources of stagnation was in turn reflected in the evolution of Gorbachev's conception of *perestroika* (restructuring). From a narrower focus on economic acceleration it expanded to encompass, in Gorbachev's words, "not only the economy but all other sides of social life: social relations, the political system, the spiritual and ideological sphere, the style and work methods of the Party and of all our cadres. Restructuring is a capacious word. I would equate restructuring with revolution . . . a genuine revolution in the minds and hearts of people."[3]

To accomplish this revolution, in Gorbachev's view, it is essential to stimulate the initiative and the creativity of the Soviet population by attacking the institutions and social norms that have long stifled it. As Nikita Khrushchev had done some thirty years earlier, Gorbachev has sought to mobilize popular support to carry out structural and policy changes, to curb the powers of officialdom, and to bring abuses of power under public scrutiny. But the novelty and significance of Gorbachev's strategy lie in its realization that Soviet society has reached a level of maturity that requires a new approach to its governance; and that the Soviet people, and above all the educated middle classes, can no longer be treated as the objects of official policy but must be treated as genuine subjects.

Khrushchev had launched this process of inclusion—a shift, however erratic, from the centralized, coercive statism of the Stalinist system to a more conciliatory and flexible approach to social forces.[4] Gorbachev has sought to extend the process of inclusion further. By contrast with Khrushchev's focus on the working class and peasantry, Gorbachev's strategy aims at incorporating the new social strata and values that are a product of the Soviet scientific-technological revolution as well as appealing to the skilled, the energetic and the creative in every walk of Soviet life. His efforts seek to overcome the alienation of key segments

of the Soviet population—from Andrei Sakharov to avant-garde writers
and artists, from the entrepreneurs of the unofficial "second economy"
to disaffected workers, peasants, and youth—and to enlist their talents
and energies in the revitalization of the Soviet system.

Gorbachev's reforms involve a redefinition of socialism itself in an
effort to tap the sources of vitality, dynamism, and innovation that have
increasingly developed outside the framework of official institutions. By
widening the boundaries of legitimate economic, social, political, and
cultural behavior, the reforms seek to draw back within these boundaries
individuals and activities that had deserted them or been excluded. In
short, Gorbachev's reforms are an effort to substitute "voice" for "exit"
in Soviet sociopolitical life.[5]

In broadening the boundaries of legitimate social activity, Gorbachev's
strategy draws on many of the ideas of leading Soviet intellectuals who
in the 1960s and 1970s were considered dissidents. Some twenty years
ago, three distinguished members of the Soviet intelligentsia—Andrei
Sakharov, Roy Medvedev, and Valery Turchin—addressed a letter to the
Soviet leadership appealing for a gradual democratization of the Soviet
system and outlining a series of measures for reform. Sakharov, Medvedev,
and Turchin compared the Soviet economy to an urban traffic intersection,
observing that when only a few cars were present, traffic police could
easily cope with their task, but when the stream of traffic increased,
fining the drivers and replacing the police no longer guaranteed a smooth
flow of traffic. "The only solution," these three intellectuals argued, "is
to widen the intersection. The obstacles hindering the development of
our economy lie outside it, in the social and political sphere, and all
measures that do not remove these obstacles are doomed to ineffec-
tiveness."[6] Gorbachev's policies not only echo many of these recom-
mendations; the policies stem from a similar understanding that economic
development and the growing maturity of Soviet society demand fundamentally new approaches to its management.

The thrust of Gorbachev's strategy is to alter the basic premise of
the Stalinist system from "all that is not permitted is prohibited" to
the principle that "all that is not prohibited is permitted."[7] But an
expansion of the public arena that broadens the scope of legitimate
activities and permits a greater degree of social self-regulation involves
a significant redefinition of the role of the Party-state. In political and
economic life as in culture, expansion of the public arena would diminish
the role of central controls and expand the role of market forces, offer
increased autonomy and resources as well as responsibility to a wide
range of organizations and individuals, and introduce a degree of "socialist
Darwinism" in promoting greater reliance on competition and self-
regulation rather than on state-sponsored protection. In short, this

181

expansion would give new impetus, and lend official support, to the emergence of an embryonic civil society.

But these changes confront Soviet reformers with an acute dilemma: the tension between the need to increase social initiative to revitalize the Soviet system and the fear that increased social autonomy will threaten central control. By simultaneously encouraging greater discipline as well as greater autonomy, and more effective central control as well as wider democratization, the current process of reform has set in motion contradictory pressures and opportunities in Soviet social life and policies, and contributes to major cleavages within the political elite.

In this exploration of the social dimensions of the process of reform, I will focus on three broad issues: the way in which broader changes in Soviet social structure and values made reform both urgent and possible; the new perspectives on Soviet society that inform the reformist program; and how societal reactions affect the prospects for a fundamental transformation of the Soviet system.

The Political Impact of Social Change

Seventy years after the victory of the Bolshevik Revolution, Mikhail Gorbachev asserts that the Soviet system stands at a crossroads, confronted by a set of choices that will determine whether the Soviet Union will enter the twenty-first century "in a manner worthy of a great power." That such an issue can even be raised is not only a measure of the gravity with which an important part of the Soviet leadership views the present situation; it also reflects a virtual revolution in consciousness within the Soviet elite. The growing conviction that domestic stability as well as international security was increasingly jeopardized by the economic stagnation, social corrosion, and political immobility of the Brezhnev era, and that only radical departures from the prevailing policies and norms would serve to avert further deterioration, reflects profound discord within the Soviet political establishment about the urgency of mounting problems, their causes, and the measures required to address them.

By the late 1970s, the erosion of confidence in the Soviet regime within the broader society, and in Leonid Brezhnev's political leadership within the broader elite, was apparent to Soviet citizens and foreign observers alike. This erosion was the product of two mutually reinforcing trends: an objective deterioration in the performance of the Soviet economy, which brought with it a mounting array of social and political problems, and a growing sense of demoralization within the Soviet elite, which reflected a shift in perceptions of regime performance.

The deteriorating performance of the Soviet economy was the key catalyst in the growing perception of failure, both in and of itself and because economic failure compounded other sociopolitical problems. But the economic slowdown and diminished international competitiveness might not have generated a sense of urgency had their presence not coincided with and contributed to a change in attitudes: an increasingly negative assessment of regime performance, which reflected a change in the criteria used to evaluate it; a growing sense of failure; and heightened pessimism about the future—in effect, a crisis of confidence within the Soviet elite. By the early 1980s, not only Western observers but key Soviet officials were in a fashion unprecedented since the early 1920s, beginning to speak of a "crisis" in order to convey the urgency of the situation.[8]

In this respect, the Soviet case resembles that of a number of authoritarian regimes that, beginning in the 1970s, underwent a series of transitions from authoritarian rule. The critical catalyst in many such cases was a deterioration of regime performance. This deterioration contributed to a loss of confidence within the ruling elite and to the development of major cleavages within it, often combined with the alienation of a growing segment of the population. In Latin America, Spain, Portugal, and Greece, authoritarian systems evolved (in however erratic and uncertain a fashion) in the direction of liberalization if not always democratization, redefining and extending the rights of individuals and groups and providing them increased protection from arbitrary state action. In the Soviet case, however, the totalitarian legacy of the Stalin era, as well as the weak development of liberalism and constitutionalism in the Russian political tradition, placed distinctive constraints on the potential for economic and political liberalization.[9] To what extent these can be overcome in the years ahead is the fundamental question of Soviet politics.

The inauguration of the process of reform in the USSR was in large measure a function of elite politics and cleavages, in which leadership succession served as a major catalyst. But the impetus for reform and the direction it is taking are a product not only of a deteriorating Soviet international position, but of fundamental changes in Soviet social structure and values in the post-Stalin period that altered the aspirations, resources, and behavior of key social groups. By undermining traditional forms of social control and motivation, these changes helped to de-legitimize traditional policies and political formulas, and to provide a rationale for fresh approaches.

The social and demographic changes from the mid-1950s to the mid-1980s transformed the passive and inarticulate peasant society of the era of Stalin into an urban industrial society with a highly differentiated social structure and an increasingly articulate and assertive middle class. The society over which Khrushchev ruled in the 1950s was still predominantly rural. By the mid-1980s, by contrast, two-thirds of the Soviet population lived in cities, and a growing percentage had been born in them. In 1959, only three Soviet cities had populations larger than 1 million; by 1985, that figure had reached twenty-two. Modernization was transforming the quality of urban life as well, while the spread of television brought urban lifestyles and values to the remotest corners of Soviet territory. When Khrushchev was dismissed in 1964, fewer than one in three Soviet families owned television sets. By 1988, television was almost universal and had not only brought a vast new universe of events and images into the Soviet household, but had rendered obsolete the system of agitation and propaganda through which the Party had for decades conveyed its message to the Soviet people.

Rapid urbanization was accompanied by a dramatic increase in the educational levels attained by the Soviet population. In 1959, two-thirds of the Soviet population over the age of ten had no more than a primary education; by 1986, almost two-thirds had completed secondary education. The combined effects of urbanization and rising levels of educational attainment transformed the Soviet working class from a relatively homogeneous body only recently drawn from the countryside to a differentiated one whose working-class membership was now increasingly becoming hereditary. Moreover, rising educational and skill levels among younger cohorts of the working class increasingly distinguished them from older generations of workers who were relegated to the ranks of the less skilled and enjoyed correspondingly lower status and pay. Younger workers also displayed a different set of orientations and values from their predecessors: a declining interest in work itself and a growing focus on family and leisure activities, including increased absorption in consumption, in the amenities made possible by the shift from communal and dormitory housing to private apartments, and by the greater range and availability of leisure activities.

Expanded educational opportunities have also sharply increased the percentage of the Soviet population with higher education. In 1959, only 5.5 million Soviet citizens had higher education; by 1986, the figure had reached 24 million. The growth in the number of "scientific workers" was particularly dramatic: from 1.5 million in 1950 to 15 million in 1986.[10] In short, not only was an increasing percentage of the Soviet working class becoming better educated; by the mid-1980s, a large urban middle class, including a substantial professional, scientific-technical and cultural intelligentsia with new cultural as well as material requirements, had emerged as a major actor on the Soviet scene.

This urban middle class, moreover, occupied an increasingly important place in both the membership and the leadership of the Communist Party itself. More than one-third of all urban males with higher education were Party members, and higher education had become the norm rather than the exception within the upper ranks of the Party, and even the Politburo itself.

The revival of Soviet sociology in the 1960s and 1970s brought the tools of social science to the study of these changes and of their likely impact on the aspirations, attitudes, and behavior of the Soviet population. Inhibited as they were by ideological and bureaucratic constraints, primitive methodological approaches, simplistic formulas about social reality, and the absence of adequate data, these sociological studies were nonetheless able to capture what was becoming a major source of social strain: the increasing tendency of the rising aspirations of the Soviet population for improved material well-being, upward social mobility, and occupational satisfaction and autonomy to outstrip the realistic possibilities for their fulfillment.[11]

For some, the demand for better and more varied food, consumer goods and services, and for higher quality education and health care, found outlets in the burgeoning second economy. For others, material dissatisfaction and frustration at limited opportunities for upward social mobility were expressed in low labor productivity, high turnover and absenteeism, rising alcoholism, and other social pathologies. The "double shift" of the female labor force, burdened by heavy household duties as well as full-time employment, took its own toll in declining birthrates. For others, disaffection took the form of emigration. Although tacit official acquiescence in these various forms of "exit" during the Brezhnev era afforded a safety valve, it offered no serious promise of future improvements.

A wide range of Soviet sources, from sociological studies to Soviet films and fiction, offered evidence that a significant shift in values was taking place in the Brezhnev era: growing pessimism about the Soviet future, increasing disillusionment with official values, and an accompanying decline in civic morale. The sources of alienation differed for different social groups and individuals, but their common thrust was a shift in the standards by which the regime's performance was evaluated. Traditional explanations of failure—the survival of capitalist remnants, growing pains, the aftermath of war, the machinations of unseen enemies—had lost their persuasiveness to a generation reared in the expectation that the Soviet Union was about to overtake the West and disillusioned by the chasm that separated myth from reality.

Indeed, it was precisely among the younger and best-educated segments of the Soviet population, including the inhabitants of its largest and most developed cities, that dissatisfaction appeared to be highest and the rejection of official norms most pronounced. This shift was a striking and new development, for these groups had traditionally provided the staunchest support for the Soviet system. By the 1980s, however, it was among young people and the better educated that new attitudes and values were taking root, and these included a more critical view of state control over economic life, greater openness to private economic activity, and greater commitment to personal freedom and individual rights.[12]

The evidence of alienation from official norms was not confined to the social science writings; it was equally apparent in Soviet cultural life. The most widely read novelists and poets and the most popular artists among the intelligentsia were not those favored by the Party and cultural establishment, but those who addressed universal moral concerns, such as the meaning of truth, the nature of good and evil, the significance of memory, and issues of national history and identity, both Russian and non-Russian. It was these themes that provoked intense discussions in Soviet literary and cultural journals and were an expression of the erosion of traditional ideological commitments and the search for new values and sources of meaning within the Soviet educated elite.

Other currents, less hospitable to tolerance or liberalization but equally alienated from the ethos of the Brezhnev era, also commanded some support in this urban milieu. One was a technocratic orientation that sought to solve current problems by applying new scientific and technological tools and managerial techniques and that saw the military economy as a possible model for emulation. Another was, if anything, antitechnological, identified with a romantic nationalism that found its symbolism in the Russian past and protested the ravages inflicted on nature and culture by the unbridled pursuit of industrialism and material progress. Even more extreme forms of nationalism and chauvinism—both Russian and non-Russian—flourished in the comparative laxity of the time, although they did not receive public expression until the era of *glasnost'*.

The spiritual alienation of important segments of the intelligentsia was further compounded by its growing exposure to the outside world. As Khrushchev's son-in-law Aleksei Adzhubei recalled recently, "When Khrushchev went to the exposition in Brussels in 1957, he decided that all the writers, managers, journalists, actors should visit the exhibit. When he visited the United States, representatives of all the professions went too."[13]

Détente extended this exposure. Scientists and scholars, students and professionals, writers and dancers and journalists took part in the expanding network of exchanges and came into contact with new ideas and approaches, alternative ways of looking at the world or of organizing professional life, and different standards of achievement. The desire for international recognition and status among professional peers, as well as the expansion of communication on issues of mutual interest, created a sense of community that transcended differing political and social systems and acknowledged that Western standards of excellence were of universal significance. Foreign radio broadcasts and letters from émigrés to friends and relatives in the USSR further pierced the Iron Curtain, bringing new sources of information about the outside world. Even in Soviet enterprises, the growing presence of Western technologies and machinery operating alongside domestic products encouraged direct comparisons with what the Soviets would later call "world standards of excellence."

These experiences provided new criteria for evaluating Soviet achievements and shortcomings. Judged by these standards, Soviet performance was increasingly found wanting, and earlier official explanations of failure were no longer convincing. Greater contact with the outside world thus contributed to the pessimism and demoralization of an influential scientific-technical and cultural intelligentsia resentful of, and frustrated by, an authoritarian, patronizing, and exclusionary pattern of political rule. This mood provided an important impetus for reform.

This transformation of Soviet attitudes had its counterpart in Soviet behavior as well. Growing alienation and a decline in civic morale contributed to a shift in expectations and energies from the public to the private realm and to the emergence of an intellectual and moral rationale for the increasing privatization of life. "Exit" became an increasingly important option for a small but significant segment of Soviet society, whether in the burgeoning "second economy"; in a blossoming popular culture; or in the emergence of a rich array of informal and unofficial groups pursuing a broad range of cultural as well as sociopolitical activities, from rock music to the preservation of historical monuments. These activities were facilitated by newly available technologies, from automobiles to videotape recorders, not readily amenable to governmental control. Ossified official norms and institutions were thus progressively supplanted by new forms of largely autonomous expression that responded to the preferences of consumers rather than officials. These trends were exemplified by the decline of the Komsomol, the official Soviet youth organization, along with the emergence of a rich and complex youth culture. But the most extreme and dramatic form of "exit" was undoubtedly the emigration of leading writers, artists, and cultural figures from the Soviet Union to escape a stifling cultural orthodoxy or political repression. This "exit" served to accelerate both the erosion of cultural vitality and the growing demoralization of those who remained behind.

What all these trends reflect is the government's decreasing ability to channel and shape the direction of social change. The very image of "revolution from above," with all its connotations of state domination of a passive society, no longer corresponds to a reality where social forces have achieved a degree of autonomy and indeed actively impinge on the political system in unprecedented ways. The erosion of political control of important sectors of Soviet life is abundantly illustrated by the evolution of the "second economy," the very existence of which epitomizes the subversion of centrally established priorities and challenges centralized control of prices, distribution of income, and the allocation of capital and labor. The spread of corruption, particularly within the political elite, threatens the organizational integrity and political legitimacy of the Party and feeds both the resentment of those excluded from patronage and the hostility of those who are critical of it.

A parallel development is visible in the escape of important dimensions of social behavior from official control. People marry, reproduce, and divorce without reference to official demographic policy; they migrate from north and east to south and west in defiance of planners' preferences; and their devotion to religious beliefs and practices resists all efforts to invigorate atheistic propaganda. A whole spectrum of social pathologies, from alcoholism and drug addiction to crime, exemplifies the limits of political control.

This entire trend has complex and contradictory implications, encompassing as it does a whole range of activities and behaviors with varying consequences. The enhanced space for autonomous social behavior allows for increased autonomy as well as corruption in Central Asia. It permits both historical preservationism and nationalistic xenophobia, Christian orthodoxy, and punk rock in Moscow. Its manifestations evoke an equally ambivalent reaction within the Soviet elite, where it is welcomed by some as an opportunity for greater social initiative and deplored by others as acquiescence in the weakening of discipline. The tension between these contradictory assessments was reflected in conflicting approaches to the process of reform itself.

Toward Socialist Pluralism:
The Social Strategy of the Reformers

Gorbachev's reform strategy involves a significantly new conception of socialism based on a novel set of assumptions about the nature of Soviet society and its relation to the political order. Although the translation of new approaches into policy remains embryonic and somewhat contradictory, support for socialist pluralism, political democratization, and legal reform reflect new ways of thinking about the Soviet system of rule and embrace a new model of socialism.

The point of departure of this new strategy is the view that Soviet development has created an increasingly differentiated, complex and modern society that remains largely unknown to the Soviet leadership and that it has been trying to govern by methods that are no longer appropriate. The "fictions" of the Stalin era have for too long been accepted as social reality, stereotypes have been a substitute for genuine social research, and unbending dogmatism has stood in the way of necessary policy reassessments. Even the tools required for effective policy-making remain inadequate and undeveloped because of Stalin's mutilation of the social sciences and the ideological and bureaucratic impediments to their revival. The primitive level of economics, not to mention sociology, demography, ethnography, psychology, and the study of public opinion, and the paucity of economic and social statistics have deprived not only policymakers but society as a whole of the self-knowledge that is a prerequisite to genuine progress. The first requirement, in the striking words of Alexander Yakovlev, is that "present-day socialism must become acquainted with itself."[14]

The changes under way in the ideological and cultural sphere and the renewal of selective de-Stalinization express a recognition that the delegitimation of key features of the Stalinist ethos—and above all its continuing legacy in the Soviet mindset—is a necessary first step in clearing the way for new approaches toward society. It has been essential to attack the equation of Stalinism with socialism and to portray Stalinism as a response to specific conditions at a particular historical moment rather than a universally valid approach to economic, social, or political dilemmas.

The renewal of public discussion of the crimes as well as the errors of the Stalin era and the presentation, in Gorbachev's speech on the occasion of the seventieth anniversary of the October Revolution, of a revised framework for the interpretation of Soviet history—one that emphasized those features of the Lenin and later periods that provide doctrinal support for *perestroika*—are an effort to gain enhanced freedom of action for new approaches.[15] The effort at delegitimization focuses on several features of the Stalinist legacy that constitute particular obstacles to sociopolitical reform: ideological dogmatism, lack of trust in Soviet society, the denial of social diversity, and an arbitrary and exclusionary pattern of centralized rule that violates fundamental norms of socialist democracy.

The delegitimation of these deeply entrenched features of Soviet ideology and practice has been accompanied by an attempt to encourage "new political thinking" in a number of areas of domestic as well as foreign policy. These new departures are obviously neither entirely novel nor completely unprecedented; in most cases they involve official endorsement of views and perspectives developed within the scholarly community and cultural intelligentsia during the Khrushchev and Brezhnev eras. In many cases these views had been sharply criticized and explicitly repudiated earlier, and their advocates treated as dissidents and expelled from their positions.[16]

Perhaps the most far-reaching feature of the reformist program is the shift from the notion of a "single truth" to a recognition of the legitimacy and indeed the necessity of divergent opinions. The entire Leninist conception of a vanguard party was premised on the need for Party tutelage over backward masses. Although the post-Stalin era was marked by a considerable broadening of the boundaries of permissible discussion on a wide range of issues, Gorbachev's call for "socialist pluralism," his insistence that open discussion was a prerequisite of scientific progress as well as of cultural vitality and should extend from technical to political issues, directly challenged the traditional claims of Party ideology.

The notion of socialist pluralism acknowledged the diversity of groups and interests as well as of ideas. The underlying assumption of socialist pluralism was clearly expressed in Gorbachev's address on the seventieth anniversary of the October Revolution when he declared: "We start from the fact that socialism is a society of growing diversity in opinions, relations, and activities of people."[17] This view of Soviet society also prompted Gorbachev's explicit call for a fundamental reassessment of socialist ideology. At the January 1987 Central Committee Plenum he criticized what he called the "schematic and dogmatic approach" to Party ideology that had prevailed in the past. He attacked the persistence of theoretical concepts that remained at the level of the 1930s and 1940s while the country's needs had fundamentally changed. He deplored the disappearance of vigorous debates and creative ideas and the absolutizing of particular authors and points of view that, Gorbachev implied, ought to have been treated as contingent and context dependent. Above all, he explicitly repudiated portrayals of Soviet social structure that denied the presence of contradictions and therefore of social dynamism, rather than presenting Soviet society as embodying diverse interests.

This view has been further elaborated and forcefully advocated by Politburo member Aleksander Yakovlev, the Party Secretary responsible for ideology. Yakovlev has repeatedly singled out dogmatism as the key obstacle to reform because "by its very nature [it] denies development." Dogmatic thinking, Yakovlev has argued, "is an inability or unwillingness to comprehend phenomena of the objective world in all their fullness and dynamism and in the contradictory nature of their development. It presents the surrounding world as an ossified formation, and science as a set of infallible 'truths' and propositions. . . . From this viewpoint, it is legitimate to describe dogmatism as authoritarian thinking elevated to a political, moral and intellectual principle."[18]

The call for socialist pluralism echoed a memorable article that had appeared in late 1986 in *Izvestiya* calling for greater debate and controversy on major issues of the day. "We must get used to the idea that a multiplicity of voices is a natural part of openness," its author had argued.

> We must treat diversity normally, as the natural state of the world; not with clenched teeth, as in the past, but normally as an immutable feature of social life. . . . We need in the economy and other areas of Soviet life a situation where multiple variants and alternative solutions are in and of themselves developmental tools and preconditions for obtaining optimal results, and where the coexistence of two opposing points of view on a single subject is most fruitful.

Reminding his audience of the high price paid in the past for intolerance toward other opinions, he concludes, "We must learn to live under democratic conditions."[19]

Official acquiescence in the necessity for, and indeed the desirability of, divergent opinions has not only widened the arena of public discussion; it has also served to legitimize the very notion of debates in Soviet public life. At a meeting with social scientists in spring 1987, Yakovlev proclaimed that "science can develop only in a process of constructive debates, in a clash of opinions. . . . We must realize that no one has a monopoly on truth, either in posing new questions or in providing answers."[20] Nor have words remained divorced from deeds. The most visible evidence of this new outlook was the dramatic transformation of the Party's theoretical journal, *Kommunist*, under the editorship of Ivan Frolov and then Nail Bikkenin, from a dreary and sterile custodian of ideological purity to a forum for lively debate on major policy issues.[21]

Formal debate has even found its way to Soviet television. Programs that present diametrically opposed positions on major issues of the day—including a debate about reform itself—and that conclude without an authoritative and final resolution of the issue are a novel departure from long-standing practices.

At the same time, the expression of multiple views is not unlimited in scope, nor does it enshrine full freedom of expression. As Gorbachev himself has affirmed, freedom extends only to those views that serve the cause of socialism. In practice, however, the limits of tolerance remain ill-defined and its boundaries fluid and hotly contested, as the controversy over the Nina Andreyeva letter in the spring of 1988 reaffirmed. But the effort to shed what some Soviets have labeled the "unanimity complex" in favor of socialist pluralism has far-reaching consequences for Soviet society and politics.

The endorsement of *glasnost'* (public disclosure), with its simultaneous connotation of both candor and publicity, constitutes a second major departure in regime-society relations. *Glasnost'* is, needless to say, a policy of preemption intended to reduce the reliance of the Soviet population on foreign and unofficial sources of information—from foreign television and radio broadcasts to gossip—to fill the voids created by Soviet silence. The Chernobyl experience gave enormous impetus to this effort. The fact that the Soviet people first learned of a major domestic catastrophe with far-reaching implications for their own health and welfare from foreign broadcasts, and that the news was initially denied by their own government, was a major political embarrassment. It dramatized as never before the high costs of traditional Soviet secretiveness, both domestically and internationally, and strengthened Gorbachev's determination to expand the flow of information and communication in order to enhance the credibility of the leadership among its citizens.[22]

Glasnost' is also a symbol of trust. It reflects a recognition by the Soviet leadership of the maturity of the Soviet population and a partial repudiation of the patronizing notion that only a small elite can be entrusted with truth. The call for greater openness in place of secrecy, for realism rather than varnishing, is thus a movement toward the normalization of Soviet public life and the potential emergence of a public sphere.

Glasnost' is equally an expression of confidence in the legitimacy of the Soviet system and its leadership, and a recognition that the pretense of infallibility is no longer necessary to command popular allegiance and support. Indeed, greater publicity for shortcomings and problems—whether the shoddy construction of nuclear power plants or the spread of drug addiction—is an indispensable precondition for successfully addressing them.

The case for *glasnost'* and its intimate connection to the prospects for reform was most eloquently put by Tat'yana Zaslavskaya, the reformist sociologist, who argued in a remarkable article in *Pravda*, "If we continue to keep from the people information about the conditions under which they live, say, the degree of environmental pollution, the number of industrial accidents, or the extent of crime, we cannot expect them to assume a more active role in economic or in political life. People will trust and support you only if you trust them."[23] *Glasnost'* is therefore indispensable for genuine feedback and for creating a mechanism for two-way communication between government and society.

Dramatic new departures in Soviet cultural policy—the most far-reaching and tangible of the changes thus far—are another expression of the new orientation toward inclusion and trust.[24] The publication of long-suppressed novels and poems and the screening of controversial films long kept from public view are not only a form of reconciliation with the intelligentsia but also an expression of a more tolerant and inclusive approach to Soviet culture, past and present. The reappraisal of the contributions of such writers and poets as Mikhail Bulgakov, Boris Pasternak, Marina Tsvetaeva, and Anna Akhmatova, once scorned for their deviation from "socialist realism," and the repudiation of measures taken against some of them, extends the boundaries of permissible literature to figures previously outside it. The process of reintegration even extends to selected figures in the emigration, which holds out the prospect of ultimately reuniting the "two streams" of Russian culture at home and abroad.

Finally and of potential significance for the future, *glasnost'* is linked to accountability. An expanded and more independent role for the media—including serious investigative reporting—is an important instrument for exposing abuses of power and position and for holding officials accountable for their actions. Needless to say, it also offers a convenient weapon for use against political opponents. It is nonetheless of great importance that *glasnost'* has extended, in however tentative a manner, to the first cautious exposés of abuses by the police and the KGB.

Even military and security affairs, traditionally forbidden territory, have begun to be opened, however tentatively, to public discussion and criticism. In a round-table discussion reported in *Literaturnaia gazeta*, a group of scientists questioned the conscription of university students, arguing "our society does not need soldiers more than it needs . . . physicists, biologists, engineers and social scientists."[25] The morality of nuclear weapons has been openly challenged in the Soviet press. A well-known Belorussian writer, Ales' Adamovich, for example, publicly argued that "for me there are no military men more courageous and worthy than those who . . . give their military expertise to the antiwar movement."[26] Even sensitive foreign and security policy issues—from Stalin's contribution to the rise of fascism, to the impact of SS-20 deployments in Europe, to the decision to intervene in Afghanistan, to the size of the Soviet military budget—have begun to be aired. Indeed, Soviet journalists and diplomats have complained publicly that excessive security hinders their work and have called on Soviet defense authorities to provide more information about the country's defense budget and military capabilities so journalists and diplomats will not have to rely exclusively on Western data.[27]

A further novel feature of the reformist program is its explicit recognition of the differentiation and complexity of Soviet society. The fiction of an essentially solidary society (consisting, in Stalinist orthodoxy, of two classes—workers and peasants—and one stratum, the intelligentsia) had already begun to dissolve in the post-Stalin era. But this fiction could not be directly challenged as long as Khrushchev's vision of communism, with its apotheosis of equality, homogeneity, and community, held sway.

With the revival of sociological research in the 1960s and 1970s, a more complex portrait of Soviet social structure began to emerge.[28] It was a portrait that recognized the evolution of a complex pattern of stratification in the Soviet Union; provided evidence of differences in earnings, status, and educational attainments among various social groups; and suggested that new forms of social differentiation might be structurally reproduced in a socialist society. The structure of power and its impact on social stratification remained a closed subject. Nor was it yet possible to acknowledge that different strata and groups might have fundamentally different social interests and that these interests might be a source of serious social antagonisms and conflict. The role of bureaucracy was equally off limits, as was any critical examination of Soviet ideology as an expression of special social interests.

The obstacles to a serious examination of these issues were illuminated by a major debate about the nature of social contradictions under socialism that erupted in the early 1980s. Prompted by the crisis in Poland and the anxieties it provoked about the potential for social instability in the Soviet Union itself, the debate engaged key philosophical journals, extended to the Party journal *Kommunist* and ultimately engaged General Secretary Yuri Andropov himself. A number of participants, most prominently Anatoliy Butenko, head of a sector in the Academy of Sciences Institute of the Economy of the World Socialist System, asserted that socialism did not automatically preclude the possibility of antagonistic contradictions and that they were not only possible but highly likely.[29] Butenko went on to argue that they were not merely the result of capitalist remnants but were generated by the development of socialism itself; that these contradictions represented not merely individual deviations but had a systemic character; and that they could be provoked by conflicting individual as well as group interests, such as a situation in which "managers" attempt to satisfy their own selfish interests at the expense of the "managed."

The proponents of this view were forced to retreat, and *Voprosy filosofii* (in an October 1984 editorial) was obliged to admit that serious ideological errors had been committed. But the Gorbachev era, with its new approach to Soviet society, has vindicated the Butenkos by giving explicit endorsement to precisely the views that were earlier criticized. Butenko himself, in a recent article in the same journal, pointedly criticized the erroneous understanding of socialism that had prevailed until Gorbachev's Political Report to the Twenty-seventh Party Congress. Butenko argued that the "theoretical dogmas, errors and prejudices that took root in the 1960s and 1970s" represented, in effect, an "ideological defense of extreme, bureaucratic centralism," which expressed the professional and social aspirations of the Soviet bureaucracy; he called for an expansion of self-government as an antidote.[30] In an interview, he asserted that Lenin's warnings of the dangers of bureaucratism and the need for public self-government had been ignored and replaced by Stalin's apotheosis of the state. Butenko concluded, "As long as a state exists whose functions are performed by special agencies and the people working in them, the possibility exists that they will become divorced from the masses and will act in their own selfish interests."[31]

The view that Soviet society encompasses diverse and potentially conflicting social interests, a view long held by Tat'yana Zaslavskaya, among others, and circulated in confidential memoranda and reports in the 1970s, has been not only legitimized but given prominence by its publication in *Kommunist*.[32] But the debate has since gone considerably further in focusing on the development of bureaucracy as the key to the emergence of the Stalinist system, and its defense of its ideological and political interests as the main obstacle to economic and political reform, thereby rekindling a debate that Leon Trotsky had launched more than a half century ago.[33]

This new approach to Soviet society is of enormous potential significance as a point of departure for the management of social and political affairs. By explicitly acknowledging the presence of conflicting interests (including bureaucratic interests), rather than obscuring and suppressing them, it not only takes another step toward the legitimation of diversity, it creates the necessary foundation for developing mechanisms for conflict management. It even acknowledges the need for some political expression of diverse views, although not of politically autonomous expression. In an unpublished talk with Soviet writers, Gorbachev himself reportedly acknowledged the need for a functional equivalent of a party opposition,[34] although other Soviet leaders clearly do not share this view. But the recognition of the need for greater political expression of social diversity provides a basis for reformers' efforts to revitalize the system of soviets, introduce competitive elections of officials, reduce the role of the Party, and, above all, of its apparatus in Soviet economic, social, and political life while sanctioning the emergence of a wide range of unofficial and nonparty organizations.

Indeed, the proliferation of informal groups and unofficial organizations concerned with a broad array of cultural, social and political issues is the most dramatic new departure on the Soviet political landscape. An officially sanctioned conference of unofficial groups in August 1987 brought together the representatives of some forty-seven such groups and generated proposals encompassing a variety of sociopolitical problems, like providing assistance to invalids and the aged, democratizing the Soviet electoral system, and building a monument to the victims of Stalinism—a proposal adopted a year later following the Nineteenth Party Conference. By 1988, the Soviet press reported that some 30,000 grassroots associations were in existence, provoking major debates about how they should be handled. By the time of the Party Conference in June 1988, a considerable number of unofficial groups and clubs had emerged with distinct political programs of their own, and some were engaged in organizing public demonstrations on environmental and political issues. Proposals were even under discussion to allow selected informal organizations to nominate candidates in local Soviet elections, posing a direct challenge to the existing *nomenklatura* system.[35]

The shift from an emphasis on social homogeneity to a recognition of social diversity and potential for social conflict, and the emergence of increasingly active unofficial organizations in defense of group interests, is especially apparent in the area of nationality problems. Khrushchev's assertion, at the Twenty-second Party Congress in 1961, that "the Party has solved one of the most complex of problems, which has plagued mankind for ages and remains acute in the world of capitalism to this day—the problem of relations between nations,"[36] marked the high tide of Soviet optimism about the achievements of Soviet nationality policy. In subsequent years the speeches of successive Soviet leaders took an increasingly sober tone. At the Twenty-sixth Party Congress in 1981 Brezhnev acknowledged that although the various nations of the Soviet Union were more united than ever before, "this does not imply that all the problems of the relations among nationalities have been resolved. The dynamics of the development of a large multinational state like ours gives rise to many problems requiring the Party's tactful attention."[37]

This sober reassessment was reaffirmed in even stronger terms by Yuri Andropov in December 1982. Using the occasion of the sixtieth anniversary of the creation of the Soviet multinational system to deliver a major address on the subject, he reminded his audience, "Soviet successes in solving the nationalities question certainly do not mean that all the problems engendered by the very fact of the life and work of numerous nations and nationalities in the framework of a single state have disappeared. This is hardly possible as long as nations exist, as long as there are national distinctions. And they will exist for a long time, much longer than class distinctions."[38]

A growing recognition by the Soviet leadership that successful management of national relations was critical to the stability of the system and demanded patient and delicate social engineering in turn generated increased encouragement and support for empirical social research on ethnic processes. Indeed, Andropov inadvertently testified to the previous shortcomings of such efforts when he called for the formulation of a "well-thought out, scientifically substantiated nationalities policy."[39]

The need for such a policy became painfully urgent following Gorbachev's accession to power. The new pressures and expectations generated by the reform process, as well as the new opportunities and diminished risks for expression of grievances that *glasnost'* appeared to sanction, brought to the surface long-simmering resentments among Russians and non-Russians alike that exploded with stunning force from Alma Ata to the Baltic to Armenia and Azerbaijan. While expressing the usual criticism of national chauvinism and narrow mindedness, Gorbachev's response also acknowledged past mistakes in nationality policy, criticized social scientists for excessively optimistic accounts of Soviet achievements, and explored new approaches for dealing with grievances.[40] Recognizing that national tensions could jeopardize his entire reform program, and ultimately his leadership as well, Gorbachev has called for a Central Committee plenum to be devoted to nationality policy. The seriousness of the issue was further underscored by the Nineteenth Party Conference, which devoted one of six final resolutions to inter-ethnic relations and called for the creation of new institutions to deal with nationality policy.

The central thrust of these emerging perspectives on national and social problems is a gradual retreat from utopia and a growing realization of the limits of social engineering. The Khrushchev era represented the height of the optimism and millenialism inspired by the Bolshevik Revolution and revived again during the era of the First Five-Year Plan. It again stimulated optimistic expectations about the future, the perfectibility of socialism, the malleability of human nature, the merging of nations, and the imminence of full communism.

That optimism has steadily receded in the post-Khrushchev era, and Gorbachev's accession dealt it a final blow.[41] The recognition that capitalism has by no means exhausted its potential—and that indeed the gap that Khrushchev so confidently expected to narrow has actually widened in the intervening period—involves a more sober assessment of international as well as domestic realities. The decision to remove from the Party program all concrete targets and explicit goals is a repudiation of a long tradition of exaggerated and unrealistic promises, just as the shift in terminology from "developed socialism" to "developing socialism" extends the time horizon for the achievement of full communism into a remote and indistinct future. Even discussions of the fate of the Soviet multinational system are more likely to emphasize the positive contribution of cultural and national diversity to Soviet life than the aspiration to create a homogeneous Soviet people.

This trend toward greater realism, and indeed outright pessimism, is accompanied by a growing realization that a wide range of social problems may well be structurally rooted in and reproduced under socialism. Where a wide variety of social pathologies—from chauvinism to corruption, from drug addiction and prostitution to crime—were once barely acknowledged and treated as "relics of the past," a phrase that implied a vast chasm would separate the socialist society of the future from its capitalist ancestry, current discussions of a wide range of social problems increasingly accept their universality in all social systems, explore why and how such behaviors are socially reproduced, and focus more on "managing" social problems than on "solving" them.

Moreover, recognizing the limited capacity and resources of the state to address a variety of social needs, and the rigidity and bureaucratization that central control entails, new thinking about social problems is directed to the potential role of voluntary associations and private initiatives in addressing them. Indeed, to the extent that *glasnost'* has focused public attention on a broad range of previously invisible and unacknowledged social problems—from unemployment to homelessness, from abandoned children to the absence of day-care centers for the aged—it has also opened the door to public discussion of how to address them. Terms like "altruism" and "charity" have reappeared in the Soviet lexicon. The campaign for democratization seeks to endow local Soviets with enhanced powers and resources that could permit new initiatives in social policy. The emergence of a wide variety of unofficial organizations creates additional frameworks for private initiatives in the name of compassion and charity. Even the Russian Orthodox Church has begun to press for the right to engage in volunteer activities such as nursing. In short, the reforms under way will both require and permit a pattern of provision for social welfare that joins public and private initiatives in novel ways.

All these trends have far-reaching implications for social science as well as for Soviet policy in the Gorbachev era. They involve the admission that Soviet social science is as yet incapable of contributing to a serious understanding of social reality or of helping to generate a suitable strategy for managing a process of reform, particularly one that demands a "civilized" rather than a forcible resolution of contradictions.

The deplorable state of the social sciences has been recognized at the highest level of the leadership. The Politburo itself met in May 1988 to discuss the need to develop serious social research and training, and a subsequent Central Committee decree spelled out a whole range of measures intended to promote serious research and training in sociology on a nationwide scale.[42]

It has become essential to the reform effort to have and to publish accurate economic and social statistics, as well as information about the needs, interests, values, and behavior of diverse social groups and the possible effects of their behavior on social processes.[43] With this objective in mind, a whole series of additional initiatives have been undertaken to give impetus to the development of the social sciences. Following a series of well-publicized criticisms of official economic and social statistics, the Central Statistical Administration was replaced by a new State Committee for Statistics, charged with "increasing the reliability of information, expanding the purview of *glasnost'*, and deepening the analysis of processes of economic and social development in the country."[44] New textbooks in social studies are being prepared and annual school examinations in history and social studies had to be cancelled in 1988. Political science as a discipline has made further strides toward institutionalization in the past few years, and its growing legitimation was symbolized by the creation, in the summer of 1988, of a new Center for Political Science Research.[45] Sociology has been given even greater prominence under Gorbachev. Not only will formal training and research be expanded in existing universities and institutes; two new institutes for sociological research have recently been established outside the framework of the Academy of Sciences. An All-Union Center for the Study of Public Opinion, under the leadership of Zaslavskaya herself, will conduct surveys designed to assist the leadership in assessing popular reactions to the reform program while the second will focus on socioeconomic aspects of *perestroika*.[46]

Ultimately, the capacity of the Soviet system to develop new mechanisms for the expression of social diversity and for the management of conflict will depend on the successful implementation of political and legal reforms. Political changes that would reduce the concentration of power in the hands of the central ministerial and Party apparatus, and movement toward establishment of the rule of law backed by a judiciary with some degree of independence, are essential to any effort to institutionalize the reform process and to provide some guarantee of its irreversibility. Both within the political leadership and among reform-minded scholars, specialists and journalists, serious attention is now being devoted to these issues; and the Nineteenth Party Conference provided some impetus to the process.[47] It is the fate of these efforts that will hold the key to the prospects of Gorbachev's reforms more broadly.

The Social Impact of the Reforms

For the first time since the October Revolution, Soviet society has emerged as a major, though not a unitary, actor on the Soviet political stage. Both its importance and its diversity have been impressed on the consciousness of the political leadership in unprecedented ways. Amorphous yet dynamic, it remains an uncertain weight on the scales of the Soviet future.

Clearly Gorbachev's reforms have been most warmly welcomed among segments of the intelligentsia. The most palpable result of these reforms has been in the cultural sphere, where they have given the cultural intelligentsia considerably enhanced autonomy and have enriched the cultural fare available to consumers of contemporary Soviet culture and the media. A dramatic rise of public interest in political affairs is perhaps the single most visible manifestation of the impact of *glasnost'* and *perestroika*. This is reflected in the soaring circulation of leading newspapers and journals during the past two years, especially those of reformist orientation.[48]

The new atmosphere has also created a degree of trust and perceived reciprocity between the intelligentsia and the regime that had heretofore been missing. Gorbachev's emphasis on the power of ideas and the call for "new thinking" in virtually every domain of Soviet life sets out an agenda that is unprecedentedly dependent on the inputs of specialists and professionals and is more responsive than in the past to their concerns as professionals. Their status and visibility have been correspondingly increased, as have their opportunities for travel abroad. Even within this group, support for the reforms is by no means universal; indeed, the intelligentsia provides leadership for antireformist currents as well. But insofar as we may take Andrei Sakharov as a bellwether of the once dissident, liberal intelligentsia, his supportive stance may be taken as an indication of the relative success of the Gorbachev regime in eliciting "voice" within this milieu.

The benefits of Gorbachev's reform program for other social and occupational groups have been far less apparent. Although the reforms hold out the long-term prospect of improvements in the supply and quality of consumer goods and services, in the short run it has raised expectations that are unlikely to be met. Indeed, the initial impact of the reforms on the economy has been sufficiently disruptive to output and wages to justify the widespread anxieties of Soviet workers. Moreover, discussion of the need for a price reform and the prospect of job insecurity threaten to jeopardize traditional and valued entitlements, whereas the promise of greater workplace democracy is unlikely to offset a real and feared decline in the standard of living. Decades of economic mythmaking have shaped popular expectations in ways that will be politically costly to undo. The simultaneous demand for low prices and abundant supplies of goods and services at those low prices is but one example of the dilemma. For the population at large even *glasnost'* must appear as a mixed blessing because the media no longer offer the comfortable assurance of success and certainty.

The process of reform is at least equally unsettling to important segments of Soviet officialdom and the many millions of state and Party bureaucrats whose role and status under the new arrangements are highly uncertain and whose power is apt to be sharply circumscribed. The widespread skepticism, anxiety, and resistance encountered even at this early stage of reform—and the relatively limited response to the new opportunities it offers for economic initiative—raise troublesome questions about how successfully the process of implementation will proceed.

Fundamental constraints on far-reaching liberalization are also imposed by the structure of the Soviet system itself. The monopoly of political power by the Party could well be maintained even with new electoral arrangements that require a greater degree of responsiveness to societal forces. Public ownership and the limited development of private property rights limits the resources that can be mobilized by independent social actors. These structural features of the Soviet system highlight the far greater obstacles to a transition from authoritarianism in the Soviet case compared to the situations prevailing in Latin America and Latin Europe.

Gorbachev's program confronts additional impediments that stem from the built-in tensions and contradictions of the reform process itself. The urgent need to overcome stagnation and social alienation by stimulating initiative conflicts with the fear of losing control. The acknowledged need for greater diversity of opinions is widely seen as threatening to the principles of socialism itself. Greater permissiveness and tolerance of various forms of social nonconformity and political protest leave unclear the boundaries of "anti-Soviet" behavior. Finally, while the reformers have come to view political democratization as a condition of economic reform, there are also obvious tensions between the two. Whether within the workplace or at a national level, a substantial expansion of political participation could well create greater constraints on the reform process.

Attitudinal constraints, deeply rooted in Soviet political culture, are a further inhibiting factor. Although neither pervasive nor unchangeable, the widespread attitude toward change appears to reflect an instinctive calculus that the danger of losses outweighs the hope of gains. Moreover, there are remnants of an anticommercial ethos long reinforced by Party ideology that inclines at least a part of the population to be suspicious of private entrepreneurship. There is also a deeply engrained tendency to equate egalitarianism with social justice, which serves as an obstacle to efforts to link rewards to performance.

What is especially striking in the Soviet case is the general poverty of sociopolitical thought, a poverty that extends even to the Soviet emigration. In the absence of more comprehensive sociopolitical programs that would offer viable alternatives to the status quo, vague sentiments that range from romantic nationalism to extreme chauvinism risk to fill the void.

A final set of constraints on potential liberalization is the depth of social and national cleavages. The chasm of mutual distrust between the Russian working class and intellilgentsia was mirrored even in the distance between the dissident intellectuals and the attempts at a free trade-union movement, although in some non-Russian republics, from the Baltic to Armenia, the force of nationalism provides precisely such a bond. Ironically but not surprisingly, the extension of *glasnost'* and "democratization" has brought national tensions and antagonisms to the surface. The Gorbachev leadership may well be persuaded that allowing the expression of grievances is a necessary first step in successfully addressing them; but new political and legal mechanisms for conflict management remain to be developed.

Notes

1. B. P. Kurashvili, in *Sovetskoe gosudarstvo i pravo*, no. 10 (1983).

2. *Pravda*, January 31, 1987. Gorbachev's remarks virtually echo the diagnoses of Soviet political, economic, and social problems in the chapters by Seweryn Bialer, Robert Campbell, and Gail Lapidus in Robert Byrnes, ed., *After Brezhnev: The Sources of Soviet Conduct in the 1980s* (Bloomington: Indiana University Press, 1983). Gorbachev's views are strikingly congruent with the those of the reformist Soviet economic sociologist, Tat'yana Zaslavskaya.

3. *Pravda*, August 2, 1986.

4. See Kenneth Jowitt, "Inclusion and Mobilization in Marxist-Leninist Political Systems," *World Politics* (October 1975), pp. 69–97, for an insightful discussion of this issue.

5. Albert Hirschman introduced these terms to describe the options available to a customer faced by deteriorating performance of a firm: to stop buying its products and turn to competitors or to express dissatisfaction to management in an effort to alter its behavior. *Exit, Voice and Loyalty* (Cambridge, Mass.: Harvard University Press, 1970), p. 59.

6. "Appeal for a Gradual Democratization," in George Saunders, ed., *Samizdat: Voices of the Soviet Opposition* (New York: Monad Press, 1974), p. 405.

7. This principle has been advocated by leading Soviet public figures, including academician V. N. Kudryavtsev, director of the Academy of Sciences Institute of State and Law. See *Voprosy filosofii*, 1 (January 1987).

8. See, for example, Konstantin Chernenko, in *Kommunist*, no. 13 (1981), pp. 10–11.

9. For a useful overview drawn from Latin American experiences, see Guillermo O'Donnell et al., *Transitions from Authoritarian Rule: Comparative Perspectives* (Baltimore: Johns Hopkins University Press, 1986).

10. Tsentral'noe statisticheskoe upravlenie, *Narodnoe khoziaistvo SSSR* (Moscow: Finansy i Statistika, 1987), pp. 523, 647.

11. These trends are discussed in some detail in Gail W. Lapidus, "Social Trends," in Byrnes, *After Brezhnev*.

12. Brian Silver, "Political Beliefs of the Soviet Citizen: Sources of Support for Regime Norms," in James Millar, ed., *Politics, Work and Daily Life in the USSR* (Cambridge: Cambridge University Press, 1987). Similar trends by age cohort were revealed in a poll of Muscovites conducted at the Institute of Sociological Research of the Soviet Academy of Sciences for the *New York Times* and CBS News in May 1988. See *New York Times*, May 27, 1988, p. A7. By contrast, among the refugees from World War II interviewed in the Harvard Project of the 1950s, regime support was greater among younger age cohorts and increased with level of education. Raymond Bauer and Alex Inkeles, *The Soviet Citizen* (Cambridge, Mass.: Harvard University Press, 1959). Support for regime norms was higher among those respondents who reported high levels of material satisfaction, but "satisfaction" was highly dependent on subjective perceptions. Recent Soviet research, for example, found that residents of Moscow and Leningrad were in fact less satisfied with the quality of life they enjoyed than were respondents from seventeen other cities because the former's higher expectations created a wider gap between aspirations and real possibilities. See also Oleg Bozhkov and Valeri Golofast, "Otsenka naseleniem uslovii zhizni v krupnykh gorodakh," *Sotsiologicheskie issledovaniia*, no. 3 (1985).

13. *New York Times*, November 4, 1987.

14. *Pravda*, April 18, 1987. Yakovlev's views are more fully developed in his "Dostizhenie kachestvenno novogo sostoianiia sovetskogo obshchestva i obshchestvennye nauki," *Kommunist*, no. 8 (1987).

15. Films such as Abuladze's *Repentance* and novels such as Anatoli Rybakov's *Children of the Arbat* helped reopen the Stalin question. Gorbachev's seventieth anniversary speech reaffirmed elements of the prevailing orthodoxy regarding Lenin and Stalin but was unflinching in referring to Stalin's "unpardonable crimes," broke new ground in defending Lenin's New Economic Policy and his essay "On Cooperation" as precedents for Gorbachev's own reforms. He also presented both Bukharin and Khrushchev in a more positive vein than has been customary. A number of articles have since appeared in the Soviet press offering a favorable appraisal of Khrushchev's contributions.

16. Indeed, a recent article explicitly blames Leonid Brezhnev and his Politburo colleague and Party ideologist Mikhail Suslov for the emergence of a Soviet dissident movement because they destroyed the key vehicle for criticism of Stalinism, namely Aleksandr Tvardovsky's journal, *Novyi mir*. Yuri Burtin as cited in Julia Wishnevsky, "A Guide to Some Major Soviet Journals," Radio Liberty Research Bulletin, RL Supplement 2/88 (July 20, 1988).

17. *Pravda*, November 3, 1987.

18. Yakovlev in *Pravda*, April 18, 1987.

19. *Izvestiya*, October 28, 1986.

20. *Pravda*, April 18, 1987.

21. See, for instance, the debates over the meaning of social justice, in *Kommunist*, no. 13 (1986). A wide array of Soviet journals now provide an unprecedented forum for discussion and debate on major issues of domestic development.

22. The argument is more fully developed in Gail W. Lapidus, "KAL and Chernobyl: The Soviet Management of Crises," *Survival* (May/June 1987).

23. *Pravda*, February 6, 1987.

24. An editorial in *Kommunist* in October 1987 defended this new orientation, contrasting Lenin's tolerant approach to culture and to the intelligentsia with Stalin's arbitrary effort to impose "bureaucratic regulation."

25. *Literaturnaia gazeta*, May 13, 1987.

26. Ibid., May 13 and June 8, 1987.

27. See, for example, V. Dashichev, in *Literaturnaia gazeta*, May 18, 1988; A. Bovin, in *Izvestiya*, June 16, 1988; V. Berezhkov, in *Sovetskaia molodezh*, August 20, 1987; and A. Bovin, in *Literaturnaia gazeta*, March 16, 1988.

28. See Murray Yanowitch, *The Social Structure of the USSR* (Armonk, N.Y.: M. E. Sharpe, 1986) for a useful collection of translations of important Soviet articles.

29. The debate was launched by academician Petr Fedoseyev in *Problemy mira i sotsializma*, 9 (September 1981), and was taken up by the journal *Voprosy filosofii* in articles by Vadim Semenov (9 [September 1982]) and Anatoliy Butenko (10 [October 1982] and 2 [1984]). Their views were attacked in a series of articles in *Pravda* and in *Kommunist*.

30. *Voprosy filosofii*, 2 (February 1987).

31. *Moskovskaya pravda*, May 7, 1987, p. 3, as quoted in *Current Digest of the Soviet Press* 39, no. 18 (June 3, 1987), p. 3.

32. *Kommunist*, no. 13 (1986). Zaslavskaya's long-standing advocacy of an "interest group" approach to the Soviet political economy is reflected in her editorship of a journal on economic sociology, which focuses on "the analysis of the development of the economy as a social process representing the specific behavior and interaction of classes, strata and groups in Soviet society." T. I. Zaslavskaya and R. V. Ryvkina, *Izvestiia sibirskogo otdeleniia akademii nauk SSSR: seriia ekonomiki i prikladnoi sotsiologii*, no. 1 (January 1984).

33. When Tat'yana Zaslavskaya first referred to entrenched bureaucratic opposition to reform (*Ekonomika i organizatsiia promyshlennogo proizvodstva*, 7 [1985], pp. 3–22), it was a striking statement. The discussion of bureaucracy and its interests has now become a staple of the Soviet media. See, for example, Vladimir Shubkin, *Znamya*, April 1987, pp. 162–186, and the roundtable on *Ogonyok*, March 12, 1988.

34. Samizdat Archive, "Beseda chlenov soiuza pisatelei SSSR s M. S. Gorbachevym," AS no. 5785 (June 19, 1986).

35. A sharp exchange over the desirability of allowing informal associations to nominate candidates to stand in new Soviet elections was carried in *Izvestiya*, March 20, 1988, p. 3.

36. *Pravda*, October 18, 1961, p. 1. For a more extensive discussion of the evolution of Soviet views, see Gail W. Lapidus, "Ethnonationalism and Political Stability: The Soviet Case," *World Politics* 36 (July 1984).

37. *Pravda*, February 24, 1981.

38. *Pravda*, December 22, 1982.

39. Ibid.

40. The new elements in the present approach involve an unprecedented acknowledgment of past errors in nationality policy, including the treatment of the Baltic states; a fresh approach to bilingualism, which offers more scope for teaching and using national languages; and a search for new procedures and mechanisms for addressing national grievances. See *Kommunist*, no. 3 and no. 13 (1987).

41. For two important treatments of this broad theme, see John Bushnell, "The 'New Soviet Man' Turns Pessimist," in Stephen Cohen et al., eds., *The Soviet Union Since Stalin* (Bloomington: Indiana University Press, 1980), pp. 179–199; and Alexander Dallin, "Retreat from Optimism," in Seweryn Bialer and Sophie Sluzar, eds., *Radicalism in the Contemporary Age*, III (Boulder, CO: Westview, 1977), pp. 117–157.

42. *Pravda*, May 13, 1988; *Izvestiya*, June 12, 1988.

43. Zaslavskaya has sharply criticized the suppression of economic and social statistics and has charged that the Soviet Union is in last place among developed countries in the level of publicly available social statistics, a criticism echoed by Gorbachev himself. (*Pravda*, February 6, 1987.)

44. *Pravda*, August 7, 1987.

45. For a useful discussion, see Archie Brown in Alexander Dallin and Bertrand Patenaude, eds., *Soviet Scholarship Under Gorbachev* (Stanford: Stanford University Press, 1988).

46. *Pravda*, March 18, 1988.

47. The need for a socialist *Rechtsstaat* (*sotsialisticheskoe pravovoe gosudarstvo*) was endorsed by the Nineteenth Party Conference, discussed on the front page of *Pravda*, August 2, 1988, and elaborated in *Kommunist* no. 11 (1988). The inadequacy of Soviet political institutions, and the need for a socialist "theory of checks and balances," was a major theme of the 1987 annual conference of the Soviet Association of Political Sciences (Archie Brown, in Dallin and Patenaude, *Soviet Scholarship Under Gorbachev*).

48. Total subscriptions have increased over 18 million in the past year alone, while the number of subscribers to *Ogonyok* doubled, from 561,415 to 1,313,349. *Novyi mir* reached a record 1,150,000 in January 1988 (*Moscow News*, no. 8 [1988], Wishnevsky, "A Guide to Some Major Soviet Journals"). The letters editor of *Ogonyok* reported that the volume of mail from readers had also increased dramatically, from 15,000 letters in 1986 to 50,000 in 1987 to 20,000 in the first three months of 1988 (*New York Times*, April 24, 1988).

Glasnost Watch

Victoria E. Bonnell

MOSCOW: A VIEW FROM BELOW

Ordinary Life in the Gorbachev Time

Visiting Moscow after an eleven-year absènce I was struck first by the freshness in the political atmosphere. The impact of *glasnost* is palpable: People talk in new ways, no longer tremulously, about the deplorable conditions in their country. The culture of deception and fear, lies and whispers, has given way to openness in public and private discourse. The mass media have become so racy that few still listen to "the voices," as foreign Russian-language broadcasts are known in the USSR. The Voice of America, once an object of official vilification, has been invited to open an office in Moscow.

A steep increase in subscriptions to newspapers and journals and the long lines at kiosks indicate that people take a lively interest in the printed word. Far less obvious, though, is the popular reaction to all this—the ways people assess what they read or. see on television. Many decades of prevarication and hyperbole have left their mark. Although nearly everyone welcomes *glasnost* to some degree, the reactions to it and to *perestroika* are more varied, complex, and problematic than a Western observer might expect.

One discovery I made is that the optimism in the West about Gorbachev's recent reforms is not quite shared in Moscow. The people I encountered had a worried and skeptical attitude toward *perestroika*—views that were not confined to intellectuals but appeared to prevail among broad strata of the population. It is hard to give a name to this set of attitudes. I refer to it as civic cynicism: a profound mistrust of political authority and official declarations.

I first saw this in 1976 and 1977, when the regime's monopoly on information was beginning to break down. For the first time since the 1920s, and on a radically new scale, people began to learn about life outside Soviet borders by means of shortwave radio broadcasts, foreign travel, and communication with recent Soviet émigrés. This loss of innocence profoundly altered popular standards for comparison; expectations for an improved standard of living rose sharply. When the ability of the regime to deliver fell far short both of these expectations and of extravagant official pronouncements, people became more and more skeptical about the promises and performance of the party-state.*

In the intervening eleven years, the mood of civic cynicism has deepened. And each day it is reinforced by the mass media, which now present scathing indictments of the Soviet system in virtually all its aspects. *Glasnost* is nurturing a mentality of cynicism at the very time when Gorbachev is attempting to create a new kind of idealism aimed at expunging the remnants of Stalinism and bringing the coun-

---

* In *Moskovskie novosti* (September 11, 1988), the historian Roy Medvedev gave this characterization of popular attitudes under Brezhnev: "Reluctance and inability to do a good job, political passivity and apathy, indifference toward the moral and political values of socialism, the moral degradation of tens of millions of people, a universal reign of mediocrity, a gulf between words and deeds, the encouragement of all sorts of lies—all this crippled the consciousness of an entire generation, which we call—sometimes not without reason—the 'lost generation.' "

try—materially and spiritually—fully into the modern age.

I say "modern age" because in the Soviet Union premodern features persist within the frame of a modern industrial society. The existence of vast urban centers, a superior space program, and military high-tech go hand in hand with preindustrial time-use (appointments are nearly impossible to schedule), consumption patterns (close to half the family budget goes for food), woefully inadequate health care (only 35 percent of rural district hospitals have hot running water; 17 percent have no running water), and an abysmally low standard of living (per capita individual consumption is about a third what it is in the United States). This incongruity produces painful contradictions. Judging by appearances, the country lags behind the West even more than in 1970 when I made my first trip there. During my recent visit I did not see a single computer; not even the banks have them. Photocopying machines are almost as scarce today as a decade ago; the telephone system is inadequate even for voice, let alone electronic data transmission. The information and communications revolutions have yet to make an appearance in the Soviet Union outside of the space and military sectors.

Civic cynicism thrives on these contradictions, undermining the logic of Gorbachev's strategy for reform. Today, as in the past, major structural changes have been initiated from above by a single formidable leader. But change from above cannot succeed without mobilizing change from below. This is a dilemma explicitly recognized by Gorbachev and some of his major policies can best be understood in this light. The problem he faces has certain similarities to that which confronted Stalin during the first Five Year Plan: how to transform the attitudes and behavior of the Soviet people in behalf of *perestroika* (the term was first used extensively during the first Five Year Plan).

Stalin's solution was to create a new kind of politics based on a combination of dictatorship, terror, *and* mass mobilization. Authoritarian and populist elements were intertwined in the Stalinist system, with participation in mass organizations a critical factor in carrying out the *perestroika* of the 1930s. Stalin utilized

popular participation to generate support for the party program while at the same time confining "all forms of public association, discourse, and public action within structures established by the regime."[1] Mass mobilization, together with mass terror, reshaped the politics of millions of Soviet citizens. These attitudes—participation without power, enthusiasm without initiative, authority without responsibility—survived well into the post-Stalin era. This is the legacy with which Gorbachev must contend.

Like Stalin, Gorbachev needs mass mobilization to carry out a vast restructuring of Soviet institutions. His approach, however, calls for a mass mobilization stimulated by policies initiated from above but sustained over the long term by institutional structures that permit autonomous political and social action. In short, it is the opposite of Stalin's recipe. Gorbachev's conception of popular participation places a high premium on the very autonomy of word and deed that the Stalinist system managed to crush for nearly sixty years. And this is precisely the area where Gorbachev's *perestroika*, with reliance on initiative from below to complement changes inaugurated from above, has run into serious obstacles. Bureaucratic intransigence is only one aspect of a monumental problem. Equally threatening is the complex set of popular attitudes—civic cynicism, inertia, and outright resistance—that are reinforced by the experience of everyday life. These have proved particularly resistant to reform.

Struggles of Everyday Life

To date *perestroika* has had little impact on the daily ordeals of ordinary citizens. Boris Yeltsin put the matter clearly at the Nineteenth Party Conference in July 1988: "As a result of restructuring, in three years we have not solved any of the problems that are tangible and real for people, let alone achieved any revolutionary transformations." Though Gorbachev was sharply critical of this statement, the press is filled with detailed reports of the appalling difficulties that people encounter as they attempt to feed and clothe themselves and send their children off to school.

The food situation, in particular, has grown steadily worse. I saw stores that had row upon row of empty shelves. The problem is not merely that basic items are in short supply (meat, sugar, milk products, fruits, vegetables, and so on) but that many items have disappeared entirely. Higher quality butter, sour cream, cheese, tea, and many other staples of the Russian diet have been replaced by poor substitutes. Everyone can see the deterioration in the quantity and quality of food products. These hardships, imposed by the scarcity and low quality of food and other basic consumer goods and services, provide the number one topic of conversation among Muscovites. More significant, and entirely unprecedented, both the people and the mass media have begun to perceive this as a systemic problem.

The extraordinary crisis in the material sphere, in combination with the general harshness of the urban environment, makes everyday life in Moscow very Hobbesian— nasty, brutish, and short. The brutishness of public life has intensified in proportion to the conditions of scarcity and the general deterioration of public facilities. The overcrowding, filth, long lines (averaging two to three hours each day for Muscovites), pushing and shoving, and sheer physical exertion required to get through an ordinary day in the capital can scarcely be comprehended by those of us who live in the Western industrialized societies. All of this takes a tremendous toll on people and, in combination with substandard medical care and alcoholism, results in a low life expectancy (the Soviet Union ranks thirty-second in life expectancy out of 126 countries) and a high level of infant mortality (fiftieth in the world, after Mauritius and Barbados).

Daily life resembles a kind of warfare, pitting citizen against citizen in a never-ending series of cruel encounters. As a means of self-defense, people have developed coping mechanisms that allow them to maneuver within established structures. "Dwelling, moving about, speaking, reading, shopping, and cooking are activities that seem to correspond to the characteristics of tactical ruses and surprises: clever tricks of the 'weak' against the

'strong', an art of putting. one over on the adversary on his own turf, hunter's tricks, maneuverable, polymorph mobilities, jubilant, poetic, and warlike discoveries."[2] These words of Michel de Certeau possess a special poignancy, because everyday life has engendered an intricate pattern of "tricks" that include conniving, hoarding and weaseling, and a generally predatory disposition.

To appreciate the significance of such practices we must bear in mind that "the structure of everyday life . . . encourages us to see the whole world as an analogy of our own everyday life."[3] Coping mechanisms, enabling ordinary citizens to "make do," have important social-psychological consequences as well as implications for conduct in the economic and political spheres. The experiences of everyday life in the Soviet Union reinforce attitudes of dependency (it's difficult to feel in control of one's life), degradation (the conditions of daily struggle are exceedingly demeaning), and desperation (no matter how hard one tries, it's difficult to cope with the most basic tasks of daily existence). Rules, both formal and informal, must be outwitted and circumvented. As an *Izvestia* correspondent put it recently: "Is it possible to rear a law-abiding citizen when everyday experience persuades him that he has no rights?" Taken together, these experiences reinforce a profound feeling of powerlessness.

Time and again I asked people why they did not protest certain injustices, why they tolerated misconduct, violations of rules, and preposterous regulations. I was told protest had no effect, that it was impossible to prosecute the guilty party, or to identify the decision-maker. Though there are notable exceptions to this pattern of resignation, such attitudes are widespread among Muscovites. Nor are the reasons difficult to detect. The Stalinist system, even in its post-Stalin manifestations, has never adequately institutionalized methods for obtaining redress of grievances—*any kind of grievances*. The system is so hierarchical and decision-making processes are often so obscure that even when fear plays no role, ordinary citizens believe that the process of redress is fundamentally hopeless, a waste of time.

Gorbachev has taken steps to promote legal reforms that provide procedures for appealing unlawful actions of officials and establish criminal liability for persecuting people for criticism. But it remains to be seen what practical effect these provisions will have.

An indispensable feature of successful social movements is the identification of "the enemy" in human form. In the Soviet Union today the system operates in such a way that it is difficult, in fact often impossible, to identify who is responsible for a given problem. To be sure, the media have focused public scrutiny and even public abuse on heads of ministries, store managers, and others. But these incidents are still episodic and there is an overwhelming impression that even highly placed officials are themselves cogs in a big impersonal bureaucratic machine. An "invisible" human agency presents a serious obstacle to autonomous political and social action.

Fear of Change

One other circumstance must be overcome by Gorbachev if he is to achieve mobilization on behalf of *perestroika:* the apprehension about, even resistance to, his reforms. The fundamental concern is one of destabilization. In the post-Stalin era there has been an unwritten social contract between the party-state and the population: The regime provides job security, a modest but steady improvement in the material standard of living, and opportunities for social mobility, and in exchange citizens cooperate at the workplace and accept a political system that rules in their name but without their effective participation.

Gorbachev now wants to rewrite the contract and many people fear that they will be victimized by these changes, just as they have been victimized in the past by grand schemes of social engineering. More concretely, the new cost accounting system (*khozrashchet*) means that job security is no longer part of the basic social contract; price reforms involve the abandonment of subsidies for basic food items and the likelihood of serious inflation. In exchange, Gorbachev is offering the possibility of genuine political participation through elections and workplace democracy. It is by no means certain that most people consider this an attractive trade-off.

How has Gorbachev attempted to surmount popular attitudes and practices that stand in the way of implementing *perestroika*? Like Stalin before him, Gorbachev has to find means to change deeply rooted ways of thinking about the world. His options are far more limited than those of the Great Helmsman. He cannot resort to terror, exhortatory propaganda, or mass spectacles. Significantly, the symbols and rituals of authority are in very low profile, while political posters, once ubiquitous, have now virtually disappeared.

Gorbachev has chosen a different path, one without precedent in Soviet experience. Influenced, most likely, by the model of interest-group politics advocated by the prominent sociologist Tatiana Zaslavskaia, he has promoted various reforms designed to democratize party and state institutions and, concomitantly, to encourage the formation of voluntary associations. These reforms recognize that, as Zaslavskaia said in a 1987 interview: "The structure of our society is made up of a great many groups whose statuses differ and which have different (sometimes opposing) interests and goals for which they struggle." Unofficial groups provide an especially important indicator of changes at the grassroots level.

Writing in the mid-nineteenth century, Alexis de Tocqueville argued that independent voluntary associations were a critical element in democratic societies. Tsarist Russia, as Tocqueville's theory would have predicted, had an exceedingly weak tradition of voluntary association. Craft guilds and mutual aid societies, so widespread in premodern Europe, appeared late in Russia's history and then only under government tutelage. Political parties and trade unions did not come to Russia until the 1905 revolution; parties and unions operated in a very circumscribed environment for only a dozen years, until the February Revolution brought down the autocracy. Following the October Revolution, voluntary associations were gradually absorbed into the one-party system. By the early 1930s, all of them, including the trade unions, had become subordinated to the party-state.

Only toward the end of the Brezhnev era did

voluntary associations begin to reappear. The late seventies and early eighties witnessed the formation of unofficial clubs among young sports fans, rock music enthusiasts, and others. These clubs, which were permitted to exist without much opposition from the authorities, focused on leisure-time activities and had a rather limited membership. The situation changed dramatically after Gorbachev came to power. More than thirty thousand grassroots organizations had come into existence in the Soviet Union by December 1987. In the fall of 1988 about five hundred unofficial groups were functioning in Moscow and several hundred in Leningrad. Membership in these groups ranges from a few dozen to several thousand.

Most voluntary associations operate on the local level; others, such as the highly successful Popular Front groups in the Baltic states, extend to an entire national republic. Three voluntary associations (devoted to a memorial for Stalin's victims, charity, and cultural preservation) currently have a national constituency. Though initially centered around leisure-time and cultural activities, voluntary associations have rapidly expanded to focus on a wide range of issues that include ecology and political reform. The appearance of politically oriented voluntary associations is certainly one of the most astonishing and potentially significant developments of the past three and a half years.

According to Boris Kagarlitsky, a leader of unofficial socialist clubs in Moscow, political groups have made substantial progress. They operate under such colorful names as "Community," "Salvation," "Epicenter," "Candle," and "Laboratory of Public Self-Management." The movement has proceeded slowly in Moscow but in provincial cities, such as Sverdlovsk and elsewhere, grass-roots political organizations have achieved a considerable following and currently occupy an important position in local politics. In the summer of 1987 a number of these groups formed the Federation of Socialist Clubs.[4]

Ferment at the Base

In contrast to the beginning of the century, Moscow and Leningrad are no longer the centers where dissident activity originates. In the 1980s, it is the periphery that has become the center of autonomous grass-roots movements for political and social change. National republics (Estonia, Latvia, Lithuania, Armenia) are generating social movements far in advance—numerically, organizationally, programatically—of those in the RSFSR. The Popular Front—a movement on behalf of *perestroika* that includes both party and nonparty elements—has achieved its greatest success not in Moscow, where its goals remain nebulous and its popular base is minuscule, but in the Baltic Republics.

Resolutions adopted by the Nineteenth Party Conference in early July 1988 lent official support to the establishment of voluntary associations "expressing the interests and aspirations of various strata of Soviet society." But the possibilities for grass-roots politics vary tremendously from one city and region to another. Recent press reports indicate that some local authorities are harshly vindictive toward these groups, while others tolerate and even support them. Moreover, not all groups have been accorded the same opportunities for public action. Certain organizations, such as the nonsocialist Democratic Union, have been sharply criticized in the press and severely treated by the authorities. While I was in Moscow a demonstration by this group was brutally dispersed on one occasion and entirely suppressed on another. The Democratic Union continues to function despite severe restrictions on its public activity, but such incidents bring to the surface the deep-seated ambivalence toward autonomous social action on the part of local authorities as well as some citizens. Yet there are indications, even in the capital, that voluntary associations are little by little moving into the interstices of public life.

Soon after my arrival in Moscow I witnessed a public demonstration in Pushkin Square, organized in behalf of a memorial to the victims of Stalinism. Several people stood with a large placard announcing the formation of a fund to build such a memorial, including a museum and library. Another member of the group collected signatures on a petition in support of the project. Police circulated in the area but did not interfere. An animated group of about one hundred people, some of them passersby, gathered around the organizers. Many signed the petition, a housewife laden with groceries and a young man in a military uniform among them. It was a moving occasion. For more than fifty years, an event of this kind could not take place in the Soviet Union; those who tried to engage in public action were severely punished. And now men and women of all ages openly demonstrated in the capital.

Public demonstrations are still far from routine in the Soviet Union, but their number has been increasing in the past several years. According to V. Kravtsov, the USSR minister of justice, there were more than two hundred and fifty sizable "unauthorized" rallies, processions, and demonstrations in Moscow, Leningrad, Sverdlovsk, and several other cities between 1986 and 1988. Law enforcement officials as well as some citizens have strong reservations about such activity, but the sanctions for such gatherings remain in force despite a recent law placing new restrictions on the demonstrators.

Nascent Cooperative Movement

Another important type of voluntary association that has appeared during the Gorbachev era is the cooperative, formed for the purpose of carrying on economic activity outside party and state auspices. Like other voluntary associations, cooperatives (involving both consumers and producers) got off to a late start in Tsarist Russia, making rapid strides only after the 1905 revolution. Cooperatives gained major importance following the introduction of the New Economic Policy in 1921, when Lenin and Bukharin advocated them as a transitional economic form between capitalism and socialism. Consumer, producer, credit, and agricultural cooperatives enjoyed a brief efflorescence in the 1920s and figured prominently in the debate over the future direction of the country's economic development. With Stalin's ascendancy in the late 1920s and the introduction of a centralized economy, the independent cooperative movement was extinguished.

Gorbachev has once again restored legitimacy to the idea of self-managed cooperatives, in fact making them a key element in his strategy for economic revival. His hope is that cooperative forms of private enterprise will bring about a swift improvement in the quantity and quality of goods and services. This policy has begun to yield results, particularly since the enactment of a new Law on Cooperatives in July 1988. By January 1989, there were more than 48,000 cooperatives in the country as a whole. Their activities are wide-ranging: restaurants, cafes, retail sales of clothing, food, and other items, plumbing and other skilled crafts concerned with household repair, typewriter repair, construction, manufacturing, tailoring, credit, car insurance, and rock music.

Like unofficial political groups, cooperatives have developed more slowly in Moscow than in some other areas, such as the Baltics. But the situation in the capital is changing rapidly. Whereas only a few dozen cooperative enterprises existed in Moscow in September 1987, one year later there were more than three thousand. During my visit, cooperative businesses, especially in the retail sector, were springing up in all parts of the city. A colorful cooperative cafe is strategically placed in front of the Intourist Hotel and a posh cooperative restaurant has opened several doors down; cooperatively owned fast-food vans can be seen in the Kremlin park and other recreational spots; cooperatives selling clothing and second-hand goods are visible in many neighborhoods. These privately owned stores, restaurants, and even public toilets were generally cleaner, more hospitable, and more expensive than their counterparts in the state sector.

The public response to these cooperatives has been mixed. High prices and lavish profits generate resentment; in many parts of the country, local authorities place obstacles in the path of these fledgling businesses. Cooperatives must contend with a deeply rooted tradition of aversion toward private enterprise, even in its collectivist forms, and toward personal enrichment through such enterprises. Finally, they are not operating within a market economy, which means that they have to wheel and deal in their relations with state suppliers, bureaucrats, and others. What is remarkable is that despite immense legal, fiscal, organizational, and ideological problems, not to speak of the Soviet

212

Mafia (yes, Mafia!) that preys on them, the number of cooperatives has been increasing and these businesses are currently taking the first steps toward collective organization.

In June 1988, the Moscow cooperative, *Fakt*, was formed to serve as an information clearinghouse for other cooperatives. Two lobbying groups—*Rossiia* and the Moscow Association of Cooperatives—have recently been created to defend the interests of cooperative businesses against the government, racketeers, and negative public opinion. There is also a new weekly newspaper for coop members, *Vestnik kooperatora:* The advent of a coordinating center, lobbying organizations, and a newspaper indicates that coops, like unofficial political groups, are beginning to achieve significant coordination outside official channels. There can be no doubt that what we see here, still in embryonic form, is the emergence of a civil society in the Soviet Union.

Cooperatives and other kinds of voluntary associations have begun to function as interest groups seeking to influence the direction of public policy and the allocation of resources. Cooperatives played an important part in achieving the withdrawal of a new tax law on private businesses in 1988; ecology and preservation groups have won important victories against local authorities; some groups aiming at political reform have become vociferous participants in the ongoing debate about restructuring party and governmental institutions; the organization seeking a memorial to Stalin's victims has garnered support from several major artistic unions and appears to be succeeding in its aims; the Popular Fronts in the Baltic states are emerging as key players in national politics. Manifestations of autonomous social action betoken a fundamental shift in the orientation of some citizens, away from civic cynicism and toward engagement in civic affairs.

Voluntary associations are still circumscribed and dependent upon official policy. Gorbachev makes appeals for "civic self-affirmation," an "active civic stance," "self-regulation and self-management," and, most often, the exercise of initiative. But paradoxically, the state itself must create a new civil society by opening up a broad sphere for independent organizations and providing the legal and institutional support for these activities. What we are witnessing in the Soviet Union today are the first decisive steps in this direction.

The liberalization in social policy cannot be explained merely as an instrumental aspect of Gorbachev's program for achieving economic reform. Nor is it just a tactical move or a grudging concession to some indigenous or foreign constituency. Gorbachev wants to arouse the population from the paralysis induced by long years of civic cynicism, fear, and general powerlessness; his goal is mobilization without regimentation. The tolerance and encouragement for autonomous organizations and for new forms of public action generated by these organizations is an intrinsic aspect of Gorbachev's strategy for change in the Soviet Union—a sine qua non of its progress. Just as it has been said of early modern Europe: "No bourgeoisie, no democracy," so today we may say of communist societies: "No voluntary associations, no *perestroika*." ◻

Notes

[1] Michael Gelb, "Mass Politics under Stalin: Party Purges and Industrial Productivity Campaigns in Leningrad, 1928–1941" (Ph.D. Dissertation, University of California at Los Angeles, 1987), p. 12. The author offers a compelling analysis of the way mass participation was engineered in the 1930s.

[2] Michel de Certeau, *The Practice of Everyday Life*, trans. by Steven F. Rendall (University of California Press: Berkeley and Los Angeles, 1984), p. 40.

[3] Agnes Heller, *Everyday Life*, trans. by G.I. Campell (Routledge and Kegan Paul: London and Boston, 1984), p. 52.

[4] Conversation with Kagarlitsky, September 13, 1988. The Declaration of the Federation of Socialist Clubs drawn up at the First Meeting of Informal Associations in Moscow is reprinted in Boris Kagarlitsky, *The Thinking Reed: Intellectuals and the Soviet State 1917 to the Present* (Verso: London and New York, 1988), pp. 349–352.

213

SOVIET STUDIES, vol. 42, no. 2, April 1990, 233-257

REVOLUTION FROM BELOW: INFORMAL POLITICAL ASSOCIATIONS IN RUSSIA 1988–1989

By Vladimir Brovkin

POLITICAL LIFE started to change rapidly in the Soviet Union in the spring of 1988 with the emergence of a myriad of informal groups and associations. The attention of the world media and of observers of Soviet affairs has been focused on the dramatic political developments in the Baltic republics, in Armenia, Georgia and Moldavia. In 1988 Popular Fronts or Independence Parties in these republics emerged as leaders of broad based popular movements for reform and national autonomy. Within a relatively short time they have become *de facto* political parties transforming the very nature of politics in these republics. Much less is known about voluntary political associations in Russia proper, especially outside Moscow and Leningrad. This is so partly because no equivalent to one unified Popular Front emerged in Russia, and the growth of informal associations was slower than in the other republics. Dozens of clubs, groups and associations of diverse political preferences appeared in many cities. Over the past year they have tried to formulate their programmes and principles of organisation and to establish contact with like-minded groups across the country. Their interaction with the authorities, their ideas and values, their programmes and goals shed light on the constellation of political forces in the largest Soviet republic. No matter how important the successes of Popular Fronts in the other republics are, the fate of the reform process in the Soviet Union as a whole will depend largely on the outcome of the struggle between reformers and conservatives in Russia. Voluntary political associations play an important if not a decisive role in this struggle. It is for this reason that this article focuses on the political associations in Russia proper. These associations represent new forces in Soviet society—forces that entered the political arena during 1988 and that have the potential, at least in parts of the country, to challenge the CPSU monopoly on political power.

Hundreds if not thousands of informal groups have emerged all over the country.[1] Their membership, organisation, political goals and activity vary to such a degree that all they hold in common is that they are outside the traditional Soviet political establishment. The very term informal—chosen by the groups themselves—carries two connotations. First, these groups emphasise their independence from the state. Second, they are not legally registered. In other words they do not officially exist. The paradox of course is that many of these groups would like to register as legal organisations and yet remain informal in the sense of independent from the state. Their identity is with society or a part of society *vis-à-vis* the state.

Any attempt to systematise the outlook of informal groups in some fashion would be inadequate both because there are so many and because the current stage of their development can best be characterised as growth pangs. Some groups unite, others break apart or grow, becoming either more cautious or more radical. Nevertheless, an attempt is made here to conceptualise the development of the informal groups over the first year of their existence within three dimensions. The chronological dimension examines the stages in their development; the second assesses their values and goals on the political spectrum; and the third discusses the CP policy towards the informal groups and their impact on Soviet politics.

The emergence of political clubs and associations

As early as 1986–87 informal groups and associations began to form in various Russian cities. At that stage they were primarily concerned with specific local issues. Central among these were environmental protection, preservation of historical monuments and investigation of crimes of the Stalin era. Only in the context of growing political awareness during the spring of 1988 did these clubs turn to explicitly political causes.

In Leningrad students campaigned to remove the name of Zhdanov from their university. In Gorky an ecological group 'Vanguard' made a debut by campaigning against the construction of a nuclear power station.[2] In Irkutsk the Baikal Popular Front was an outgrowth of the powerful movement to protect lake Baikal.[3] In Krasnoyarsk a 'Committee to Aid Restructuring' was formed in 1988 and in the spring of 1989 it launched a campaign against undemocratic election procedures.[4] In Kalinin and in Kirov we encounter the same name, 'Committee to Aid Restructuring', but with a pointed use of the pre-Bolshevik names of these cities: 'Tver Committee' and 'Vyatka Committee'.[5]

Perhaps the most important political event that triggered the politicisation of existing clubs and the formation of new ones all over the country was the publication in mid-March of the Nina Andreeva letter. *Pravda* called it a platform of anti-restructuring forces on 5 April 1988. The letter was perceived as an attempt by party conservatives to roll back the process of reform. The supporters of reform now felt it was their duty to defend what had already been gained and to make sure that the reforms would continue. That could only be achieved if the 19th Party Conference endorsed Gorbachev's plans. This prospect seemed far from assured in May 1988. The extent to which corrupt local party mafias controlled centres of power is often underestimated. Boris Eltsin's frank description of corruption in the Moscow party organisation sheds some light on this problem:

Question: What mistakes did you make when you were the first secretary of the Moscow city party committee?
Answer: I underestimated the influence of organised mafia in Moscow, in all spheres. As soon as we touched the trade organisations, the food services, police, and the KGB, everything got into motion. And all of them are interconnected to such a degree. When you pull out one thread, another bogs down. This was perhaps the main mistake. At that time in the trade sector alone, two thousand people were arrested. In the police

apparatus, we replaced the main directorate. In food services, it was also replaced. The leadership of the KGB—also replaced.[6]

Discussion clubs began to pay close attention to the composition of delegations from their provinces to the 19th Party Conference. According to Boris Kagarlitsky, one of the leaders of the Federation of Socialist Clubs, several months before the conference, Tatyána Zaslavskaya first expressed the idea of creating clubs to defend restructuring.[7] Initially the idea did not find much support. Only in the climate of acute danger did the supporters of reform organise. As Kagarlitsky put it:

> In fact, the Popular Fronts movement emerged spontaneously, from below. Moreover, no one from among liberal experts [like Zaslavskaya] took part in its creation. Furthermore, the activists of the Popular Front, who had a bitter experience of the three years of restructuring, were not inclined to trust official liberals, fearing treason on their part. These fears were only strengthened after the Party Conference.[8]

Student activists in Moscow used a favourable moment at the end of May in the context of President Reagan's visit. They reckoned that the authorities would not dare to apply force while the attention of the world media was focused on Moscow. They began weekly gatherings and rallies on Pushkin square in Moscow.[9] On 14 June my friends from the Federation of Socialist Clubs invited me to come along to their rally. Several hundred people assembled in front of the *Izvestiya* building. Despite *glasnost'*, *Izvestiya* functionaries did not consider the rally worth reporting in their paper. Leaders of the Federation held up placards: 'Down with the temporary rules on demonstrations!', 'Down with bureaucracy!', 'Down with the KGB!'. Moscow police slowly surrounded the crowd and pushed passers-by aside. A police officer repeated through a loudspeaker: 'Your gathering violates the decisions of the Moscow Soviet. If you do not stop the unsanctioned rally, we will apply force.'. The crowd chanted: 'Con-sti-tu-tion!'. The police moved in, grabbing those who held the placards, and pushing them into unmarked buses, waiting around the corner. Eight people were detained.

In Moscow, Leningrad, Yaroslavl' and Sverdlovsk a boisterous campaign started against local mafias who packed delegations to the Party Conference. In Sverdlovsk the huge Uralmash plant demanded the inclusion of Boris Eltsin in the province delegation.[10] As Eltsin explained:

> Moscow collectives put forward my candidacy—it did not go through. The Sverdlovsk collectives put forward my candidacy— it did not go through. The Bureau of Sverdlovsk obkom supported the inititive of 15,000 Communists from the Uralmash plant, who had voted for my candidacy. It was nevertheless rejected. Only at the last moment, when there was no longer time to wait, was I sent to Karelia, where they received me well and elected me as one of 13 delegates.[11]

Party organisations in the provinces were as much controlled by conservatives as in Moscow. They certainly tried just as much as the Moscow apparatus did to discredit Eltsin and to bar reformists from being elected to participate in the Party Conference.

As in other cities, the Popular Front in Yaroslavl' emerged in the wake of the

June Party Conference. Initially the city authorities did not object to the formation of the PF. They wished to keep it from meeting in the centre of town and the city stadium was assigned to it as a meeting place. As one *samizdat* author pointed out, this proved to be a mistake, because 'instead of 500–700 people, 7,000–8,000 people began to come to the PF meetings'.[12] On 8 June a protest rally against the election of local functionaries to the Party Conference gathered 6,000 people.[13] In the early summer of 1988 these meetings at the stadium turned into the Hyde Park Corner of Russia. Speakers replaced each other in a steady flow, all discussing democratisation, relations with local authorities, crimes of Stalinism, and a programme for the Yaroslavl' PF. As one of the activists related, most of these proposals were incorporated into a collective programme of action: 'Democratisation of Society and Reform of the Political System'.[14] The Yaroslavl' authorities showed a remarkable degree of tolerance. The obkom secretary received the representatives of the Popular Front, but prohibited the PF from displaying its own news bulletin board in town. The PF managed to make arrangements with the city information office to put up its bulletins for a fee on the city information stands. This relatively amicable co-existence of the PF with the communist authorities in Yaroslavl' grew much more tense in the autumn. Local authorities have been much more hostile and repressive elsewhere.

Throughout 1988 obkom secretaries in the provinces continued to talk about restructuring and democratisation but in fact tried to suppress unsanctioned initiatives from below. For example, in Kuibyshev the obkom first secretary, E. F. Murav'ev, banned the play 'Democratisation' in early 1988.[15] In the context of talk about democratisation, such actions galvanised public opinion and gave the first impetus to organise public pressure in defence of *glasnost'* and restructuring. As in so many other cities, the party elections of candidates to the 19th Party Conference gave rise to a popular protest movement. Like so many other first secretaries, Murav'ev included his cronies and subordinates in the delegation from Kuibyshev. What infuriated the local people most was that he also included five ministers who had no relation to Kuibyshev province. The delegates nominated in Kuibyshev itself were simply ignored.[16] On 22 June a rally of 10,000 people gathered in the city's main square despite the authorities' ban. The rally was sponsored by a Marxist group 'Perspective'.[17] Murav'ev called this unsanctioned rally an 'ideological act of sabotage'. The crowds chanted: 'Restructuring yes! Murav'ev no!'. The next day one local paper did not come out. Another wrote about subversive activity and the radio spoke about 'extremists and provocateurs'.[18] In the wake of the rally the Popular Front was formed; its first major victory was that Murav'ev was forced to resign.[19]

In Khar'kov relatively moderate informal associations were formed: the 'April' club, which favoured a socialist state with the rule of law, and 'Chance', an ecological preservation group. Even that was too much for the obkom first secretary, V. P. Mysnichenko, who said: 'The lack of offensive ideological work is reflected in the fact that all kinds of unsanctioned associations and groups arise with negative orientation'. If the ecological group and the 'April' club were tolerated askance, the group 'For Civil Rehabilitation' of victims of the Brezhnev era repressions was threatened with imprisonment for anti-Soviet activity.[20]

In Magadan, in Siberia, the reaction of the authorities to local initiatives was even more repressive. An unsanctioned group, 'Democratic Initiative', demanded the abolition of privileges for the party bureaucracy. For this appeal activists were fined, dismissed from jobs and imprisoned. The local press published letters from indignant workers demanding that 'the traitors' be confined in psychiatric clinics. Teachers in schools were instructed to announce that an anti-Soviet organisation was active in town.[21]

In Rostov-on-Don the local 'Defence' club found itself in open confrontation with the city party chief, V. D. Kozlov, in the autumn of 1988. The club activists tried to explain to citizens that the city first secretary had assumed an anti-restructuring position. Even some communists accused him of inaction in regard to the local trade mafia. Heavy police force was Kozlov's answer. The club tried to appeal to Ligachev during his visit to Rostov and finally sent a letter to Gorbachev.[22]

Patterns of interaction between the new clubs and fronts and the authorities vary in detail and in degree of suppression, but not in substance. The authorities did not know how to respond to the new reality. In some places they tolerated the Popular Fronts, as in Yaroslavl. In others they tried to suppress them, as in Magadan. By their actions they managed only to radicalise the emerging political society. Whatever method they chose to use, they tried to retain control over the new societal forces. A *samizdat* article described how Komsomol functionaries in Leningrad tried to coopt the Federation of Socialist clubs:

> What have they not promised us in the Komsomol obkom! They promised a xerox machine, and freedom of the press and a circulation of 300 copies for our paper, with one condition only, that we work under the auspices of the obkom.[23]

In the summer the party bureaucracy was so frightened by the turmoil that it managed to pass two important pieces of legislation: the rules on how to conduct public demonstrations, and the creation of a special riot police force in July 1988. A decision was clearly made at the top to stop weekly demonstrations on Pushkin square in Moscow. The authorities' first attempt at a crack-down on informals came at the end of August. The newly created riot police was thrown into action to disband the demonstration commemorating the 20th anniversary of the Soviet occupation of Czechoslovakia on 21 August. A participant described the riot police actions:

> ... they did not ask any questions and did not give any warning. They simply attacked those who did not please them, the members of the Democratic Union and chance people on the streets. People were dragged along the pavement by the hair, hit against the asphalt with their heads, hit by metal objects in the face. Once in buses, they beat them with clubs. The beating with clubs continued in the cells as well.[24]

A total of 156 people were arrested. The hot summer was over. The message to society was unambiguous. The party bureaucracy did not want any initiatives from below. It was concerned not with restructuring but with retaining full control.

Political spectrum of informal groups

The appearance of informal groups, clubs, and associations is a symptom of the ideological vacuum created by the death of Marxism-Leninism. The informal groups phenomenon is itself a manifestation of the fact that old answers no longer satisfy various strata of Soviet society. Gorbachev's reforms opened a Pandora's box, so that old problems and grievances have come out into the open. Soviet society is looking for an answer to the question so often posed in Russian history: What is to be done? Where do we go from here?

The mainstream among political associations can be characterised as liberal. These are primarily 'Popular Fronts', 'Democratic Restructuring' clubs, 'Alternative' clubs, 'Elections 89' committees in Moscow, Leningrad, Kharkov and some other cities, as well as the 'Memorial' society, the informal association 'Moscow Tribune', the 'Federation of Socialist Clubs' and some others. The very diversity of names indicates that these groups have not yet coalesced into national or all-Union organisations. Like islands they exist primarily in big cities (with the exception of the Baltic republics) and are trying to create all-Union organisations. All of these mainstream groups are resolute supporters of Gorbachev's reforms and are dissatisfied with how little has been achieved. Their goal is to quicken the pace of the reform process in the direction of profound democratisation. They would all subscribe to the goals of establishing the rule of law in the Soviet Union, institutionalisation of a government accountable to the people, transferring political power to multi-party freely elected soviets, dismantling the party's monopoly on power, the *nomenklatura* system and all the vestiges of Stalinism. Within these broad parameters, however, there are significant differences on a variety of problems even within these groups.

As early as the spring and summer of 1988 city-based informal groups began establishing contact with groups of similar political outlook in other cities. A process of alliance building and political differentiation began. In this political context the socialists played an important role. In many Russian cities groups were formed that called themselves socialists or social democrats: the Union of Social Democrats in Leningrad, for example. In the spring of 1988 they united into the Federation of Socialist Clubs, which appeared at many boisterous rallies in the summer of 1988. Composed primarily of students and young people, the FSC sees itself as a counterpart to the Komsomol. It consists of clubs with great diversity of ideological orientation: 'Commune', 'Civic Dignity', 'Alliance', 'Che Guevara', 'Socialist Initiative', Social Democrats, anarcho-syndicalists and so on.[25] The FSC clearly does not speak with one voice. It reflects the diversity of interests and orientations existing among young people. At the same time it is an indication that Marxism-Leninism and the Komsomol, the hierarchical, bureaucratised youth organisation, are losing their appeal among the young. They are searching for new ideas and for new organisations. They are trying to define their role in society and to answer difficult questions. What is socialism? Why did it fail? It seems that all young socialists agree that the system created by Stalin, whose many elements are still in effect today, had nothing to do with true socialism. Echoing the views of the Mensheviks in the 1920s, A. Grishin wrote in a *samizdat* journal: '... the concept of democracy is inseparable from the concept of socialism and socialism is unthinkable without democracy'.[26] Since the Soviet system is no democracy it is not socialism either. The draft of the FSC programme stated: 'Restructuring is the beginning of the revolutionary process, the essence of which is the establishment of the original democratic principles of socialism'.[27]

It is not clear what the authors meant by the word 'original'. Most probably it was left unexplained because various factions would explain differently when the original elements of socialism were subverted. The draft programme went on: 'We are for a true socialist democracy based upon elected and capable soviets which would have broad economic authority'.[28] This is an almost verbatim repetition of the Mensheviks' programme of 1924, which the authors of this draft did not cite. They are Mensheviks but they do not know it. Repeating another plank in the Menshevik platform, they demand '... equality of all political and societal organisations before the law and the restoration of real independence of the courts'.[29] The young socialists are unequivocal in their demands for political freedom: 'It is necessary to guarantee a real transition from the policy of *glasnost'* to true freedom of the press'.[30]

Just like the Mensheviks, today's socialists favour a combination of democracy in politics and socialism in economics, socialism not in the sense of a centralised planned economy, but a version of market socialism. 'We favour rejection of the ministerial system of directing the economy'.[31] What they understand by market socialism is a system of guarantees that prevent market forces from hurting the workers: 'We are categorically against the liberal interpretation of the reform which is designed to widen social inequality and create privileges for the technical elite'.[32] By the 'liberal interpretation' the young socialists mean the interpretation by some Soviet economists who favour restoration of a free market economy.

On 21 August 1988 the FSC convened a conference to work out its programme. The conference was originally planned with the participation of the Komsomol, but a week before the conference the Moscow Soviet banned it and the Komsomol withdrew. The conference assembled despite the ban; 200 delegates from 70 cities took part.[33] It was decided that the Federation of Socialist Clubs would retain a decentralised structure with a variety of factions and differences of opinion. Nevertheless a joint declaration on the anniversary of the Nazi–Soviet pact and the occupation of Czechoslovakia were worked out. Analysing the development of Socialist clubs, one *samizdat* observer compared them to Marxist circles at the turn of the century. It was a period of ferment and search. It was necessary, he argued, to build a powerful and united movement.[34]

An attempt was made at the end of August 1988 to coordinate the activity of all city-based Popular Fronts. On 26–29 August a conference of Popular Fronts convened. Representatives of 70 local organisations from seven Union Republics and 40 cities attended.[35] Some of the participants were communists. The socialists from the FSC were there as well. The representatives of PFs did not think of themselves as an organisation opposing the CP. On the contrary, they saw their goal in supporting Gorbachev's policy of restructuring. The conference adopted a General Declaration, a resolution on the nationality question, and a draft for reform of the electoral law. An attempt to create an all-Union or even an all-

Russian Popular Front failed. Disagreements over specific issues were insurmountable. Discussing the causes for the conference's inability to unite various PFs, Kagarlitsky, of the FSC, pointed out that a popular mass movement had emerged during the summer of 1988. These new Popular Fronts were essentially different from the 'old' clubs. They were frightened by a wide popular base and afraid of losing leadership of this movement.[36] Aside from the conflict between the new and the old clubs, the Popular Fronts by their very nature comprised supporters of restructuring whose ultimate objectives were quite diverse. Should the Union Republics be allowed to secede? Should a multi-party system be introduced? Should anti-socialist clubs be admitted to Popular Fronts? For many communists in the Popular Fronts it was difficult if not impossible to answer these questions in the affirmative in August 1988.

The 'Moscow Tribune' club is the closest to what could be called a loyal opposition. Such prominent people as R. Z. Sagdeev, Roy Medvedev and Tat'yana Zaslavskaya are members, as was the late Andrei Sakharov. The club had a total of 100 members at its founding in October 1988.[37] Now that all of the above-mentioned activists have been elected to the Congress of People's Deputies, thanks largely to pressure from the informal groups, they are entering the stage of formal politics in the legislature. Their agenda includes democratisation of electoral law, broadening of the rights of nationalities and disengagement of the bureaucracy from directing the economy.[38] This group of former political exiles, outcasts, and mavericks is turning into a small core of liberal legislators which has made common cause with Eltsin and the Baltic representatives in the Congress in the summer of 1989. No doubt the Popular Fronts which now exist in many Russian cities will attempt to unite into an all-Union organisation which will serve as a political base for the liberal constructive opposition of Eltsin. Summing up the development of Popular Fronts in 1988, a *samizdat* journal wrote:

> From young people's political clubs and their associations, to the Popular Fronts movement of many thousands, which has arisen in the majority of regions of the country—this is the evolution of our movement in just half a year.[39]

The 'Memorial' society is very similar to the Popular Fronts in its spirit. In fact, many students, professors, and intellectuals I spoke to were enthusiastic supporters of both. 'Memorial' sees its task as somewhat different from the Popular Fronts. Its top priority is profound destalinisation. At its founding congress in January 1989, the society decided to erect a monument to the victims of Stalinism, to establish a library, and an archive. Groups of volunteers across the country are collecting information on the tragic events of the past. The chapter of 'Memorial' in Odessa, for example, has made it known that it received numerous letters from concerned citizens about sites of executions during the Stalin era.[40] A core of 'Memorial' enthusiasts is based at the Historical Archival Institute led by Yurii Afanas'ev, himself an uncompromising supporter of reforms, and a member of 'Memorial' and of the 'Moscow Tribune'. They are creating an oral history library, interviewing hundreds of people on collectivisation, the purges, the war, and executions. A young historian called D. Yurasov is the epitome of the 'Memorial' enthusiast. He has collected data in the archives on thousands of victims of Stalin's purges. When I talked to him last year he was fully immersed in his search for relatives of camp survivors, for missing documents, in reconstruction of biographies, places and dates of executions during the Great Terror. People like Yurasov are driven by a thirst for truth, to make the tragedy of the past public knowledge.

As is widely known, groups of people and individuals in various parts of the country have been doing this for years, including Yurasov himself. The search for the truth about the past did not start with Gorbachev's restructuring. Discovery of execution cites near Minsk and in the Ukraine,[41] and the new light shed on the execution of the Imperial family, are only the most recent reminders that individuals have been working on their own for years.[42] Restructuring has made it possible for these people to come out into the open and to coordinate their activity. During my discussions with some 'Memorial' members in January 1989 they told me that the thorniest problem at their recent meetings was the question of how to define the term 'victims of Stalinism'. Were these only the people who were persecuted during the 1929–1953 period? Or should political prisoners under Lenin and Stalin's successors be included as well? I was told that the majority was inclined in favour of the latter but was afraid of retaliation by the authorities.

'Memorial's' concern to reveal the truth about the past should be seen in a broader historical context. It is a part of a much larger cultural trend to rethink and rediscover not only Soviet but Russian history. The outward manifestations of this trend are the appearance of groups all over the country seeking to restore old Russian names to their cities and towns. An informal group is lobbying to restore the old Russian name Tver' to the city of Kalinin, Vyatka to Kirov, and Ekaterinburg to Sverdlovsk. A *samizdat* journal *Samara* makes the same point in Kuibyshev, *Peterburg* in Leningrad.[43] And even in a place where one would least expect a movement in favour of the old name, Kaliningrad, a group of informals is seeking to restore the name Königsberg.[44] A special commission was formed recently to consider the problem of renaming.[45] Informal groups have generated enough interest and pressure from the public that in some cases communist names were dropped, like that of Zhdanov from Leningrad University. Yet the broader implications of this movement are much more profound. It is a repudiation of the Bolshevik legacy and a search for pre-revolutionary identity.

If the 'Moscow Tribune' and the Popular Fronts concentrate on constructive engagement and specific legislative proposals, and 'Memorial' on the search for historical truth, other informal groups in the liberal mainstream put an emphasis on what for them are priority issues. Among those are Helsinki Human Rights groups and the Vienna Committee set up in the spring of 1989 to monitor Soviet compliance with international agreements on Human Rights.[46] An informal group, 'Trust', seeks to promote trust and cooperation between East and West. The Human Rights groups are similar to the Popular Fronts and 'Memorial' in their basic intellectual outlook and in their political values. Yet they are slightly more critical of the Soviet authorities and see their role in systematic and consistent criticism of all the violations of human rights which are still frequent in the Soviet Union.

The most prominent personalities in these groups are Sergei Grigoryants, Editor of the *samizdat* journal *Glasnost'*, Lev Timofeev, editor of the *samizdat* journal *Referendum*, and Aleksandr Podrabinek, an editor of *Ekspress Khronika* and a frequent contributer of articles to *samizdat* journals. These people are connected to the Human Rights movements of the 1970s and 1980s, hence they are sceptical of Gorbachev's administration. To be sure, they also consider themselves a loyal and constructive opposition.[47] But they are much more outspoken and uncompromising in their critique than Sakharov before his death, Eltsin, Medvedev, Zaslavskaya and other prominent figures in 'Moscow Tribune'. In their analysis of the current change, the authors in these journals reiterate that too little has been accomplished so far:

> It is difficult to believe the General Secretary because even though a number of good laws were passed, . . . so far no economic and legal foundations have been created for the improvement of the economy. . . . The law on the enterprise has been passed but is not implemented. And how can it be implemented if there is no system of wholesale trade. A system of unemployment insurance—none. A law on bankruptcy—none. A law on share holding—none. Whatever one needs for improvement of the economy does not exist . . . . Only a free market economy can lead the country out of the economic crisis.[48]

Despite the rhetoric of reform, human rights violations continue. Week after week the pages of *Ekspress Khronika* are full of reports of demonstrations disbanded, fines imposed on activists, arrests and other repressive actions by local authorities. Human Rights activists subjected the new legislation adopted or prepared by the Supreme Soviet under Gorbachev's leadership to profound criticism. Aleksandr Podrabinek wrote, for example, that the rule of law, Gorbachev style, was going to be a system whereby new laws would be introduced which were more restrictive and less democratic than under Brezhnev. Society would be forced to comply with these draconian laws while the West would acknowledge that the rule of law had been established in the USSR.[49] According to Podrabinek the law on elections to the Congress of People's Deputies was indeed worse than under Brezhnev. It introduced corporate and indirect elections, trying to secure absolute control for the CP.[50] Similarly the new Ukaz of 8 April 1989 on anti-Soviet activity criminalises 'discrediting' of Soviet public officials and organisations, which is hardly better than the anti-Soviet activity and propaganda clause in article 70 it has replaced.[51] People grouped around these journals are sceptical but cautiously optimistic. They distinguish two political groupings within the CP, one, a party of repentance, and the other the party relying on force.[52] Their hope is that the party of repentance will prevail.

Within the general spectrum of political opinion in the USSR the Democratic Union seems to be even more critical than the Human Rights groups and the more modest Popular Fronts, 'Memorial' and Restructuring clubs. The Democratic Union also supports the establishment of a market economy, the rule of law and a multi-party system.[53] Yet its final goals would lead not to restructuring but to replacement of the Soviet system. For the Democratic Union restructuring is too half-hearted, too uncertain and too limited. Evgenii Debryansky said at its founding congress in May 1988:

...the CPSU leadership offers us only one variant of restructuring without having published the entire programme of how it intends to lead the country out of the current crisis. It is trying to carry out reforms on the basis of existing economic, political and societal relations.[54]

Such restructuring is doomed to failure, because it is not restructuring. All these social relations have to be changed. The Democratic Union's criticism of restructuring nevertheless pales in comparison with its denunciation of the Leninist-Stalinist legacy:

We consider that the social and political order which was established in the country as a result of the state overturn in October 1917 and which has, for a number of reasons, strengthened itself in the course of historical development, is a system of stagnant totalitarianism in the conditions of omnipotence of the *nomenklatura*.[55]

Contrary to the now official line of Gorbachev's reformers on history, which stipulates that only in 1929 did the Stalinists distort the 'Leninist democratic' principles, the Democratic Union uncompromisingly condemns the entire Leninist legacy, from the very first days of the October seizure of power. One of the Democratic Union's most important actions was a rally on the 70th anniversary of the Bolshevik proclamation of Red Terror. The Democratic Union reminded the public that Bolshevik state policy was to seize hostages from among the 'class' enemy, and that thousands were executed on the 'class' principle:

On 5 September 1918 the Bolsheviks launched Red Terror. Tens of thousands of innocent people were executed... Thousands of hostages were seized, including women and children, who were later killed.[56]

In a number of articles in their *samizdat* journals Democratic Union authors discussed Lenin's legacy in a knowledgable and sophisticated manner. One author, for example, argued that the so-called October revolution which proclaimed soviet power was not a revolution at all and did not transfer power to the soviets. In fact, according to the author, the October *coup d'état* was directed against the soviets. Prior to October, the soviets had expressed the will of society through several political parties. The October *coup* aimed to smash the soviets from within and establish a one-party dictatorship. As a result, the expression 'soviet power' has been used to disguise the actual dictatorship of the privileged elite.[57] The Democratic Union rejects and denounces communist totalitarianism in no uncertain terms. Stalinism was nothing more than a return to the War Communism of Lenin. The author saw one as an extension of the other. He defined Bolshevism as the 'turning off of all moral restraints', as self-assuredness in righteousness, and as the mentality 'Victors are not judged', that allowed communists to conduct their brutal experiments on the Russian people.[58]

In the general spectrum of political opposition in the Soviet Union, the Democratic Union is much closer to independence parties and movements in the republics than to Popular Fronts and pro-restructuring groups, both in Russia and in the other republics. The Democratic Union and the Independence parties share total rejection of the entire Soviet system of government and economy. One of the Democratic Union's factions has even adopted the name 'Constitutional Democrats', the name of the Russian Liberal party which was destroyed by the Bolsheviks.[59] They refer to the CP as a dictatorship of partocracy and openly advocate a Western-type market economy.[60] Some in the Popular Fronts, both in Russia and in the other republics, may also share these goals but they are more pragmatic. They abjure the Democratic Union's rejectionist posture. In a sense, the Democratic Union reflects the views of frustrated young people, intellectuals who realise that so little has changed and so little can be done under current conditions. Unlike the Popular Fronts in the Baltic, the Democratic Union does not have masses of people behind it. It is a radical but relatively impotent young people's protest association.

In January 1989 I asked some activists in the Leningrad Popular Front what they thought of the Democratic Union. One replied: 'What they say is pleasant to hear, of course. They denounce the communists, they call things with their right names'. But their methods were not to his liking. The Democratic Union was too radical. It was not open to constructive engagement with reformers inside the CPSU. There was no hostility towards the Democratic Union on his part. Rather he perceived their tasks as complementary. It was good that the Democratic Union provided a little bit of a kick against the bosses, he said. It was also necessary to work within the system against Solov'ev and Co. Thus it is not so much in goals that the Democratic Union differs from the Popular Fronts as in tactics and in style of activity. It does not want to ask anything of the authorities. It makes demands. As Valeriya Novodvorskaya declared at the founding congress:

> Political struggle means something other than appeals to the ruling party with requests and pleas; political struggle means an appeal to the people and the organisation of such resistance to totalitarianism that it would compel the party to adopt reforms.[61]

A vigorous debate ensued in *samizdat* journals between Novodvorskaya and activists in the Human Rights movement. In her article: 'What is the Difference Between Political Struggle and Human Rights Activity?' Novodvorskaya rejected the old forms of struggle, typical, as she thought, of Human Rights activists. They were always appealing to the authorities. They were full of illusions. They tried to remedy the consequences of the regime rather than to attack the root causes. They should not write petitions but raise the people in universal protest action against totalitarianism:

> If all took part in a democratic strike, no authority would be able to withstand the pressure. Clearly our predecessors, the Socialist Revolutionaries and the Social Democrats, understood this. It would not have occurred to them to write letters to ministers or to kneel down at the feet of the Tsar.... What has happened to us if after 71 years of this horrible system, some still have the naivete to entreat the authorities for anything?[62]

Kiril Podrabinek defended the Human Rights activists' approach and criticised the Democratic Union. He had great reservations about its claim that it is or would like to become a political party. Clearly it was not yet a political party. Its members were groups of impatient intellectuals. By proclaiming a party and by claiming to formulate the tasks of political struggle for the entire people, they were in fact usurping the right of the people to decide for themselves. The Democratic

Union's programme had already been formulated without any participation by the people. This smacked of the Bolsheviks' approach to politics whereby a small party claimed to speak on behalf of the people, never asking their consent. Enough of parties speaking for the people. The Democratic Union might be acquiring features of those against whom it struggled. The Human Rights approach was the best one. It sought to create guarantees for the people to exercise their political rights by themselves without any intermediaries speaking for them.[63] Despite their different approaches, priorities, and tactics, all these groups are heirs to the Westerniser tradition in Russian intellectual history. All are for some form of democratic elected representative government.

All of the above-mentioned groups, clubs, and associations are essentially composed of the intelligentsia. These are students, professors, journalists, writers, lawyers, professional people, engineers—in other words, Russia's educated society. In many cases membership of one of those groups or clubs goes hand in hand with membership of another. Young socialists I spoke to were affiliated with the FSC, 'Memorial', Popular Front, and ecological groups. The term 'membership' is hardly applicable. Aside from a group core, most others can be better defined as supporters. They are clustered primarily in big cities and very few workers and even fewer farmers seem to have been involved during the first year of the informal groups' existence. Whereas in the Baltic and in Armenia Popular Fronts managed to become broad-based popular movements, in Russia proper political associations remained relatively isolated from the populace throughout 1988. They often complained of apathy and passivity among Russian workers.

The situation began to change in the spring and especially in the summer of 1989 during a wave of workers' strikes. During the elections to the Congress of People's Deputies the first contacts with wider audiences were made. To their great surprise, many intellectuals from various clubs discovered that the workers listened to their appeals with great interest. Yurii Afanas'ev received an enthusiastic reception at the Electrical plant in Moscow in May 1989. A new stage in the relationship between the political clubs and the broader electorate commenced, a stage of competition with the official candidates for popular support.

A group that stands apart from all others is *Pamyat'* (Memory). It calls itself a Russian patriotic organisation but what distinguishes it from Popular Fronts in the other republics, which also consider themselves patriotic, is that *Pamyat'* is openly anti-Semitic. It grew out of a movement to protect the Russian cultural heritage in the 1970s and 1980s. In its early stages *Pamyat'* advocated the preservation of Russian historical monuments. It was concerned with the preservation of the Russian village, Russian customs, dialects, traditions, and way of life. In recent times, though, especially from 1986 onward, *Pamyat'* has been evolving in the direction of Russian chauvinism and rabid anti-Semitism. The communists and the Jews are to blame for Russia's misfortunes. Russia was a victim of a Marxist-Jewish conspiracy.[64] *Pamyat'* held a number of rallies in Moscow and Leningrad over the last year and voiced these ideas to chance audiences in the streets. Like the liberal and the socialist currents in the new political spectrum, *Pamyat'* is also splintered into several regional organisations which are autonomous from each other. These are the National Patriotic Front

Pamyat', headed by Vasil'ev, in Moscow; the World Anti-Zionist and Anti-Mason Front, headed by V. Emel'yanov; the National Patriotic Front, led by N. Zherbin, in Leningrad, as well as 'Patriots' (Leningrad), 'Fatherland' (Sverdlovsk), 'Homeland' (Chelyabinsk) and some other groups. Some *samizdat* observers feared that the appeal of *Pamyat'* might yet turn out to be the greatest among the ordinary people. These fears seem to have been exaggerated, at least in the context of 1989. If the elections to the Congress were a barometer of popular attitudes, then *Pamyat'* did very poorly. Only a handful of its candidates were elected. It is more significant that the liberal reformers' candidates defeated *Pamyat'* people in numerous districts.

Interaction with the authorities

The communist authorities have obviously been uneasy about the activities of the unsanctioned associations. But they did not display any consistent policy. The groups were neither suppressed nor allowed to function openly. The policy seems to have been one of petty harassment, fines, and short-term imprisonment of activists. In chronological terms, the summer of 1988 was a time of relative permissiveness in the climate of the party conference. The autumn of 1988 was a period of rough treatment. Beginning with the election campaign to the Congress of People's Deputies in January 1989, unsanctioned associations began to function more openly again. In the aftermath of the election defeat of party functionaries, however, the authorities began a new campaign against the associations.

On 28 August 1988 a rally was organised in Leningrad by the Union of Social Democrats to discuss rising prices and the falling standard of living. It was forcibly disbanded by the newly created riot police.[65] Similarly, on 3 September in Leningrad at the Kazan' cathedral, police attacked Democratic Union activists, arrested 24 people, and imposed heavy fines.[66] On 5 September a rally to commemorate the victims of Bolshevik Red Terror organised by the Democratic Union was also brutally disbanded.[67] Fifty people were detained at a similar demonstration in Moscow. Democratic Union activists wore black cloth over their mouths with the inscription 'glasnost'.[68] The riot police were very tough. Their tactics, according to an eyewitness, were to isolate the crowds from the activists and to intimidate them by beating.[69]

On 5 September 1988 a joint meeting of several informal groups was held in the Kirov Palace of Culture on the occasion of the Red Terror anniversary. The 'Alternative' club, the Leningrad 'Popular Front', the 'Democratic Restructuring', club, the Democratic Union and others took part.[70] The Democratic Union spokesman proposed honouring the victims of Bolshevik Red Terror by a minute of silence. Half the audience remained seated. The author of the *samizdat* article describing the event came to the conclusion that they were functionaries and KGB agents.[71] However, the authorities were more cautious when several unsanctioned associations acted together. On 9 October the authorities allowed a public meeting in Leningrad sponsored by the Club of Democratisation of Trade Unions, the Union of Social Democrats and the Democratic Union. It was decided to create a strike fund to help workers if and when they went on strike and to express support for the Polish Solidarity movement.[72]

When various clubs and groups coordinated their efforts they were able to force the authorities to grant concessions. Perhaps the most remarkable example of this was in connection with the Constitution day rally in Leningrad. Thirteen informal groups and clubs organised several meetings in September 1988 in various enterprises and houses of culture protesting against the July *ukaz* of the Supreme Soviet on the conduct of rallies and demonstrations. They also formed an 'Organisational Committee' which decided to stage a city conference on 7 October on Constitution day in the Il'ich house of culture. The clubs and informal groups applied to their district executive committees of soviets for a permit and in most cases the permits were not granted. On 28 September representatives of the 'Democratic Restructuring' club, the Popular Front, and the 'Rejuvenation' club sent a delegation to the obkom to inform it that if the rally was not allowed, they would take part in an unauthorised rally.[73] The obkom granted permission for a rally in the 'Locomotive' stadium. The clubs invited the CP authorities to take part in this gathering as well, but the obkom refused. About 10,000 people were present at this rally. The Democratic Union decorated the podium with traditional Russian national flags (white, blue and red) and representatives of the Estonian Independence party displayed the Estonian national flag.[74] The speakers criticised the new *ukaz* as unconstitutional, since it violated basic provisions on the freedom of speech and assembly. On 30 October in Leningrad the protest action was repeated; this time it was a silent vigil in front of the Kazan' cathedral—300 people stood with candles in honour of Soviet political prisoners.[75] The police moved in quickly, disbanding the vigil and imposing heavy fines.

One can cite dozens and dozens of similar occurrences across the country in the autumn of 1988: unauthorised rallies, riot police, clubs and beatings, arrests and fines. These became familiar elements of political life in Russia. Among the Democratic Union activists alone, several tens of thousands of fines were imposed in 1988.[76] To pay the fines, informal groups began to collect donations, establishing a fund to help those arrested and fined. At the end of the year a further step was taken. An unsanctioned group called 'Civic Dignity' created a 'Committee of Civic Defence' to provide legal aid to those whose rights had been violated by the state and party apparatus.[77]

Examples of joint political actions by several informal associations demonstrate that on such issues as freedom of speech and assembly, and struggle against unconstitutional actions by local authorities, the Democratic Union finds much in common with more moderate associations like Restructuring and the Popular Fronts. However, it has established close contact with Independence parties and movements in the Baltic republics and Georgia, and with the Armenian Karabakh Committee. At the Democratic Union's second congress in February 1989 representatives of these parties and movements were present as guests and observers. The Democratic Union unequivocally recognised the rights of these republics to self-determination, including secession from the Soviet Union. Their main slogan is: 'For Your Freedom and Ours!'[78] Other mainstream liberal clubs are certainly not ready to go that far. If the summer of 1988 was a period of euphoria and consolidation, the autumn of 1988 was a period of political differentiation and radicalisation. What was inconceivable a year earlier was now on the agenda.

Confrontation and elections, spring 1989

In the summer and autumn of 1988 the activities of unsanctioned associations and especially those of the Democratic Union were regarded by the authorities as irritating and embarrassing but hardly dangerous. They thought they were dealing with intellectuals, 'demagogues' and 'extremists'. It is now apparent that apparatchiks contemplated a number of measures against informal associations as early as late autumn 1988. A *samizdat* journal reported that at the Moscow telephone exchange they diligently began work to make it possible to disconnect 90% of private telephones 'in case of emergency'. Lists of those whose phones would not be turned off were provided to the telephone exchange.[79] In Leningrad the second secretary of the obkom, Degtyarev, addressed the issue of unsanctioned associations on 16 September. He called the Democratic Union an anticonstitutional organisation and accused the PF of sharing some of its objectives.[80] Shortly thereafter, the Leningrad KGB started the so-called case No. 64 against the activists of the Democratic Union for 'disseminating documents discrediting Soviet social order'.[81]

At the beginning of December 1988 a representative of the Komsomol CC came to Gorky with an instruction to the Komsomol first secretary, Suvorov; the instruction was reported to have been to cease any support they might have rendered to the unsanctioned associations and to prepare for a sharp change of policy in regard to informal associations.[82] The Internal Affairs directorate in Gorky established permanent supervision over the following leaders of political clubs: Stas Klokov from 'Vanguard', Stas Petrichevsky from 'Nizhegorodsky Council on Ecology', and Sergei Tsvetkov of the Federation of Socialist Clubs.[83] In Kharkov a closed party meeting took place in response to the publication of the programme of the Ukrainian People's Movement for Restructuring.[84] 'The opinion was expressed that this movement claims to be an alternative political party whose goal is to spread Ukrainian nationalism and in the future to detach the Ukraine from the USSR'.[85]

In early February 1989 a curious document appeared in several cities. In *Pravda* references were made to an obkom plenum in Leningrad which discussed measures to be taken to stop the creation of 'structures opposing the Communist Party'.[86] The wrath of party functionaries was directed against the informal groups and associations. Unfortunately very little was reported in the official Soviet press on the substance and especially the origins of the obkom decisions. From *Pravda* one gets the impression that this was a decision of local Leningrad party officials. Yet in the unofficial, *samizdat* press an interesting document described similar decisions adopted in Minsk. As an article in *Referendum* related, on 6 February the first secretary of the Central Committee of the Belorussian CP, E. Sokolov, read to newspaper correspondents excerpts from a document he called a 'closed' (*zakrytoe*) decision (*postanovlenie*) of the Politbureau: 'Concerning Measures on

Counteracting Attempts to Create Political Structures Opposing the CPSU'. The Democratic Union and Popular Fronts were mentioned. Sokolov said that the document was signed by Gorbachev. This document was also read in the Minsk obkom and there the letter was said to have been prepared by Medvedev, a Politbureau member, and his Ideological Commission. The document was referred to as a 'letter' on one occasion and as a 'decision' on another. In both cases the document spoke about attempts by extremists to blacken soviet and communist leaders and their attempts to push through their people at the elections.[87]

Regardless of where the document originated and who signed it, the fact remains that measures against informal associations were discussed at least in Leningrad and Minsk at the same time. According to the author in *Referendum*, Sokolov presented it in Minsk as a decision of the Politbureau in order to cool down the support of the Writers' Union and other public organisations for the informal associations. The author argued that Gorbachev perhaps could not prevent such a move by conservatives in the party leadership and in the Central Committee and had to go along with it. What is most remarkable is the way Sokolov interpreted the meaning of the document to Minsk party officials. He is reported to have said: 'Hit them so hard that they will not get up' (*Dat' po zubam tak chtob ne vstali*).[88]

All these pronouncements, threats and measures clearly indicate that the party was alarmed by the rise of new social forces, especially in the face of elections to the Congress of People's Deputies in full swing in February and March 1989. The stage was set for the first trial of strength between the party apparatus and the popular initiative groups across the country, in the context of elections. It is important to stress here that by the spring 1989 elections the local party bureaucracy and the unsanctioned clubs had a year of rising tensions behind them. Prohibitions, disbandments and fines were well remembered. The question: 'Why do we have to ask for permits from them?' gave way increasingly to the slogan: 'No to Elections Without Choice!'.

The election campaign triggered the informals into action. All across the country they began to enjoy a new and exhilarating experience—the right to campaign in elections and support candidates opposed to the local hierachies. In addition to the existing informal associations, new ones emerged in many cities. These were primarily the so-called 'Residents' Initiative Groups'. Their task was to mobilise residents in their electoral districts for alternative candidates. As is well known, the party bureaucracy succeeded in eliminating alternative candidates from the ballot and in placing unopposed single candidates in 399 electoral districts.[89] As Eltsin acknowledged, 'the party organs have made it possible only for those whom they considered appropriate to go through'.[90]

Local authorities systematically violated electoral law by packing nomination meetings with their men, intimidating opposition candidates and disrupting residents' nomination initiatives. That gave rise to the slogan: 'Let's Throw the Bastards Out!' On 15 March 1989 in Leningrad a rally took place attended by 1,000 people. It was sponsored by the 'Alternative', 'Democratic Restructuring' and 'Memorial' clubs. It was decided to convene a Forum of Leningrad Society, and to work for a united front of all clubs against the apparatus. Slogans were chanted: 'Long live Unsanctioned Restructuring!'[91] To coordinate the efforts of all the clubs a new committee, 'Elections 89', was formed. It printed leaflets and set pickets against the uncontested candidate, obkom first secretary Solov'ev. Some picketers were detained by the KGB 'for anti-Soviet agitation and propaganda'.[92] This only added fuel to the fire. It was the 'Elections 89' Committee that played such a crucial role in defeating all the Leningrad party bosses in the elections.

In Moscow a rally sponsored by 'Memorial' in mid-March was attended by 3,000 people. They held posters proclaiming 'Russian Popular Front for the Trial of Stalinism'. Evgenii Evtushenko spoke about attempts by the authorities to ban the rally. Prominent figures like Vasilii Selyunin and S. I. Grigoryants demanded the publication of Solzhenitsyn's *Gulag Archipelago* and the resignation of Ligachev.[93] Moscow was unrecognisable in those days in March: meetings and rallies at enterprises, televised debates among candidates, activists from various clubs passing leaflets at metro station entrances and a bitter campaign against Eltsin by the party apparatus.

The more popularity and authority the Popular Fronts acquired, the more suspicious the party authorities were of their intentions. Coexistence turned into open political struggle. Yaroslavl' was one of the few Russian cities where the Popular Front had become popular and strong enough to participate actively in the election campaign. That made all the difference. The authorities could not dismiss names of alternative candidates or refuse registration to them as easily. The Popular Front was watching very closely for any violations of electoral law. Moreover, there were newspapers which were willing to publish such information. In the eyes of many sincere supporters of reform the Popular Front emerged as a defender of electoral law against the machinations of the party apparatus.[91]

But the Yaroslavl' example was an exception to the rule. In most cities the party authorities managed to dismiss alternative candidates arbitrarily. A catalogue of all violations of the law would take many pages. As an observer in a *samizdat* journal put it: 'Do not forget, our democracy is a socialist one. This means not the total absence of democratic procedures, but total possibility for the dictatorship to render them meaningless'.[95] This is exactly what happened in Ryazan'. The Residents' Initiative Group sent a petition to the electoral district commission for a permit to hold a residents' nomination meeting in accordance with the electoral law. The electoral district commission and the city authorities ignored the petition. The Initiative Group responded with an ultimatum: 'We resolutely protest against the dragging out of a decision on this matter. We give notice that voters from the electoral district No. 279 will assemble outside the city hall at 6 p.m. on 5 April 1989 to obtain an answer to their application.'[96] The city authorities banned a rally and refused to schedule a nomination meeting. Voters assembled despite the ban. The Initiative Group leader, A. Gavrilov, contacted the city authorities again, but to no avail:

A. Gavrilov told those assembled that they had been given no answer at all, and he suggested that they assemble the next day at the Radio Institute Stadium to collect signatures for a petition to the Central Electoral Commission. In the meantime two policemen twisted his arms behind his back and dragged him inside a vehicle. That was the signal. The police advanced on the crowd . . .[97]

Despite such heavy-handed interference, or maybe because of it, the party bureaucracy suffered a crushing defeat in the elections; 35 obkom secretaries and 200 other high ranking functionaries and military officers across the country were defeated. The victory of Eltsin in Moscow stunned the bureaucracy. A new political situation was created. The informal associations realised their potential and their power. If these were the results at a stage when the informal groups movement was still in its infancy, without any all-Union organisation or independent press, what would the result have been if they had been able to nominate their own candidates in truly free contested elections? The prototype of what could happen was seen in Lithuania, where Sajudis supported candidates virtually swept away the CP functionaries in a landslide.

The party apparatus strikes back

The Communist Party bureaucracy was shocked by the election results. A new offensive against the informal associations was launched. The Democratic Union activists were beaten up and fined again.[98]*Pravda* reported that top officials blamed informal associations, not themselves, for their defeat: 'The informal associations which had in the beginning come out under the banners of restructuring... have in fact created an anti-restructuring atmosphere and blame the party organisations for it'.[99] In other words, the press and the informals were to blame, not the party.

Similarly, in Leningrad the joint city and province CP plenum after the elections attributed the defeat of the party to a better organised campaign by the informal associations. The 'extremists and demagogues' managed to create a negative image of a party functionary.[100] What must have frightened the party officials most was the realisation that ideas, unthinkable only yesterday, were becoming popular. Gerasimov, the city party chief, admitted in an interview that the people in Leningrad found the idea of a multi-party system attractive. Nevertheless he was against it and for more resolute struggle against 'extremists'.[101] The journal *Agitator*, for party propagandists, urged its readers to begin a resolute struggle against the 'antisocial' unsanctioned associations.[102]

If in Leningrad the party resorted to threats and warnings, in Georgia it resorted to shooting. The CP response on 9 April must be seen in the context of a growing fear of the new forces challenging its authority. It is important that each time in the course of 1988–89 that popular movements arose to the point of not merely criticising the CP but challenging its power, the answer was violent suppression. In 1988 it was in Armenia when the Karabakh committee was arrested. In April 1989 it was the massacre in Georgia and the arrest of leaders of the Independence movement, and in January 1990 in Baku.

Can the party retain control? What should the policy be towards unsanctioned associations? These and similar questions were debated at the April 1989 Central Committee plenum. The speeches of party functionaries portrayed the attack upon them as an attack on Soviet power. The first secretary of the Moscow obkom, Mesyats, argued:

... it has become fashionable in Moscow to disseminate leaflets, posters, and all kinds of appeals. And I will tell you. These are not child's play. These are political slogans, which call for the overthrow of Soviet power, overthrow of the party.[103]

The speaker called for immediate measures against informal associations, especially against the Democratic Union. The first Secretary of the Azerbaidzhan CP, Vezirov, spoke in the same vein:

We cannot close our eyes to the fact that certain forces aim to deprive our party of the leading role.... This is ideological AIDS... ... Restructuring must be defended from the attacks of openly anti-socialist forces, who are trying to shake the foundations of the state and seize political power.[104]

What is clear from these hysterical appeals is that the party apparatchiks are frightened. Are 'demogogues' and 'extremists' isolated enemies or are they powerful forces threatening the power of the CPSU? The first secretary of Krasnodar obkom, Poloznikov, argued:

Events of the last years, and especially of the last few months in the Baltic, Caucasus, in Moscow and Leningrad, in Moldavia and in other regions, as well as the slogans that are now openly printed in our press, the slogans of the Democratic Union and of some other informal associations, do not provide ground for either calm or contemplation. Some of those who call themselves communists, like Nesterov and Alekseev from the Leningrad 'Restructuring' club, and many others, consider the entire Communist Party guilty of Stalinist crimes. They are talking about splitting the USSR, about removing the CPSU from power, or even hanging the communists. They call on people not to fulfil government decisions, but to sabotage Soviet laws.[105]

The speaker concluded with an appeal: 'It is time to act!'

Although many speakers tried to limit the scope of the problem to the activity of informal groups it is clear that the implications of their speeches were much broader. Restructuring permitted these groups to form. Restructuring allowed the press to reveal to young people that the CP committed crimes. P. N. Fedoseev of the Presidium of the USSR Academy of Sciences put it this way: 'a part of our youth has formed an impression that the CPSU has turned out to be a party of mistakes and crimes against the people'.[106] In almost all speeches the unmistakable theme was enough is enough. The party was not going to give up power voluntarily. It was not going to turn into a discussion club. Vezirov even said that some CP organisations had started forming their own detachments (druzhiny). The plenum showed that the CP is in a deep crisis. It has discovered, as Gorbachev put it, that it did not know the society in which it lived.[107] It has discovered that those whom it had considered demagogues and extremists were able to mobilise a majority vote against the CP bureaucracy. No wonder the communists' instinctive reaction is to suppress.

On the eve of the opening of the Congress of People's Deputies on 21 May 1989 all liberal and socialist associations in Moscow coordinated their activity for the first time. They sponsored and organised an impressive rally attended by tens of thousands of people. It was not easy for different groups to work together. Some people from the Moscow Tribune were against participation by the Democratic

Union spokesman. Nevertheless, he was admitted and all liberal and socialist groups cooperated on this occasion. The speakers called for the end of the *nomenklatura* system, separation of the party and the state and introduction of a multi-party system. Some went as far as to suggest that the new Congress should proclaim itself a Constituent Assembly. This rally marked the beginning of the new stage in the history of informal political associations in contemporary Russia. For the first time, the leaders of these groups spoke to tens of thousands of people. Thanks to TV coverage they became known to even broader strata. The rally marked the transition from discussion groups politics to mass politics.

Conclusion

The rise of informal political associations in the USSR is a sign of the awakening of Soviet society. It is discovering its strength, it is searching for new ideas, it is crystallising into new political organisations and parties. This brief survey of the new political forces on the Russian political horizon suggests that we are witnessing a rebirth of the pre-1917 political society. Russia is returning to itself, to its history, religion, customs and traditions. It is returning to pre-Bolshevik norms of behaviour, to pre-Bolshevik moral and ethical values, to pre-Bolshevik political culture. We are witnessing a great historical turning point in the history of Russian culture.

The CPSU has taken the role of the autocracy, the establishment which is clearly perceived by society as the cause of the problem. Just as in 1917 the liberals are ready for a constructive dialogue and reform. The right wing (then Black Hundreds, now *Pamyat'*) is blaming the Jews and Marxists. And the socialists (the SRs and Mensheviks then and the Democratic Union and new Social Democrats now) are more uncompromising and aspire to lead the people against what was then tsarist and is now communist autocracy.

Yet there is a significant difference between the aspirations of Russian society in 1917 and now. There are no Bolsheviks any more, in the sense that there are no people who are convinced that by the laws of history they are destined to lead Russia by means of dictatorship of the proletariat. Neo-Stalinist conservatives who want to preserve their privileges are not sure, as the Bolsheviks were, that history is on their side. In fact, they may be starting to realise that history is against them. The emergence of new political groupings akin to Russia's prerevolutionary political parties which the Bolsheviks brutally crushed during the civil war, heralds not only the demise of Stalinism, but also the end to the 1917 Bolshevik revolution. Perhaps it is better to refer to it as Bolshevik counter-revolution. The real revolution was not in 1917 but in the 1860s–1880s, a revolution of Westernisation started by Alexander II. The Bolsheviks destroyed the attributes of European political culture, the parliament, the parties, and the independent press. They disrupted the process of Westernisation for many decades but they have proved powerless to stop it.

The second and perhaps crucial difference between 1917 and 1989 is that the man at the head of the conservative establishment today, unlike in February 1917, is the leader of reform. Gorbachev started a revolution from above, yet he unleashed forces of society from below. In the course of 1988 and 1989 these new forces were becoming increasingly assertive and independent of party control. It is a revolution from below. The paradox of the political development during this time is that the party conservatives contributed more to the growth of the informal associations than the reformers. It was their machinations with the elections to the Party Conference that gave birth to the protest movement. It was their repression in the autumn of 1988 that radicalised many clubs. It was their manipulations at the Congress elections in the spring of 1989 that turned political clubs into competitors for public office. And finally it was their failure to improve the economic situation that made the workers become interested in opposition and go on strike.

Informal political associations are indeed embryos of future political parties. The CP is reluctant to admit it, but it realises that it must deal with the situation. The conservatives clearly want to roll *glasnost'* back, the reformers want to go full steam ahead. An open split within the CP is not impossible. Gorbachev has the unenviable task of manoeuvring between an increasingly assertive society and an increasingly frightened party apparatus. Instead of the party and the people united as the communist dogma reiterates, todays political scene in Soviet Russia is one with a variety of political forces.

The days of unchallenged supremacy of the Stalinist-Brezhnevist CP are gone. One can put it in the words of Trotsky, which he too hastily addressed to the Mensheviks in 1917: 'Your role is played out, your place is in the dustbin of History'.

Kennan Institute

[1] In Leningrad alone a Soviet observer has counted 1,300 informal groups. V. Lisovsky, '"Neformaly"—Za i Protiv', *Agitator*, 1989, No. 9 (9 May) pp. 26–28, here p. 27.

[2] *Ekspress Khronika*, 1988, No. 38 (18 September).

[3] *Ekspress Khronika*, 1988, No. 48 (27 November).

[4] *Ekspress Khronika*, 1988, No. 34 (21 August), p. 12.

[5] For data on Tver' Committee, see: *Ekspress Khronika* 1989, No. 11 (13 March) and on Vyatka Committee 'Vibor', in *v gorode Kirove*, *Levyi Povorot*, *samizdat* journal of the FSC, 1988, No. 14 (Moscow), p. 4.

[6] 'Pozitsiya Nashego Kandidata', (An interview with Boris Eltsin), *Propeller*, newspaper of the Aviation Institute named after Sergo Ordzhonikidze, 1989, No. 15 (21 February) (Moscow), p. 4.

[7] Boris Kagarlitsky, 'Narodnyi Front i krizis perestroiki', in *Materialy Samizdata*, Radio Free Europe–Radio Liberty, 1989, No. 4 (27 January) Arkhiv Samizdata No. 6332, p. 7.

[8] *Ibid.* p. 8.

[9] For a description of the first FSC demonstration in May 1988, see: S. Mitrokhin, 'Pikety', *Khronograf, samizdat* journal of the FSC, 1988, No. 7 (4 June) (Moscow, pp. 1–10. in: *Materialy Samizdata*, Radio Free Europe–Radio Liberty, 1988, No. 53 (17 December) Arkhiv Samizdata No. 6316.

[10] Kagarlitsky, 'Narodnyi Front...'.

[11] 'Pozitsiya....'.

[12] 'Yaroslavl'', *Levyi Povorot*, *samizdat* journal of the FSC, 1988, No. 14 (Moscow), p. 34. The Soviet official media estimate of participants in the rally was 5,000 people, see: Yana Nikitina, 'Diskussii na stadione', *Ogonek*, 1988, No. 34 (20–27 August).

[13] Kagarlitsky, 'Narodnyi Front...'. For a Soviet official media report on the June rally, see. A. Zhuravel' and N. Chulikhin, 'Golos Naberezhnoi. Po povodu mitinga v Yaroslavle', *Sotsialisticheskaya industriya*, 10 June 1988.

[14] 'Yaroslavl''... See also: V. Kosarev, 'Kto zhe oni—neformaly?' *Krasnaya zvezda*, 21 January 1989.

[15] Anatolii Cherkasov, 'Budet li prodolzhena "Demonstratsiya"', *Referendum, samizdat* journal 1988, No. 4 (January), (Moscow), p. 5-6.

[16] Anatolii Cherkasov, 'Miting ne smotrya ni na chto', *Referendum, samizdat* journal, 1988, No. 13-14 (June), (Moscow), pp. 10-12.

[17] Kagarlitsky, 'Narodnyi Front...'.

[18] Cherkasov, 'Miting...'.

[19] Kagarlitsky, 'Narodnyi Front...', and official media source: Zhan Mindubaev, 'Uroki odnoi otstavki', *Politicheskoe obrazovanie*, 1989, No. 1, pp. 23-30.

[20] E. Zakharov, 'Neformaly i Khar'kovskie vlasti', *Referendum, samizdat* journal, 1988, No. 22-23 (December), (Moscow), p. 11.

[21] Arnold Eremenko, 'Magadan—Severnaya bastiliya Sovetskogo Totalitarizma', *Ekspress Khronika*, 1989, No. 1 (January), p. 6.

[22] 'Rostov-na-Donu', *Moskovskii vestnik, samizdat* journal of the Moscow Popular Front, 1989, (January), (Moscow), pp. 7-8.

[23] 'Ofitsial'naya pechat' o neformalakh i nezavisimoi presse', *Vestnik Kluba Nezavisimoi Pechati*, 1988, No. 1 (10 October), p. 23; Arkhiv Samizdata, No. 6286.

[24] 'V Aiove vse spokoino', *Levyi Povorot, samizdat* journal of the FSC, 1988, No. 14 (Moscow), p. 37.

[25] S. Mitrokhin, 'Znamya Anarkhii v tsentre Moskvy', *Khronograf, samizdat* journal of the FSC, 1988, No. 7 (4 June), (Moscow), p. 3. in: *Materialy Samizdata*, Radio Free Europe–Radio Liberty, 1988, No. 53 (17 December), Arkhiv Samizdata No. 6316.

[26] A. Grishin, 'Vremya konferentsii', *Levyi Povorot, samizdat* journal of the FSC, 1988, No. 14 (Moscow), pp. 22-31, here, p. 31.

[27] 'O programme FSOK', *Khronograf, samizdat* journal of the FSC, 1988, No. 1 (28 May), (Moscow), pp. 14-19, here p. 18. in: *Materialy Samizdata*, Radio Free Europe–Radio Liberty, 1988, No. 53 (17 December), Arkhiv Samizdata No. 6315.

[28] *Ibid.* p. 15.

[29] *Ibid.* p. 17.

[30] *Ibid.* p. 14.

[31] *Ibid.* p. 17.

[32] *Ibid.* p. 16.

[33] 'Informatsionnoe soobshchenie po itogam Ob"edinennoi Vsesoyuznoi konferentsii Federatsii Sotsialisticheskikh Obshchestvennykh Klubov i Vsesoyuznogo Sotsial'no-Politicheskogo kluba', *Levyi Povorot, samizdat* journal of the FSC, 1988, No. 14 (Moscow), p. 20.

[34] Boris Kagarlitsky, 'Posleslovie k konferentsii', *Levyi Povorot, samizdat* journal of the FSC, 1988, No. 14 (Moscow), p. 33.

[35] 'Informatsionnoe soobshchenie...', pp. 21-22.

[36] Kagarlitsky, 'Posleslovie...', p. 32.

[37] 'Kul'tura i obshchestvennaya zhizn'.Moskva', *Ekspress Khronika*, 1988, No. 42 (16 October) p. 8. See also 'Intellektualy sozdayut politicheskii klub', *Referendum, samizdat* journal, 1988, (1-15 October), (Moscow), p. 6.

[38] This agenda was summarised in the election programme of Andrei Sakharov; see: 'Predvybornaya programma', *Materialy Samizdata*, Radio Free Europe–Radio Libery, 1989, No. 4 (27 January) Arkhiv Samizdata No. 6335. p. 1. Specific plans for legislative activity by members of the Moscow Tribune were discussed at its session at the end of April. See: 'V preddverii s"ezda—o s"ezde", *Moskovskie novosti*, 1989, No. 18 (30 April), p. 2.

[39] Editorial, *Moskovskii vestnik, samizdat* journal of the Moscow Popular Front, 1989, (January), (Moscow), p. 1.

[40] 'Odessa', *Ekspress khronika*, 1989, No. 13 (26 March), p. 2. The 'Memorial' society in Moscow began publishing its own *samizdat* newspaper: *Vedomosti Memoriala*. For a photocopy of the first page of the first issue, see: *Materialy Samizdata*, Radio Free Europe–Radio Liberty, 1989, No. 11 (24 March), p. 13.

[41] See for example, 'Exhumation of Bykovnya Graves in Ukraine Described', *FBIS: Daily Report*, 4 May 1989, p. 65, a reprint from: *Literaturnaya gazeta*, 26 April 1989, p. 2.

[42] 'Zemlya vydala tainu', *Moskovskie novosti*, 1989, No. 16 (16 April), p. 16.

[43] For photocopies of the title pages of these journals, see: *Materialy Samizdata*, Radio Free Europe–Radio Liberty, 1989, No. 11 (24 March).

[44] Vadim Khrappa, 'My—Narod K'onigsberga', *Referendum, samizdat* journal, 1988, No. 10 (April), (Moscow), pp. 12-13.

[45] This commission was formed under the auspices of the Soviet Culture Fund and the Academy of Sciences. Restoration of the old names for 20 cities was considered, including Nizhnii Novgorod (Gorky), Samara (Kuibyshev) and Tver' (Kalinin). It is important that the restoration of the name Sankt Peterburg for Leningrad was not considered. See: 'Nazvat' svoimi imenami', *Moskovskie novosti*, 1989, No. 18 (30 April), p. 2.

[46] 'Kluby i ob"edineniya. Leningrad', *Ekspress Khronika*, 1989, No. 12 (19 March), p. 2.

[47] See: 'Activist Timofeyev Interviewed on Plans', *FBIS Daily Report*, 7 June 1988, p. 56.

[48] 'Vremya polnoe sobytii, eshche ne razrazivshikhsya', *Referendum, samizdat* journal, 1988, No. 17 (16–30 September), (Moscow), p. 2.

[49] Aleksandr Podrabinek, 'Vybory, est' li vybor?', *Ekspress Khronika*, 1989, No. 13 (26 March), p. 5.

[50] *Ibid.*

[51] For a critique of this *ukaz*, see: 'Trudnosti zakonotvorchestva', and 'Za strokoi Ukaza', *Moskovskie novosti*, 1989, No. 16 (16 April), p. 2.

[52] 'Politika razuma i politika sily', *Referendum, samizdat* journal, 1988, No. 13–14 (1–30 June), (Moscow), pp. 1–3.

[53] 'Programma Demokraticheskogo Soyuza', in 'Demokraticheskii Soyuz. Paket dokumentov', *Materialy Samizdata*, Radio Free Europe–Radio Liberty, 1988, No. 24 (6 June), Arkhiv Samizdata No. 6217. See also: 'Pervoe Soveshchanie Koordinatsionnykh Sovetov, DS,' *Svobodnoe slovo, samizdat* journal of the DU, 1988, No. 2 (26 October), p. 2.

[54] 'Obzor Byulletenya Demokraticheskogo Soyuza', *Demokraticheskaya oppozitsiya, samizdat* journal of the DU, 1988, No. 11 (September), (Leningrad), p. 2.

[55] *Ibid.*

[56] Cited in: 'Monolog sud'i', *Levyi Povorot, samizdat* journal of the FSC, 1988, No. 14 (Moscow), p. 47. For the entire text see, '70 let nachala Krasnogo terrora', *Demokraticheskaya oppozitsiya, samizdat* journal of the Democratic Union, No. 12, 1988, (September), (Leningrad), p. 2.

[57] Sergei Skripnikov, 'Vlast' Sovetam, no kakim?', *Antitezis, samizdat* journal of the Communists-Democrats, a faction of the Democratic Union, 1989, No. 1 (January), (Moscow), pp. 1–2. I was pleased to recognise in the author's argument some of my own ideas on the destruction of the multi-party system in Russia, which I expressed in my book: *The Mensheviks After October. Socialist Opposition and the Rise of the Bolshevik Dictatorship* (Ithaca, NY: Cornell University Press, 1987).

[58] Andrei Novikov, 'Tak li zakalyalas' stal'?', *Antitezis, samizdat* journal of the Communists-Democrats, a faction of the Democratic Union, 1989, No. 1 (January), (Moscow), p. 2.

[59] For the programme of the Constitutional Democratic faction of the Democratic Union, see: 'K natsional'nomu vozrozhdeniyu Rossii, (Leningrad, noyabr' 1988)' and 'Osnovy politicheskoi platformy', in *Materialy Samizdata*, Radio Free Europe–Radio Liberty, 1989, No. 1 (2 January) Arkhiv Samizdata Nos. 6325 and 6326.

[60] 'Chto takoe DS i chego on dobivaetsya?' *Svobodnoe slovo, samizdat* Journal of the Democratic Union, 1988, No. 1 (15 October), p. 1. in: *Materialy Samizdata*, Radio Free Europe–Radio Liberty, 1989, No. 1 (2 January) Arkhiv Samizdata No. 6324.

[61] 'Obzor Byulletenya...', p. 2.

[62] Cited in a review of the monthly Bulletin of the Democratic Union, *Ekspress Khronika*, 1989, No. 39 (25 September), p. 12.

[63] Kiril Podrabinek, 'Politcheskoe op'yanenie', *Ekspress Khronika*, 1988, No. 43 (23 October), pp. 12–16.

[64] On the *Pamyat'* demonstration on 22 October 1988 and alleged contact with the KGB, see: *Ekspress Khronika*, 1988, No. 48 (27 November).

[65] 'Khronika', *Demokraticheskaya oppozitsiya, samizdat* journal of the Democratic Union, No. 11 (September), (Leningrad).

[66] *Ibid.*

[67] 'Khronika', *Demokraticheskaya Oppozitsiya, samizdat* journal of the Democratic Union, 1988, No. 12 (September), (Leningrad), p. 4.

[68] *Ekspress Khronika*, 1988, No. 37 (11 September), p. 16.

[69] Sergei Mitrofanov, 'S privetom ot Urfina Dzhiusa', *Referendum, samizdat* journal, 1988, No. 15–16 (15 August–15 September), (Moscow), pp. 1–2.

[70] 'Khronika', *Demokraticheskaya oppozitsiya, samizdat* journal of the Democratic Union, 1988, No. 12 (September), (Leningrad), p. 4.

[71] *Ibid.*

[72] 'Leningrad', *Ekspress Khronika*, 1988, No. 40 (2 October), p. 4.

[73] 'Leningrad', *Ekspress Khronika*, 1988, No. 39 (25 September), p. 8.

[74] Rostislav Evdokimov, 'Neobychnyi miting', *Referendum, samizdat* journal, 1988, No. 18 (1–15 October), (Moscow), pp. 11–12.

[75] '30 Oktyabrya—den' politzaklyuchennogo', *Ekspress Khronika*, 1988, No. 45 (6 November), pp. 1–2.

[76] *Vtoroi s"ezd Demokraticheskogo Soyuza*, p. 2.

[77] 'Samizdat', *Ekspress Khronika*, 1989, No. 1 (1 January), p. 3.

[78] 'Printsipy natsional'noi politiki', in *Programma DS, Demokraticheskii Soyuz, paket dokumentov, Materialy Samizdata*, Radio Free Europe-Radio Liberty, 1988, No. 24 (6 June) Arkhiv Samizdata No. 6217, here pp. 24–26.

[79] *Ekspress Khronika*, 1988, No. 38 (18 September), p. 17.

[80] 'Kul'tura i obshchestvennaya zhizn'', *Ekspress Khronika*, 1988, No. 39 (25 September), p. 10.

[81] 'Delo No. 64', *Ekspress Khronika*, 1989, No. 52 (25 December), p. 8, and 'Leningrad', *Ekspress Khronika*, 1989, No. 1 (January), p. 1.

[82] 'Raznoe, Gorky', *Ekspress Khronika*, 1988, No. 52 (25 December), p. 4.

[83] 'Gorky', *Ekspress Khronika*, 1989, No. 1 (January), p. 1.

[84] For the Programme of the Ukrainian People's Movement for Restructuring, see the Soviet source: *Literaturna Ukraina*, 16 February 1989, reprinted in: *Soviet Ukrainian Affairs*, 2, Winter 1988, (London) pp. 20–23.

[85] 'Raznoe, Khar'kov', *Ekspress Khronika*, 1989, No. 13 (26 March), p. 2.

[86] 'Perestroike, sotsial'nye orientiry', *Pravda*, 25 March 1989.

[87] 'Chteniya nakanune repressii', *Referendum, samizdat* journal, 1989, No. 27 (16–28 February), (Moscow), p. 3.

[88] *Ibid.* See also a report of the representative of the Belorussian Movement in Support of Restructuring, I. Yakovlev, to the Latvian Popular Front on the repressive measures of the Belorussian authorities, in: *Atmoda*, Information Bulletin of the Latvian Popular Front, 20 February, 1989, (Riga), p. 4.

[89] Dmitry Kazutin, 'Surprises of Political Spring', *Moscow News*, 1989, No. 12 (26 March–2 April), p. 3. and 'V Tsentral'noi izbiratel'noi kommissii', *Sovetskaya Rossiya*, 11 March 1989, p. 1.

[90] 'Pozitsiya . . . .

[91] 'Leningrad', *Ekspress Khronika*, 1989, No. 12 (19 March), p. 2. The Leningrad authorities labelled activists from the 'Elections 89' committee as 'demagogues', see: 'Razum protiv demagogii', Leningradskaya Pravda, 21 March 1989.

[92] 'Pikety v Leningrade', *Ekspress Khronika*, 1989, No. 11 (12 March), 11.

[93] 'Mitingi Memoriala', *Ekspress Khronika*, 1989, No. 11 (12 March), p. 1.

[94] On the initiatives of the Yaroslavl' Popular Front during the elections, see: M. Ovcharov, 'Kommissya obretaet svoe litso', *Izvestiya*, 3 February 1989 and Kosarev, 'Kto zhe oni . . . '.

[95] Valerii Senderov, 'Est' li prok ot proshedshikh vyborov', *Ekspress Khronika*, 1989, No. 14 (2 April), p. 3.

[96] 'Clubs Used Against Ryazan' Rally Participants', *FBIS Daily Report*, 19 April 1989, pp. 64–65, reprint from: *Sovetskaya Rossiya*, 15 April 1989, p. 2.

[97] *Ibid.*

[98] 'Posle uroka net peremeny', *Moskovskie novosti*, 1989, No. 18 (30 April), p. 2. and 'Democratic Union Leaders Arrested, Face Charges', *FBIS Daily Report*, 2 May 1989, p. 49.

[99] V. Drozd, 'Vyvody bez deistviya', *Pravda*, 30 April 1989, p. 2.

[100] N. Volynsky and V. Loginov, 'Zatyanuvshayasya pauza', *Pravda*, 20 April 1989, p. 2.

[101] 'Leningrad's Gerasimov Queried on Election Defeat', *FBIS Daily Report*, 25 April 1989, p. 47; reprint from *Izvestiya*, 24 April 1989, p. 2

[102] Lisovsky, '"Neformaly"—Za i Protiv',

[103] 'Vystupleniya v preniyakh na Plenume TsK KPSS', *Pravda*, 27 April 1989, p. 7.

[104] *Ibid.* p. 6.

[105] *Ibid.* p. 5.

[106] *Ibid.* p. 4.

[107] *Ibid.* p. 2.

The Heralds of Opposition to *Perestroyka*

Yitzhak M. Brudny[1]

Abstract: A review and analysis is presented of substantive material published in the journals *Nash sovremennik* and *Molodaya gvardiya* from Gorbachev's advent to power through roughly October 1989. The size of the journals' circulations is noted to assess the influence of writers who are in the vanguard of opposition to *perestroyka*. The article includes a section devoted to the tradition of Russian "thick journals." It concludes by examining the popularity and power of Russian nationalism in relation to *perestroyka* and the nature of the opposition to it as reflected in both journals. *Journal of Economic Literature*, Classification Number: 052.

"We live, in pluralism, the devil take it"
—Yuriy Bondarev at the election rally in Volgograd.

"You forced upon the country the pluralism of morality which is more dangerous than any bomb"
—Valentin Rasputin at the Congress of People's Deputies.

In March 1985, at the time Mikhail Gorbachev became General Secretary, there were five Soviet literary monthlies, or "thick journals," as they are known in the USSR, which had a clearly defined Russian nationalist orientation. These journals were: *Molodaya gvardiya, Nash sovremennik, Moskva, Sever*, and *Don*. Their combined circulation was well over one million copies per year. Most important among them were the Moscow journals *Nash sovremennik* (circulation 220,000 copies) and *Molodaya gvardiya* (circulation 640,000). In four full years of Gorbachev's leadership these two journals became the leading organs of various Russian nationalist groups which oppose *perestroyka* and *glasnost'*.

This paper analyzes the fiction and non-fiction published in these two journals between March 1985 and May 1989, as well as the size of their circulation and subscription. This analysis provides a fairly clear picture of the nature, strategy, arguments, and popularity (at least among the Russian reading public) of the Russian nationalist opposition to ongoing reforms. The paper is divided into four basic sections: the first briefly

[1]Harvard Academy for International and Area Study, Harvard University, 1737 Cambridge Street, Cambridge, MA 02138.

162

Soviet Economy, 1989, 5, 2, pp. 162-200.

describes the tradition of the Russian "thick" journal from pre-revolutionary times to the end of the Khrushchev era; the second analyzes manifestations of Russian nationalism on the pages of the journals *Novyy mir* and *Molodaya gvardiya* from the mid-1950s to the late 1960s; the third discusses the politics of *Nash sovremennik* in the Brezhnev era; and the final section portrays the politics of these two journals and measures the degree of popularity and power of this nationalist message from the time Gorbachev took office to May 1989.

THE TRADITION OF THE "THICK JOURNAL"

The pre-revolutionary Russian and post-revolutionary Soviet state did not allow (with the exception of the short period between 1905 and 1922) and still does not allow the formation of Western-style political parties. The function of parties as institutions which aggregate and promote the socio-political concerns of social and intellectual elites is performed, because of the highly politicized nature of Russian literature, by the so-called "thick journals" (*tolstiye zhurnaly*). These are monthly publications, several hundred pages long, with sections of prose, poetry, literary and social criticism, economics and politics.

To be more precise, in Russia and the Soviet Union the "thick journals" were and are: (a) a well-recognized means of shaping public opinion, (b) accepted arenas of permitted socio-political debate, and (c) important institutional bases of informal groups of politically like-minded members' of the intellectual elite, usually headed by its leading representative. In 19th-Century Russia, such publications as *Sovremennik*, *Sovremennyye zapiski*, *Moskvityanin*, and *Vremya* created and perpetuated this tradition. In the Soviet Russia of the 1920s, the journal *Krasnaya nov'*, edited by the old Bolshevik intellectual Aleksandr Voronskiy, continued to a large degree the pre-revolutionary tradition of the "thick journal" (Maguire, 1968).

In Stalin's Russia, open and even semi-open political debate disappeared. Literary journals were closely monitored by the party ideological apparatus in order to prevent any deviation from the party line and the enshrined principle of "socialist realism." In the post-war years, Politburo member Andrey Zhdanov was entrusted with the supervision of Soviet cultural life. Under Zhdanov, Stalinist intolerance toward the slightest deviation from the prescribed norm reached its apogee.

Thick journals were the primary victims of Zhdanov's cultural policies. On August 14, 1946 the Central Committee issued a decree entitled "Resolution on the Journals *Zvezda* and *Leningrad*" which fully revealed the Stalinist approach to the thick journals. The decree proclaimed that:

> Our journals are a mighty instrument of the Soviet state in the cause of the education of the Soviet people, and Soviet youth in particular. They must therefore be controlled by the vital foundation of the Soviet order—its politics. The Soviet order cannot tolerate the education of the young in the spirit

of indifference to Soviet politics, in the spirit of a devil-may-care attitude and ideological neutrality. . . . Consequently any preaching of ideological neutrality, of political neutrality, of "art for art's sake" is alien to Soviet literature and harmful to the interests and the Soviet state. Such preaching has no place in our journals (Swayze, 1959, p. 37).

The resolution was prompted by the publication in the above-mentioned journals of works of Mikhail Zoshchenko and Anna Akhmatova. In the aftermath of the decree the journal *Leningrad* was shut down permanently, while *Zvezda*'s editorial board was purged.

During the first post-Stalin decade the number of "thick journals" drastically increased. According to a Soviet source, from 1955 to 1957 alone twenty-seven new "thick journals" appeared (Bocharov, 1988, p. 99). More importantly, in this period the journals again became institutions of aggregation and articulation of ideas prevailing in the intellectual elite and, thus, major forums of socio-political debate.

There were two main reasons why in the post-Stalin era Soviet leaders tolerated the publication in "thick journals" of ideas which implicitly or explicitly challenged, both from the nationalist "right" and liberal "left" perspective, official policies. First Khrushchev and later Brezhnev and Suslov (the party chief overseer of cultural life) might have reached the conclusion that it is impossible to suppress such ideas effectively, if they prevail in large segments of society, without a revival of the terror. The post-Stalin consensus in the political leadership was, however, to prevent a recurrence of the terror. Second, in the post-Stalin era the scope of views prevailing among members of the political elite was very similar if not identical to that which prevailed among members of the intellectual elite (Cohen, 1985, p. 133). Competing political leaders could, therefore, perceive the socio-political debate among members of the intellectual elite as an important extension of their own debates.

In the late Khrushchev-early Brezhnev era, the leading "thick journal" of the anti-reformist and orthodox Stalinist end of the political spectrum was *Oktyabr'*, headed, from 1961 to 1973, by Vsevolod Kochetov. At the other, reformist and anti-Stalinist end of the spectrum stood the journal *Novyy mir*. Konstantin Simonov, chief editor from 1954–1958, and especially Aleksandr Tvardovskiy, chief editor from 1950–1954 and again from 1958–1970, turned *Novyy mir* into a major participant in the socio-political debate by publishing some of the most important anti-Stalinist fictional and non-fictional works of the period (Spechler, 1982).

RUSSIAN NATIONALISM IN *NOVYY MIR* AND *MOLODAYA GVARDIYA*, 1956–1970

In order to understand the present politics of *Molodaya gvardiya* and *Nash sovremennik*, one should go back to the literary politics of the years

1956–1970. The two main "thick journals" which published works of Russian nationalist writers and critics in the years 1956–1970 were *Novyy mir* and *Molodaya gvardiya*. *Novyy mir* was not simply an anti-Stalinist journal which called for socio-political reform. It was the very first institutional basis of an emerging Russian nationalism in the post-Stalin era. Between 1953 and 1970, the journal published a series of fictional and non-fictional works whose common denominator was a sharp criticism of various aspects of Stalin's legacy in the countryside, be it the methods of party management of agriculture, the harsh living conditions of the peasantry, or even collectivization itself. Because of its subject matter, this genre became known as "village prose" [*derevenkaya proza*].[2]

Although all "village prose" writers who contributed to *Novyy mir* were extremely critical of party policies in the countryside, in retrospect one can discern very meaningful differences of opinion among them. By the mid- to late-1960s there were two "faces" to the "village prose" appearing in *Novyy mir*, which in fact represented two distinct types of Russian nationalism. The first type of "village prose" might be called "liberal-nationalist." It developed from the Valentin Ovechkin school of agrarian journalism of the early post-Stalin era.[3] Its leading exponents were such writers as Fyodor Abramov, Efim Dorosh, Boris Mozhayev, and Sergey Zalygin. Their prose was essentially an effort to write the true history of party policies in the countryside under Stalin and Khrushchev and their effect on the lives of Russian peasants.[4]

The second type of *Novyy mir* "village prose," which emerged in the early 1960s, could be called "conservative nationalist." Its leading exponents were such writers as Vasiliy Belov, Viktor Likhonosov, Aleksandr Solzhenitsyn, and Aleksandr Yashin. These writers equated Russian national identity with traditional peasant identity. They gave a highly idealized description of the traditional peasant way of life and morality, and presented its rapid disappearance as a national tragedy. Often this prose contained strong anti-urban and even anti-intellectual sentiments.[5]

From 1966 to 1970, another major Russian nationalist "thick journal" was *Molodaya gvardiya*, the organ of the Komsomol Central Committee.[6] *Molodaya gvardiya* was the first journal with an exclusively Russian nationalist orientation in the post-Stalin era. The Russian nationalism of

---

[2]On the "village prose" of the 1960s–1970s, see Hosking (1980, Ch. 3), Brown (1978, Ch. 12), Lowe (1987, pp. 81–95), Žekulin (1971), and Lewis (1976).

[3]The September 1952 issue of *Novyy mir* contained a semi-fictional essay by Valentin Ovechkin (1904–68) entitled "District Weekdays" [*Rayonnyye budni*]. Through the portrayal of a confrontation between District Party Secretary Borzhov, the local Stalinist bully, and reform-minded Second Secretary Martynov, Ovechkin blasted Stalinist methods of agricultural management. This essay became a landmark in Soviet social criticism since it gave birth to a school of agrarian journalists known at the time as "essayists" [*ocherkisty*]. On Ovechkin and the "essayist school," see also Garden (1976) and Vilchek (1988).

[4]See Abramov (1968), Dorosh (1958–1970), Mozhayev (1966) and Zalygin (1964).

[5]See Belov (1968), Likhonosov (1963, 1967), Solzhenitsyn (1963) and Yashin (1962).

[6]For an analysis of several major essays published in *Molodaya gvardiya* in the late 1960s, see Yanov (1987, Ch. 10).

Molodaya gvardiya also had two "faces," although these were very different from the "faces" of *Novyy mir*. The common denominator of the two types of nationalism found in *Molodaya gvardiya* was a rejection of the reformist politics of *Novyy mir*, an ecological orientation, and a concern for the preservation of the architectural remnants of pre-revolutionary Russia, in particular, ancient Russian churches.

One type might be called a "neo-Stalinist nationalism." Ecological orientation and preservationist concerns distinguished the neo-Stalinist nationalists of *Molodaya gvardiya* from the orthodox Stalinists of *Oktyabr'*. Neo-Stalinist contributors to *Molodaya gvardiya* did not limit themselves to praising Stalin's revival of the military and state-building traditions of the Russian tsars, but especially praised Stalin's retreat from the Bolshevik idealism of the revolutionary era. Moreover, they presented the Russian Revolution as a Russian national revolution. The second type of Russian nationalism appearing in *Molodaya gvardiya* might be called "radical Slavophilism." The representatives of this type sharply attacked *Novyy mir* not for its anti-Stalinist stance but for what they perceived to be its pro-Western liberalism. In their essays, they combined strong anti-urban and anti-intellectual rhetoric with a highly idealized view of the Russian Orthodox Church and traditional Russian peasantry as it was portrayed in the "village prose."[7]

NASH SOVREMENNIK, 1970–1985

In 1970, Aleksandr Tvardovskiy and Anatoliy Nikonov, the editors of *Novyy mir* and *Molodaya gvardiya*, were replaced and the editorial boards of the journals purged as a part of a crackdown on both the liberal and nationalist intelligentsia. In 1972, the orthodox Stalinist writer Anatoliy Ivanov (b. 1928) was appointed editor of *Molodaya gvardiya*, a position he still holds as of this writing (May 1989). Although neo-Stalinist nationalists and radical Slavophiles continued to publish in the journal, it ceased to be their primary publication. In addition, after Tvardovskiy's departure, liberal and conservative "village prose" writers largely stopped contributing to *Novyy mir*. In the 1970s, the journal which emerged as the main Russian nationalist publication was *Nash sovremennik*.

The transformation of *Nash sovremennik* began in August 1968 with the appointment of the poet Sergey Vikulov (b. 1922), until then deputy chief editor of *Molodaya gvardiya*, as chief editor of the journal. Vikulov purged the editorial board of the journal, dropping ten of the twelve members of the old board and bringing in thirteen new writers and critics. From the very beginning, Vikulov brought to *Nash sovremennik* both the "village prose" writers of *Novyy mir* and the Russian nationalist historians and literary critics of *Molodaya gvardiya*.[8] This proved to be the key to the

---

[7]For examples of neo-Stalinist nationalism, see Sakharov (1970), Semanov (1970); for examples of radical Slavophilism, see Glinkin (1967), Lobanov (1968), Chalmayev (1968), and Zhukov (1969).

[8]See Abramov (1972), Zalygin (1975), and Rasputin (1976) [liberal nationalist and conservative national-

journal's success. It acquired the status of the most important Russian nationalist journal publishing views of all segments of the Russian nationalist movement, from the liberal nationalists to the neo-Stalinists. In short, *Nash sovremennik* became the leading institution of the Russian nationalist intelligentsia.

By the early 1980s, *Nash sovremennik* had become very popular among the Russian reading public. Its steadily growing circulation was a good indication of the popularity of the ideas identified with the journal. The circulation of *Nash sovremennik* rose from 60,000 copies in October 1968 (the last issue of the pre-Vikulov era) to 336,000 copies in February 1981.[9]

Such significant growth in the circulation of *Nash sovremennik* was combined with an official recognition of the journal's contributors as being among the most important Soviet writers. This recognition came in the form of the very prestigious RSFSR State, USSR State and Lenin Prizes, which were awarded to the Russian nationalist writers closely associated with the journal, and the reprinting of their works in millions of copies.[10] The growth in circulation and official recognition bestowed upon its authors reflected the important role *Nash sovremennik* and its contributors were to play in Brezhnev's and Suslov's efforts to co-opt into the system those Russian nationalist intellectuals previously excluded from it.[11] This inclusionary strategy pursued two aims: (1) to gain popular support for Brezhnev's policies of heavy investment in agriculture; and (2) to regain the ability to mobilize the ethnic Russian population through appeals to its nationalist sentiments since official Marxist-Leninist ideology could no longer perform this function.[12]

I call Brezhnev's politics of inclusion a "political contract," to distinguish it from Brezhnev's labor and social policies, conceptualized by

---

ist "village prose"]; Mikhaylov (1969), Paliyevsky (1973), and Chivilikhin (1978-1984) [radical Slavophile and neo-Stalinist prose and literary criticism].

[9] The interim statistics of *Nash sovremennik*'s circulation are: 70,000 copies in January 1969; 100,000 copies throughout 1973; in the period between the January 1975 issue and the November 1979 issue the circulation grew from 119,000 copies to 205,800 copies; throughout 1980 the circulation was 300,000 copies; in January 1981 it was increased to 333,000 copies.

[10] Vladimir Soloukhin (1979) and Georgiy Semenov (1981) were awarded the RSFSR State Prize. Fyodor Abramov (1975), Gavriil Troepolskiy (1975), Valentin Rasputin (1977), Viktor Astaf'yev (1978), Pyotr Proskurin (1979), and Vasiliy Belov (1981), all received the USSR State Prize for literature. Yuriy Bondarev (1972) and Vasiliy Shukshin (1976) were awarded the Lenin Prize. Between 1967 and 1977 Astaf'yev's books were printed in 3,608,400 copies; Bondarev's in 3,419,700 copies; Soloukhin's in 2,850,200 copies; Shukshin's in 2,744,000 copies, Abramov's in 2,629,000 copies; Belov's in 2,598,210 copies; Proskurin's in 2,441,000 copies; Rasputin's in 1,427,000. These statistics do not include reprints of works of these writers in the popular *Roman-gazeta* series. Each work in this series is printed in 2.5 million copies and sits virtually in every Russian peasant's and worker's living room. Works of Bondarev, Soloukhin, Shukshin, Abramov, Belov, Proskurin, and Rasputin were reprinted in these series (see Mehnert, 1983, pp. 36, 239, 268).

[11] Jowitt interpreted the process of inclusion of members of social elites (he calls them "articulated audiences") into Communist regimes as "the attempt to control society 'from within,' as opposed to commanding it from an insulated position" (see Jowitt, 1975, p. 86).

[12] On agriculture as Brezhnev's highest investment priority, see Gustafson (1981, Ch. 2).

Hauslohner and others as a "social contract" (Hauslohner, 1987). Like the policies associated with the "social contract," the "political contract" failed because by the end of the 1970s Russian nationalists refused to be a partner. This was due to two factors: a rising level of expectations among the Russian nationalists, fueled by the "political contract," in such areas as protection of the environment and historical monuments, and a revitalization of the countryside, expectations which the Brezhnev government could not or did not want to fulfill; and secondly, the continuation of negative social trends including an overwhelming increase in the incidence of alcoholism, a continuous depopulation of the countryside, and the Russian demographic decline, all processes which Brezhnev's efforts could not reverse.

Using the 600th anniversary of the Kulikovo Field Battle (1980) and 160th anniversary of Dostoyevsky's birth (1981) as a pretext, Nash sovremennik began to publish a series of essays very critical of the social and political realities of the Brezhnev era. The repercussions quickly followed. On February 1, 1982, Pravda sharply attacked an essay of the radical Slavophile literary critic Vadim Kozhinov, published in the December 1981 issue of Nash sovremennik, as a part of its Dostoyevsky anniversary celebrations. This attack was followed shortly by lengthy attacks on Kozhinov and Nash sovremennik in other thick journals (Kozhinov, 1981; Kuleshov, 1982; Surovtsev, 1982). This signaled the end of the "political contract." Apparently Andropov was the man who stood behind this decision since he replaced Suslov as the party's chief ideologue at this time. In late July 1982, the Central Committee, for the first time in more than ten years, issued a resolution which contained an explicit condemnation of Russian nationalism. In January 1983, the circulation of Nash sovremennik was cut from 335,000 to 220,000 copies, a fact which points to Andropov's determination to crack down on Russian nationalism. These policies continued, although in a less harsh form, under Chernenko.[13]

The policies of the "political contract," nevertheless, transformed the Russian nationalists from being one among many groups within the Russian intellectual elite at the beginning of the Brezhnev era to being the most influential group (at least by perception) at its close. Environmentalism and the preservation of historical monuments, two issues with which Russian nationalism was very closely identified, had gained enormous popularity within Soviet society by 1985. Andropov and Chernenko recognized this reality and, unlike Brezhnev in 1970, did not try to eliminate the main institutional basis of Russian nationalism. The question of how to deal with Russian nationalist intellectuals and their institutional bases was left to Mikhail Gorbachev.

---

[13]The relationship between Russian nationalism and the Soviet state in the years 1981–1984 is fairly well described in Dunlop (1985, Ch. 1–3).

NASH SOVREMENNIK AND *MOLODAYA GVARDIYA* UNDER GORBACHEV

In the period under review (March 1985–May 1989), one can distinguish three stages in the development of Russian nationalism as it appears in the journals under review. At every stage the publication policies of *Nash sovremennik* and *Molodaya gvardiya* dutifully presented the positions of the different types of Russian nationalism toward Gorbachev's policies in general and his cultural policies in particular.[14]

The First Stage: March 1985–March 1987

Perhaps because Russian nationalists were allowed to be the most active political group throughout most of the Brezhnev era, they appeared to be better prepared for political action than the non-nationalist members of the Russian intelligentsia. They demonstrated this in the first year and a half of Gorbachev's leadership. While *Molodaya gvardiya* remained politically ineffective in this period, different groupings of the Russian nationalist movement successfully used *Nash sovremennik* to shape the terms of the socio-political debate.

Soon after Gorbachev took power, *Nash sovremennik* turned ecology, and especially the project to divert Siberian rivers to Central Asia, into one of the main issues on the political agenda.[15] In fact, the journal led the nationalist campaign against the project. In its July 1985 issue, *Nash sovremennik* published a "Round Table," in which twelve highly respected Soviet scientists warned that the river diversion would not bring the promised economic benefits, but could lead to ecological disaster (*Zemlya i khleb*, 1985). This was the beginning of a long campaign which ended on August 15, 1986, when the Politburo announced the halt of all field work on the project in order to reevaluate its economic and ecological consequences. This was in effect the cancellation of the project. Moreover, the opposition to the project was rewarded: one of the project's major opponents and an important contributor to *Nash sovremennik* in the 1970s, the liberal nationalist writer Sergey Zalygin, was appointed chief editor of *Novyy mir* a week before the cancellation was announced.

In addition to the environmental issue, *Nash sovremennik* soon brought the subject of moral corruption in Russian society to the center of the political debate. *Nash sovremennik*'s success in raising the issue of moral corruption was a result of the publication in the journal of the works of such conservative nationalist "village prose" writers as Valentin Ras-

---

14On Russian nationalism under Gorbachev, see also "Russian Nationalism Today," *Radio Liberty Research Bulletin*, December 19, 1988 (special edition of *RL Bulletin* which contains essays of John B. Dunlop, Darrell P. Hammer, Andrei Sinyavsky, Ronald Grigor Suny, and Alexander Yanov).

15On the river diversion project in general and the Russian nationalist campaign against it in particular, see Petro (1987), Darst (1988), and Micklin and Bond (1988).

putin, Viktor Astaf'yev, Vasily Belov, and Aleksandr Astrakhantsev. Rasputin, in the novel *Fire* (Rasputin, 1985), Astaf'yev, in the collection of short stories *Place of Action* (Astaf'yev, 1986), Belov, in the novel *Everything Lies Ahead* (Belov, 1986), and Astrakhantsev, in the novel *Parting of the Ways* (Astrakhantsev, 1986), all portrayed Russian society as morally corrupt and argued that without a revival of traditional moral values, Gorbachev's reforms were doomed to fail. They searched for the agents of the moral corruption of Russia and found them in the Communist Party, the urban intelligentsia, urban emancipated women, rock music, and the national minorities, especially Jews and Georgians.[16]

During this period, *Nash sovremennik* did not limit itself to the publication of conservative nationalist critiques of Russia's moral corruption. Rather, *Nash sovremennik* was the very first journal in the Gorbachev era to publish neo-Stalinist and anti-Semitic attacks on the new, liberalizing trends in Soviet cultural life. In the June 1985 issue of the journal, the theater critic Mark Lyubomudrov lashed out at those theater directors who staged plays which gave a more realistic account of Soviet reality (Lyubomudrov, 1985). These plays, Lyubomudrov claimed, rather than giving Russia a clear national ideal to strive for, were exclusively preoccupied with the darker sides of Soviet life. In many ways this article set the standard for all subsequent neo-Stalinist critiques of Gorbachev's *glasnost'* policies.

The radical Slavophiles in this period also used *Nash sovremennik* to revive the debate about the Slavophile legacy and its crucial importance in the present. They did so in order to suggest that Gorbachev would lose his mandate to rule if the essence of his reforms were the simple adoption of Western social, political, and cultural models. The historian Apollon Kuzmin stated that by borrowing Western values and culture, the post-Petrine autocracy and the aristocratic elite separated themselves from the rest of the Russian nation and became, in fact, "rootless cosmopolitans." Progressive forces in Russian society, such as the Decembrists, turned against the autocracy because it was a cosmopolitan institution bent on weakening and betraying the Russian state (Kuzmin, 1985, p. 189; Kuzmin, 1986, pp. 189–190).

By using the concept "cosmopolitans"—the euphemistic sloganeer of Stalin's anti-Semitic campaign, Kuzmin implied that those elites who wanted to introduce Western or Western-like models to the Soviet Union were alien social elements, as Jews are, and should be treated the way Jews were treated in the late 1940s–early 1950s. Kuzmin's argument was supported and elaborated by another radical Slavophile historian, Vadim Pigalev (Pigalev, 1986). In an essay on the Slavophile legacy, he asserted

---

[16]For his novel *Fire* [*Pozhar*], Rasputin received the State Prize in 1987. Astafiyev's collection of short stories was preceded by the publication in the *Oktyabr's* January 1986 issue of his novel *The Sad Detective Story* [*Pechal'nyy detektiv*] which dealt with the same issues. At the May 1987 discussion of journal publication in the RSFSR Writers Union Secretariat, *Nash sovremennik* was praised for being in the forefront of the ecological campaign and the struggle against moral corruption. See "Obsuzhdeniye raboty zhurnala 'Nash sovremennik'," *Literaturnaya Rossiya*, May 15, 1987.

that the Russian nation is anti-bourgeois and anti-capitalist in its nature. The only way to undermine its strength is to turn the Russian people into "consumerist-philistine cattle." Thus Gorbachev was warned of the danger of turning Russia into a Western-style consumer society.

The Rise of Aleksandr Yakovlev

The ability of *Nash sovremennik* to set the agenda for socio-political debate, however, progressively diminished after the autumn of 1986. This was due to the fast rise in the Kremlin hierarchy of Aleksandr Yakovlev, a committed reformer and a long-time foe of Russian nationalism.[17] In March 1986, at the end of the 27th Party Congress, he was promoted to the position of Secretary of the Central Committee in charge of cultural life and in January 1987, he became a candidate member of the Politburo, rising to full membership six months later.

Yakovlev knew that control of the cultural realm was crucial for creating wide popular support for *perestroyka*. In order to achieve this he made several key appointments over the course of 1986. Vasiliy Shauro, Russian nationalist sympathizer, and a leading supporter of the policies of the "political contract" in the party apparat, was replaced by Yuriy Voronov in the position of head of the Cultural Department of the Central Committee, and Vasiliy Zakharov replaced another Brezhnev, appointee, Pyotr Demichev, in the post of Minister of Culture.

More important, Yakovlev handed control of several Moscow newspapers, popular magazines and literary journals to the reform-minded intellectuals. Vitaliy Korotich replaced an old Stalinist, Anatoliy Sofronov, as chief editor of the popular, mass-circulation weekly *Ogonyok*, while Albert Belyayev and Yegor Yakovlev became chief editors of the newspapers *Sovetskaya kultura* and *Moskovskiye novosti*. Yakovlev seized the opportunity of the vacant positions of chief editor at the journals *Znamya* and *Novyy mir* to appoint Grigoriy Baklanov as the chief editor of *Znamya* and Sergey Zalygin as the chief editor of *Novyy mir*. Finally, Yakovlev used his influence to support the election of Elem Klimov as the first secretary of the Filmmakers' Union (May 1986) and of Kiril Lavrov as the first secretary of the newly created Union of Theater Workers (December 1986), thus helping supporters of cultural liberalization to gain control of these two important artistic unions.

These nominations signified the beginning of the Gorbachev "political contract." The beneficiaries of Gorbachev's "contract" were liberal and liberal-nationalist members of the intellectual elite. Not only did they control important newspapers and journals, but the circulation of these pro-reform publications was allowed to skyrocket while the circulation of *Nash sovremennik* essentially remained frozen at its 1983 level.[18]

---

[17]See his two-page essay "Protiv antiistorizma," *Literaturnaya gazeta*, November 15, 1972.

[18]The circulation of *Ogonyok* rose from 1,500,000 copies in 1985 to 3,350,000 copies in 1989; the

Liberal-reformist circles of the intelligentsia were quick to utilize effectively their newly acquired power and, by early 1987, were able to dictate the agenda of the socio-political debate. Such subjects as Stalinism and the Stalinist legacy, as well as the direction of the political and economic reforms, became dominant in the discussion. At the same time, *Ogonyok*, *Znamya*, and *Novyy mir* started publishing previously forbidden literary works of living and deceased Russian writers. Other popular thick journals such as *Yunost'*, *Druzhba narodov*, *Oktyabr'*, and *Neva* quickly followed the lead.

The winter of 1987 found Soviet society in the midst of what the poet Andrei Voznesensky termed "a revolution by culture" (Voznesensky, 1987, p. 811). This "revolution" was expressed in the constantly expanding range of permissible authors, subjects, styles, and genres in literature, theater, television, the visual arts, and popular music. This expansion created a pluralism of cultural forms and content and undermined the Stalinist orthodoxy which viewed such plurality as inimical and dangerous to socialism. It also undermined the almost twenty-year period of privileged access to mass media and literary journals enjoyed by the Russian nationalists. They, however, were not ready to accept the change of circumstances as a *fait accompli*.

Literature turned out to be the sphere of cultural life in which Russian nationalist resistance to the "revolution by culture" was the strongest. By early 1987, the Russian nationalist opponents of *glasnost'* firmly controlled the Russian Republic Writers Union and its publication, the weekly *Literaturnaya Rossiya* (circulation 150,000 copies). Despite the fact that the Russian nationalist opponents of *glasnost'* had lost the weekly *Ogonyok*, they were able to keep three Moscow literary journals under their control. Russian nationalist chief editors and editorial boards of *Moskva*, *Nash sovremennik*, and *Molodaya gvardiya* remained untouched. This gave the Russian nationalist foes of *perestroyka* a forum upon which to stage a frontal attack on Gorbachev's cultural policies.

The Second Stage: March 1987–March 1988

Russian nationalists reacted in different ways to these developments in the cultural realm. In fact, the period between March 1987 and March 1988 was crucial in the development of Russian nationalist attitudes toward Gorbachev's reforms. During this time liberal nationalists like Likhachev, Zalygin, and Mozhayev became leaders of the pro-Gorbachev coalition among the intelligentsia. At the other end of the Russian nationalist spectrum, radical Slavophiles and neo-Stalinist nationalists formed an anti-*perestroyka* alliance and fought hard against the liberalization of culture.

---

circulation of *Znamya* went up from 175,000 copies in 1985 to 980,000 in 1989; the circulation of *Novyy mir* increased from 425,000 in 1985 to 1,573,000 copies in 1989. In comparison, in the same period of time the circulation of *Nash sovremennik* grew only from 220,000 to 250,000.

At the beginning of the period, the leading conservative nationalists and members of *Nash sovremennik*'s editorial board, Rasputin, Belov, and Astaf'yev, adopted a position of political "fence sitting." They supported some aspects of *perestroyka*, such as the anti-Stalinist campaign, reform in the countryside, tough anti-alcohol policies, and publication of previously forbidden works of literature, and opposed others, such as the opening up of Soviet society to Western cultural influences, in general, and the legitimation of rock music, in particular. Later on, however, they joined another prominent conservative nationalist member of the *Nash sovremennik* editorial board, Yuriy Bondarev, who by March 1987 had become the unchallenged leader of the united Russian nationalist opposition to Gorbachev's cultural policies.

Progressively losing the ability to shape the agenda of the sociopolitical debate and increasingly repulsed by events in Soviet cultural life, the conservative nationalists, radical Slavophiles and neo-Stalinist nationalists launched a frontal attack on the liberalization of cultural life and, by implication, on *perestroyka* in general. This assault began in March 1987 at a meeting of the Secretariat of the Russian Republic Writers' Union. On this occasion, Bondarev, one of the secretaries of the Union, spoke of the "pseudo-democrats of literature, who have lit over an abyss the light of *glasnost'* which they stole from justice and truth." He equated the situation of Russian national culture today to that of Russia in July 1941, when it was on the brink of defeat by Nazi Germany. He called upon the nationalist opponents of reform to rally for a "cultural Stalingrad" (*Literaturnaya Rossiya*, March 27, 1987).

In the months following the meeting of the RSFSR Writers Union, there was a "revival" of *Molodaya gvardiya*. It not only joined *Nash sovremennik* as a very important forum of Russian nationalist reaction to the cultural liberalization but, in fact, it became the most important publication of the neo-Stalinist nationalists who opposed Gorbachev's reform projects. The publication of hitherto forbidden works of literature, avant-garde art, the liberalization of Soviet television, the acceptance of rock music, the liberal reformist intelligentsia, and newspapers and journals which supported the reforms were all assailed with increasing intensity (Pisarev, 1987; Andreyev, 1987; Baigushev, 1987a). The leading voice in this campaign was Vyacheslav Gorbachev, the deputy editor of *Molodaya gvardiya*. In a series of essays, he defended Stalin, extolled traditional family values, criticized the publication of Nabokov's works and the exhibition of Chagall's paintings, attacked Jews, freemasons, rock music, the liberal reformist intelligentsia and its newspapers and magazines such as *Ogonyok*, *Moskovskiye novosti*, *Sovetskaya kultura*, and *Nedelya* (Gorbachev, 1987a; Gorbachev, 1987b; Gorbachev, 1987c).

After *Ogonyok* sharply responded to Vyacheslav Gorbachev's vicious attack in the July 1987 issue of *Molodaya gvardiya*, the party apparatus, fearing that the situation was getting out of hand, intervened to stop the infighting between the journals. A high party official, in an article in

Pravda which he signed under the pseudonym "Vladimir Petrov," called upon both *Molodaya gvardiya* and *Ogonyok* to restrain themselves. The neo-Stalinists of *Molodaya gvardiya*, however, insisted on having the last word in this confrontation. In the September 1987 issue of the journal, twenty-two nationalist historians, writers and literary critics elaborated in sixty-eight pages Vyacheslav Gorbachev's arguments against Mikhail Gorbachev's cultural policies. This was the strongest attack (until March 1988) on Mikhail Gorbachev's reform program since his rise to power.[19]

In essay after essay, the contributors assailed the Soviet press for its reports on drug addiction and prostitution, criticized rock music, the publication of forbidden works of literature (especially those of Nabokov), and the exhibition of avant-garde art (especially that of Marc Chagall), demanded the cessation of attacks on Stalin, and argued against the rehabilitation of Bukharin and Trotsky. Mikhail Gorbachev's idea that the radical restructuring of Soviet society requires the encouragement of diverse social and political views was proclaimed to contradict the Russian historical experience and its national traditions. As one of the contributors bluntly stated: "cultural 'pluralism,' the uninterrupted 'free competition' of different, [and] at the same time, entirely contradictory points of view, tastes and predilections, implies the rejection of the main idea which unifies the Soviet people, of traditional spiritual values, and of deviation from the main road of our history" (Fomenko, 1987, p. 280).

The principle of democratization was assailed as leading to social anarchy, and the liberal-reformist intelligentsia, which pressed for the democratization of Soviet politics, was accused of undermining the strength of the Russian state. What Russia really needed was, as another contributor asserted, "a strong and responsible state power, which knows the troubles and the needs of the nation" (Karpets, 1987, p. 243). In the next six issues of *Molodaya gvardiya* (October 1987–March 1988), the attacks continued on various aspects of *perestroyka* and *glasnost'*, be it the publication of Pasternak's *Doctor Zhivago*, works of fiction and literary criticism of liberal reformers, rock music and the content of Soviet television programs, or Nikolay Shmelev's proposals for radical economic reform (Markova, 1987; Lisenkov and Sergeyev, 1987; Khatyushin, 1987; Doronin, 1987; Baigushev, 1987b; Bushin, 1988a; Antonov, 1988; Trukhin, 1988).

Nash sovremennik tried to keep up with *Molodaya gvardiya* in its attacks on *perestroyka* and *glasnost'*. The two journals, however, opposed Gorbachev's reforms from different Russian nationalist viewpoints. As mentioned earlier, the *Molodaya gvardiya* perspective was definitely that of the neo-Stalinist nationalist. Despite the fact that *Nash sovremennik* also published neo-Stalinist attacks on *perestroyka* (Shevtsov, 1986; Lyubomudrov, 1987; Baigushev, 1988), it served primarily as a forum for the radical Slavo-

---

[19]*Ogonyok*, No. 30, 1987, pp. 26–27; Vladimir Petrov, "Kultura diskussii," *Pravda*, August 3, 1987; "V otvete za vremya," 1987.

philes. This line of the editorial board of *Nash sovremennik* meant the end of the journal as a forum for all branches of the Russian nationalist movement. From late 1986 on, such prominent liberal nationalists as Dmitriy Likhachev, Sergey Zalygin, Boris Yekimov, and Boris Mozhayev no longer contributed to *Nash sovremennik*. In fact, the column on agrarian journalism was the only section of the journal which continued to publish liberal nationalist journalists. It was *Novyy mir* which became, from the time of Zalygin's appointment as its chief editor, the main liberal nationalist journal.[20]

The contributors to *Nash sovremennik* in particular saw a grave danger to Russian national existence in the pluralism of cultural forms which Gorbachev encouraged. They pointed to the policy of removing all obstacles from the performance of rock music as an example of how *perestroyka* contributes to the spread of harmful Western political and cultural values among the Russian youth. And as in the case of *Molodaya gvardiya*, the attack on rock music as a symbol of Gorbachev's cultural policies went on in *Nash sovremennik* simultaneously with vicious attacks on the reformist intelligentsia (Dunayev, 1988; Kazintsev, 1986, 1988a; Bushin, 1987). Another device used by contributors to *Nash sovremennik* to attack *perestroyka* was to discredit the recently rehabilitated Bukharin and his legacy. They portrayed Bukharin as a Trotskyite in disguise, a man who hated Russia, who organized the persecution of leading representatives of Russian national culture, and even as an enemy of NEP and the Russian peasantry (Dubrovina, 1987, pp. 181–183; Kozhinov, 1987, pp. 164–165; Kuzmin, 1987, p. 176).

During this period, however, *Nash sovremennik* tried to do more than simply criticize Soviet reformers. As in the preceding stage, the journal attempted to concentrate on one policy area around which most Russian nationalists, as well as wide sections of the general public, could unify in order to create strong pressure in favor of a major policy change. If in 1985–1986, *Nash sovremennik* was campaigning for the cancellation of the river-diversion projects, in 1987–1988, the journal lobbied for the imposition of a "dry law" on Soviet society.

On May 17, 1985, the Politburo announced a policy severely restricting production and sales of alcoholic beverages. These restrictions were accompanied by the creation of a voluntary Sobriety Society, known after its Russian acronym of VDOBT (*Vsesoyuznoye dobrovolnoye obshchestvo borby za trezvost'*), the aim of which was to spread the idea of sobriety among the masses. By mid-1987, it was clear that the policy was not only failing to achieve its goals but also causing serious damage to the Soviet economy. In many places local authorities quietly increased sales of alcoholic beverages. Moreover, instead of becoming an aggressive Russian nationalist organization, the VDOBT turned out to be a very ineffective institution staffed with ex-party and government bureaucrats.

---

[20]On Zalygin and his editorial policies at *Novyy mir*, see Brudny (1988).

All these developments prompted *Nash sovremennik* to start a campaign for the imposition of a total ban on the production and sales of alcohol and for the revitalization of the VDOBT. The campaign began with the publication in the July 1987 issue of the journal of an essay by Dr. Fyodor Uglov, a member of the Soviet Academy of Medical Sciences and the chief Russian nationalist spokesman on problems of alcoholism. In the essay, Uglov notes that alcoholism threatens the very existence of the Russian nation (Uglov, 1987). He insists that the income the state generates from alcohol sales cannot outweigh the damage alcohol abuse inflicts on the economy and national defense.

Uglov brings up two main causes of the evident failure of the May 1985 policies. First, these policies were at best only half-measures. Second, there is a conspiracy between bureaucrats who see in alcohol sales the easiest way to generate revenues, and ethnic non-Russians in the mass media who oppose the idea of a sober Russian nation.[21] The only way to save the Russian nation from physical extinction is, in his view, to reimpose the complete ban on the production and sales of alcohol which existed in Russia in the years 1914-1925, and to transform the VDOBT into a grass-roots movement led by prominent Russian nationalist advocates of "dry law" policies.

Uglov's ideas were elaborated and defended by Lapchenko and Kovalenin in the March 1988 issue of *Nash sovremennik*. In his essay, Boris Lapchenko argues that the policy of restricting production and sales of alcohol is bound to remain ineffective while an acute shortage of consumer goods exists (Lapchenko, 1988). Lapchenko calls for a complete ban on alcohol production and sales, combined with a saturation of the market with consumer goods. The essay by A. Kovalenin, a member of the Novosibirsk chapter of the VDOBT, contains a detailed program to fight alcoholism (Kovalenin, 1988). At its center stands a proposal to elect Uglov and other well-known Russian nationalists to head the VDOBT, to have new elections in all regional chapters of the society, and to impose a total ban on the production and sales of alcohol by December 19, 1989, the 70th anniversary of the Bolsheviks' decision to continue pre-revolutionary "dry law" policies.

Finally, the period between March 1987 and March 1988 witnessed the emergence in the Soviet political arena of a new form of Russian nationalist opposition to *perestroyka*. Exploiting Gorbachev's policy of permitting the formation and activities of non-official societies with a political agenda, the nationalist and rabidly anti-Semitic Moscow organization *Pamyat'* was able to transform itself from a small cultural club into a very visible, if not significant, factor in Soviet politics. Although the leaders of *Pamyat'* presented themselves as ardent supporters of *perestroyka*, through their arguments about a pervasive Judeo-Masonic conspiracy against

---

[21]In his 1986 book (Uglov, 1986), Uglov openly blames pre-revolutionary alcoholism in Russia on Jews.

Russia, they in fact challenged *perestroyka* from radical Slavophile positions taken to the very extreme.[22]

It was natural that *Nash sovremennik* would be the first journal to defend *Pamyat'* from its liberal critics. The first to address the subject of *Pamyat'* on the pages of the journal was the leading radical Slavophile theorist, Vadim Kozhinov. He rejects many of *Pamyat'*'s arguments because they contain, in his words, too much "ignorance" and "infantilism" which find its expression "in all kinds of emblems, myths, [and] fantastic images." Kozhinov refused, however, to condemn *Pamyat'*, claiming that its extremism is an unavoidable by-product of the ongoing transformation of Russian nationalism into a mass movement. Finally, this refusal to denounce the organization went hand-in-hand with a long and harsh attack on *Pamyat'*'s critics (Kozhinov, 1987, pp. 167–172).[23]

This defense was seconded by that of the conservative nationalist Valentin Rasputin in the January 1988 issue (Rasputin, 1988, p. 171). Rasputin spoke about "the left-leaning (*davshaya levyy kren*) press" which violates the principles of *glasnost'* by attaching to *Pamyat'* the label of the "Black Hundreds," and by denying *Pamyat'* the right to defend itself in print. *Pamyat'* ought to be defended, Rasputin argues, because behind attempts to discredit and crush the organization stands a desire to discredit and crush the entire Russian nationalist movement.

The Third Stage: March 1988–May 1989

It was not surprising that *Nash sovremennik* defended *Pamyat'* regularly, beginning in late 1987. This was a period of growing confrontation between the supporters of *perestroyka* and its opponents. One of the most important arenas for this confrontation was a meeting of the governing board of the USSR Writers Union, which took place on March 1–2, 1988. Russian nationalist opponents of *perestroyka* used the forum to attack the reforms. As in March 1987, the assault was led by Yuriy Bondarev, who portrayed *glasnost'* as "unruliness of all-negating emotions," and accused reformers of depicting all Russian and Soviet history exclusively in black colors. He openly labeled the historian Yuriy Afanas'yev, one of the main spokesmen of reformers, as the "apostle of sensation and slander." Other nationalist writers and critics defended *Pamyat'*, criticized the rehabilitation of Bukharin, and blamed the reforms for weakening the state and thus setting the stage for the Nagorno-Karabakh affair.[24]

This confrontation at the meeting of the Writers Union's governing board was an ominous prelude to the publication of an essay by a college teacher, Nina Andreyeva, entitled "I Cannot Give Up Principles" (*Ne mogu*

---

[22]For a useful recent summary of Soviet and Western writings on Pamyat', see Laqueur (1989, pp. 135–145).

[23]For a similar attack on Pamyat' critics, see Kuzmin (1988, pp. 154–156).

[24]Literaturnaya gazeta, March 9, 1988. In addition to Bondarev's speech, see also the speeches of Prokhanov, Kunyayev, and Prokushev.

postupitsya s printsipami). Spread over a full page in the March 13, 1988 issue of the daily *Sovetskaya Rossiya*, it was a frontal attack on *perestroyka* made from the neo-Stalinist nationalist point of view. Andreyeva defended Stalin as the leader who turned Russia into a superpower, criticized *glasnost'* policies, and accused reformist writers Shatrov and Rybakov of falsifying Soviet history in their recently published works. The essay was rabidly anti-Semitic: it emphasized the Jewishness of Trotsky and even argued that Jews are a counterrevolutionary nation. The unprecedented length of the essay and the fact that it was reprinted in regional newspapers throughout the Soviet Union and in Eastern Europe clearly pointed to Yegor Ligachev, the second ranking Politburo member at the time, as its main sponsor.[25]

Despite official condemnation of Andreyeva's article in *Pravda* (April 5, 1988), its publication encouraged the editors of *Molodaya gvardiya*, who, sensing the support for their ideas within the Politburo, to intensify their assault on *perestroyka*. In its April 1988 issue, the journal published an essay by Mikhail Malakhov, the deputy head of Gosplan under Khrushchev. It was the first serious effort to forge an alliance between Russian nationalist intellectuals and the anti-reformist forces in the Soviet political elite (Malakhov, 1988).

The content of the essay is very similar to that of Andreyeva's. It is an outright apology of Stalinism. It praises collectivization and industrialization and the principles of Stalinist industrial management. In the same breath, Malakhov sharply criticizes the de-Stalinization reforms of Khrushchev. Finally, Malakhov warns that Gorbachev's re-opening of the Stalin question would inevitably lead to anarchy and the undermining of socialism.

Alongside Malakhov's essay, *Molodaya gvardiya* resorted to a strategy of selectively publishing readers' letters in order to renew its attacks on such manifestations of *perestroyka* and *glasnost'* as the rehabilitation of Bukharin, private businesses, rock music, and the publication of formerly forbidden anti-Stalinist works of fiction. As before, the reform-minded intelligentsia bore the main brunt of the attack. They were accused of undermining national morale by filling literary journals with works which "attempt to prove that the last seventy years were the most dirty and disgusting in the history of our nation." They also were found guilty of weakening the Russian state by using the existing freedom of expression to preach ideological rapprochement with the bourgeois West (Khochu, 1988; Nesti, 1988; Podmena, 1988; Kak nashe, 1988).

Like *Molodaya gvardiya*, *Nash sovremennik* made an effort to establish a tie with the anti-reformist forces in the Soviet political elite. *Nash sovremennik* tried to present Ligachev and his appointees as leaders whose records show a deep understanding of Russian nationalist concerns. The May

---

[25]According to a prominent reformist intellectual, Vasiliy Selyunin, Ligachev himself praised the essay in two meetings with Soviet press editors and pressed them to reprint it. See *Christian Science Monitor*, April 27, 1988, pp. 1, 10.

1988 issue of the journal contained Yevgeniy Chernykh's essay about the anti-alcohol policies of the Tomsk regional party secretaries, Ligachev, and his successor (and presumably appointee) Zorkaltsev. Chernykh claims that already in the 1970s, Ligachev, on his own initiative, severely restricted the number of alcohol sales outlets and their working hours. As a result of this policy, the consumption of vodka in the region fell by one-third in the period 1974–1984. After the introduction of the anti-alcohol policies in May 1985, Zorkaltsev closed several main alcohol producing facilities in the region, left open only a few liquor stores and restaurants which serve liquor, and banned deliveries of alcoholic beverages from outside the region (Chernykh, 1988, pp. 156, 158–159). The message of the article is clear: Ligachev and his people deserve Russian nationalists' strongest support.

Alongside the promotion of Ligachev, *Nash sovremennik*'s publication policies between April and June 1988 were aimed at strengthening the unity of the Russian nationalist opposition to *perestroyka* on the eve of the 19th Party Conference. As a symbolic act of solidarity with the editorial line of *Molodaya gvardiya*, *Nash sovremennik* carried in its May 1988 issue a long interview with Anatoliy Ivanov, the chief editor of *Molodaya gvardiya*, which contained a straightforward apology for Stalinism and a harsh attack on *perestroyka*. Ivanov tries to shift the blame for the violence which accompanied collectivization, and for the destruction of several Moscow churches in the 1930s, from Stalin to his Jewish lieutenants, Yakovlev and Kaganovich, and justifies the terror of the 1930s as a defensive act against internal enemies. The terror, he declares, saved the Soviet Union from a counterrevolution of the kind East Germany experienced in 1953, Hungary in 1956, and Czechoslovakia in 1968. Finally, like the rest of the neo-Stalinists, he repeats the warning that the reforms are leading Russia to anarchy, as they did in Eastern Europe (A. Ivanov, 1988).

Ivanov's neo-Stalinist and anti-Semitic assertions were seconded by the radical Slavophile stance of Vadim Kozhinov. The April 1988 issue of the journal contains his programmatic essay in which he blames the Jews for terrorizing the Russian peasantry during collectivization and for blowing up Moscow's churches in the 1930s. Contrary to Ivanov, Kozhinov is not apologetic toward Stalin. He presents Stalin as a good Leninist and as a man who merely perfected the machine of terror which Lenin built during the Civil War. Moreover, he stated that both Lenin and Stalin were only executioners of the will of the world Communist movement which was under Jewish domination (Kozhinov, 1988).

Publication of the articles of Ivanov and Kozhinov reflected the strategy of *Nash sovremennik*'s editors. Anti-Semitism was to serve as the "glue" of the nationalist opposition to the reforms. Indeed, in the months preceding the 19th Party Conference, anti-Semitic attacks on *perestroyka* in *Nash sovremennik* reached an unprecedented level. *Nash sovremennik* now openly endorsed a theory of Judeo-Masonic conspiracy by publishing

Viktor Ivanov's novel *The Day of Judgment* (V. Ivanov, 1988). The novel, of a kind which had not appeared in print in the Soviet Union since Ivan Shevtsov's rabidly anti-Semitic novels of the 1960s, portrayed the subversive activities of a Judeo-Masonic espionage network in the Soviet Union of the Khrushchev era. *Nash sovremennik* also rallied in defense of Vladimir Begun, the leading anti-Semitic theorist in the Soviet Union, from attacks by reformers who accused him of plagiarizing from Hitler's *Mein Kampf*. The *Nash sovremennik* editors not only published a letter in defense of Begun but also endorsed it (Protiv, 1988).

The anti-Semitic line of *Nash sovremennik* was quickly picked up by *Molodaya gvardiya*. The July 1988 issue of the journal, which appeared during the Party Conference, carried a dialogue between Ivan Shevtsov himself and Air Force Marshal Ivan Pstygo. They assail "Zionism" and present it as "the agency of world imperialism" and as the most vicious enemy of the Soviet state. Moreover, the authors openly praise *Pamyat'* for its efforts to make the public aware of the "Zionist" threat. Shevtsov and Pstygo, indeed, go on to present *Pamyat'* as a patriotic society which deserves the open and unqualified support of the party and the military (Shevtsov and Pstygo, 1988, pp. 226–228).

The 19th Party Conference proved that Russian nationalist opposition to *perestroyka* has substantial support inside the party. Such prominent opponents of *perestroyka* as Yuriy Bondarev and Anatoliy Ivanov were elected to the Conference as delegates. In his speech before the Conference, Bondarev defended the publication policies of *Molodaya gvardiya* and *Nash sovremennik* and viciously attacked *glasnost'*. He accused the reformist newspapers and journals of propagating national nihilism and immorality, Western ideas and values, and warned that *glasnost'* was destabilizing the Soviet state. Bondarev's ideas found support among many delegates who interrupted his speech with applause, and who booed Baklanov, the editor of *Znamya*, who sharply criticized Bondarev's speech (*Pravda*, July 2, 1988).

While broad support of Russian nationalist opposition to *perestroyka* was evident among the delegates, this was not reflected in the Conference resolutions. In fact, one resolution contained an implicit condemnation of Russian nationalist opposition; the policies of *glasnost'* were upheld while the "activities aimed at . . . stirring up national and racial hatred" were condemned (*Pravda*, July 2, 1988). Moreover, in early fall 1988, the Russian nationalists suffered a major defeat: Gorbachev disregarded the renewed pressure of *Nash sovremennik* to impose a total ban on alcohol production (Khukhry et al., 1988; Dusha, 1988) and cancelled the 1985 anti-alcohol policies.

Despite the defeat of the anti-alcohol campaign, Russian nationalists were extremely encouraged by the hostility of the Conference delegates toward reformist Moscow intellectuals. To them, this was the best indicator of the views prevailing among the party elite. Moreover, Ligachev openly expressed his support of their views by endorsing Bondarev's

Conference speech at a meeting with local journalists in Gorkiy in August 1988.[26]

At the September 1988 meeting of the Secretariat of the RSFSR Writers Union in Ryazan', the leaders of the coalition of Russian nationalist opponents to *perestroyka*, encouraged by this endorsement, began a new assault on Gorbachev's cultural and economic policies. It is worth pointing out that the intensity of the assault did not diminish after Ligachev lost his position as the second-ranking Politburo member in the September 30, 1988 Politburo reshuffle.

Rasputin, in the meeting's keynote address, spoke about the destructive impact on Russia and its culture of such Western imports as rock music, beauty contests, sex education, and the defense of homosexuality. The radical Slavophile economist Mikhail Antonov attacked the legalization of joint ventures and the move toward integration into the world economy as leading to the transformation of Russia into a "colony of multi-national corporations." Another leading radical Slavophile, the literary critic Anatoliy Lanshchikov, added to Antonov's argument a warning that Gorbachev's policies would cause Russia to fall victim to "Western 'peaceful' technological aggression and the equally 'peaceful' Eastern demographic aggression." He, as well as other participants, also complained about the anti-Russian nature of *Ogonyok* and other leading reformist publications.[27]

Elaboration of Rasputin's argument that *perestroyka* undermines the moral health of the Russian nation by exposing it to Western cultural aggression fit perfectly into the aim of the editorial boards of *Nash sovremennik* and *Molodaya gvardiya* to redefine the nature of the sociopolitical debate. Already the October 1988 issue of *Nash sovremennik* featured a special section dedicated to the dangers of rock music to Russian youth. The contributors present rock music as the Western "Trojan Horse" which destroys from within the most basic unit of Soviet society, the family, and call for enactment of legislation limiting the activities of rock bands (Chistyakov and Sanachev, 1988; Chirkin, 1988; Gunko, 1988). Both *Nash sovremennik* and *Molodaya gvardiya* followed Rasputin in attacking "pornography" in Soviet cinema, theater, and arts, the defense of homosexuality, and sexual education as leading to the corruption of youth (Andreyev-Rayevskiy, 1988; Lyubomudrov, 1989, pp. 177–179; Lugovoy, 1989; Matveyets, 1989; Shiropayev, 1989, pp. 183–184; Zelenevskiy, 1988).

Of equal if not higher importance to the campaign against rock music

---

[26]Answering a reporter who praised Bondarev's speech at the Party Conference and complaining that *Ogonyok* is engaging in sensationalism and destructive criticism of Soviet achievements, Ligachev argued that the Party Conference rejected reformers' attempts to portray Soviet history exclusively in negative terms. He went on to emphasize that during the Stalin and post-Stalin periods, the Soviet Union transformed itself from a backward country into a world superpower (see Povyshat', 1988, p. 5).

[27]An abridged stenographic report of the Ryazan' meeting of the RSFSR Writers Union Secretariat was published in the October 28, 1988 issue of *Literaturnaya Rossiya*.

and sexuality in arts, was the journals' effort to discredit the radical reformers and their publications both in the eyes of the party elite and the general public. Between October 1988 and May 1989, almost every issue of both journals printed polemical essays and readers' letters which violently attacked *Ogonyok* and *Znamya*, their leading contributors, and their editors, Korotich and Baklanov. The strategy was to blend character assassination with political accusations. So, Korotich's reformist credentials were challenged on the ground that in the past the *Ogonyok* editor had praised Brezhnev's literary genius. *Ogonyok* itself was denounced as "an omnipotent ideological narcotic" which demoralizes Russian people by denying their past achievements and undermining their belief in the idea of socialism. Baklanov, the editor of *Znamya*, in turn, was accused of distorting the history of World War II, especially Stalin's war record, and spreading malicious allegations against *Pamyat'* (Bushin, 1988b; Bushin, 1989a; Bushin, 1989b; Ekologiya, 1988, pp. 245-250; Fed, 1989a, pp. 13-16, 1989b, pp. 175-179; Gorbachev, 1989, pp. 250-257; 1989, pp. 277-281; Kozhinov, 1989, pp. 143, 173-175; Lapin, 1989; Litsom, 1989, pp. 217-226, 228-232).

The same basic strategy was applied against the liberal Moscow intelligentsia and cultural avant-garde associated with it. *Molodaya gvardiya* published letters from readers in which the Moscow intelligentsia was labeled "intellectual bourgeoisie" and was accused of attempting to take from the party its control over the nature of the reform process (Litsom, 1989, pp. 228, 233). In addition to these political accusations, *Molodaya gvardiya* portrayed the avant-garde poetry and prose of young members of the Moscow intelligentsia as elitist and detached from the concerns of the people (Bulin, 1989; Khatyushin, 1988; Savetskiy, 1989).

Anti-intellectualism also constituted an important dimension in *Nash sovremennik*'s and *Molodaya gvardiya*'s evaluation of Stalinism, its roots, and the political and economic alternatives to it. It is clear that the two journals would like to avoid extensive treatment of Stalinism, since it meant both the acceptance of the agenda of the socio-political debate set by radical reformers and the danger of a potential breakdown of the Russian nationalist alliance over this issue. Stalinism and its political, social, and economic legacy, indeed, was not discussed at the Ryazan' meeting.

Russian nationalists, however, were dragged into this very debate because of the extremely wide publicity which accompanied publication of such anti-Stalinist works of fiction as Grossman's novel *Life and Fate* or Voinovich's *Life and Adventures of Ivan Chonkin*; the foundation by leading members of Moscow reformist intelligentsia of the *Memorial* society dedicated to commemorating the victims of Stalinism in the fall of 1988; and an intensification, due to the progressively worsening food supply situation and the sharply diminishing availability of consumer goods, of the debate about the potential of a command economy and the future direction of economic reform.

Although the strategy of *Molodaya gvardiya* and *Nash sovremennik* in dealing with the issue of Stalinism and the Stalinist legacy differed significantly, both journals heavily emphasized anti-intellectual and anti-Semitic elements in order to keep the nationalist alliance together. *Molodaya gvardiya*'s policy primarily was to publish essays and letters of orthodox Stalinists, be it simple workers, intellectuals, or former high party officials (Benediktov, 1989; Konotop, 1988; Matveyets, 1988; Mostafin, 1989; Zhitnukhin, 1988).[28]

The orthodox Stalinists aggressively justify all aspects of Stalinism, including collectivization and the terror, as the necessary price Russia had to pay to become a superpower. They follow the editor of *Molodaya gvardiya*, Ivanov, in transferring the responsibility for the excesses of the terror from Stalin to his Jewish subordinates, Mekhlis and Yakovlev, and to Jewish officers in the security police. Finally, this defense of Stalinism includes a justification of the command economy, created by Stalin, and criticism of Khrushchev's reforms and their apologists among the liberal Moscow intelligentsia. These reforms, they argue, only undercut the vitality of the command economy by weakening discipline in the party and in the society as a whole. The solution to the Soviet Union's economic problems is not its marketization but rather a strengthening of the work ethic and the selection of proper party cadres to supervise the economic sphere (Benediktov, 1989, pp. 19-21, 62-64; Konotop, 1988, pp. 237-243).

In the period between fall 1988 and late spring 1989, *Nash sovremennik*'s approach to dealing with Stalinism and its legacy was far more sophisticated than that of *Molodaya gvardiya*. The orthodox Stalinist defense of collectivization, the terror, and the command economy was entirely absent from the *Nash sovremennik* pages. What the journal published instead were essays by conservative nationalists and radical Slavophiles which attempted to discredit the reformers' view of Stalinism and its origins, the nature of the command economy, and the desired direction of economic reform. All the essays effectively deny Stalin's responsibility for collectivization and the terror by tracing the foundations of the Stalinist system back to the politics and ideas of the 1920s, or even to the revolution itself.

The conservative nationalist Soloukhin and the radical Slavophile Lanshchikov thus follow up Solzhenitsyn and reject the reformers' attempt to attach the label "Stalinist" to such events as collectivization, industrialization, and the terror. Reformist intellectuals from *Ogonyok* and the *Memorial* society employ the term "Stalinist" in order to white-

---

[28]Among these neo-Stalinist essays, that of the late (d. 1983) Ivan Benediktov (Benediktov, 1989), Commissar and Minister of Agriculture in the years 1938-1958 and later Soviet ambassador to India and Yugoslavia, clearly stands out. The essay is based on a series of interviews with Benediktov conducted in 1980-1981 but published only in April 1989. This is the most elaborate defense of Stalinism published in the USSR in the post-Stalin era. Recently it was claimed that the Benediktov essay was a fabrication (see Gennadiy Vychub, "Maket krasiv, A dal'she?" *Sovetskaya kul'tura*, December 9, 1989, p. 3).

wash the record of their spiritual and biological fathers, the party intellectuals who perished in the purges of the 1930s. This party intelligentsia, however, was responsible for the murder of the tsar and his
family, and for millions of victims during the Civil War and collectivization.

While Soloukhin does not mention Lenin explicitly, Lanshchikov does.
It was Lenin, according to Lanshchikov, who came up with the idea of the
rapid collectivization of the Russian peasantry. During the NEP, this idea
was ignored by the party until Stalin reintroduced it. The idea of a
breakneck pace for industrialization was not Stalin's invention either,
but was borrowed from Trotsky. There was no such thing as the Stalinist
terror, they argue, only a Communist terror, which eventually justly
victimized its initiators. The attempt of the reformers to distinguish
Stalinism from other forms of socialism, Lanshchikov and Soloukhin
imply, is merely a strategy to legitimize Western-oriented socialism
which combines political and cultural pluralism with market economics
(Lanshchikov, 1988; Soloukhin, 1988).

The radical Slavophiles Kunyayev and Kozhinov elaborate this argument while Kozhinov, together with two other radical Slavophiles,
Antonov and Kazintsev, link it to the ongoing debate about the direction
of economic reform. In his poetry and criticism, Stanislav Kunyayev
aggressively put forth the idea that the terror of the 1930s was fair
retribution for the crimes against Russia, which were committed by
communist intellectuals of predominantly Jewish origin from the time of
the revolution to collectivization. Moreover, the reformist intelligentsia
today, the so-called "children of the Arbat," must bear the responsibility
for the crimes of their fathers.[29]

Trotsky, Bukharin, and other Jewish Communists are Kunyayev's
main targets. It was not Stalin but Trotsky, whom he calls Leib Bron-
shtein to emphasize his Jewishness, who invented the concentration
camp system in the early 1920s. Kunyayev carefully singles out all senior
NKVD officers in the early 1930s with Jewish-sounding names to assert
that Jews played a key role in the emerging GULAG system. Bukharin,
the only non-Jewish Communist attacked by Kunyayev is found guilty
of initiating the terror against Russian national culture in the 1920s
(Kunyayev, 1988a, 1988b).

Jewish intellectuals, Bukharin, and the NEP era also appeared on Kozhinov's list of villains. In the 1920s and the 1930s, he stated, Jewish
intellectuals eagerly destroyed Russian national culture by branding it as
anti-Semitic. Moreover, according to Kozhinov, Jewish intellectuals
were the beneficiaries of Stalinism, not its victims. Even in 1950 and
1951, during the anti-cosmopolitan campaign, a third of the Stalin Prizes

---

[29] In August 1989 Sergey Vikulov resigned as chief editor of *Nash sovremennik* and recommended Stanislav
Kunyayev to be appointed as his successor. Vikulov's recommendation was approved by the Secretariat
of the RSFSR Writers Union. Kunyayev unveiled his plans for the 1990 *Nash sovremennik* in the interview
to *Literaturnaya gazeta*. See *Literaturnaya gazeta*, August 16, 1989.

for Russian-language literature was awarded to Jews (Kozhinov, 1989, p. 170).

Bukharin, however, is a far more important target of Kozhinov's attack than the Jewish intelligentsia. Bukharin, he argues, provided the ideological justification for a drive to transform radically Russian society and destroy its centuries-old national traditions as well as the intellectuals defending these traditions. There were no principal disagreements between Stalin and Bukharin about the collectivization of the peasantry, only disagreements about tactics. Bukharin was concerned not with the fate of millions of Russian peasants as such, but with the impact of collectivization upon the tempo of economic development and the stability of Soviet power (Kozhinov, 1989, pp. 151–153, 155, 157).

Kozhinov's attack on Bukharin and the NEP era is not simply an academic effort to present the Russian nationalist views of Soviet history. It is an integral part of his debate with the liberals about the desired course of Gorbachev's economic reforms. While in the 1920s Bukharin sought the destruction of Russian national traditions, Bukharin's modern day followers attempt to use his ideas in order to justify the introduction of Western-type economic models and American-style family farm agriculture, both of which are alien to Russian national traditions. The Russian economy, concludes Kozhinov, ought to rely on centuries-old Russian national traditions (Kozhinov, 1989, pp. 167, 173–174).

This linkage between Bukharin's ideas and the current debate over the direction of the economic reforms is the central subject of Mikhail Antonov's essay. Although Antonov's interpretation of Bukharin's ideas completely contradicts that of Kozhinov's, their conclusions are identical. According to Antonov, the main spokesman for Bukharin on economic questions was the famous economist Kondratiev. Bukharin and Kondratiev came up with an interpretation of the economic principles of NEP which fundamentally differed from that of Lenin. While Lenin's conception of NEP never envisioned the unrestricted development of market relations, Bukharin's and Kondratiev's did. If their ideas were accepted by the party, Antonov asserts, Russia soon would have fallen prey to Western economic imperialism (Antonov, 1989, pp. 136–138).

In rejecting Bukharin's idea of market socialism, Antonov does not accept the Stalinist model of the command economy. The latter, in addition to being an economic failure, is responsible for the systematic destruction of the environment and ought to be dismantled (Antonov, 1989a, pp. 126–133).[30] The Stalinist command economy, however, should not be replaced by the contemporary versions of Bukharin and Kondratiev ideas. Shmelev, Abalkin, Aganbegyan, Bogomolov, and other champions of market economics and Soviet integration into the world

---

[30]Mikhail F. Antonov, the head of a section at the Institute of World Economics and International Relations (IMEMO), is the main Russian nationalist speaker on questions of economic reforms. His August 1987 essay contains the most elaborate Russian nationalist analysis of the failures of the command economy. See Antonov (1987).

economy are wrong, Antonov argues, because their program does not go beyond the narrow framework of Western economic theory.

The primary purpose of the economic reforms must not be the attainment of capitalist-level efficiency and productivity, or growth of the GNP, but the "real improvement of the physical and spiritual health of our compatriots and an increase in their well-being." Relying on this definition, Antonov argues that the true indicators of socio-economic development of the country should be demographic growth, levels of fertility and mortality, average life span, health situation of the population, real income of the population, changes in land yield, changes in the ecological situation, morality of the population, and the rates of crime. In order to achieve very positive results on all these indicators, the Russian national economic model should rely neither on command-administrative methods, nor on the market mechanism, but on "socio-political means based on spiritual and moral values which include both economic and administrative means" (Antonov, 1989a, p. 147).

Antonov, however, does not go beyond this extremely vague statement, or the equally ambiguous assertion that Russian economics should be based on millenium-old Russian national traditions. Neither here, nor in any of his numerous essays published elsewhere, does he explain how economics based on Russian national traditions ought to function or how it would be different from the existing system. However, he spares no effort in criticizing market economics as socially unjust, and works to politically discredit the Soviet supporters of a market system. Since market economics and plutocratic and individualistic Western democracy are inseparable, the hidden agenda of the reformist economists is to turn Russia into a province of the West (Antonov, 1989a, pp. 143, 146, 149–150).[31]

If Antonov's argument against the ideas of Bukharin and Abalkin stops short of providing a clear answer how Russian nationalist economics should function, then Kazintsev's attack on the anti-Stalinist writings and liberal dissidents does provide at least a partial answer. In many ways he carries the ideas of Kozhinov, Antonov, and other radical Slavophiles to their logical conclusion. The specific targets of the deputy editor of *Nash sovremennik* are several anti-Stalinist fictional works, especially those of Grossman and Voinovich.

Under the guise of portraying the evils of Stalinism, these writings slander the Russian people as a whole and its millenium-old history. Publication of these "Russophobic" works, Kazintsev asserts, is an integral part of the reformers' drive to discredit Russian national traditions and its defenders, past and present, in order to justify imposition of Western-type pluralism. The next stage of this drive is already on the

---

[31]In his speech at the Ryazan' plenum and in his other essays, he very passionately argues against the policy of foreign investments and joint ventures as leading to the effective transformation of the Soviet Union into a Western colony. See Antonov (1989b).

way with the forthcoming publication of the writings on contemporary Russian nationalism of the emigre scholar Alexander Yanov (Kazintsev, 1988b; Kazintsev, 1989).

The marketization of the Soviet economy and the growth of private business are as dangerous to the Russian people and their traditions as the reformers' literary politics. This situation requires the unity of all forces opposing the reforms. Russian nationalists, therefore, must make the painful choice between the bureaucratic command economy and the socially unjust market system. Both are evils, asserts Kazintsev, but the bureaucratic command economy is definitely the lesser. We will be able to compromise with the bureaucrat, who is now scared of the reformers, but not with the emerging Soviet entrepreneur. Thus, Kozhinov's and Antonov's Russian national economics, as interpreted by Kazintsev, is merely a modification of the existing command economy (Kazintsev, 1989, pp. 167–168).

Kazintsev's justification for the alliance between Russian nationalists and anti-reformist forces in the political elite and his readiness to accept the essentials of the Stalinist economic structure had yet another very important reason: the fast growth of the anti-Russian nationalist movements in the Caucasus and, especially, in the Baltic republics in the second half of 1988 through the spring of 1989. Kazintsev implicitly accuses reformers of a willingness to accept the secession of the Baltic republics from the Soviet state (Kazintsev, 1989, p. 161). Indeed, as nationalist movements in the Baltics became stronger and more aggressive in their demands, *Molodaya gvardiya* and *Nash sovremennik* increasingly challenged these claims and called for strengthening the alliance with the anti-reformist wing of the party.

If in January 1988, *Molodaya gvardiya* argued that the only Soviet nationality problem is the problem of the demographic decline of ethnic Russians by November and December 1988, it already admitted that a lack of knowledge of the Estonian language by local Russians constituted a legitimate basis for the natives' discontent. This admission, however, was made under the assumption that the language question is the only aspect of the nationality problem which Russians are willing to recognize and discuss. Those members of the Estonian nationalist movement who call for secession from the Union are labeled "anti-Soviet" and "anti-communist" (Troitskiy, 1988; Teterin, 1988a, 1988b).

In January 1989, *Nash sovremennik* openly proclaimed that the concepts "Russophobia" and "anti-Soviet activity" are one and the same and accused the nationalist movements in the Baltics of both. The author also identified the reformers in Moscow as supporting the demands of local nationalist movements (Kuzmin, 1989). In other words, the journal asserted that the preservation of the integrity of the Soviet state is of major interest to the Russian nationalist movement and the anti-reformist forces in the party.

Finally, in April 1989, *Molodaya gvardiya* published a long essay on the

situation in Lithuania which harshly attacked the policies of the local
Communist Party and the Lithuanian National Front (Sajudis). The
author, a Russified Dagestani who lives in Lithuania, accused the local
party of imposing discriminatory language requirements on the Russian-speaking population. He followed the pattern established by Nash
sovremennik and argued that Sajudis, in its essence, is both an anti-Russian and anti-Soviet secessionist movement. The implicit agenda of
this essay is clear: it is a call to the party in Moscow to suppress nationalist movements in the Baltics and restore to the Russian-speaking population in these areas the rights it enjoyed prior to perestroyka (Kaziyev,
1989).

The Russian nationalist positions on Gorbachev's cultural, economic,
and nationality policies were aired at the Congress of People's Deputies.
Vasiliy Belov and Valentin Rasputin, both members of the Nash sovremennik editorial board, argued that policies of cultural pluralism are forcing
upon Russia dangerous "pluralism of morals." They complained about
the "spread of Russophobia" in the Baltics and the Caucasus, criticized
the cooperative movement, and openly expressed their support for Ligachev and the anti-reformist wing of the party (Izvestiya, June 3, 1989; June
7, 1989).

In sum, between March 1985 and May 1989, the Russian nationalist
movement split between the reform-supporting minority and the
reform-opposing majority. This majority consisted of three groups with
very different opinions, but these differences were outweighed by strong
opposition to Gorbachev's cultural, economic, and nationality policies.
Molodaya gvardiya and Nash sovremennik played crucial roles in Russian
nationalist politics during this period. Their editorial policies were aimed
at: maintaining the unity of the Russian nationalist opposition to radical
reforms; forging an alliance between this opposition and the opponents
of radical reforms in the political elite; discrediting leading reformist
intellectuals, their journals, and their causes; and convincing the party to
limit, if not to reverse, Gorbachev's policies of cultural pluralism, economic reforms, and greater autonomy for the non-Russian republics. The
fourth and final section of this paper examines the popularity of the ideas
published in Molodaya gvardiya and Nash sovremennik.

POPULARITY OF RUSSIAN NATIONALIST
APPEAL

There is still no adequate procedure for measuring the degree of
popularity of Russian nationalist (or reformist) appeal. Poor showing of
Russian nationalist candidates at the elections to the Congress of People's Deputies is a very misleading indicator, since most Russian nationalists showed a Slavophile-like disdain for the election process, and because
most of their outspoken opponents were elected in Moscow, which is

hardly representative of the RSFSR as a whole.[32] Those Russian nationalists who were elected turned out, however, to be popular among the
delegates to the Congress: Vasiliy Belov, the only Russian nationalist
candidate to the Supreme Soviet, was elected to the Council of Nationalities with a vast majority of 1,984 to 165 votes, while Boris Yeltsin and
most of the reformist Moscow candidates failed to win seats (*Izvestiya*,
May 28, 1989). Incidentally, Belov was elected to the Congress from the
Party list. Both of these facts suggest that Russian nationalist ideas are
popular among the party elite.

As for the ability of Russian nationalists to influence the policy process,
the results are very inconclusive, at least for now. It is true that Russian
nationalists were in the forefront of the successful campaign against the
river diversion projects, but these were always very controversial. They
failed to reverse Gorbachev's cultural policies and they were defeated in
their attempt to force the party to impose a total ban on the production of
alcohol. Yet, on June 6, 1989 the Supreme Soviet of the RSFSR went
along with Russian nationalist demands and imposed high taxation on
the gross income of cooperatives. The cooperatives, however, are very
unpopular both among the Russian general public and the RSFSR
bureaucracy. The decision to tax them highly may have to do as much
with these factors as with the Russian nationalist campaign against
cooperatives.

Finally, the data on the circulation and subscription to *Molodaya gvardiya*
and *Nash sovremennik* could provide some very useful insights into the
question of the popularity of Russian nationalism among the Russian
population. This is especially true because both journals refuse as a
matter of principle to publish previously forbidden or unpublished works
of fiction and non-fiction, which is one of the main causes of the meteoric
increase in circulation of such reformist journals as *Znamya*, *Druzhba
narodov*, and *Novyy mir*, as well as the Russian nationalist journal *Moskva*.

Analysis of circulation and subscription to *Molodaya gvardiya* suggests
that orthodox Stalinist and neo-Stalinist nationalist ideas which dominate the journal are not very popular among the Russian reading public,
especially among Moscovites. The journal's circulation fell from 870,000
copies in 1981 to 655,000 in 1989.[33] Moreover, most of its still large
circulation list consists of institutional subscribers: *Molodaya gvardiya* is a
required subscription in all military and Komsomol libraries.

Beginning in 1987, based on data about the size of personal and general
library subscriptions in Moscow, it is known that *Molodaya gvardiya* had
only 5,900 personal subscribers and 1,900 general library subscriptions,

---

[32]This disdain for parliamentary politics was expressed even by Russian nationalist delegates to the
Congress. Rasputin, for example, called the legislative activities of the Congress "legislative chicanery"
(*zakonodatel'nuye kryuchkotvorstvo*). See *Izvestiya*, June 7, 1989.

[33]All the data in this section are based on Bocharov, 1988; Gudkov and Dubin, 1988; Gudkov, 1988;
"Struktural'nyye izmeneniya tirazhey zhurnalnoy periodiki," *Sotsiologicheskiye issledovaniya*, 6:60–62, 1988;
"Ob itogakh podpiski na tsentral'nyye gazety i zhurnaly," *Izvestiya TsK KPSS*, 1:138–139, 1989.

the lowest by comparison to other Moscow "thick journals." The total size of the 1987 distribution of the journal in Moscow, which includes sales at newsstands, was only 7,941 copies, i.e., only 1.2 percent of total circulation. From rather fragmentary data we also know that in 1988 the distribution of the journal in Moscow was still only 1.5–2.0 percent of its total circulation. In comparison, in 1988, 23 percent of the circulation of the reformist *Novyy mir* was distributed in the capital.

At the same time, an analysis of the subscriptions and circulation of *Nash sovremennik* suggests that the popularity of the conservative nationalist and radical Slavophile ideas associated with the journal is meaningful and growing, even in Moscow. Although in 1989 the journal did not reach its 1982 level of 335,000 copies, its circulation stood at 250,000 copies, including 243,000 (mostly personal) subscriptions. Moreover, in 1986 and 1987 *Nash sovremennik* was the second most popular journal in Moscow after *Novyy mir*: it had 13,000 personal subscribers in 1986 and 16,000 in 1987.[34]

It is true that a circulation of 250,000 copies is rather small in comparison to the journals of the reformers. One should add, however, that the journal's circulation is still very tightly regulated. *Nash sovremennik*'s editors complained that while all other "thick journals" were permitted unrestricted subscriptions for their 1989 issues, *Nash sovremennik* was allowed only a 20 percent increase (*Nash sovremennik*, 1:192, 1989). This suggests that reformers in the party leadership are trying to limit the spread of ideas associated with the journal.

Today *Nash sovremennik* is clearly the most important journal of the Russian nationalist opposition to the reforms. Its future positions will provide a clear indication of the direction of Russian nationalist politics. Changes in its editorial board and its circulation figures may also serve as a measure of the popularity of the Russian nationalist appeal and the support it enjoys in the political elite.

Afterword

After this article was accepted for publication, the author spent four weeks in the Soviet Union, returning on October 14, 1989. During his stay in Moscow, he interviewed a dozen of the leading Russian nationalist contributors to *Molodaya gvardiya* and *Nash sovremennik*. The author visited the editorial offices of *Nash sovremennik* twice and had lengthy talks with its new chief editor, Stanislav Kunyayev, and especially his deputy, Aleksandr Kazintsev.

Nash sovremennik contributors and editors said that at present there is an intense competition for the hearts and minds of ethnic Russians. This competition is intensified by the deepening economic crisis and efforts of

---

[34]In comparison, *Znamya* had 10,000 subscribers in 1986 and 13,500 in 1985; *Druzhba narodov*, 4,800 and 8,100; and *Oktyabr'*, 6,600 and 9,700, respectively. See Bocharov (1988, p. 99).

nationalist movements in the Baltics and the Caucasus to secede. The current situation, they said, calls for the transformation of Russian nationalist-controlled newspapers and journals into considerably more effective media capable of shaping the political views of ethnic Russians than they have been heretofore. *Nash sovremennik* plays a very important role in this new strategy.

In order to broaden the support among the members of their traditional constituency, the middle classes and the intelligentsia of provincial Russian cities, and to reach constituencies with no significant Russian nationalist following (the Russian working class and Russian-speaking population of the Baltic republics), the RSFSR Writers Union replaced Vikulov, the chief editor of *Nash sovremennik*, in August 1989. City-born, Moscow University-educated, and younger than Vikulov by ten years, Kunyayev (b. 1932), the new chief editor, calculates that he can broaden the journal's appeal by publishing in 1990 Solzhenitsyn's *October 1916* and new novels of Bondarev and Pikul', two Soviet writers especially popular among members of the Russian working and middle classes. These forthcoming publications, combined with a conspicuous absence of works by the well-known "village prose" writers, the mainstay of the journal's prose section in the Vikulov era, clearly point to *Nash sovremennik*'s shift from a rural to urban focus.

As the author of this paper was told by the editors, the commissioned non-fictional works on economics and politics will emphasize the ideas most popular with the urban Russian-speaking population, such as: (a) the integrity of the Russian-dominated Soviet state; (b) support of the authoritarian one-party system; (c) defense of the Soviet military from attacks by the reformers; (d) social justice as the guiding principle of economic reforms; (e) and a very high priority for ecological concerns. The content of the August and September issues, effectively co-edited by Vikulov and Kunyayev, already illustrates this shift.[35]

Another part of the new strategy is a sharp increase in the number of speaking engagements by *Nash sovremennik* editors and contributors, and a diversification of the audiences. In the summer and early fall of 1989, they appeared before employees of science institutes, KGB and MVD officers, factory workers, and high school and university students, to name a few.[36] These meetings took place in Moscow, various provincial Russian cities, the Ukraine, and even the Baltics. This overall strategy seems to be very successful. The 1990 subscriptions to the journal jumped by 97 percent in comparison to the 1989 subscriptions and

---

[35]See Solzhenitsyn's essays (1989), Antonov's programmatic article on the subject of economic reform (1989c), and readers' letters dealing with such questions as the construction of nuclear power stations, activities of cooperatives, and even price formation of heavy industrial goods (Iz nashey, 1989).

[36]According to People's Deputy Yuriy Shchekochkin, the Political Administration of the MVD held regular meetings with *Nash Sovremennik* editors between June 1989 and January 1990. See *Radio Liberty Daily Report*, No. 20 (January 29, 1990).

reached 480,000 copies. This was the biggest increase among Moscow and Lengingrad "thick" journals (*Literaturnaya gazeta*, January 10, 1990).[37]

In recent months *Nash sovremennik* as an institution and its leading contributors as individuals not only are attempting to shape public opinion favorable to Russian nationalist ideas but also to create a powerful coalition capable of making a serious impact on the direction of political and economic reforms. This coalition includes, in addition to Russian nationalist institutions and societies, workers, trade unions, conservative party officials, intellectuals, economists and their publications, and members of the Supreme Soviet.

This coalition uses the umbrella of the United Front of Russian Workers (*Ob"yedinennyy front trudyashchikhsya Rossii* or OFT), a working-class organization founded in Leningrad in June 1989 with the support of the local party organization. In early September 1989, OFT convened its First All-Russian Congress in Sverdlovsk at which Anatoliy Salutskiy, one of the leading writers of *Nash sovremennik* on the question of economic reform, took an active part (on the Sverdlovsk conference, see Salutskiy, 1989). Soon after the Congress, the Sixth Plenum of trade unions decided to give OFT full financial and organizational support (see *Trud*, September 9, 1989).

Headed by Venyamin Yarin, a rolling mill operator from Nizhniy Tagil and a Supreme Soviet deputy, OFT demands an increase in the percentage of workers in the Supreme Soviet. The OFT platform calls for the election of two-thirds of deputies to local and republican Soviets from workplaces and only one-third from territorial districts. It also demands a restriction in the activities of cooperatives and proclaims that the cost of economic reform will not fall on the shoulders of Soviet workers. With the support of Moscow trade unions, on October 3, 1989 OFT staged a mass rally with 10,000 to 20,000 participants, in which its principal demands were aired.[38]

Salutskiy claims to have been instrumental in introducing the OFT leadership to such conservative communist intellectuals as the former *Kommunist* editor, Richard Kosolapov and the economists Aleksey Sergeyev and Vladmir Yakushev. As a result of Salutskiy's mediation, Kosolapov became the movement's chief ideologue, while Sergeyev and Yakushev took charge of developing the alternative model of economic reform which was presented at the OFT conference in Leningrad on October 21, 1989 (*Sovetskaya Rossiya*, October 22, 1989). Their main economic publications will be *Ekonomicheskiye nauki* and *Planovoye khozyaystvo* (see Sergeyev, 1989; Salutskiy, 1989), *Trud*, and *Sovetskaya Rossiya* appear to be the news-

---

[37]The aggressive nationalism of *Molodaya gvardiya* also seems to gain popularity with the Russian readers: the 1990 subscriptions to the journal rose by 11 percent, in comparison to 1989, and reached 697,000 copies (*Literaturnaya gazeta*, January 10, 1990). Since institutions are no longer requesting new subscriptions, this increase reflects a growth in individual subscriptions.

[38]For more information on this demonstration, see *Trud*, October 5, 1989 and *Moskovskiy komsomolets*, October 6, 1989.

papers which are going to publish materials supportive of OFT positions (see *Trud*, September 10, 1989, October 15, 1989; *Sovetskaya Rossiya*, October 22, 1989, November 24, 1989, December 30, 1989).

Concluding Note

In late October 1989, the coalition between the Russian nationalist intellectuals writing for *Nash sovremennik*, the OFT, and conservative members of the Supreme Soviet from the Russian Republic acquired an organizational form. On October 20-21, a group of 51 People's Deputies from the RSFSR met in the city of Tyumen' (for an account of the meeting, see Pavel Emelin, "Russkiy vopros," *Literaturnaya Rossiya*, November 17, 1989). At the end of the meeting 28 deputies signed a programmatic declaration, published in the front pages of the December issue of *Nash sovremennik*. The content of the declaration was remarkably similar to the ideas Russian nationalist intellectuals have articulated in their thick journals.

The declaration main points are as follows: it a) protests the discrimination of Russians in the Baltic republics and Georgia and claims that they are lacking legal protection and representation; b) charges that the financial resources of the RSFSR are being pumped into the other republics; c) expresses concern over the reformers' efforts to discredit the military, denounces Gorbachev's policies of unilateral disarmament, and calls for education of Soviet youth in the idea of territorial integrity and strength of the Soviet state; d) demands the creation of a RSFSR Academy of Sciences, RSFSR radio and television agency, and new RSFSR newspapers and publishing houses; and e) appeals for the adoption of new educational and cadre policies based on the principle of proportional representation of each nationality in the Soviet population. Citing the lack of action on these issues by the RSFSR Council of Ministers, the declaration calls for the formation of a club of RSFSR People's Deputies which would defend the national interest of ethnic Russians (*Nash sovremennik*, 12:3-6, 1989).

On October 24, 1989, the founding meeting of the Deputies Club "Rossiya" took place in Moscow. The "Rossiya" Club was sponsored by OFT, *Sovetskaya Rossiya*, and such Russian nationalist institutions as the Russian Republic Writers Union, the journal *Nash sovremennik*, the *Unity* ["Edinstvo"] society, and the "Committee for Rescuing the Volga River" (*Sovetskaya Rossiya*, October 25, 1989). Yarin was elected the chairman of the club, Salutskiy as one of the co-chairmen, and the chief editor of *Nash sovremennik*, Kunyayev, as a member of the club's executive council. "Russia" was clearly designed to be both the alternative to the "Inter-regional" group of radical deputies and the coordinating forum of institutional and individual participants in the conservative alliance on the eve of the March 4, 1990 elections to the local and RSFSR Supreme Soviet.

On December 29, 1989, this alliance, which began to call itself the *Bloc of Social-Patriotic Movements of Russia* ["blok obshchestvenno-patrioticheskikh dvizheniy Rossii"], published its electoral platform. The platform represents a further elaboration of the ideas of the Tyumen' declaration. Challenges to the policies and ideas of radical economic reform occupy major parts of the platform. It claims that the economic crisis deepened because of the senseless effort to destroy the existing economic structure and to replace it with an unregulated market mechanism. The platform expresses its opposition to the policies of free-economic zones, concessions, and "semi-colonial-type joint ventures" which would turn Russia into a supplier of raw materials and a dumpster for the nuclear and chemical waste of capitalist countries.

The document declares the Bloc opposition to the legalization of private property (even though it does support private agriculture) and demands that the issue be subject to a national referendum. Hand-in-hand with its declared opposition to private property comes a proposal for currency reform officially aimed at killing the "shadow economy." This reform would consist of exchanging old rubles for new ones of the same value up to the level of 10,000 to 15,000. A declaration on the sources of income would be required for those wishing to exchange amounts above this ceiling. The introduction of a progressive inheritance tax is proposed as a supplement to the monetary reform.

In the sphere of political reform, the platform demands the creation of the RSFSR Communist Party, RSFSR Academy of Sciences and research institutes similar to those of the USSR Academy. Like the Tyumen' document, the platform calls for the creation of an RSFSR radio and television agency. Since they propagate values of "immorality and individualism, pornography and violence," the All-Union radio and television would stop broadcasting all but the news in the Russian republic. RSFSR radio and television would operate in accordance with a new RSFSR "law on morality" which would protect Russians from propagation of immorality.

In the realm of inter republican relations, the platform concedes for the first time the possibiliy of secession of republics from the Union, but calls for reconsideration of the republics' borders since they were arbitrarily established in the 1920s and later. The program reiterates the Tyumen' declaration demand to halt the subsidization of republican economies and the standard of living of citizens of other republics beginning in 1991, and adds to this a call for all All-Union organizations, ministries, and legislative organs located in the RSFSR to pay rent for their facilities. Finally, the platform proposes designating Moscow as the sole capital of the RSFSR and moving the All-Union capital elsewhere ("Za politiky narodnogo soglasiya i rossiyskogo vozrozhdeniya," *Literaturnaya Rossiya*, December 29, 1989; for further analysis of this document and some of its implications, see Paul Goble, "A Program for Russia: The Appeal of the Bloc of Russia's Social-Political Groups," *Radio Liberty Report*, January 3, 1990).

The impact of these developments on the pace of the economic reforms is hard to judge at this point. However, it does not appear out of line to argue that this emerging conservative alliance does present a very serious challenge to the successful execution of radical economic reform. The author takes this opportunity to address himself to those fellow Sovietologists who tend to minimize the significance of Russian nationalist journals and their contributors. The author believes that the ability of the two "heralds of opposition" to shape public opinion and promote successful political alliances which could affect the nature of *perestroyka* should not be underestimated.

REFERENCES

Abramov, Fyodor, "Pelageya (Pelageya)," *Novyy mir*, 6:31-70, 1969.

Abramov, Fyodor, "Al'ka (Al'ka)," *Nash sovremennik*, 1:2-36, 1972.

Andreyev, Aleksey, "Vospitaniye krasotoy i agressivnost' bezobraznogo (Education by Beauty and Aggressiveness of the Ugly)," *Molodaya gvardiya*, 7:264-271, 1987.

Andreyev-Rayevskiy, Aleksey, "S kogo zhe delat' zhizn'? (On Whom to Model Life?)," *Molodaya gvardiya*, 11:247-257, 1988.

Antonov, Mikhail, "Tak chto zhe s nami proiskhodit? (So What Happens to Us?)," *Oktyabr'*, 8:3-66, 1987.

Antonov, Mikhail, "Idti svoim putyom (To Follow One's Own Path)," *Molodaya gvardiya*, 1:195-200, 1988.

Antonov, Mikhail, "Nesushchestvuyushchiye lyudi (Nonexistent People)," *Nash sovremennik*, 2:125-150, 1989a.

Antonov, Mikhail, "Speshim—kuda i zachem? ([We] Are Rushing—Where and Why?)," *Literaturnaya Rossiya*, March 31, 1989b.

Antonov, Mikhail, "Vykhod yest'! (There Is a Solution!)," *Nash sovremennik*, 8:71-110, 9:138-158, 1989c.

Astaf'yev, Viktor, "Mesto deystviya (The Place of Action)," *Nash sovremennik*, 5:100-140, 1986.

Astrakhantsev, Aleksandr, "Razvilka (A Parting of the Ways)," *Nash sovremennik*, 12:53-82, 1986.

Baigushev, Aleksandr, "Preodoleniye (Overcoming)," *Molodaya gvardiya*, 4:227-253, 6:232-254, 1987a; 12:229-251, 1987b.

Baigushev, Aleksandr, "Letopis' pokoleniya (The Chronicle of a Generation)," *Nash sovremennik*, 1:185-191, 1988.

Belov, Vasiliy, "Plotnitskiye rasskazy (A Carpenter's Stories)," *Novyy mir*, 7:7-56, 1968.

Belov, Vasiliy, "Vse vperedi (Everything Lies Ahead)," *Nash sovremennik*, 7:29-106, 8:59-110, 1986.

Benediktov, Ivan, "O Staline i Khrushcheve (On Stalin and Khrushchev)," *Molodaya gvardiya*, 4:12-67, 1989.

Bocharov, A., "Zhurnaly v fokuse mneniy (Journals in the Focus of Opinions)," *Literaturnoye obozreniye*, 1:98-100, 1988.

Brown, Deming, *Soviet Literature Since Stalin*. Cambridge: Cambridge University Press, 1978.

Brudny, Yitzhak M., "Between Liberalism and Nationalism: The Case of Sergei Zalygin," *Studies in Comparative Communism*, **21**, 3/4:331–340, 1988.

Bulin, Yevgeniy, "Otkroyte knigi molodykh! (Open the Books of the Young!)," *Molodaya gvardiya*, 3:237–248, 1989.

Bushin, Vladimir, "S vysoty svoyego kurgana (From the Heights of One's Hill)," *Nash sovremennik*, 8:182–185, 1987.

Bushin, Vladimir, "Yesli znat' i pomnit' (If One Knows and Remembers)," *Molodaya gvardiya*, 2:269–279, 1988a.

Bushin, Vladimir, "S vysoty nasypnogo Olimpa (From the Heights of an Artificial Olympus)," *Molodaya gvardiya*, 10:262–280, 1988b.

Bushin, Vladimir, "Kak Arkadi Mikhailovich uzh bol'no shibko Grigoriya Yakovlevicha nastroshchal, a tot yego za eto na poltora goda upek (How Arkadi Mikhailovich Scared Grigoriy Yakovlevich to Death and the Latter Sent Him off for Year and a Half in Jail for This)," *Nash sovremennik*, 1:190–191, 1989a.

Bushin, Vladimir, "Deyaniya svyatogo otkazchika (Acts of a Holy Renouncer)," *Molodaya gvardiya*, 2:254–262, 1989b.

Chalmayev, Viktor, "Neizbezhnost' (Inevitability)," *Molodaya gvardiya*, 9:259–289, 1968.

Chernykh, Yevgeniy, "Nastupleniye prodolzhayetsya (The Offensive Continues)," *Nash sovremennik*, 5:150–160, 1988.

Chirkin, Albert, "Podrostok, semiya i rok-muzika (The Adolescent, Family, and Rock Music)," *Nash sovremennik*, 10:141–149, 1988.

Chistyakov, V. and I. Sanachev, "Troyanskiy kon' (The Trojan Horse)," *Nash sovremennik*, 10:126–141, 1988.

Chivilikhin, Vladimir, "Pamyat' (Memory)," *Nash sovremennik*, 1, 1978; 8–12, 1980; 5–6, 10–11, 1983; 3–4, 1984.

Cohen, Stephen F., *Rethinking the Soviet Experience*. New York: Oxford University Press, 1985.

Darst, Robert G., Jr., "Environmentalism in the USSR: The Opposition to the River Diversion Projects," *Soviet Economy*, **4**, 3:223–252, July–September 1988.

Doronin, Anatoliy, "O roke—bez prikras (On Rock Music Without Embellishment)," *Molodaya gvardiya*, 12:213–228, 1987.

Dorosh, Yefim, "Derevenskiy dnevnik (A Village Diary)," *Novyy mir*, 7, 1958; 7, 1961; 10, 1962; 6, 1964; 1, 1965; 1, 1969; 9, 1970.

Dubrovina, Elida, "Ne otgoryat ryabinovyye kisti (The Ashberry Bunches Shall Not Burn)," *Nash sovremennik*, 9:180–187, 1987.

Dulayev, Mikhail, "Rokovaya muzyka (Fatal Music)," *Nash sovremennik*, 1:157–168, 2:163–172, 1988.

Dunlop, John B., *The New Russian Nationalism*. New York: Praeger, 1985.

"Ekologiya pravdy (The Ecology of Truth)," *Molodaya gvardiya*, 12:238–257.

"Dusha dorozhe kovsha (The Soul Is more Valuable than the Ladle)," *Nash sovremennik*, 9:142–172, 1988.

Fed, Nikolay, "Poslaniye drugu, ili pis'ma o literature (Message to a Friend, or Letters about Literature)," *Nash sovremennik*, 4:3–20, 1989a; 5:169–185, 1989b.

Fomenko, Aleksandr, "O samom glavnom (Of the Greatest Importance)," *Molodaya gvardiya*, 9:278–281, 1987.

Garden, Patricia, "Reassessing Ovechkin," in Richard Feeborn, R. R. Millner-Gulland, and Charles A. Ward, eds., *Russian and Slavic Literature*. Columbus: Slavica, 1976, 405–424.

Glinkin, Pavel, "Zemlya i asfal't (Earth and Asphalt)," *Molodaya gvardiya*, 9:240–255, 1967.

Gorbachev, Vyacheslav, "Chto vperedi? (What's Ahead?)," *Molodaya gvardiya*, 3:250–277, 1987a.

Gorbachev, Vyacheslav, "Perestroyka i nadstroyka (Restructuring and Superstructure)," *Molodaya gvardiya*, 7:220–247, 1987b.

Gorbachev, Vyacheslav, "Prinyat' k deystviyu (To Take Action)," *Molodaya gvardiya*, 8:228–245, 1987c.

Gorbachev, Vyacheslav, "Arendatory glasnosti? (The Renters of Glasnost'?)," *Molodaya gvardiya*, 1:229–267, 1989.

"Granitsy prilichiya (Limits of Decency)," *Molodaya gvardiya*, 4:260–288, 1989.

Gudkov, Lev and Boris Dubin, "Chto my chitayem? (What Are We Reading?)," *Literaturnoye obozreniye*, 1:93–97, 1988.

Gudkov, Lev, "O chem skazali tirazhi (What Circulations Said)," *Sovetskaya kul'tura*, September 22, 1988.

Gunko, Boris, "Dve estetiki (Two Aesthetics)," *Nash sovremennik*, 10:121–125, 1988.

Gustafson, Thane, *Reform in Soviet Politics*. New York: Cambridge University Press, 1981.

Hauslohner, Peter, "Gorbachev's Social Contract," *Soviet Economy, 3,* 1:54–89, January–March 1987.

Hosking, Geoffrey, *Beyond Socialist Realism*. New York: Holmes & Meier, 1980.

Ivanov, Anatoliy, "Cherny khleb isskustva (The Black Bread of Art)," *Nash sovremennik*, 5:171–179, 1988.

Ivanov, Viktor, "Sudnyy den'" (Day of Judgment), *Nash sovremennik*, 4–6, 1988.

"Iz nashey pochte (From Our Mailbox)," *Nash sovremennik*, 9:180–192.

Jowitt, Kenneth, "Inclusion and Mobilization in European Leninist Regimes," *World Politics*, 28, 1:69–96, 1975.

Karpets, Vladimir, "Povorot k nravstvennosti (A Turn to Morality)," *Molodaya gvardiya*, 9:241–245, 1987.

Kazintsev, Aleksandr, "Litsom k istorii: Prodolzhateli ili potrebiteli (With the Face to History: Continuers or Consumers)," *Nash sovremennik*, 11:166–175, 1986.

Kazintsev, Aleksandr, "Ochishcheniye ili zlosloviye? (Purification or Vilification?)," *Nash sovremennik*, 2:186–189, 1988a.

Kazintsev, Aleksandr, "Istoriya—ob"yedinyayushchaya ili razobshchayushchaya (History—Unifying or Setting Apart)," *Nash sovremennik*, 11:163–184, 1988b.

Kazintsev, Aleksandr, "Novaya mifologiya (The New Mythology)," *Nash sovremennik*, 5:144–168, 1989.

"Kak nashe slovo otzovetsya (How Our Word Will Be Received)," *Molodaya gvardiya*, 6:265–278, 1988.

Kaziyev, Bagautdin, "Tolcheya na puti k pravde (A Crowd on the Way to the Truth)," *Molodaya gvardiya*, 4:235–250, 1989.

Khatyushin, Valeriy, "O novykh veyaniyakh v kritike (On the New Trends in Criticism)," *Molodaya gvardiya*, 10:243–255, 1987.

Khatyushin, Valeriy, "O mnimom i podlinom v poyezii (On the Imaginary and the Real in Poetry)," *Molodaya gvardiya*, 9:260–275, 1988.

"Khochu vyskazat' svoye mneniye (I Want to Express My Own Opinion)," *Molodaya gvardiya*, 4:276–278, 1988.

Khukhry, A., A. Tarakanov, and I. Ivanov, "Tuman nad alkogolnoy propost'yu (Fog over the Alcoholic Abyss)," *Nash sovremennik*, 8:92–97, 1988.

Konotop, Vasiliy, "V chiikh interesakh traktuyutsya nashi idealy i interesy? (In Whose Interests Are Our Ideals and Interests Interpreted?)," *Molodaya gvardiya*, 10:230–244, 1988.

Kovalenin, A. V., "Trezvost'—oruzhiye perestroyki" (Sobriety—the Weapon of *Perestroyka*)," *Nash sovremennik*, 3:143–145, 1988.

Kozhinov, Vadim, "I nazovet menya vsyak sushchii v ney yazyk . . . (And Each of Its People Shall Speak My Name . . .)," *Nash sovremennik*, 11:153–176, 1981.

Kozhinov, Vadim, "My menyayemsya? (Are We Changing?)," *Nash sovremennik*, 10:160–174, 1987.

Kozhinov, Vadim, "Pravda i istina (Truth and Rightness)," *Nash sovremennik*, 4:160–175, 1988.

Kozhinov, Vadim, "Samaya bolshaya opasnost' . . . (The Greatest Danger . . .)," *Nash sovremennik*, 1:141–175, 1989.

Kuleshov, V., "Tochnost' kriteriyev (Accuracy of Criteria)," *Pravda*, February 1, 1982.

Kunyayev, Stanislav, "Razmyshleniya na Starom Arbate (Reflections on the Old Arbat)," *Nash sovremennik*, 7:26–27, 1988a.

Kunyayev, Stanislav, "Vse nachinalos' s yarlykov (It All Started with Labels)," *Nash sovremennik*, 9:180–189, 1988b.

Kuzmin, Apollon, "V prodolzheniye vazhnogo razgovora (The Continuation of an Important Conversation)," *Nash sovremennik*, 3:182–190, 1985.

Kuzmin, Apollon, "Otvety, porozhdayushchiye voprosy (Answers Which Beg Questions)," *Nash sovremennik*, 5:189–190, 1986.

Kuzmin, Apollon, "Meli v eksterritorial'nom potoke (Shoals in the Exterritorial Torrent)," *Nash sovremennik*, 9:173–179, 1987.

Kuzmin, Apollon, "K kakomy khramy ishchem my dorogy? (To Which Temple Are We Searching a Path?)," *Nash sovremennik*, 3:154–164, 1988.

Kuzmin, Apollon, "Kto vinovat i komy eto nuzhno? (Who Is Guilty and for Whom Is It Necessary?)," *Nash sovremennik*, 1:191–192, 1989.

Lanshchikov, Anatoliy, "My vse glyadim v Napoleony . . . (We Are All Looking to Become Napoleons . . .)," *Nash sovremennik*, 7:106–142, 1988.

Lapchenko, Boris, "Ne oboronyat'sya—nastupat'! (Not to Be on the Defensive—to Advance!)," *Nash sovremennik*, 3:130–143, 1988.

Lapin, V., "Pust' ne drognet pistolet progressa (The Pistol of Progress Should Not Shake)," *Molodaya gvardiya*, 3:268–270, 1989.

Laqueur, Walter, *The Road to Freedom. Russia and Glasnost.* New York: Scribners, 1989.

Lewis, Philippa, "Peasant Nostalgia in Contemporary Soviet Literature," *Soviet Studies*, 28, 4:548–569, 1976.

Likhonosov, Viktor, "Bryushkiin (Reyki nzh. I olk)," *Novyy mir*, 11:142–145, 1963.

Likhonosov, Viktor, "Rodnyye (Relatives)," *Novyy mir*, 2:145–159, 1967.

Lisenkov, Anatoliy and Yuriy Sergeyev, "Kolovert bespamyatsva (The Whirling [Forces of] Delirium)," *Molodaya gvardiya*, 10:256–270, 1987.

"Litsom k pravde (With a Face Turned to the Truth)," *Molodaya gvardiya*, 3:212–236, 1989.

Lobanov, Mikhail, "Prosveshchennoye meshchanstvo (Educated Philistines)," *Molodaya gvardiya*, 4: 294–306, 1968.

Lowe, David, *Russian Writing Since 1953*. New York: Ungar, 1987.

Lugovoy, E., "Bilet na poshost' (The Ticket to Vulgarity)," *Molodaya gvardiya*, 4:287–288, 1989.

Lyubomudrov, Mark, "Teatr nachinayetsya s Rodiny (Theater Starts with the Motherland)," *Nash sovremennik*, 6:163–178, 1985.

Lyubomudrov, Mark, "Kak nashe slovo otzovetsya (How Our Word Will Resound)," *Nash sovremennik*, 7:167–175, 1987.

Lyubomudrov, Mark, "Izvlechem li uroki? (Will We Learn the Lessons?)," *Nash sovremennik*, 2:170–183, 1989.

Maguire, Robert A., *Red Virgin Soil: Soviet Literature in the 1920s.* Princeton: Princeton University Press, 1968.

Malakhov, Mikhail, "Smysl nashey zhizni (The Meaning of Our Life)," *Molodaya gvardiya,* 4:257–275, 1988.

Markova, Yekaterina, "Otbleski golubogo ekrana (Reflections of the Blue Screen)," *Molodaya gvardiya,* 10:228–242, 1987.

Matveyets, G., "Ne v nem odnom delo (He Was Not the Only One),"*Molodaya gvardiya,* 12:240–244, 1988.

Matveyets, G., "Dorogoye udovol'stviye za 30 kopeyek (A Costly Pleasure for 30 Kopecks)," *Nash sovremennik,* 4:192, 1989.

Mehnert, Klaus, *The Russians and Their Favorite Books.* Stanford: Hoover Institution Press, 1983.

Mikhailov, Oleg, "V chas muzhestva (In the Hour of Courage)," *Nash sovremennik,* 4:106–114, 1969.

Micklin, Philip P. and Andrew R. Bond, "Reflections on Environmentalism and the River Diversion Projects," *Soviet Economy,* **4**, 3:253–274, July–September 1988.

Mozhayev, Boris, "Iz zhizni Ivana Kuzkina (From the Life of Ivan Kuzkin),"*Novyy mir,* 7:42–118, 1966.

Mustafin, Dmitriy, "Narod pomnit vse (People Remember Everything)," *Molodaya gvardiya,* 3:234–236, 1989.

"Nesti lyudyam slovo dobroye, svetloye (To Bring People the Good and Bright Word)," *Molodaya gvardiya,* 5:265–279, 1988.

Paliyevskiy, Pyotr, "Mirovoye znacheniye M. Sholokhova (The World Significance of M. Sholokhov)," *Nash sovremennik,* 12:167–173, 1973.

Petro, Nikolai N., "The Project of the Century: A Case Study of Russian Nationalist Dissent," *Studies in Comparative Communism,* **20**, 3/4:235–252, 1987.

Pigalev, Vadim, "Chto oni ishchut u slavyanofilov? (What Are They Looking for in the Slavophiles?)," *Nash sovremennik,* 10:156–162, 1986.

Pisarev, Yuriy, "Nuzhna li nam rokovaya muzika? (Do We Need Rock Music?)," *Molodaya gvardiya,* 7:273–278, 1987.

"Podmena (Substitution)," *Molodaya gvardiya,* 6:250–264, 1988.

"Povyshat' sozidatel'nuyu rol' pressy (Promoting a Constructive Role for the Press)," *Zhurnalist,* 9:1–9, 1988.

"Protiv podmen (Against Substitutions)," *Nash sovremennik,* 5:189–190, 1988.

Rasputin, Valentin, "Proschaniye s Matyoroy (Farewell to Matyora)," *Nash sovremennik,* 10:3–71, 11:17–64, 1976.

Rasputin, Valentin, "Pozhar (Fire)," *Nash sovremennik,* 7:3–38, 1985.

Rasputin, Valentin, "Zhertvovat' soboyu dlya pravdy (To Sacrifice Oneself for the Sake of Truth)," *Nash sovremennik,* 1:169–176, 1988.

Sakharov, A. N., "Istoriya istinnaya i mnimaya (True and Imaginary History),"*Molodaya gvardiya,* 3:297–320, 1970.

Salutskiy, Anatoliy, "Poiski istiny i 'pop-nauka' (Searches of Truth and "Pop-Science"), *Ekonomicheskiye nauki,* 10:78–85, 1989.

Semanov, Sergey, "O tsennostyakh otnositel'nykh i vechnykh (On Relative and Eternal Values)," *Molodaya gvardiya,* 8:308–320, 1970.

Sergeyev, Aleksey, "Iz segodnya v zavtra ili pozavchera? (From Today into Tomorrow or into Yesterday?)," *Ekonomicheskiye nauki,* 9:121–131, 1989.

Shevtsov, Ivan, "Spolokhi (Lightening)," *Nash sovremennik,* 12:174–187, 1986.

Shevtsov, Ivan and Ivan Pstygo, "Vospitat' patriota (To Educate a Patriot),"*Molodaya gvardiya,* 7:221–230, 1988.

Shiropayev, Aleksey, "Kozlinnyy dukh, ili na dvore 'dvadtsatyye gody'? (The Goat Spirit, or Are the 'Twenties' Back?)," *Nash sovremennik*, 1:180-185, 1989.

Slavetskiy, Vladimir, "Ishchu stikhi! (Searching for Poems!)," *Molodaya gvardiya*, 1:279-282, 1989.

Soloukhin, Vladimir, "Pochemy ya ne podpisalsya pod tem pismom (Why I Did Not Sign That Letter)," *Nash sovremennik*, 12:186-189, 1988.

Solzhenitsyn, Aleksandr, "Matryonin dvor (Matryona's Home)," *Novyy mir*, 1:42-63, 1963.

Solzhenitsyn, Aleksandr, "Pomenal'noye slovo o tvardovskom (Eulogy for Tvardovskiy)" and "Zhit' ne po lzhi (Live Not on a Lie)," *Nash sovremennik*, 9:159-162, 1989.

Spechler, Dina R., *Permitted Dissent in the USSR*. New York: Praeger, 1982.

Surovtsev, Yuriy, "V stile ekstaza (In the Style of Ecstasy)," *Znamya*, 3:202-224, 1982.

Swayze, Harold, *Political Control of Literature in USSR, 1946-1959*. Cambridge, MA: Harvard University Press, 1959.

Teterin, Igor, "Realisty protiv ekstremistov (The Realists Against the Extremists)," *Molodaya gvardiya*, 11:196-209, 1988a; 12:218-237, 1988b.

Troitskiy, E., "Russkaya sotsialisticheskaya natsiya segodnya (Russian Socialist Nation Today)," *Molodaya gvardiya*, 1:277-287, 1988.

Trukhin, Aleksandr, "Sem' raz otmer (Measure Seven Times)," *Molodaya gvardiya*, 1:217-225, 1988.

Uglov, Fyodor, "Glyadya pravde v glaza (Staring Truth in the Eye)," *Nash sovremennik*, 7:150-157, 1987.

Uglov, Fyodor, *Iz plena illyuzii (From the Captivity of Illusions)*. Leningrad: Lenizdat, 1986.

Vilchek, L. Sh., *Peyzazh posle zhatvy (The Landscape After the Harvest)*. Moscow: Sovetskiy pisatel', 1988.

Voznesensky, Andrei, "A Poet's View of Glasnost'," *Nation*, June 13, 1987.

"V otvete za vremya (Responsibility for the Times)," *Molodaya gvardiya*, 9:219-287, 1987.

Yanov, Alexander, *The Russian Challenge and the Year 2000*. Oxford: Blackwell, 1987.

Yashin, Aleksandr, "Volgodskaya svad'ba (The Vologda Wedding)," *Novyy mir*, 12:3-26, 1962.

Zalygin, Sergey, "Na Irtyshe (On the Irtysh)," *Novyy mir*, 2:3-80, 1964.

Zalygin, Sergey, "Komissiya (Commission)," *Nash sovremennik*, 9-11, 1975.

Žekulin, Gleb, "The Contemporary Countryside in Soviet Literature: A Search for New Values," in James R. Millar, ed., *The Soviet Rural Community*. Urbana, IL: University of Illinois Press, 1971, 376-404.

Zelenevskiy, V., "A vy izuchaite nas! . . . (Study Us! . . .)," *Molodaya gvardiya*, 12:273-287, 1988.

Zhitnukhin, Anatoliy, "Sokhranyaya preemstvennost' (Keeping the Continuity)," *Molodaya gvardiya*, 10:23-33, 1988.

Zhukov, Dmitriy, "Svyaz' vremen (The Link of Times)," *Molodaya gvardiya*, 6:300-304, 1969.

2

SOVIET HISTORY

Alexander Dallin

In the late spring of 1988, primary and secondary school students and teachers throughout the Soviet Union learned to their intense relief that examinations in Soviet history had been suspended. With the hemorrhaging of revelations about the Stalin era, the old textbooks turned out to be worse than useless. "Today [*Izvestiia* remarked] we are reaping the bitter fruit of our moral compromises and are paying for those things that we mutely accepted and supported and...for which we blush today and do not know how to explain to our children."[1] As the Gorbachev era unfolded, more and more subjects were opened up to public scrutiny, and Soviet history was by no means the least of these.

This, after all, was the Orwellian dimension. A people was coming face to face with its past, a past full of unpersons and unevents, along with myths and fictions that had oddly remained in limbo all these years. And the suspension of prior belief—of a single truth, previously unchallengeable and obligatory—was a good metaphor for the novel search for honesty about the past, the uncertainties and confusions that it engendered, and the unprecedented opportunities for revelations and public debate. For many in the Soviet Union, Stalin in particular was a quintessentially emotional subject that their sense of loyalty and legitimacy was closely bound up with, not a matter of remote, academic scholarship but something that had touched—nay, grabbed—their lives and those of their loved ones.

History had always been a subject of particular sensitivity for Soviet scholarship, education, and propaganda. This reflected the profound but unresolved tension between the professional historians' integrity—their characteristic search for sources, documents, and archives; their commitment to reconstruct the past as they see it—and the traditional Bolshevik view of history as a weapon—as part of the "superstructure," inevitably controlled by the ruling class, much as education, law, and art had been seen as instruments to be wielded by those in political charge.[2] Nowhere did scholarship and politics coexist more awkwardly and uncomfortably than in treating Soviet history since 1917.

On the other hand, under Gorbachev the seventy years of Soviet history were bound to become the battlefield among contending political factions and orientations: every group, every politician would hark back to the Lenin years in search of legitimation—and each would find a different "Lenin" to invoke and cite. And, as the debate over *perestroika* expanded in scope and publicity and as its participants tested the waters and gained civic courage, they would not only fill in some of the previously suppressed "blank pages" in Soviet history, but would argue over their meaning—the lessons of the New Economic Policy of the 1920s, the need for the forcible collectivization of agriculture, the scope and causes of the purges, Stalin's blunders before and during the Great Fatherland War, and much else—issues from which lessons could be drawn for what the country faced in the 80s and the years ahead.

Just as is in other issue areas and disciplines, the process has gone further than had ever been intended when the Gorbachev team took over in March-April 1985. Characteristically, it required a signal from the top of the political pyramid to unleash and legitimate the search for a truer past. Just as characteristically, there were those who tested and stretched the limits of the permissible in the highly new atmosphere of *glasnost'* and what more recently has been sanctioned as "socialist pluralism."

At first Mikhail Gorbachev had no time for those who pressed for historical revisionism; this would only "set people at each other's throats." Let bygones be bygones: why dig up the past (and make more enemies in the process)?[3] In fact, faithful to the semantic code dating back to the Khrushchev era, he denied that there was such a thing as "Stalinism": it was a notion invented by the enemies of communism, widely used to "blacken" the Soviet Union.[4]

Not only did Gorbachev not want to create more problems for himself by promoting historical revisionism (other than by designating the Brezhnev era as the years of stagnation), he apparently failed as yet to understand that (a) to win over the creative intelligentsia to his cause, some constraints on free speech had to be removed and the festering Stalin question had to be reopened, and (b) more specifically, Soviet history could be made into an ally of perestroika, showing the legitimacy of reform and the roots of what had gone wrong: it is not for nothing that NEP—the New Economic Policy of the 1920s—had for many years been the codeword for a new reform, hinting at a greater role for private initiative and individual rights.

By early 1987 Mikhail Sergeyevich had come around to argue that if previous Soviet leaders had made mistakes, this must be acknowledged: the past must be seen as it really was. The key figure here in persuading the boss (as in general in the intellectual opening up) was Aleksandr Yakovlev.[5] Soon legal and political rehabilitations began—posthumously—and were given due publicity. For instance, the charges against the prominent economists Chayanov and Kondratyev, and therewith the 'little' trials of the early '30s (against the so-called Toiling Peasant Party and the Industrial Party) were in effect declared to have been phony. That process of formally reversing the verdicts of the Stalinist purges has of course continued, notably with the rehabilitations of Bukharin, Rykov, and Rakovsky in February 1988.

Significantly, the sweeping reversals went beyond the circle of those Bolsheviks who, like Bukharin, could now be made positive heroes. If some rehabilitations were politically instrumental, others served more broadly to undo the earlier tragic miscarriages of justice. After the reaffirmation of the innocence of the military commanders— Tukhachevsky, Yakir, Gamarnik, and Kork were perhaps the best known—and of the victims of the "Leningrad affair" of 1950, the rehabilitations of Zinoviev, Kamenev, Radek and Piatakov, in June 1988, dramatized this shift in official Soviet history.

Thus Gorbachev came to espouse a more comprehensive view of the need for historical candor, just as he had adopted a more comprehensive view of what *perestroika* was to mean. He and his allies now explicitly demanded that the "blank pages" and the "forgotten names" of Soviet history be filled in. That was the signal that was needed, although careful observers soon detected that there was all manner of opposition to such an unraveling—opposition typically coming from those who feared that political and cultural liberalism and tolerance would mean a loss of control and the triumph of anarchy. These were views most clearly identified, at the apex of the Soviet *apparat,* with Politburo members Yegor Ligachev and Viktor Chebrikov, and were echoed by a number of political, artistic, and academic incumbents at lower levels. They have stressed the other side—the patriotic-pedagogical uses of the past: Soviet history was not a "chain of unrelieved mistakes." "There is not a single year [of the Soviet past] that we cannot be proud of." The conservative critics have charged that some of the reformist "nihilists" want to depict all of Soviet history as a failure and a mistake; that dilettantes have gotten into the history business to create false sensationalism; that revisionism in history has gone much too far. In fact Gorbachev's November 2, 1987 speech on the 70th anniversary of the Revolution (right after the ouster of Boris Yel'tsin) gave internal evidence of a forthright speech having been truncated and toned down by Politburo decision before being delivered. To a detached historian its treatment of a number of questions in Soviet history, such as collectivization, Trotsky, and a number of foreign policy issues, remained highly unsatisfactory.

Still, the general mood has been intoxicatingly permissive. In 1988 candor has grown even more; there hardly seemed any limits that writers or scholars needed to respect; and some writers were publishing obsessively (Mikhail Shatrov is a good example), as if revelations might soon go out of style. That of course is precisely what some citizens feared as the political struggle gained in fierceness in 1987-88. Yet the momentum of the new spirit, even if inhibited and constrained on several occasions, sufficed to carry the campaign to new heights.

In this climate the professional historians have flunked. As a group they failed to rush to the front ranks of the movement. If they welcomed the new opportunities, they were not seen to be using them. In fact, some of the leading historians were content to equivocate in terms which the impatient reformers perceived as evasive doubletalk. If the scholars agreed with the new line, their voices were at first surprisingly muted, divided, and unsure.

There are good and bad reasons for their attitude (and there are of course exceptions). As professionals historians are cautious by nature and habit, and, unlike some journalists, will typically not make assertions without being able to document them. They suffer from a lack of sources and from barred access to Soviet archives (as we do). Many of them have been burned in the past when it came to interpreting Soviet history. Many of the "liberals" among the historians, who had come out of the closet in the post-Stalin years, had been slapped down or silenced during the partial return to orthodoxy after Khrushchev's ouster. And for the others, the establishment historians who had earlier committed themselves to the official line in the Brezhnev years, to endorse the present revisionism would mean publicly to stand on their head.

As an organization the Soviet historical craft (unlike the writers or even more the cinematographers) has been establishment-oriented, averse to risk-taking, and rather bureaucratic. Nor has the study of recent Soviet history attracted the best and the brightest among younger Soviet historians, and one can hardly blame them for that choice.

The result is a situation where others in the Soviet intelligentsia see the historians as having abdicated. An editorial note in *New Times* introducing the translation of Mikhail Shatrov's sensational play, "Dal'she, dal'she, dal'she [Onward, onward, onward]," says: "Our readers evince great interest in 'blank spots' in history. It must be admitted, however, that our social sciences [and that includes history] lag behind this growing public interest. So more often than not Soviet historical fiction provides answers to such questions."[6] Even more bluntly, other Soviet publications declare that "Soviet historical science has found itself...on trial." Illustrative of letters to the editor concerning a round-table of historians defending themselves from attack (primarily by invoking their specialized professional skills) was one from two computer specialists: The "historians' contemptuous judgments of 'people who have no command of methodology and methods' suggest a caste-like, priestly arrogance...."[7] Thus it has remained for others to seize the opportunity—for publicists, novelists, memoirists, playwrights, film and television writers—to do what was to have been the historians' job.

Those who follow Soviet affairs are familiar with the publication of Anatoli Rybakov's *Deti Arbata [Children of the Arbat]*–a work written largely in the 1960s and only now allowed to be published; and with Tengiz Abuladze's film, "Pokayanie" ["Repentance"]: I mention these as examples of an increasingly numerous Soviet genre that clearly sheds light on history, but in one case chooses to be surrealist and symbolic and in the other produces a fictionalized version that is open to criticism from literal-minded historians trying to protect their turf from artistic intruders.

Though some of it has been mediocre, a good part of the recent work has been clever and imaginative.[8] Shatrov's play on the Treaty of Brest-Litovsk was the first to bring back to the stage Trotsky and Bukharin as dedicated comrades in situations where Lenin is not infallible and Stalin is trivial. His "Dal'she, dal'she" pushes further still (and in fact, it has so far not been performed in Moscow): its cast of characters includes Kerensky and Spiridonova, Plekhanov, Krupskaya, Denikin, Markov, Kornilov, Zinoviev, and Trotsky, in a very clever dialogue, assessing their successes and failures, both dedemonizing and deromanticizing the events of October and what came before and after. If nothing else, it stimulates thinking by the reader or theater-goer, and perhaps the most important achievement is the emergence of publicly-available, printed or performed versions of history that diverge from what used to be called the "general line" (as well as often rather outspoken criticism of these versions). The same is true of documentary films, such as "Protsess" [meaning both "The Process" and "The Trial"], a vivid indictment of Stalinism shown in Moscow in May 1988, apparently after encountering a good deal of resistance to its release.

Magazines and journals have been publishing documented stories, memoirs, and interviews. *Pravda* has had full-page articles, on Fridays, devoted to such topics as Lenin's (previously suppressed) political testament and to the Sixth Party Conference (Prague, 1912). Perhaps the most sensational in this series was an account of the Tukhachevsky purge in 1936, by the military procurator who reviewed the case in 1955, citing passages from interrogations of key figures, confirming the arbitrary, almost accidental nature of the process, and of course establishing the innocence of all the victims.[9] A revised, unexpurgated version of the memoirs of Anastas Mikoyan (edited by his son Sergo) includes fascinating revelations bearing on the Seventeenth Party Congress and the circumstances leading up to the Kirov murder. Hard as it is to believe it, they have begun to serialize translations of Stephen F. Cohen's *Bukharin*, George Orwell's *Animal Farm*, and Arthur Koestler's *Darkness at Noon*.

Some of the magazines have begun concentrating on the lesser characters, such as Piatnitsky, Kosarev, Osinsky, and Khodzhaev, often providing excerpts from their diaries or testimony by their children or other family members. *Moscow News* carried the story of five teen-age girls, daughters of victims of the purges such as Putna and Krestinsky, who were themselves picked up for counter-revolutionary activity—now in their 60s all reunited and retelling what they know or remember of the past. *Dialog* (the former *Bloknot agitatora*) had a couple of articles giving the fullest (to date) account of the "Leningrad affair."[10]   *Ogonyok* has published letters from Kapitsa to Stalin and Beria on Lev Landau, the prominent physicist arrested in the '30s; and articles on Vavilov and on Lysenko—incidentally, producing an interesting controversy in the letters to the editor, with Lysenko's son rallying in defense of his father and a number of people from all over the country denouncing him rather colorfully. Similarly, Dudintsev's play, "Robed in White," provides another revelation of Lysenkoism.

Little by little, revisionism has invaded the history of Soviet foreign policy, too, though still more cautiously than domestic affairs.[11]   The war years—previously, the prime exhibit for Stalin's greatness—are now open to criticism. Scholars and journalists have finally challenged the authorities to produce the documents (read: the secret protocol) relating to the Nazi-Soviet Pact of 1939.[12] Aleksandr Samsonov and others have blamed Stalin for the purge of the Red Army command which was responsible for the heavy devastation and defeats of the first months of the war—precisely the sort of charge for which Aleksandr Nekrich was pilloried in 1965.[13] The famous Order #227 ("Ni shagu nazad!"), threatening Soviet troops who retreated at the height of the crisis before Stalingrad—of course known to millions and later published abroad but never printed in the Soviet Union—can now be discussed in print. The number of prisoners of war is still not available, perhaps not known, but it is discussed. The same is true of the number of people who have gone through the GULag: different approximations, perhaps guesses. Similarly, on the 1937 census, at least a few details have appeared on what had been expected and what was found in the figures that were never released. Thanks to the efforts of a Polish-Soviet commission of historians, a number of sensitive issues are being raised, and even responsibility for the Katyn massacre (traditionally attributed to the Nazis) has emerged as a question that requires a new, honest look.[14]

And at last there is a soul-searching discussion of the causes of Stalinism. What was it—in Bolshevism, in Russia's political culture or in its underdevelopment, in the unique historical setting, in Stalin himself—that had caused what is now acknowledged as a tragedy? Had it all been necessary, even inevitable, or avoidable? If there are no good, no simple, no official answers, perhaps that is healthy too.[15]

Nor have the revelations been limited to the Stalin years. Fyodor Burlatsky gives a revealing portrait of Khrushchev in a full-page article in *Literaturnaya gazeta,* based no doubt on his own experience, but perhaps also on the still unpublished Khrushchev memoirs.[16] Survivors tell of Beria's career—and of his arrest.[17] Others deal with corruption and indolence in the Brezhnev years.[18] All along Lenin had been the unquestioned icon, but now the first hints have appeared about his responsibility (though not in the mass media). At least a few essays and articles cautiously but seriously weigh the effects of coercion and overcentralization under Lenin as trends that perhaps paved the way for Stalinism.[19]

The professional historians could scarcely expect to have been given a dispensation of immunity *sine die*. Early on there were some efforts among them to climb aboard the bandwagon or at least to stagger behind it. There were also a few attempts to discuss what was wrong with Soviet historiography. It is instructive to observe to what extent an awareness of scholarship abroad—including Western writings on Soviet history—has provided a standard and a challenge to the more open-minded, self-conscious among Soviet scholars.[20] Most interesting has been the use of Western works by Danilov to familiarize Soviet readers with data not otherwise available to them.[21]

None has been more courageous than the historian Yuri Afanasyev, the rector of the State Historical-Archival Institute who has become known for his frank pronouncements on behalf of intellectual *perestroika*. In 1987 the journal *Istoriia SSSR* held a high-powered conference and in 1988 published a thirty-page summary of the remarks made there on "Contemporary Non-Marxist Historiography and Soviet Historical Science"—in itself something of an event, and especially so because it lacked the combative tone assailing non-Soviet writings that had been mandatory for many years. While opinions among the participants varied, there was recognition that much of what were revelations to Soviet society had been well known abroad. Indeed, now it had to be acknowledged that for many years Soviet historiography had isolated itself from the mainstream of world scholarship, which had in the meanwhile forged ahead on many fronts. Afanasyev went a step further in opposing the traditional division into "us and them": because of the ideological biases prevalent since the early 1930s, he said,

> the third generation of Soviet historians is entering into [professional] life essentially ignorant of trends in humanitarian and social thought abroad. We have lived without Durkheim, Mosca, Weber, Toynbee, Freud, Croce, Spengler, Braudel, Sorokin, Marcuse, without Collingwood, Jaspers, Althusser, Jacobson,

Gourvitch, Carr, Saussure, Trubetskoy, Boas—I could prolong this list....

Most Soviet historians have been passed by...by the most important developments in historical science, entire directions such as, for instance, structural linguistics, ethnology, psychoanalysis, historical demography, historical anthropology, contemporary theories of evolution, the history of mentalités, historical geography, and along with these, entire worlds that had been unknown to 19th century man [i.e., to Marx]: the biological and subconscious in man and society, mythological reasoning, and so on.[22]

Other participants at the conference enumerated American scholars working on the Soviet Union who, in the new era, should be invited to contribute to Soviet journals and scholarly enterprises. How soon all this can be remedied and whether anything comes of it all, remains to be seen, but clearly—despite resistance and uneasiness on the part of some Soviet academics and academic bureaucrats—it is the most promising and ambitious effort to remove the dead hand of the past half century or more.

The listing of revisionist writings could readily be extended. It is encouraging and significant. It grows with every passing month. There is a commitment by some people to get the truth out. But there remains the tension between the search for truth and the political uses of history. There is also bitter resistance, footdragging and doubletalk.[23] There are revelations but as yet scarcely any monographs or any serious, detailed, documented studies.[24] Although new legislation concerning archives has been drafted, there is still no regular access to them. And there are the remaining "blank pages," now limited to a few particularly neuralgic points for the regime (such as alternatives to the October Revolution, anti-Jewish measures, Trotsky, and the Cold War).

All in all, in spite of all these problems, these are developments that most of us, here and there, would not have dared expect even a few years ago. The sad fact, of course, is that such attitudes and initiatives can thrive only so long as they are congruent with the official political course; they might still be terminated if the whole enterprise of *glasnost'* should be aborted from above. But we can hope that they have indeed learned from their own history.

COMMENT

Terence Emmons

Alexander Dallin describes very well current developments in the Soviet public's recently commenced, ongoing rediscovery of the recent past. I have no quarrel with his judgments about either the impetus or the impediments involved in this remarkable process; a few points of amplification do come to mind.

To appreciate the "Orwellian dimension" of Soviet history as it has been propagated officially until very recently, we may do well to recall that Soviet history has not merely been bent to the usual instrumentalist requirements of civics and ideology of an authoritarian regime, but was the instrument of a regime espousing an historicist philosophy; a regime which has defended its legitimacy in historical-law terms; a regime whose official historians have for decades ritualistically declared their task to be to demonstrate that the Bolshevik revolution (read: everything that has happened from 1917 to the present) was both "necessary and inevitable." Therefore, as Martin Malia strikingly put it in his remarks to this conference, the history of the Soviet Union from 1917 to the present has been, until a few short months ago, a "sacred history."

We need to bear all this in mind in order to appreciate the nature of the impediments to *perestroika* in Soviet historiography, to some extent as a whole, but especially that of the Soviet period. In order to go along with the "new revisionism," historians who have made careers out of writing on the Soviet period would have to repudiate not only the official line of the Brezhnev years, but the entire rationale and *modus operandi* of Soviet historiography since at least the time of the *Short Course*, that is, since the mid-1930s.

By the same token, introduction of new ways of thinking about the Soviet past is confronting not only the resistance of ingrained individual habits of mind and *amour propre*, but complex institutional impediments. Revisionist historians are, of course, perfectly aware of these impediments, and the first months of 1988 have witnessed the commencement of an effort to remove them, as signalled, for example, by the installation of a new editor-in-chief and editorial board of *Voprosy istorii* and penetrating published criticism of the editorial practices of that and other historical journals; by attacks on policies governing archival access (sometimes with reference to the U.S. Freedom of Information Act); and by some scathing criticism of the monopolies exercised in large areas of historical scholarship by academicians and their entourages.

It seems to me that one of the most encouraging signs of awareness of the task at hand is the widespread recognition in the Soviet press discussion of teaching Soviet history in the schools that the very notion of a *single* textbook on Party history or general history must be rejected.

With a "best scenario option," I would anticipate the appearance in the pages of the professional historical journals of some serious new monographic articles (as opposed to "out of the drawer" items or programmatic discussions) on the Soviet period by late 1988. Allowing lead time for research and production, revisionist book-length studies are not likely to be rolling off the presses for another two or three years at best, allowances made for a few command performances.

In the meantime, as Professor Dallin writes, the task of re-examining recent history is being shouldered by writers and critics in the pages of mass-circulation papers, magazines, and the "fat journals" such as *Znamya, Druzhba narodov*, and, of course, *Novyi mir.* By mid-1988 the boldness and even sensationalism of this enterprise has reached heights that were surely unimaginable to serious students of Soviet affairs as recently as a year ago. *Neva,* we read in the newspaper, is serializing Koestler's *Darkness at Noon.* In discussions of the history of Soviet foreign policy of the 1930s and 1940s, not only do we have a revival of Aleksandr Nekrich's 1965 charges against Stalin for the devastations of the first months of the war, but arguments that Stalin was in fact responsible for the war—by having paved the way for Hitler's rise to power with his policies on "social-fascism" in the early 1930s, and then at the end of the decade by being responsible for the miserable performance of the Soviet army in the "winter war" against Finland, thereby encouraging Hitler to think he could win a war on two fronts. And so on. This is truly the slaughtering of the sacred cow of Soviet history.

For those of us fortunate enough to live in a society that has been unmarked by wrenching political-institutional discontinuities in recent times but is nevertheless changing rapidly, dicta about the "lessons of history" and the need to understand the past in order to confront the future may seem little more than pious conventions. Observance of the ongoing confrontation with the uses and abuses of history in the Soviet Union should stimulate reflection on their profound meaning.

Nicholas V. Riasanovsky

My first observation, in reacting to such works as Shatrov's "Dalshe, dal'she, dal'she," is that these basic views on how the Revolution went—whether its costs can be justified, whether they were inevitable, what mistakes were made—are so strikingly (and somewhat crudely) presented. Of course all this has been discussed outside the Soviet borders for all these decades. For instance, much of it reads like Menshevik literature. Pavel Miliukov is mentioned by name, and even if few of them contributed as much, I think a few Western specialists belong in this discussion.

What that implies, of course, is that we might be headed towards a single universe of discussion—not Soviet historiography separately, not non-Soviet historiography separately. And perhaps the biggest single issue for historians—and by now we know that what historians say and do is of some importance to others—is whether we shall indeed attain this one world of historiographic knowledge and research. As of now, I would have to say, there are still very great limitations to it.

I do not know how to predict, and I do not know which way it will turn out, As has been indicated here, there is now observed there is much more variety, freedom, truth in the Soviet treatment of important matters. It is also evident that this is even more the case *informally*. This has always been the case, but apparently it has escalated so that in conversations with Soviet historians you can now discuss topics such as the purges and much else. And yet these are still different worlds—theirs and ours—and I am looking earnestly for signs of changes along certain lines. Let me indicate two.

I am still looking for a real criticism of Lenin, beyond what we find today, which is something like Lenin saying in a play, 'I haven't done enough about Stalin because of this accursed illness of mine.' Of course, he could not control his illness. Not too long ago I read an interesting interview of Soviet historians with foreign correspondents.

Question (approximately): "Haven't you been too dogmatic and narrow in treating Lenin?" Answer (approximately): "Oh, yes, we have, and that is why we have failed to present the manysidedness of his genius."

Another example. I am curious whether in any important sense the Soviet Union is willing to criticize its own foreign policy—again, not in the sense of, let us say, the need to strive even harder for peace, but substantively—the sort of thing that is very common in the West. I am waiting for them to say, "That's where we made a mistake, that's why we were aggressive."

These are only two of the items that separate our two worlds, and I am sure many people can think of others. Let me repeat that the central question is to what extent the separation between these worlds has diminished and will diminish.

I can only add that it is nice to have more personal contact with Soviet colleagues, but that too is not especially new, and that too has its ups and downs. In the last years of Stalin, when I wrote an article on the *Petrashevtsy*, I was referred to as "*izvestnyi belogvardeets* [the famous White-Guardist] Nikolai Riasanovsky." I wanted to send a letter to the editor saying that unfortunately I was born much after the Civil War and thus could not be a "White Guardist." The last time I was in the Soviet Union, I gave a talk at an institute of the Academy of Sciences and was introduced (in Russian) as "an outstanding bourgeois historian who has learned our language very well." From what we have heard today I have concluded that I may next be promoted from "bourgeois" to "non-Marxist" historian. Let us welcome that and wait to see what follows.

Martin Malia

Let me begin with a couple of quotations. First of all, the title of this conference—Knowledge, Power and Truth—echoes Sir Francis Bacon, who spelled out long ago that knowledge is power and so is truth. Then, to quote George Orwell, who is still much cited in Eastern Europe—indeed in some of the items mentioned in Robert Davies's article referred to by Professor Dallin—"He who controls the past controls the present." In other words, when we are talking about history in the Soviet Union today, we are talking about much more than an academic subject, or scholarship and the humanities. We are talking about politics and power, something the Soviets themselves are quite aware of: as Pokrovsky once put it, "History is present politics projected into the past." And Terence Emmons just informed me that Karelin already had said the same thing in the 19th century, while Trevelyan in England came close with his dictum: "History is past politics." Thus some measure of this attitude is inevitable whenever we are writing about history; we are always also writing about the present, indeed about power relations in the present.

In the Soviet case, however, we have a much more extreme example of this phenomenon. Soviet history is not just the civil history of the Russian past, or of filling in "blank spots" or "white spots" (in Gorbachev's phrase) in the empirical record of that past. It is a question of the sacred history of "real" socialism. So when people start talking about what order Stalin issued to the troops in 1942, or whether Ordzhonikidze shot himself or (as is now maintained in the Soviet Union) he was shot by Stalin, or whether there were so many million victims of collectivization, they are raising a hand to the sacred history of socialism, that is, how the existing order was built, on what it rests, and what its legitimacy is.

The regime has always recognized this. The sacred history in question was codified for the first time in the famous *Short Course* of 1938. The Soviets revised this *Short Course* once under Khrushchev. They are in the process of revising it again. This new history of the Soviet Union has already been referred to by Yuri Afanasyev in one of his published declarations as simply a revised version of the old. The framework of historical writing in the Soviet Union is thus to this day still that of the *Short Course*. Certain empirical or civil details have been modified, but the basic structure of the sacred history has not changed.

The central dilemma of this sacred history is this: The Soviet Union has a criminal past extending from at least 1929 to 1953, and the people working on filling in the "blank spots" of this era want to fill in the civil details of this criminal past. However—and this brings us to what one speaker [actually Afanasyev] called the "on-the-one-hand, on-the-other-hand approach"—this criminal past is at the same time the centerpiece of Soviet history, its great period of achievement from 1929 to 1945. So if one fills in the "white spots" of this era and gives an honest empirical or civil account of those years, what does one do to the sacred history of the regime? And what does one do to the legitimacy of the Soviet system? This is what the recent struggle between Ligachev and Gorbachev over the Nina Andreyeva letter in *Sovetskaya Rossiia* in March-April was all about. For how far can one go in filling in the famous "blank spots," by rewriting the civil history of the Soviet Union, without undermining its indispensible sacred history?

To put it in a slightly different way, if you fill in all the "white spots," simply by translating not just Stephen Cohen (as is being done), but Merle Fainsod, Adam Ulam, Robert Conquest, and a few others— even Isaac Deutscher and E. H. Carr—you don't even have to go to the archives to fill in the main "blank spots." So a further question arises: Is the long period of the "blank spots," the scholarless period of 1929-1953, just the result of the "cult of personality" or is it the product of the system? Precisely this question is now being raised. Take for instance a review of Aleksandr Bek's novel, *Novoe naznachenie*, by the reform economist Gavriil Popov, who asks outright: Could the Stalinist period just be a product of Stalin the man? If it was, how can a Marxist understanding of the role of personality in history be reconciled with the extraordinary significance thereby attached to a specific person over so many years? Next, how should one interpret the hero of the novel, Anisimov—who is in fact modeled on Ordzhonikidze—who tries to reform things after Stalin's death, and comes to grief, but never understands why? The conclusion of the novel suggests to Popov that Anisimov's mistake was to identify what he calls the "administrative system"—in fact, the Soviet system *per se*— with one of its specific forms, that is, Stalin and Beria.

In a similar review of Abuladze's film "Repentance," the reviewer explicitly mentions that the state depicted in George Orwell's *1984* has a special department, the Ministry of Truth, concerned with the correction of the past. But, the author adds, a lie about the past is a lie about the present. But if one says that a lie about the past is a lie about the present, and if one starts rewriting Soviet history by going beyond the "white spots" of the period 1929 to 1953, one raises two vexing questions. One is the question of origins, which Professor Riasanovsky referred to. Where did the "administrative system" come from, and how was Stalin possible? This means raising the question of Lenin and the nature of Leninism, of the most basic structures of the regime. Next, by challenging both present and past lies, one gets into the mind-boggling issue of what to do now about setting all this aright. And the implications of correcting the lies are positively revolutionary, for they imply an upset to the whole system.

I would like to conclude by presenting something from *The New York Times* as a small example of the questions this could lead to if raised in the Soviet Union. The U.S. Senate has now voted money reparations to some 60,000 survivors out of 160,000 Japanese-Americans deported from California, unjustly and unconstitutionally, in World War II. Even if it was "only" 160,000 people, it should not have been done. If now someone were to start raising similar questions in the Soviet Union about the millions of victims of the past, where would things stop?

So this whole bundle of questions—knowledge, power, and truth; the "white spots"; Stalin vs. the system; the origins of the "administrative system" and Leninism—this is an absolutely explosive and revolutionary affair. Frankly, I don't see how the Soviets can get out of it without the regime's deliberately waiting so many generations that many of these issues become, if not totally moot, then so muted as to be harmless in the present. Thus I do not expect the "white spots" to be filled in in the near future outside the pages of the "thick reviews." I don't expect an attack upon those institutional and structural factors that produced the "black holes" of the regime's record in the first place.

NOTES

1.   *Izvestiia*, June 10, 1988.

2.   On problems of Soviet historiography in general, see Nancy W. Heer, *Politics and History in the Soviet Union* (MIT Press, 1971); John Barber, *Soviet Historians in Crisis, 1928-1932* (Macmillan, 1981); Samuel Baron et al., *Windows on the Russian Past: Essays on Soviet Historiography Since Stalin* (AAASS, 1977); Cyril E. Black, ed., *Rewriting Russian History* (2d ed., Vintage, 1962); John Keep et al., *Contemporary History in the Soviet Mirror* (Frederick A. Praeger, 1964); Hans Rogger, "Politics, Ideology and History in the USSR," *Soviet Studies*, January 1965; Konstantin Shteppa, *Russian Historians and the Soviet State* (Rutgers, 1962); Kurt Marko, *Sowjethistoriker zwischen Ideologie und Wissenschaft* (Wissenschaft und Politik, 1964); and Lowell Tillett, *The Great Friendship: Soviet Historians on the Non-Russian Nationalities* (University of North Carolina Press, 1969).

3.   Samizdat transcript of Gorbachev remarks, "Beseda chlenov SP SSSR s M.S. Gorbachevym," Moscow, June 19, 1986, *Arkhiv Samizdata*, no. 5785.

4.   Interview with *L'Humanité*, February 4, 1986, in M.S. Gorbachev, *Izbrannye rechi i stat'i*, III (Moscow, 1987), p. 162.

5.   On Yakovlev, see Timothy Colton, *The Dilemma of Reform in the Soviet Union* (rev. ed., Council on Foreign Relations, 1986); Seweryn Bialer et al., eds., *Gorbachev's Russia and American Foreign Policy* (Westview, 1988), *passim;* also Jerry Hough, *Russia and the West* (Simon and Schuster, 1988). On developments in historiography, see the thorough treatment in Robert W. Davies, "Soviet History in the Gorbachev Revolution: The First Phase" (University of Birmingham, Centre for Russian and East European Studies, October 1987); and Stephen Wheatcroft, "Unleashing the Energy of History, Mentioning the Unmentionable and Reconstructing Soviet Historical Awareness, Moscow [January-June] 1987," *Australian Slavonic and East European Studies*, vol. I, no. 1 (1987), pp. 85-132; and "Steadying the Energy of History and Probing the Limits of Glasnost': Moscow July to December 1987," *ibid.*, vol. I, no. 2 (1987), pp. 57-114. See also Vera Tolz, "'Blank Spots' in Soviet History," Radio Liberty Research (Munich), RL 119/88 (March 21, 1988).

6.   *New Times*, 1988, no. 1, p. 26.

7.   "Soviet Historical Science on Trial," *Moscow News*, 1968, no. 15, p. 2. The original round-table appeared under the title, "Stopping History or Marching On?" *Moscow News*, 1988, no. 10, p. 12.

8.   On the politics of the artistic output, see John B. Dunlop, "Soviet Cultural Politics," *Problems of Communism*, November-December 1987, pp. 34-56; and Nancy Condee and Vladimir Padunov, *Soviet Cultural Politics and Cultural Production* (IREX Occasional Papers, December 1987). See also the discussion by Geoffrey Hosking of seven recent Soviet novels dealing with the Stalin years, in the *Times Literary Supplement* (London), October 9-15, 1987, pp. 1111-12; see also Wheatcroft and Davies, cited above.

9.   For instance, "Leninskoe zaveshchanie," *Pravda*, February 26 and March 25, 1988; "Shestaia, prazhskaia," *ibid.*, April 8, 1988; and Boris Viktorov, "<Zagovor> v Krasnoi Armii," *ibid.*, April 29, 1988.

10.   *Dialog*, 1987, no. 18 and 19. On the so-called Doctors' plot, see *Druzhba narodov*, 1988, no. 4; and Natalia Rapoport in *Yunost'*, April 1988.

11.   See also A. Roshchin, "V Narkomindele nakanune voiny," *Mezhdunarodnaya zhizn'*, April 1988. The most farreaching critique of earlier Soviet foreign policy is Vyacheslav Dashichev, "Vostok-zapad: poisk novykh otnoshenii," *Literaturnaya gazeta*, May 18, 1988.

12.   See the sweeping article by Alexander Bovin, "Let's Break the Ice on Foreign Policy," *Moscow News*, 1988, no. 24, which also refers to the articles on the Nazi-Soviet Pact by "Ernst Henri," in *Moskovskaya Pravda*, May 18-19, 1988.

13.   See, e.g., *Argumenty i fakty*, 1987, March 14-20 (trans. in *Current Digest of the Soviet Press*, vol. 39, no. 12; also V. Kulish, in *Nauka i zhizn'*, 1987, no. 12. The reference is to Aleksandr Nekrich's *1941, 22 iyunia*; see Vladimir Petrov, ed., "*June 22, 1941*" (University of South Carolina Press, 1968). See also Lt.Gen. Nikolai Pavlenko, "Na pervom etape voiny," in *Kommunist*, 1988, no. 9, pp. 88-94.

A good sample of current criticism by non-historians is this excerpt from a political essay: "What we are now reaping in the economy is what we sowed in 1927-1929 when we abandoned the principles of the New Economic Policy. The press has carried a number of letters whose authors, longing for a historical rehabilitation of Stalinism, defend the management methods established in our country in the 1930s....Their arguments exhibit a failure not of history but of elementary logic the basic fallacy of *post hoc ergo propter hoc*. Logically, the fact that we defeated fascist Germany after carrying out collectivization does not mean that the former resulted from the latter. Our victory in the war may just as well have been accomplished despite collectivization, or it may have had nothing to do with it.

"'If there had been no 1937, there would have been no autumn of 1941,' K[onstantin] Simonov has observed. There are grounds for arguing even further that if there had been no 1929, there would have been no 1933. What I have in mind is that...fascism might never have taken hold in Europe (or in Germany)...." (Andrei Nuikin, "Idealy ili interesy?" *Novyi mir*, January 1988 [trans. in *Current Digest of the Soviet*

Press, vol. 40, no. 21, June 22, 1988]).

14.   The issues that the Polish scholars insisted on bringing up included, among others, the dissolution and purge of the Polish Communist Party ordered by Stalin in 1938, the Nazi-Soviet Pact and the ensuing Soviet occupation of Eastern Poland, the fate of Poles imprisoned and exiled in 1939-41, the Soviet role at the time of the Warsaw uprising in 1944. See *Pravda,* March 12, 1988.

The Polish press meanwhile has openly reported on the demand to air the Katyn question. See *Trybuna Ludu,* March 12-13, 1988. On Stalin's purge of the Latvian communists, see *Ogonyok,* 1988, no. 15.

15.   Two particularly searching and original analyses that went beyond the question of Stalinism, were Igor' Kliamkin, "Kakaia ulitsa vedet k khramu?" *Novyi mir,* 1987, no. 11; and Sergei Andreyev, "Prichiny i sledstviia," *Ural,* 1988, no. 1.

There has been no book-length biography of Stalin published in the Soviet Union since Stalin's death. A full-length reinterpretation of Stalin and his role, *Triumf i tragediia, by* Dmitri Volkogonov (newly appointed head of the Institute of Military History of the USSR Ministry of Defense) has not yet appeared; however, an interesting condensed version of his preface appeared in *Literaturnaya gazeta,* December 9, 1987. See also *Izvestiia,* May 4, 1988.

16.   Fyodor Burlatsky, "Khrushchev," *Literaturnaya gazeta,* February 24, 1988.

17.   A fascinating piece on Beria by Nikolai Zhusenin (*Nedelya,* February 22-28, 1988) includes excerpts from interviews with the sons of Mikoyan, Khrushchev, and Malenkov, the widow of Marshal Bliukher, the daughter of Marshal Konev, and several retired military commanders. The surviving relatives of the victims of Stalinist purges have become the subjects of interviews and articles in Soviet media. (See, e.g., Anatoli Golovkov, in *Ogonyok,* 1988, no. 18.) An article about Anna Larina, Bukharin's widow, in *Ogonyok* (1987, no. 48) provoked considerable response (e.g., Yu. Maksimov in *Literaturnaya gazeta,* 1988, no. 14) and a rebuttal in *Ogonyok,* 1988, no. 17, including the text of Bukharin's testament. There also appeared a (less exciting) report on the sister of Marshal Tukhachevsky (*Ogonyok,* 1988, no. 17), which was introduced by the following editorial note (p. 20):

"Today the historians, as probably never before, are intensively reconstructing our recent past. Like restorers of art they are removing, one by one, the layers of lies from events, facts, phenomena, and are presenting to us—their contemporaries—a picture of the past not nearly so happy as we find it in the textbooks on the history of our country. Documents come to light which had been carefully hidden, guarded until better times arrived—which our days have fortunately turned out to be. For just saving them in those dreary times one could pay with one's freedom. And of course there survive live witnesses—if one may so label those who managed behind barbed wire to preserve their life and faith...."

On Andrei Zhdanov, see Yuri Karyakin, in *Ogonyok*, 1988, no. 19.

18.   The Soviet press has been full of accounts of corruption in high places in the Brezhnev years, including prominent Party functionaries, officials close to him, as well as members of his family. On the suicide of General S.M. Krylov, aide to MVD minister Shchelokov, see *Ogonyok*, 1988, no. 25.

19.   Vasilii Selyunin, "Istoki," in *Novyi mir*, May 1988, pp. 162-189.   In all fairness, this is but a subordinate theme in this remarkable essay on coercion and incentives in Russian history.

20.   "Stopping History or Marching on? Historians Exchange Opinions," *Moscow News*, 1988, no. 10, p. 12.

21.   V.P. Danilov, "Diskussiia v zapadnoi presse o golode 1932-1933 gg. i 'demografii kolkhoznitsii,'" *Voprosy istorii*, 1988, no. 3, pp. 116-21, a path-breaking piece by the leading Soviet specialist on collectivization, reviewing various Western estimates and debates on the scope and nature of Soviet population losses in the hunger of 1932-33.

22.   "Sovremennaia nemarksistskaia istoriografiia i sovetskaia istoricheskaia nauka: beseda za 'kruglym stolom,'" *Istoriia SSSR*, 1988, no. 1, pp. 172-202, cited at pp. 185-86. See also the interview with Afanasyev in *Sovetskaya kul'tura*, March 21, 1987. For earlier conferences and "round-tables" with historians, see "Istoriko-partiinaia nauka: puti perestroiki i dal'neishego razvitiia," *Voprosy istorii KPSS*, 1987, no. 7, pp. 137-52; and "Osnovnye etapy razvitiia

sovetskogo obshchestva," *Kommunist,* 1987, no. 12, pp. 66-79.

Afanasyev has been one of the more ardent reformers who have shown impatience with compromises, for instance, with what they regard as a standard ploy by the apologists: the use of the "on the one hand...on the other hand" argument (such as: Stalin violated legality, but he built up the armed forces). See in particular the exchange in Afanasyev, "Perestroika i istoricheskoe znanie," *Literatur- naya Rossiia,* June 17, 1988; and Pobisk Kuznetsov, "Voprosy istoriku," *Pravda,* June 25, 1988. The partial defense of the achievements under Stalin naturally shades over into political territory, as exemplified by the now infamous "Nina Andreyeva" article (*Sovetskaya Rossiia,* March 13, 1988) that the reformists branded as a manifesto of their political adversaries.

23. In addition to the preceding note, see e.g., L.N. Bezvestnyi, "Videt' i druguiu storonu," *Voprosy istorii KPSS,* 1988, no. 4, pp. 107-110; B.N. Ponomarev, "Nekotorye problemy istoricheskogo opyta KPSS i sovremennost'," *Voprosy istorii KPSS,* 1988, no. 4, pp. 29-41. Ponomarev, of course, is one of the surviving members of the Soviet leadership whose experience goes back to the Stalin era.

24. Book-length monographs making at least some use of Soviet archives are beginning to appear. See, e.g., Galina Makarova, *Narodnyi Komissariat po delam natsional'nostei RSFSR 1917-1923 gg.* (Nauka, 1987); and Aleksandr Kavtaradze, *Voennye spetsialisty na sluzhbe Respubliki Sovetov 1917-1920 gg.* (Nauka, 1988).

Russia After Perestroika

Abraham Brumberg

1.

On April 24, 1991, *Pravda* published the text of a joint statement signed by Gorbachev and Boris Yeltsin, the chairman of the Supreme Soviet of the Russian Federal Republic, as well as the leaders of Byelorussia, Ukraine, Kazakhstan, Uzbekistan, Azerbaijan, Tajikistan, Kirgizia, and Turkenistan. Georgia and the Baltic Republics were notably absent, but nine out of the fif-teen Soviet republics signed the statement, representing 98.6 percent of the USSR's territory and 92.7 percent of its population.[1]

That Yeltsin had called for Gorbachev's resignation only a few days before made the publication of the joint declaration seem all the more dramatic; for it said, in effect, that whatever their former differences, the signers were now determined that the country recover from a deep crisis—

specifically, "social and interethnic conflicts, plummeting production, decline in people's living standards," and the "serious disruption of law and order." The government's own "mistakes committed in the course of perestroika" had contributed to the crisis, the statement admitted, and it proposed a broad five-point program aimed at resolving it.

On the one hand the declaration promised to rescind the highly unpopular 5 percent sales tax, imposed last January to soak up money, and to lower the price increases on foodstuffs and other consumer goods that had gone into effect only three weeks earlier, supposedly in order to encourage farmers to put more food in the shops (e.g., a 100 percent increase in the price of milk and eggs, 200 in the price of meat, and 300 of rye bread). It also proposed to improve the production and distribution of consumer goods.

On the other hand, the declaration spoke vaguely of the need for a "special work regime"—which sounded like the old Stalinist talk of strict factory discipline—in certain key industries, and called for a ban on all acts of "civil disobedience," another ominous-sounding restriction in a country where public meetings in recent years have generally been allowed to take place. Specifically, it urged the nation's coal miners, as well as other workers then on strike, to go back to work and "to make up for the losses they had caused in the immediate future."

In one of its most unexpected passages, the joint declaration stressed the need for greater independence and autonomy on the part of the republics. Each must have the right, for instance, to control its own exports and properties. While a new Union treaty and a new USSR constitution must be created as soon as feasible, the republics should be free "to adopt additional economic measures" as they see fit. The republics that refused to sign the statement—the Baltic countries, Moldavia, Armenia, and Georgia—will be able "to independently decide" whether or not they want to join the Union. Gorbachev for a long time seemed to regard the quest for independence as some kind of malignant growth either to be cured or excised (as he apparently attempted to do by sending troops to repress the independence movements in Vilnius and Riga last January). He now in effect provided independence with a mantle of legitimacy. Moreover, the agreement between Gorbachev and the republican leaders may also prepare the way for direct presidential elections in 1992, rather than (as the present constitution states) in 1995.[2]

The joint declaration is one of the more surprising events of recent months. Only a week earlier, Boris Yeltsin, while on a visit to France, had urged the European Parliament and the French government to bypass the Soviet authorities and deal directly with the Russian Republic—a demand that both Enrique Baron, president of the European Parliament, and President François Mitterrand pointedly rejected.[3] On April 22, the Democratic Russia Movement (DRM), which Yeltsin heads, had called for Gorbachev's resignation and endorsed the miners' strike. Yet Yeltsin not only signed the agreement, but called it "a tremendous victory," praising Gorbachev, and supporting the ban on strikes.[4] Small wonder that his new position caused some consternation among his colleagues and admirers, including the Russian Orthodox priest Gleb Yakunin, a leader of the DRM, who called Yeltsin's signature on the agreement his "greatest error and a colossal blunder."[5]

On the day the text of the joint declaration appeared in *Pravda*, a plenary session of the Party's Central Committee opened in Moscow. Gorbachev's hard-line enemies in the Communist party organizations, the army, and the KGB were hopeful that the meeting would vote to severely censure the General Secretary, or, if possible, to expel him from office. They had been waiting for a long time. Last February, Ivan Polozkov, the first secretary of the Russian Republic's Communist party, attacked Gorbachev for "giving priority to planet-wide values rather than class interests," for "robbing the people of their past and their present" without providing them with any "convincing account of what they can expect in the future." Gorbachev, he charged, was weak, irresolute, indecisive. He had brought the Soviet Union to the brink of disintegration, and permitted

> our pseudodemocrats (i.e., the liberal forces) to use any method— slander, defamation, fabrications, blackmail—to discredit socialism.[6]

On April 24 the same accusations filled the Central Committee meeting hall. Indeed, the atmosphere became so nasty that Gorbachev, on the second day of the session, offered to resign—perhaps a shrewd bluff, perhaps a genuine offer. Either way, his threat to leave sufficiently frightened Party members that he was given an overwhelming vote of confidence. This was not the first time that Gorbachev offered to resign. He did so at the 28th Party Congress last July, and was re-elected with a larger mandate than before.[7] In both cases the hard-liners backed off, terrified lest Gorbachev's departure lead to a schism in the Party and the country, and eventually to their own political demise. Indeed, at the April 24 meeting the hard-liners retreated to the point where the plenum voted to invite representatives of other political parties and movements for political talks, possibly leading to some kind of "coalition government." However calculated the offer

may have been, however unlikely such a coalition, the Communist party had never gone so far before.

Gorbachev's victory at the Party plenum and the obviously well-timed joint declaration took the wind out of the sails not only of his Party opponents, but of his foes in the Supreme Soviet as well. Just three days before the declaration, on April 20, the second congress of the hard-line "Soyuz" group of USSR Supreme Soviet deputies had met in Moscow, and heard its chairman, Yuri Blokhin, call for what amounted to a removal of Gorbachev from power, for an immediate state of emergency, with a moratorium on strikes and rallies, the suspension of the activity of all political parties, and military control over transportation. The extreme rightist Colonel Viktor Alksnis, one of Gorbachev's bitterest enemies, demanded a special session of the USSR Congress of People's Deputies in order to oust Gorbachev from the presidency—a proposal endorsed by the delegates. After the Central Committee meeting on April 24, however, Blokhin asserted that the joint declaration was acceptable insofar as it contained ideas shared by Soyuz, such as the introduction of a "special work regime" in basic industries, such as power, transport, and communications. The declaration does indeed refer to the need for "a special work regime" in certain industries, but according to Yeltsin those industries will be given "most-favored status" by way of incentives ("various benefits, financing, and taxes") and the new "order and discipline" must be predicated entirely on these incentives.[8] The request for a "special session" of the Congress of People's Deputies, Blokhin said, would be scrapped.

The import of these events soon became evident. After months in which every decision Gorbachev made seemed to push him further to the right, he named several well-known reformers as his aides, among them the jurist Vladimir Kudryavtsev, the economists Leonid Abalkin and Yuri. Yaremenko, and the Ukrainian writer Boris Oleynik. Within two weeks of the declaration of April 24, Yeltsin, despite criticism among his own supporters, was able to use his immense authority among workers to settle the coal mine strike. At the same time, the central government agreed to cede control of the Russian mines (among other industries) to the Russian Federal Republic, with the understanding that the coal fields could be privatized if the miners so desired. (Several of the mines have long been unprofitable, subsidized by the state because of the disastrous consequences to be expected if they were closed down. That now has become Yeltsin's problem.) In addition, Yeltsin and the KGB chief, Vladimir Kryuchkov, agreed to establish a separate KGB under the jurisdiction of the Russian Republic.

An even more remarkable sequel to the declaration came in May, nearly a month later, when the Soviet government announced that thirteen of the fifteen republics had agreed on the details of the "special work regime." The new agreement made it clear that a ban on strikes would be counterbalanced by incentives such as wage increases tied to higher productivity, and the right of enterprises to sell a part of their products on the open market, rather than (as has been the case so far) on terms strictly dictated by the state. Most startling was the fact that thirteen out of the fifteen Soviet republics, with the exception of Georgia and Estonia, agreed to the new economic measures. Equally if not more startling was the trip by Grigory Yavlinsky, the reformist economist, and six other economists, to the United States to discuss with a number of Harvard economists a new plan designed to transfer the USSR to a market economy. As *Moscow News* reported in the May 26–June 2 issue, the new Yavlinsky effort is supported fully by both Gorbachev and Yeltsin, and Gorbachev has expressed "his interest and eagerness to see the results." All of this illustrates how grave is the economic crisis and how momentous the accord reached on April 24.

2.

The events of late April and early May make up what the Russians call a *povorot* (reversal) or, more strongly, a *perevorot* (overturn), and it is one in the direction of the left. It followed an earlier *povorot*, to the right, in November and December 1990, and five months that were, for most Soviet citizens, the grimmest in recent memory. A look at the earlier reversal of direction is necessary to understand the recent one.

Beginning in November 1990, events seemed to point only to one conclusion: that perestroika was finished, and that a new ominous era, routinely referred to as "post-perestroika," had begun. One telling straw in the wind was Gorbachev's shift on the "500-Day Plan"—the economic program drafted jointly by a group of economists headed by Stanislav Shatalin and Grigory Yavlinsky. Initially a supporter of the plan, Gorbachev reversed himself and flatly rejected it. In the months that followed, Gorbachev was vested with additional power, and a series of presidential decrees virtually put an end to the Supreme Soviet's legislative functions. Shadowy, unconstitutional, yet officially recognized "salvation committees" in the Baltic Republics mocked the promises of a "law-based state"; so did the bloodshed when Soviet troops were sent in to repress supporters of independence in Vilnius and Riga. As the liberals, or "demo-crats," resigned their positions—most dramatically Foreign Minister Edvard Shevardnadze, and also Shatalin him-self—they were replaced by promi-nent hard-liners such as KGB Major General Boris Pugo and Army Colonel General Boris Gromov, pro-moted to minister and deputy minister of Internal Affairs respectively, and the former finance minister, Valentin Pavlov, promoted to prime minister.[9]

By the end of March of this year, Gorbachev's approval rating dropped to below 14 percent—"a negative *rey-teeng*," the highly respected sociolo-gist Tatyana Zaslavskaya told me. (Since then, it has shrunk to about 10 percent.) The public preferred, among others, Solzhenitsyn and Shevardnadze. Five months earlier I still heard people defending Gorbachev, saying: "Well, he did try, at first,..." but when I came back in March, the tone had be-come overwhelmingly abusive.

Indeed, for most people, the culprit solely responsible for the right-wing *povorot* was Gorbachev himself. He was seen by most of the democrats I have mentioned as an incipient dictator, a man who never had any use for genuine reforms, a Party appa-ratchik, whose perestroika was one more in a long history of attempts to prop up a failing then altar a rotten system. His was perhaps a more serious attempt, but then the situation was graver than ever before. As soon as the process threatened the foun-dations of the Soviet system, as well as Gorbachev's own power, he turned, apparatchik-like, to the traditional methods of intimidation, censorship, and, in the economic domain, to the "administrative-command" system.

Whatever the merits of that view, it rests in part on an underlying sense of personal betrayal. This is how the writer Lyudmilla Saraskina put it in her article "Comforted by Lies" in *Moscow News* (March 24–31, 1991):

> We cherished and maintained our delusions mainly out of a desire "to participate in creating a new life," and rationalizing lies as tac-tical ruses against hard-liners.... We have corrupted the authorities by our laissez-faire attitude, so that they no longer feel hypocriti-cal about their treatment of us and they cast off the pretense that they have our interests at heart. Their pleasant face in a bad game has been changed into a cynical and shameless scowl.

Tatyana Zaslavskaya, who together with other reformers like Abel Abeg-anyan strongly influenced Gorbachev's early reforms, told me that she

> believed in Gorbachev for a long time, and tried to excuse his reluc-tance to act firmly on crucial matters such as private land own-ership, full economic decentral-ization, or curbing the power and prerogatives of the party apparat. I harped on his difficulties; the ob-durate resistance of the bureau-cracy, the pressure he'd been under. I was never "the lady who has the ear of Gorbachev" as some of the W...... ....me. In fact, I have never seen him alone. Still, I attended several meetings with Gorbachev, and was impressed—a common phenomenon among people des-perately wanting to believe, after years of *Brezhnevshchina*, that a new day was dawning. But now I have changed my mind. Sure he's been under pressure, but often he uses "pressure" as an excuse for doing what he wants to do anyway.

> Others saw Gorbachev's tilt to the right as a reflection of authoritarian

views and the habits bred by Russia's political culture, whether tsarist or Marxist-Leninist. Gorbachev, on this view, was merely reacting in traditional fashion. "Democracy," said Leningrad's mayor, Anatoli Sobchak, in a characteristic remark, "has never sunk roots in our country. So it isn't surprising that Gorbachev is not behaving in a democratic fashion."

Others turned that same argument around. Gorbachev, in their view, became little more than the official head of a nation incapable of transforming itself politically, unable to outgrow deep-rooted mental attitudes: a nation, as one writer observed only semi-facetiously, not of workers (*rabochye*) but of slaves (*raby*).[10] But some of the politicians and writers who knew him best scoffed at the idea of Gorbachev as a born-again rightist. In the light of the April 24 agreement, it is worth recalling that even some of Gorbachev's severest critics—Shevarnadze, Anatoli Sobchak, Yegor Yakovlev (editor of *Moscow News*), and Shatalin—considered his turn to the right, however reprehensible, a tactical step, rather than a reflection of a change of heart. "The idea," Shatalin told me,

> that Gorbachev has suddenly turned into a rightist, or that he had always been a rightist in disguise, is absurd—as absurd as the tendency, prevalent in the West, to lump all army officers into one huge monolithic right-wing camp. I know the army, and I can assure you this is simply not so. And I know the KGB, too—even there, plenty of people want to turn the KGB into a normal and decent organization, and who support democratic reforms in general.

Shevardnadze, who had warned of the dangers of "dictatorship" when he resigned in December, rejected the notion that Gorbachev had become a "rightist" when I talked to him in late March. "If he really became one," Shevarnadze told me in late March, "he would have to shoot himself."

On March 12 in *Nezavisimaya gazeta* ("Independent Newspaper"), one of the best of the new Soviet publications, the editor in chief, Vitali Tretyakov, published an article entitled "Apologia for Gorbachev or Perestroika's Epitaph," which was remarkable both because Tretyakov, formerly an editor of *Moscow News*, has been a consistent critic of Gorbachev, and because among the intelligentsia—which makes up most of *Nezavisimaya gazeta*'s readership— any kind word about the president was regarded as a well-nigh unpardonable sin.

The author listed "forty-six theses in defense of Gorbachev." (He could, he said, just as easily have listed 146 against, but he felt that a corrective to the widespread view of the president as a hopeless "rightist" was in order.) Gorbachev embarked on many of his policies, said Tretyakov, not because of "objective circumstances," that is, not because (as the conventional view would have it) he had no choice, but out of conviction and his own moral sensibility:

> Gorbachev had other options, he could have smothered the new child [perestroika]; instead, he helped the baby get on its feet and develop its own character.

Among the "theses," in effect accomplishments, listed by Tretyakov were the "destruction of the totalitarian regime in the Soviet Union and thus also of totalitarian regimes in Eastern Europe," loosening the Party's monopoly of power, weakening the instruments of mass repression, and forcing the nomenklatura to engage in an open contest for power.

Referring to the constitutional clause mandating a direct presidential election, and the elimination of "safe" seats, he wrote, "Thank God he has created a system which will eventually allow us to get rid of the imbeciles sitting on the necks of the people."

Tretyakov's defense was unusual. The most common refrain was that Gorbachev had finally "shown his true face," or, more charitably, that he had become a *zalozhnik*, "hostage," of the right (the army, KGB, and the Party apparat)—"if you will, a voluntary hostage," in the words of the political scientist Yevgeni Ambartsumov.

Though the "hostage" theory struck me as rather far-fetched insofar as it suggested Gorbachev's utter dependence on his putative "captors," I found its emphasis on the vast, powerful, and anxious bureaucracy considerably more persuasive than the speculations on the weight of history or Gorbachev's personal proclivities. Certainly, Gorbachev has long been the target of conservative hostility. The attacks I have mentioned by Ivan Polozkov, the first secretary of the Russian Federal Communist Party, were typical. At the 28th Congress of the Soviet Communist Party, held in June and July 1990, Gorbachev and the liberals who were then his allies—Aleksandr Yakovlev, Leonid Abalkin, and Edvard Shevardnadze—were harshly attacked by hard-line Party leaders and army officers, and indirectly but unmistakably by KGB chief Vladimir Kryuchkov. They were blamed for damaging Soviet security by "losing" Eastern Europe and dissolving the Warsaw Pact, "heaping mud" on Lenin's memory, and betraying Soviet workers via "capitalist" reforms. When Colonel Viktor Alksnis criticized first Yakovlev and then Gorbachev for encouraging Baltic separatism, the applause was so loud that Gorbachev had to request that the chief of the general staff restore order.[11]

On November 13, Gorbachev faced a hostile audience of 1,100 army officers and other defense officials. They charged him with neglecting the elementary needs of the military (housing, schooling, and so on), allowing "antipopular, antisocialist, and separatist forces" to "wage a determined struggle for power," and for advocating military cuts that would endanger national security.[12]

The pressure on Gorbachev continued unabated. On December 22, 1990, the newspaper *Sovetskaya Rossia*, the unofficial organ of Russia's nationalists, reactionaries, and anti-Semites, published an open letter to Gorbachev asking him to declare a state of emergency so the country would not fall prey to a "dictatorship" of "separatists," "antipopular and antisocialist" forces, and "criminal wheeler-dealers." The fifty-three signatures were said to be those of "public figures," though few of them had any claim to either fame or accomplishment. The one interesting exception was the Russian Patriarch, Aleksy II—interesting in the light of the tendency of some Western observers to see the "increased role of religion in the USSR" as an unmitigated blessing.

3.

Pressure alone, however, could not make Gorbachev a hostage of such reactionary forces. Did a right-wing cabal actually present Gorbachev with an ultimatum at the end of 1990, as some of my informants believed: an ultimatum that he either reject the 500-Day program, suppress the Baltic independence movements, and censor outspokenly critical television programs, or else be driven from office? There was much speculation about such an ultimatum, but no evidence that it was actually issued or that the right-wing forces had the power to make good on it. Moreover, such a challenge does not explain Gorbachev's previous reluctance to carry out Shatalin's plan and his failure to reach a working accord with his democratic supporters. (Indeed, his anger had exploded on many occasions: in the summer of 1989, for instance, Gorbachev bitterly criticized reformists in the USSR Supreme Soviet and several outspoken periodicals for their "inflammatory" and "irresponsible" articles that "endanger perestroika."[13]) For this reason, the threat—tacit or explicit—of coercion from the right seems a less convincing reason for Gorbachev's turn to the right last autumn than a more complex combina-

Boris Yeltsin

tion of reasons: Gorbachev's uneasy relationship with the liberal intelligentsia, on the one hand, and the purely pragmatic dividends to be gained from leaning on the right, on the other.

It is probably true, as many people who know him well believe, that Gorbachev has never felt entirely at home with liberal, and particularly flagrantly anti-Communist, intellectuals. Yet the democrats themselves have contributed in some measure to the breakdown of the alliance with Gorbachev. The historian and philosopher Alexander Tsipko, who has written some of the most astringent criticism of Marxism to have appeared in the Soviet press, cites the failure of many democrats to present Gorbachev with clear alternative programs. The complaints of such democrats as Arkady Murashov, secretary of the Interregional Group of People's Deputies or of the well-known jurist Victor Sheynes "that their pleas for collaboration had been wilfully ignored," he told me, "are not quite true. The pleas were always accompanied by innuendoes and abrasive comments that Gorbachev must have found insulting." Shevardnadze was blunter: "The democrats have always been too disorganized to give Gorbachev the support he needed."

The Interregional Group of People's Deputies, founded in July 1989 and one of the first groups to set itself up as part of the democratic opposition, is a case in point. Consisting of both USSR Congress and Supreme Soviet deputies, some of them, like Sakharov, nationally and internationally famous, and others novices, the group has resolutely rejected setting itself up as a political party, and has from the first been divided by controversy over political and economic issues. In the spring of 1990, some of its members were in favor of vesting Gorbachev with more power, while others regarded this as a step toward Gorbachev's personal dictatorship.[14] Later the group disagreed—over the 500-Day Plan, and the extent to which the struggle for the independence of the republics should be encouraged.[15] These and other controversies have prevented the group from adopting clearly defined programs.[16]

In addition, the inflammatory rhetoric of some of their leaders has often dismayed members of the group. In July 1989, when reaching an accord with Gorbachev was high on the Interregional Group's agenda, Yuri Afanasyev, who had just been elected the group's co-chairman, was so sweeping and unrelenting in his attacks (he asserted, for example, that Gorbachev's rule was "illegal") as to stymie all efforts at collaboration.[17] Afanasyev's tendency to make wholesale indictments has undermined his influence. Viktor Danilov, author of some of the best works on the collectivization of agriculture, told me that at a conference of historians Afanasyev disparaged colleagues who had written Party-line propaganda, forgetting that he had done exactly the same thing before Gorbachev had come to power. The death of the Interregional Group's chairman, Andrei Sakharov, deprived the Interregional Group and the democratic movement in general of their most illustrious leader. It also led to an erosion of the group, which has shrunk to half its original four hundred or so members.

The relationship between the democrats and Gorbachev also became frayed for purely pragmatic reasons. The right wing, as the political scientist Igor Klyamkin put it pungently, has all the necessary levers of power—the army, the KGB, the Party apparat, control over finances, and to a considerable extent control over the public media. "What do the democrats have to offer? Next to nothing that can be used to implement political change." The opinion polls supporting the democrats' view of the right wing have only been converted into power locally, as in the Baltic countries and the miner's strikes.

It is easy to see the appeal of this argument, however self-serving, for Gorbachev in the autumn of 1990. The Union was coming apart at the seams. The central government's power, like his own, was crumbling. So·was the economy. The 500-Day Plan, supported by some economists, was criticized as impractical by others, and—to judge by the results of a similar plan in Poland—was likely to produce high unemployment, social unrest, and political backlash, not exactly a comforting prospect.

And so Gorbachev chose "stabilization"—that is, law, order, and avoidance of contentious reforms, and an alliance to the forces that could bring it about—the army, the KGB, and the Party apparat. It is only in the light of such developments, it seems to me, that Gorbachev could have been seen as a *zalozhnik* of the right. In early December 1990, at a meeting with industrial managers, one of the speakers warned him that he had to "decide whom to turn to in a difficult moment—to Communist executives or to someone else."[18] The "difficult moment" had arrived; he turned to "Communist executives."

4.

The *povorot* of April 24 is clearly an attempt to mend fences with at least some portion of the broadly defined democratic opposition. But what instruments had the opposition fashioned to achieve its goals? The goals are admirable—authentic political pluralism, an end to the power and privileges of the Communist party apparat, complete freedom of information, a market, or "mixed," economy, public control over the military and intelligence services. But how are they to be realized? Some would say through the political parties, more than one thousand of which (not all, certainly, democratic in character) have sprung up since the end of 1989, and especially since the passing of the law on public associations in June 1990, which legalized political parties for the first time since 1918, except in the Baltic Republics and Georgia, where political parties took part in elections and were granted legal status in 1989. [19]

Last November I talked to some of the leaders of the Russian left-of-center groups--the Democratic, Social Democratic, Christian Democratic, Socialist, Green, Anarcho-Syndicalist, Constitutional Democratic (Kadet) parties and some members of the Interregional group of deputies in the USSR Supreme Soviet, all organized in the Russian Republic—so far there are no Soviet-wide parties. The parties are small. They have not as yet been able to run in elections, but most expect to put forward candidates for the election to the Supreme Soviet of the USSR and the Supreme Soviets of most of the republics, now scheduled for 1994, but likely to be held in 1992.

Everyone seems to agree that the Democratic party is the largest, with perhaps 30,000 members. To judge by the attendance at its meetings, the Social Democratic party is also fairly popular but it has only about 5,000 members. As the Leningrad political journalist Sergey Andreyev recently argued, these democratic political parties often fail to take into account the concrete interests of social groups. It would, he believes, make more sense to have separate parties representing the workers, the peasants, the intelligentsia, and so on.[20] Their programs tend to be wordy and vague: "The Declaration of Principles" of the Party of Free Labor (Partiia Svobodnovo Truda), for instance, speaks of the

> values that are embodied by the party—the values of world civilization, those that are usually called "humanitarian," but which in point of fact have been engendered by societies with market economies and democratic political structures. Hence our ideal is a free market and a democratic state.

But "a free market and a democratic state" are also the basic principles of the Democratic party, as its leader Nikolay Travkin assured me. Indeed, these very words appear in the Democratic party's platform, as well as in the platforms of the Social Democrats and other similar parties. There are distinctions, to be sure: the Democratic party wants to get rid of any "government interference in the economy, politics and private life [of the citizens]," while the Social Democrats "are not so enamored of private property as is the Democratic party. We fear," one of their leaders, Pavel Kudikin, told me, "that a rush to the free market, such as the one advocated in the 500-Day Plan, may lead to the emergence of a rapacious capitalist alone, and we place great emphasis on the need for adequate social safeguards."

In the end, however, differences among the parties are obscured by lofty declarations and by personal squabbles among the leaders. An article in *Moscow News* early this year reported that Nicolay Travkin and G. Khatsenkov, leaders of the Democratic Party of Russia, were quarreling over their party's financial affairs and that the leaders of Shchit (Shield), the union in defense of army men, were also badly split. The revolutionary Leningrad city council attacked its respected chairman, the lawyer Anatoli Sobchak, and was itself accused of corruption on the TV program *600 Seconds*.

The only group that has tried to combine several parties in a large coalition is the Democratic Russia Movement (DRM), which includes the Democratic party, the Social Democrats, the Republicans (formerly Democratic Platform), and Christian Democrats. But as its name signifies, it sees itself as a broad and loosely linked "movement," rather than as a political party with a well-defined political and economic program. Some of its members have accused one another of ties with the KGB.

New parties, however small, insignificant, or ineffective, are organized every week. "Aren't you a Western journalist?" a man in his late forties asked me in the Rossia Hotel, where I went to interview several leaders of the miners' hunger strike. He then announced proudly that he had just formed a new party. "It's called the Conservative party," he said, "and I have written a terrific political and economic program. Could you have it printed in the West?" I asked whether he might not be the only member of his party. "Oh, yes," he replied without hesitation, "but you must understand that my program is better than any other—any other!"

A number of party leaders have become widely known. One of them is Oleg Rumyantsev of the Social Democratic party, a principal author of the new liberal constitution of the Russian Republic, still to be passed by Russia's parliament; and one hears much talk about Nikolay Travkin, leader of the Democratic party, who, unlike almost all of the other leaders, comes from a working-class background. Travkin has been accused of being power-hungry and authoritarian, but I found him clearheaded and sensible. "The business of a political party," he told me, "is to take power. That's why I put such an emphasis on organizational matters. Our party must be democratic, open to differing views, but at the same time disciplined, centralized, and capable of acting effectively once a decision is reached." When I said that this made him sound suspiciously "Leninist," he grinned and replied that "the only good thing Lenin ever did in his life was to create a political party."

The Democratic Platform, a social democratic faction that split off from the Communist Party of the Soviet Union and later rechristened itself as the Republican party, was in the news a year ago but its membership has since fallen from 30,000 to 20,000.[21] A great many liberal-minded Party members have been reluctant to join the Democratic Platform because its leaders are unimpressive. In the words of Yegor Yakovlev, the liberal Party members would "be only too ready to leave the sclerotic hard-liners to their own designs and rally around Gorbachev, if he only were to issue the call for a new and reformed Party." (Yakovlev himself quit the Party after the Lithuanian crackdown this January.)

A year ago Gorbachev could have forced a significant split within the USSR Communist Party. At its last congress, in June and July 1990, his prestige was still high, and the other liberal democrats high in the party— Aleksandr Yakovlev, Sobchak, and Shatalin, possibly even Yeltsin— would have joined him. Since then, an estimated two million Party members have quit, the conservatives have become more powerful, and most of the remaining rank and file make their feelings of apathy plain. No doubt there are still dissidents in the Party. The Russian Federal parliament, for instance, includes a group of 179 deputies who are members of the Communist party, but who call themselves "Communists for Democracy." But there is little chance that the dissidents would form a new "social democratic party," as Shatalin and the editor of *Literaturnaya gazeta*, Fyodor Burlatsky, have urged.[22]

5.

The fragility of the democratic opposition suggests that the democrats would have done better to consolidate their ranks before challenging an enemy who, whatever his standing in the polls, was still firmly in control of the central mechanisms of power and thus capable (as experience has shown) of sabotaging the democrats' best laid plans. Many talk of the urgent need to create a party open to representatives from many different republics that would stand for at least basic ideological and strategic principles; but all attempts to organize such a group have failed. Most recently, forty-one parties participated in the "Congress of Democratic Forces," held in Kharkov, Ukraine, on January 27 of this year. Only twenty-six of the parties, some of them so small as to be nearly invisible, agreed to sign the final platform.

Such efforts consistently founder on the nationalities problem—that is, the difficulty of reconciling the aspirations and demands of individual republics. According to both Sobchak and the chairman of the Ukrainian "Green World" party, Yuri Shcherbak, the only agreement on human rights that was passed in Kharkov was a statement to the effect that such rights were a good thing. Some of the participants demanded that the statement condemn violations "wherever they occur," but a majority of the participants said the republics might resent having their actions criticized—and that any such discord should be avoided. A number of representatives

311

found objectionable even the hollow statement that was finally passed, and they withdrew from the congress. Among the parties that refused to sign the resolutions, for instance, was Lithuania's Sajudis.

The representatives of the republics can be capable of ugly, undemocratic, and nationalistic intolerance. Vytautas Landsbergis, Lithuania's president, for instance, is greatly admired for his courage and firm defense of his country's interests. Nonetheless, liberals (within and outside Lithuania) criticize his lack of tolerance of political opponents, his encouragement of a

Moscow, May 1990

"cult of personality," his reluctance, even refusal, to cooperate with democrats in other republics. And after the Congress of Democratic Forces, Gavriil Popov, the liberal mayor of Moscow, criticized "with bitterness and distress" the refusal of Sajudis and other republican parties to sign the Kharkov documents.[23]

To be sure, Landsbergis is not to be compared with Zviad Gamsakhurdia, the one-time chairman of the Georgian Helsinki Committee, who was elected chairman of the Georgian parliament last year and president of the country on May 26 of this year. Gamsakhurdia has turned into a ruthless and chauvinistic autocrat, appointing local prefects responsible only to himself, and arresting his political rivals as "enemies of the Georgian people." He has placed the republic's press under government control and expelled several foreign reporters. Gamsakhurdia is also a nasty demagogue, combining religious with nationalistic rhetoric in his frequent speeches. "Let the whole world be aware," he said recently,

> that we struggled and continue to struggle for the rebirth of the religious and national ideals of our ancestors, and that the Almighty has endowed Georgia with a great mission. We are struggling against the eternal night of godlessness and injustice, our righteous cause is protected by the Almighty, and this is why we shall triumph.

(The Patriarch of All Georgia, Catholicos Iliya II, strongly supports the Georgian president. He recently announced that "whoever kills a Georgian, regardless of the latter's guilt, will be regarded by the Church as an enemy of the Georgian people."[24])

Nowhere is Gamsakhurdia's religious and nationalistic fanaticism more evident than in his dealings with the Georgian Muslim minorities, which make up nearly 20 percent of the country's population. When the South Ossetian Autonomous Region declared independence this year, he used Georgian troops to bloodily suppress the Ossetians, in fact killing more people than the Soviet troops did on the streets of Tbilisi in 1989.[25]

None of this prevented Boris Yeltsin from traveling to Georgia in March, and signing an agreement with Gamsakhurdia establishing joint police and army patrols "in the territory of the former South Ossetian region."[26] Yeltsin acted unilaterally, without the consent—or even, apparently, the knowledge—of the Russian Supreme Soviet. As the constitutional expert Oleg Rumyantsev, a Social Democrat and a consistent admirer of Yeltsin, commented disapprovingly, "Boris Yeltsin, I am afraid," he said, "takes more and more steps without taking anyone into account, for which I can find no justification."

Since he signed the Joint Declaration on April 24, and since Gorbachev's substantial concessions to him, Yeltsin seems stronger than ever. He was ready to join with Gorbachev in endorsing the Shatalin plan last autumn and was cast aside; but now he has an apparent alliance with him that incorporates some of his principal aims. As a result, he seems to have shelved the demand he made early in March for a new united political party. He clearly commands a larger following than any other leader, at least in Russia. He is the man who has stood up to Gorbachev, who has courageously attacked the corruption and privileges of the Communist party, who wants a strong Russia, and who promises to bring both freedom and bread to its citizens:

Yet Yeltsin has also been criticized for the coarseness of his populist slogans and his demagogic proclivities. His March 8 speech, in which he called Gorbachev a "liar," and his political critics "enemies who must be fought, not embraced—even women" (sic) dismayed many of his supporters—so much so that he was forced to apologize for his remarks a few days later.

Some critics maintain that Yeltsin is trying to imitate if not outdo Gorbachev. Gorbachev demanded presidential powers: so has Yeltsin. Gorbachev has opposed "excessive" demands for sovereignty within the USSR: Yeltsin, who endorses the Baltic demands for independence, has denounced similar demands of the Tatar Autonomous Republic, on the grounds that the time for granting more autonomy to the Tatars "has not yet arrived." Gorbachev tries to convert indecisiveness into a virtue: Yeltsin refuses either to endorse or repudiate the March 17 referendum.

In a recent issue of *Moscow News*, deputy chief editor Stepan Kiselyov called Gorbachev and Yeltsin "Siamese twins" dealing in "demagogy and lies." He was particularly scathing about Yeltsin's practice of

> playing up the separatist tendencies in the union republics with a view to weakening his rival [Gorbachev]. By so doing, Yeltsin is planting a time bomb under his own state. The nationalist conflicts that have undermined Gorbachev's power may soon flare up inside Russia. Then Tataria or North Ossetia [the part of Ossetia inside the RSFSR] may one day become hotbeds of unrest like today's Georgia or Lithuania. And that may wake up the terrible beast—Russian nationalism—which would not go back to its lair until it tears the whole country apart.[27]

Notwithstanding Yeltsin's success in settling the miners' strike, his great test may well come later this year, when having been elected president of the Russian Republic, he finds himself demonstrably unable to make good on his promises. As Igor Golumbiovsky, deputy editor of *Izvestia*, who recently survived a campaign by apparatchiks to dislodge him, told me: "The country knows him as a fighter, but thus far not as a *deyatel*" (roughly, "doer"). This may be unfair, but it suggests the current tone of the Soviet populist politics.

6.

The common thread in many criticisms of Gorbachev, particularly since the *povorot* of last winter, including his use of force in the Baltic Republics and the stream of presidential decrees, was the charge that he has been heading toward a dictatorship.[28] Yet quite apart from Gorbachev's indignant denials of any such intent,[29] the plain fact is that his power has not increased, but manifestly declined. Paradoxically, in fact, the more de jure powers he gained, the less power he had de facto. Gorbachev has been issuing one ukase after another, but many of them have been calmly ignored. What recent events illustrate above all is the strength of the forces unleashed by Gorbachev and of the institutions they have produced, particularly in the press and television. The Soviet state and the CPSU still control most publishing facilities and distribution of paper. But since the press law went into effect in June 1990, the grip of the central authorities has loosened to a remarkable extent. (The law confines the censorship apparatus, Glavlit, to strictly limited military and security matters, removes Glavlit's representatives from publications and gives the editors the right to name their founders [*uchrediteli*], which is important for making contracts on their own.) Many newspapers have become more radical; many new publications have appeared, such as *Nezavisimaya gazeta, Kuranty, Kommersant, Stolitsa, Megapolis EXPRESS, Moskovskii kurier,* and *Russki kurier.* No longer sold only by individual vendors clustered around Pushkin Square, they are widely available in newspaper kiosks and bookshops.

Television freedom is far more constrained. When Gorbachev appointed the pliant bureaucrat Leonid Kravchenko as head of Gostelradio (now All-Union Television and Radio Company), Kravchenko took the popular Friday evening show *Vzgliad* ("View") off the air, and turned the lively and informative daily news program *Vremya* ("The Times") into a tool of pre-perestroika-like agitprop. In addition, he fired a number of talented news broadcasters.

I experienced the new television climate when I agreed to be interviewed for the daily program "120 Minutes," only to find after the show that some of my critical remarks had been cut. One of my interviewers, a smooth young man with an unctuous grin, who had assured me that my tape "would not be tampered with," now explained that "Mr. Kravchenko, as head of the company, feels he has the right to decide what should and what should not go on the air." In doing so, he was repeating Kravchenko's line, which is that as a "company director" he is not duty-bound "to serve anyone but his chief."

Such squalid tactics, however, may prove to be no more than a temporary nuisance. Kravchenko has been violently criticized in the press, and on April 12 he was expelled from the USSR Journalists' Union. Nearly all the republics have their own radio and television stations, which are not subordinate to Gorbachev's man in

Zviad Gamsakhurdia and Boris Yeltsin in Kazbegi, North Ossetia, March 1991

315

Moscow. The Leningrad radio and TV stations, though nominally responsible to Kravchenko, have successfully defied him, and according to Sobchak set themselves up as independent shareholding companies fully independent of the central authorities (their signal strength extends to Moscow and other areas far away from Leningrad). At the end of March, a newly formed independent television company began to operate in Siberia. Its head, Vladimir Mukusev, has announced that he would run a program under the name of *Vzgliad*, and probably employ some of its Moscow staff.[30]

Most important, the Russian Republic has now formed its own television company. While its management is still bickering with Kravchenko in order to get exclusive control of the one available channel, it has already begun broadcasting several hours every day, without any censorship from Kravchenko. Its morning and evening new programs increasingly resemble the outspoken national news show *Vremya* before Kravchenko censored it. Russian television will probably obtain a whole channel for its own use before very long. When it does, most of the broadcasters from Central TV will join the Russian Republic company (as many have already), and Kravchenko, although still in control of widely broadcast programs, may be left looking for a staff.

Not only did Gorbachev's attempts to control the media fail. Discussions between the central authorities and representatives from the Baltic states resumed in March and now seem more likely to open the way to eventual independence. Gorbachev's two most notorious decrees—establishing joint army-police patrols to enforce "law and order," and authorizing the militia and KGB to enter any establishment suspected of engaging in "speculation" and inspect its books—have become a dead letter. Except in small provincial towns, where the local Communist authorities retain considerable power, the patrols are nowhere to be seen, and no businesses have been invaded by the KGB during the past few months.

In fact, the evolution toward a rule of law continues, and the courts continue to function. Work on the revised Russian Republic criminal code is nearly finished. Last autumn one of *Pravda*'s writers, Vladimir Petrunya, accused several "democrats," including Galina Starovoitova, a radical USSR Supreme Soviet deputy, of deliberately creating food shortages in Moscow in order to prepare a "counter-revolutionary coup." Starovoitova sued Petrunya and *Pravda* for slander. The court found *Pravda* guilty, and ordered it to publish an apology. If *Pravda* fails to obey the order, Starovoitova has vowed she will sue the newspaper for damages—and "keep suing it until the end of my life."[31] In February of this year, the journal *Ogonek* won a similar slander charge against the military journal *Voenno-istorichesky zhurnal*, which had accused the authors of a declaration by the DRM published by *Ogonek* of holding Nazi views.

Another notable development has been the activity of the USSR Supreme Soviet Committee for Constitutional Oversight, which has nullified several presidential decrees as unconstitutional, including Gorbachev's decree that established "military political organizations" in the armed forces. The organizations must therefore be abolished. According to many observers in and outside the Soviet Union, this prepares the way for abolishing Communist party control over the army—one of the major demands of the democrats.

7.

The reversals of power and policy during the past eight months should be suggestive for understanding other *povorots* to come.

First, the tendency to interpret every disturbing or reprehensible development in the USSR, whatever its magnitude, as yet another indication of the intransigent nature of Soviet totalitarianism should now be seen as the superflous remnant of a bygone era. Worrying as the situation was in the winter of 1990, it was by no means as calamitous as many people in and outside the Soviet Union imagined. Those who murmured darkly about the "resurgence" of Stalinism, or an impending "dictatorship," or the strangling of democratic institutions, failed to take into account the fact that these are no longer realistic possibilities, that Soviet society can not be regimented as it once was, and that the incipient "dictators" have so far lacked the means, the strength, the nerve—perhaps even the wish—to bring them about.

Second, just as the alarms about the impending death of democracy in the Soviet Union proved premature, so too are any excessive expectations about the new turn to the left likely to be disappointed.

The second *povorot* of April 1991 was caused by the dismal failure of relying on right-wing forces to bring about the necessary economic and political changes, and by the widespread anger and frustration that failure aroused. But right-wing forces—and here I am speaking particularly of the huge bureaucratic apparat—are still very much a part of the Soviet scene, and not about to relinquish their power. In spite of their recent setbacks, they will do their best to undermine Gorbachev and the democrats by exploiting economic difficulties and the conflicts between national groups. Soviet life, with its immense unresolved economic, ecological, ethnic, religious, and political problems, will continue to be subject to instability and tension.

A closer collaboration between Gorbachev and the "democrats"—if the democrats can agree on a common stratgey—would no doubt alleviate some of those problems, and every setback for the right is a victory for its opponents. The attendance of both Gorbachev and Yeltsin on May 21 at the Andrei Sakharov Memorial Congress, presided over by Elena Bonner, seemed to suggest that a new phase of collaboration between Gorbachev and the democrats has already begun. But the problems will remain.

Third, some of the conventional views of Mikhail Gorbachev, too, should be put aside. He has never been the tyrant, "dictator," or "dogmatic Leninist," that many in the West and in the USSR claim him to be, in spite of his sponsorship of glasnost and perestroika; nor has he ever justified the adulation he has often inspired in the West. His role, however central until now, will probably diminish in the years or perhaps even months ahead. His critics both on the right and left may still consider him, all their objections notwithstanding, as indispensable to Soviet stability, but they are likely, in my opinion, to revise their view in the very near future.

Gorbachev is not likely to be removed from power by a political plot. He is not likely to resign, as urged upon him recently by the miners and some radical intellectuals. Nor is his popularity rating about to improve more than marginally. Rather, the revolution that he unleashed and for several years marked with his powerful impulses and visions will find new channels and new leaders as elections take place nationally and in the republics. The latest accord between Gorbachev and the republics sets the stage for the passing of the Soviet empire. Open and direct elections for a new president could provide a legitimate and democratic way for Gorbachev to turn over power to a federal candidate whose name will not be predictable for months to come. (Yeltsin, if he becomes president of the Russian Republic, is not likely to run for president of the USSR.) If elections do indeed take place in 1992 as reported, Gorbachev will be owed much for having lasted so long without being a "hostage" to anyone except himself. □

[1] See "Joint Declaration on Urgent Measures for the Stabilization of the Situation in the Country and for Overcoming the Crisis," *Pravda*, April 24, 1991, p. 1.

[2] See interview with Sergei Grigorev, a Gorbachev aide, in *The Washington Post*, May 1, 1991.

[3] *Le Monde*, April 17 and 18, 1991.

[4] On May 11, Yeltsin went one step further, calling Gorbachev "an ally" of the democratic movement and "clearly in favor of reforms." (*The New York Times*, May 12, 1991, p. 13).

[5] Among other critics were Lev Ponomarev, a DRM leader, who said the joint declaration "smelt of 1937," as well as the chairman of the DRM, Yuri Afanasyev, and the economist Vasili Selyunin, who accused Yeltsin of helping to keep Gorbachev in power (TASS, April 25 and 27, 1991; and *Komsomolskaya pravda*, April 30, 1991).

[6] *Sovetskaia Rossia*, February 2, 1991.

[7] See *Pravda*, July 10, 1990.

[8] Interview with Boris Yeltsin on Radio Russia, May 5, 1991, FBIS-SOV, May 7, 1991, p. 40.

[9] The word "liberals" and the more widespread term "democrats" are often used interchangeably in the USSR today for the democratic "camp." There are former Communist party members (e.g., Yeltsin, Leningrad mayor Anatoli Sobchak, Moscow mayor Gavriil Popov, *Moscow News* editor Yegor Yakovlev, and the historian Yuri Afanasyev) who had hoped to reform the party "from within" and now consider themselves democratic socialists, or social democrats. There are unreconstructed liberals of the Manchester School variety, such as Nikolay Travkin, head of the Democratic party. There are former dissidents, former conformists, atheists, and Christians and people eschewing any political or confessional labels. They all subscribe to several basic principles: authentic political pluralism; an end to the power and privileges of the Communist party apparat; complete freedom of information; a market—or "mixed"—economy; public control over the military and intelligence services.

[10] The brilliant young writer Tatyana Tolstaya agrees, writing in these pages ("In Cannibalistic Times," *The New York Review*, April 11, 1991) that the Soviet state and the mentality of its citizens "did not emerge out of thin air" but out of "the bleak depths of Russian history" and the savagery of its leaders is the newest emanation of "a longstanding tradition in the Russian state," and popular attitudes—intolerance, senselessness, and cruelty—have similarly been around since time immemorial.

For a more scholarly analysis of historical parallels, especially between perestroika as a "revolution from above" and the policies of Ivan the Terrible and Peter the Great, see the discussion between Aleksey Shishov, political editor of the new weekly *Russki kurier*, and the historian Yevgeni Anisimov in *Russki kurier*, No. 4, February 1991, pp. 8–9. In the West, *The Economist* (April 27, 1991, pp. 11–12) persistently if not obsessively champions the view that "Leninist" dogmas constitute the single most tenacious obstacle to genuine reforms.

[11] See Alexander Rahr, "A Pyrrhic Victory for Gorbachev?" *Report on the USSR*, July 20, 1990.

[12] For a translation of some of these speeches, see "Gorbachev Fields Military's Complaints," *The Current Digest of the Soviet Press*, Vol. XLII, No. 47, 1990, pp. 7–14.

[13] *The New York Times*, October 18 and 19, 1989.

[14] See, for instance, the account of a discussion on this subject in my article "The Turning Point?" *The New York Review* (June 28, 1990), pp. 52–53.

[15] See "Inside the Interregional Group," by Alexander Rahr, *Report*

on the USSR, October 26, 1990, pp. 1–4.

[16]In March 1990, the distinguished economic historian Vasili Selyunin, one of the fiercest critics of Gorbachev, told me much the same thing. "The curse of my democratic friends in the parliament," he said, "is that they keep bickering among themselves instead of uniting and presenting the country with a concrete alternative program." Selyunin's trenchant essay, "How to Convert the Soviet Economy into a Free Market," is available in what is otherwise an appallingly edited grabbag, *The Anti-Communist Manifesto*, published by The Free Enterprise Press, Bellevue, Washington, 1990.

[17]See Vera Tolz, "The Implications for Glasnost of Gorbachev's Attack on Reformists," *Report on the USSR*, October 27, 1989, p. 6.

[18]*Izvestia*, December 7, 1990.

[19]For a discussion of the events preceding the legalization of political parties, see my article "The Turning Point?" pp. 52–54.

[20]In fact, a party representing private peasants has just been formed, headed by the USSR Supreme Soviet Deputy Yuri Chernenko.

[21]See *The New York Review*, March 29, 1990, p. 27, for the text of the Democratic Platform's program document.

[22]See "The Alternative to the Break-Up of Left Forces—a Movement towards Social Democracy," a discussion by Burlatsky, Shatalin, and Sergey Alekseyev, chairman of the USSR Constitutional Supervisory Committee, *Literaturnaia gazeta*, January 30, 1991, pp. 1 and 5.

[23]Gavriil Popov, "No Freedom for Solitary Fighters," *Moscow News*, No. 3, 1991. Landsbergis sponsored a republican law establishing the death penalty for "treason of the motherland," a law taken intact from the Criminal Code of the USSR, adopted under Stalin and abolished several years ago. He has spent republican funds on publishing his collected works (see "Who Needs a Volume of Landsbergis' Speeches?" *Literaturnaia gazeta*, February 2, 1991). When I was in Vilnius a few months ago, I talked to two eminent Lithuanian philosophers and Sajudis members, Arvydas Juozaitis and Arvydas Sliogeris, both of whom felt that Landsbergis was "a chauvinist and a dictator at heart." The former Lithuanian prime minister, Kazimiera Prunskiene, who disagreed with Landsbergis's attitude towards Moscow, arguing for a more pragmatic approach, has been the subject of violent attacks in the Lithuanian press.

[24]See interview with Gamsakhurdia in *Ogonek*, No. 9, February 1991, pp. 4–5.

[25]See, for instance, "Gamsakhurdia's First 100 Days," by Elizabeth Fuller, *Report on the USSR*, March 8, 1991.

[26]*Izvestia*, March 25, 1991.

[27]Stepan Kiselyov, "Siamese Twins," *Moscow News*, No. 12, 1991.

[28]See, for instance, Yuri Afanasyev, "The Coming Dictatorship?" and Peter Reddaway, "Empire on the Brink," *The New York Review*, January 31, 1991.

[29]See, for instance, "Mikhail Gorbachev: I Will Not Be a Dictator!" *Golos*, 1, January 5–11, 1991.

[30]*Izvestia*, March 25, 1991

[31]As related to me by the jurist Boris Zolotukhin.

I

Thinking About the Soviet Future

GEORGE W. BRESLAUER

University of California at Berkeley

The question, "can Gorbachev's reforms succeed?" cannot be addressed without specifying what we mean by "Gorbachev's reforms," and what we mean by "success." Let me take these issues in turn.

Three Russian-language terms usually summarize the changes that Gorbachev has advanced as his program: glasnost, *demokratizatsiia,* and perestroika. Glasnost refers to the liberalization of public expression. *Demokratizatsiia* refers to democratization of the political order's norms of association, representation, competition, and accountability. Perestroika refers to the decentralization of authority to make major economic decisions, and to the creation of markets to coordinate those decisions. In a sense, all three terms refer to a process of marketization: the public arena as increasingly a marketplace of ideas; the political process as increasingly a marketplace of competition for office, status, and power; the economy as increasingly a marketplace for the creation and exchange of wealth.

Gorbachev probably did not anticipate how far he would go in these directions when he took office in March 1985; nor did he know when he began to radicalize his policy advocacy during the winter of 1986-87. But social, economic, and political circumstances appear to have pushed him toward support for increasingly radical reform. We cannot know at any point in time what Gorbachev defines as the nonnegotiable limits of reform. He has probably made a virtue of necessity on many occasions and publicly justified degrees of marketization he had previously ruled out. It seems safe to guess, however, that he is enough of a product of his past, and enough of a politician, not to favor any of the following: dissolution of the Soviet Union, anarchy, or a mass-revolutionary overthrow of the system; a multiparty system with minority status for the Communist Party; an arena of public discourse in which "anything goes"; or a free-market system in which private ownership of the means of production is the norm, rather than the exception. He or his successors may ultimately be forced to accept one or the other of these extremes, as, for example, is currently taking place in Poland and Hungary. But Gorbachev's behavior thus far suggests that he is committed to avoiding these outcomes in the USSR.

Thus, when we speak of Gorbachev's reforms, we have in mind a process of liberalization, democratization, and economic decentralization that goes well beyond our previous definitions of "minor reforms," "moderate reforms," or "tinkering with the system." We instead have in mind a process of marketization that continues or deepens the challenge to political, ideational, and economic *monopoly* that characterized the Brezhnevite order.

In the area of glasnost we have already witnessed radical reform. The Soviet print and electronic media's treatment of domestic issues is almost as diversified and innovative as that in any liberal democracy. Of late, even Lenin and Gorbachev have come under public attack (though not frequently). On matters of foreign policy, diversity of public expression is less fully developed. The recent televising of debates in the Congress of People's Deputies and in the Supreme Soviet, however, dramatically expanded the limits of permissible criticism on foreign and defense policy as well, which may have an impact on the editorial policy of newspapers and journals.

Political democratization has taken off during 1989. Many obstacles to democratic competition, representation, and accountability remain, all the more so in the provinces. But the institution of competitive elections, the creation of a power structure to rival that of the Party-State apparatus (the Congress of People's Deputies and the soviets at all levels), the legitimation of informal organizations of all sorts (now numbering well over sixty thousand), the creation of popular fronts in many republics, the networking, coordination, and publicity available to lobbying and mass-action organizations in varied locations—all these constitute a radical departure from the norms of Brezhnevism, indeed of Leninism as well. The development of new legal codes to institutionalize a more democratic order proceeds apace as well, though it is a lengthy, less dramatic, and less public process. But if it eventually parallels the political changes now taking place, it could substantially constrain political or bureaucratic arbitrariness, insulate the judiciary from regular political intervention, and take a big step toward the "law-based state" Gorbachev proclaims as his goal. Whether this will also involve an independent legal order and the "rule of law" as understood in liberal democracies remains to be seen.

Radical changes have also taken place in the economy, especially in the partial legalization of private enterprise in town and countryside (cooperatives, leasing of land and of industrial plant), as well as in changes in the foreign trade sector. But otherwise, while important changes in both law and, to a lesser extent, behavior have been instituted in the socialized and state-run sectors, the most crucial issue—price reform—has not yet been addressed. Indeed, the regime appears to be so wary of the political, social, and economic disruptions that could result from price reforms that it has formally postponed dealing with the issue until at least 1991. In the meantime, the economy continues to stagnate. The cooperative sector has expanded greatly during 1988-89, but it is mostly small-scale, contributes as yet little to the GNP or standard of living, and is widely resented by officials and public alike. The failure to deal with price reform has kept the state-run economy in a condition of impasse. In sum, one could well argue that widespread movement toward marketization has not taken place in the economy to a degree even comparable to that which has occurred in political expression and competition. The economy has not yet been radically reformed, an observation that is related to, but distinct from, the observation that the condition of the consumer sectors remains appalling.

This has created a situation in which public discontent can be expressed, often vociferously, while economic improvements are not yet available to cushion the force of those expressions and prevent their escalation beyond established limits. The result has been an interesting dynamic. Demands for political participation have escalated virtually out of control, while pessimism and cynicism about the prospects for economic perestroika appear to be spreading and intensifying among the population. Gorbachev's response has been typically to use those demands (such as the recent major labor strikes in Siberian and Ukrainian coalfields) to justify radicalization of reform of the polity or economy. He is seeking to create channels for the institutionalization of more democratic and market-oriented procedures to keep pace with escalating demands and frustrations. At the same time, he has sought thereby to prevent demands for secession from the USSR, or for a multiparty system, from becoming widespread.

DEFINING SUCCESS

There are, in principle, many alternatives to continued or further movement in the direction of radical reform. A minimalist, negative definition of "success" might simply mean avoidance of those alternatives: systemic breakdown; a conservative restoration (whether Brezhnevite or in the form of a militarized regime); or a fascist backlash (be it Russite-fundamentalist, Stalinist, or populist-other variant). Any of these would represent the failure of reform. Or failure could be defined as the indefinite perpetuation of the current situation, with a stalemate in the economic and ethnic situations, and a continuing condition of social turmoil in many locales.

A more positive definition of success would envisage the creation of a relatively stable system that represents some variant of a democratic polity and a marketized economy. Politically, this might entail a multiparty system, or possibly only competitive and public politics within the context of a dominant party system. Economically, marketization might result in free-market capitalism or, short of that, some variant of market socialism or regulated capitalism.

Pessimists who believe in the unreformability of the Soviet system have low expectations about what can be achieved, and might, therefore, view the avoidance of basic alternatives to reform as the most that one can hope for. Optimists, on the other hand, are more likely to embrace more ambitious reform scenarios as the measure of success. The choice between a pessimistic-negative and an optimistic-positive measure may hinge on the political preferences or personal temperament of the analyst, on that individual's perception of the relative strength of pro-reformist and anti-reformist interests in Soviet officialdom and society, or on the observer's theory of the prerequisites for radical reform in analogous milieux historically and in the contemporary world.

I will not speculate about the biases or temperaments of analysts. I will instead focus on the second of these considerations: the image of Soviet social structure and popular attitudes, of Soviet political structure and official attitudes, and of the impact of the international context on prospects for successful radical reform. I will treat each of these topics in turn, specifying how one's perceptions of each can be the basis for counsels of alarm (pessimists) or counsels of hope (optimists). I will then turn to several other issues that feed into pessimistic and optimistic forecasts, not in order to determine who is right, but rather to lay bare the varieties of assumptions that can underpin pessimism and optimism about the Soviet future. Throughout, I will emphasize the importance of leadership and leadership strategies as intervening variables that may be decisive in determining the success of reform.

SOCIAL STRUCTURE AND ATTITUDES

Obstacles to Radical Reform

One's image of Soviet social structure, and of present attitudes toward reform on the part of different groups, contributes greatly to one's conception of the chances that reform can succeed. In contrast to Blair Ruble's emphasis in chapter 5 on social factors facilitating, or even pushing, reform, pessimists such as George Feiffer would emphasize social and attitudinal obstacles to reform.[1] One such obstacle is the widespread social demoralization that many observers perceive among large segments of the population. Under Brezhnev, this expressed itself in an epidemic of alcoholism. Among the professional classes, the same phenomenon expressed itself in a loss of faith in the reformability of the system, a loss of optimism about the future, and a sense of anomie.[2] Young people became cynical and self-regarding, placing rock 'n roll and jeans over public causes and work satisfaction in their hierarchy of values.

A second ingredient in counsels of alarm is the purported conservative effect of the Brezhnevite welfare-state on attitudes, particularly among the working class. Brezhnevism provided a spare cradle-to-grave social security for the population. It subsidized prices on basic commodities, rent for state apartments, job security in one's place of current employment, and relatively low wage differentials between productive and unproductive employees. It discouraged risk-taking by providing incentives for managerial and worker risk-avoidance. Moreover, it reinforced in its propaganda, policies, and organizational structure a deep-seated Russian (and, globally, peasant), sense of envy. Definitionally, envy differs from jealousy. Those who are jealous of someone else want to have what that other person has. Those who are envious want that other person not to have what they have; that is, they want to drag that person down to their level. Clearly, jealousy is compatible with, indeed functional for, a market economy, envy is dysfunctional, for it encourages leveling downward, rather than aspiration and achievement. All these features of the Brezhnevite welfare-state frustrate the search for economic efficiency through marketization. And Gorbachev's reluctance to tackle the issue of price reform, to sanction widespread bankruptcies of inefficient enterprises, and to struggle very hard on behalf of the cooperatives, which are the objects of widespread envy and complaint, is a major constraint on reform.

Counsels of alarm along this dimension also sometimes point to a xenophobic and authoritarian political culture that provides the basis for an intolerance of the diversity and openness that political-economic marketization would engender. At best this could frustrate the reform process; at worst it could provide the social basis for a right-wing reaction.³ The problem is compounded by its overlap with the issue of inter-ethnic relations. The Russian chauvinist tendency in both Russia and the minority republics is a powerful support for reactions against both the traumas of austerity and transition, and the rapidly growing assertiveness of ethnic minorities throughout the Soviet Union. Directly and indirectly, these tendencies have been coupled to a siege mentality, a Manichean worldview, a missionary urge, and a severe distrust of foreigners. In its most extreme form, this has facilitated regime-initiated pogroms. In its less extreme forms, it has facilitated official efforts to justify a repressive authoritarian regime.

In addition to being xenophobic, both Russian and Soviet political cultures have been authoritarian, paternalistic and regimented, instilling in many people a belief that the only alternative to order is anarchy, and that a strong boss is needed to ensure social cohesion. These anti-liberal features have been further reinforced by a culture that never extolled the notion of individual rights, individualism, or contracts, and which embraced substantive, rather than procedural, definitions of justice (i.e. "who wins" is more important than "fair play"). To the extent that radical reforms move the system toward rule of law, contracts, commercialism, procedural definitions of justice, and so on, they will have to overcome or circumvent these biases of the mass political culture.

The final social structural basis for pessimism is the ethnic situation. Although the bases and nature of ethnic assertiveness vary both between and within republics, the counsel of alarm emphasizes the apparent intractability of the ethnic problem as a whole. Ethnic assertiveness in the Baltic states has reached the point of secession, an outcome that Moscow presumably cannot live with. A top Party leader, Politburo-member Alexander Yakovlev, has suggested the acceptability of a relationship of suzerainty between center and periphery, wherein Moscow continues to control only foreign affairs, defense, and macro-economic planning. Presumably, Moscow could live with a loose federal or confederal arrangement, and with a political process that adopts features of the "consociationalism" analyzed in Western democracies by Arend Lijphard.⁴ But it remains to be seen whether confederalism would be workable given the interdependencies in the USSR's

industrial economy. And even if workable, it is not clear that
Baltic separatists, for example, would be willing to settle for consociationalism rather than full independence. Finally, this "solution" clashes with the issue of the rights of ethnic out-groups
within the minority republics (Russians in Estonia; Armenians in
Azerbaidzhan), the bolstering of which has been integral to Soviet
nationality policy for almost sixty years. Any solution to one
ethnic problem appears to create another ethnic dilemma. The
burden of argumentation would appear to fall on those who claim
that the ethnic situation is ultimately manageable.

Facilitators of Radical Reform

Counsels of alarm are rooted in, among other things, a
particular perception or image of Soviet social structure and popular orientations. Counsels of hope, on the other hand, are rooted
in a very different image of the same phenomena. First, optimists
such as Ruble argue that Soviet social structure has been transformed dramatically by modernization and education.[5] A new
social structure has been created, which includes the "new middle
class," skilled blue-collar strata, and, from a generational standpoint, the "yuppies." Collectively, these strata number in the tens
of millions, many of whom are purportedly eager to employ their
skills and initiative in a context that will promise a payoff (whether
public or private). True, these are the strata that were demoralized,
or had turned cynical, under Brezhnev. But it does not necessarily
follow that they are irredeemable.

Gorbachev has clearly targeted these strata as the people he
hopes to inspire and reactivate on behalf of entrepreneurialism
and political initiative. He has been attempting, through glasnost,
laws on cooperatives, multi-candidate elections, the encouragement of informal groups, and other measures to create an environment in which independent political and economic initiative will
prove rewarding. Optimists argue that the social demoralization
of earlier years, and the widespread fears of risk-taking, were
rational situational responses to the structure of incentives under
Brezhnev; S. Frederick Starr would go further and argue that
informal groupings abounded under Brezhnev and that mass communications, licit and illicit, were abundant, as the populace took

advantage of modern technology to mobilize itself.[6] Moreover, the scope of the second economy under Brezhnev belied the notion that either a commercial spirit or the work ethic had been destroyed in the USSR. And Paul Gregory's findings from émigré interviewing support the proposition that low labor exertion under Brezhnev was more often a product of the incentive structure than of alcoholism or sloth.[7] Since Brezhnev, changes in the structure of incentives, which is what reform is all about, have changed both behavioral tendencies and attitudes. Certainly the explosion of informal groups in the USSR (well over 60,000), the recent doubling in the number of individuals working in cooperatives and "individual labor activity," and the widespread political mobilization connected with elections to the Congress of People's Deputies and the local soviets encourages us to think of the Soviet middle classes as active not passive, potentially entrepreneurial not hopelessly risk-averse. A recent public opinion poll at a Soviet vocational-technical school found that 44 percent of the students looked forward to making their careers in the cooperative sector.

Even at the mass levels, the process of moving toward reform, and the glasnost campaign's elevation of popular consciousness, can erode the passive, authoritarian mentality of the traditional political culture. We have seen this in the political maturity of mass demonstrations in the Baltic states, the Ukraine, Moldavia, and Armenia, where the middle and lower classes have joined forces to exploit new opportunities for political empowerment. We have seen it in the level of discipline and sophistication displayed by workers in the major coal miners' strikes in the Kuzbass and Donbass regions. And we see it in a recent nationwide poll following the televised proceedings of the Congress of People's Deputies. 53 percent of respondents agreed in full with Andrei Sakharov's characterization of the war in Afghanistan as a "criminal war," while an additional 15 percent agreed with him "in part." As a leading Soviet analyst of public opinion concluded: the masses were not conservative or reactionary, they were sleeping under Brezhnev. Now they are waking up, and their level of political consciousness is rising rapidly, while their level of political liberality is perhaps higher than we had assumed.

Contrasts between the optimistic and pessimistic images of Soviet society are striking, but they are not irreconcilable.

Optimists do not deny that xenophobia, social demoralization, a risk-averse, welfare-state mentality, envy, Russian chauvinism, and xenophobia are features of Soviet society. However, optimists rebel against the tendency to feature these as the *dominant* tendencies, to treat them as immutable or as incapable of being neutralized, or to view them as attitudes divorced from their social context. For example, while optimists might concede the existence of intense anti-reform sentiments, they would insist on a more complex portrait of the distribution of such sentiments, and of their social roots. Among which social forces, in what geographic locales, are xenophobia, Russian-chauvinism, and envy most prevalent? Counsels of hope are based on an image of Soviet society that displays the "modernizing" tendencies as actually or potentially dominant—strong to begin with, and getting stronger. Optimists view the process of reform as one during which the structure of political and economic incentives reinforces modernizing attitudes. Counsels of alarm, in contrast, view the "drag" of traditional attitudes as great enough to lace the reform process with compromises, hesitations, and contradictions that will prevent it from effecting a decisive breakthrough in a marketizing direction.

Clearly, we do not have sufficient evidence about the actual distribution of attitudes within the Soviet social structure to resolve this clash between optimists and pessimists. But, accepting the probability that both traditional and modernizing tendencies are *widespread* in the USSR, it is reasonable to suggest that the future will hinge in part on the leadership strategies employed to reinforce modernizing, and undermine traditional, attitudes. It will be necessary to structure incentives to offset social demoralization, risk-aversion, and the welfare-state mentality. It will be necessary to offset or insulate xenophobic tendencies. And, if economic reform is to succeed, it will be necessary to change envy into jealousy through transformative leadership that seeks to alter popular biases—a function of transformative leadership to which I will return below.

The nationalities problem appears to be more intractable, for it adds a centrifugal component to the impact of modernization and education that may not be containable. However, for Gorbachev (or his successors) to manage (not solve) the ethnic crisis, they will probably have to follow some of the suggestions offered by Lapidus and Ruble in their contributions to this volume. They will have to forge a *differentiated* strategy that takes cognizance of the diversified character of the "nationality problem" in different republics, that accommodates aspirations for autonomy while refusing to accommodate intercommunal violence, that establishes institutions of conflict management that gain legitimacy as they seek to temper passions. And they will need luck, both at home and abroad. I know of no Western expert on the Soviet nationalities problem who is genuinely optimistic that the crisis will be successfully managed. Experts divide more between counselors of alarm and counselors of despair.

THE PARTY-STATE AND OFFICIAL ATTITUDES

Obstacles to Radical Reform

Counsels of alarm are typically based on distinctive perceptions of the party-state. One feature of that perception is bureaucratic entrenchment and corruption. Deeply entrenched party and economic bureaucracies, stretching over a huge land mass, and widely corrupted by the indulgence of the Brezhnev era, constitute a formidable obstacle to reform. Both political accountability and a genuinely free market would undermine the political autonomy and status of bureaucrats who have much to lose from such a change. Not only would it threaten their career prospects, their rights to control political and economic relationships in their domain, and their self-conception, it would also threaten their socio-economic privileges, on which they, their families, and their friends have come to depend, either (in somes cases) for a decent standard of living or (in other cases) for a luxurious standard of living.

This resistance will be difficult to break. Bureaucratization per se is not the problem. It is bureaucratic entrenchment and corruption that is difficult to dismantle. One need only think of Soviet public administration as dominated by corrupt political machines to envisage the problem. Tammany Hall, the Chicago machine—each required autonomous public movements, drawing upon the coercive resources and political muscle of other levels of government, to break their power.

331

Another dimension of this image of the party-state is a perception that the military and KGB are institutions that are not comfortable with the implications and side-effects of glasnost, political democratization, or consumer sovereignty. Military leaders have long enjoyed privileged access to scarce resources, both during the decision-making processs over investment priorities and during the subsequent struggle to fulfill the plan. Any move toward consumer sovereignty, as an adjunct to economic reform, would threaten that access. The KGB, in turn, must fear an environment of openness toward the outside world, as well as manifestations of disorder at home. In part this stems from an ethos that the KGB shares with the military, and with most militaries in the world: a passion for discipline and order. In part, though, it stems from the profoundly unsettling ambiguity facing KGB, MVD, and military officials, as they try to distinguish political from non-political crime, anti-state from within-system behavior (especially in the minority republics), and illegitimate police behavior from legitimate during this period of glasnost, "learning democracy," and transition to a "legal state." In a liberalizing and destabilized political milieu, some cops are eager to bash heads; others are afraid of being accused of police brutality; all are ambivalent or hostile toward the process that made the new milieu possible. Whether as a result of a KGB-military alliance or not, the prospect of praetorianism looms large in the counsels of alarm.[8]

Counsels of alarm also emerge from the images of the Soviet political order propounded by theorists who characterize the Brezhnevite system as partocratic or neo-traditional.[9] Kenneth Jowitt's is the most subtle and convincing of these theories, combining a complex characterization of the Soviet party-state with a theory of modernization that attempts to explain and predict the evolution of this type of state.[10]

From Jowitt's perspective, the widespread corruption of party and state officials has been proceeding apace during the past twenty-five years. He explains this corruption not in the general terms of Lord Acton ("power tends to corrupt, and absolute power corrupts absolutely"), but as stemming from features more distinctive to this political order. He argues that the elitism intrinsic to Leninism, based on party officials' self-proclaimed higher insight into historical necessity, provides a basis for aristo-cratization. Such a process was held in check under Stalin by the combination of a heroic "social combat task" (e.g. collectiviza-tion) and terror. But in the post-Stalin era, when each of these has been largely eliminated, party officials became corrupted, demanding "tribute" and other concrete demonstrations of defer-ence and recognition of their higher worth, as substitutes for the heroic roles they once performed. The result of spreading cor-ruption, nepotism, and aristocratization is that modernizing tendencies in the post-Stalin era come to be embedded in, and dependent upon, a political-cultural and political-institutional context that is the decisive determinant of what is possible. Put differently, this context ensures that, whatever the distribution of traditional and modern attitudes across society, the ability to act upon these attitudes will be shaped and skewed by the dominant institutional context. Generational change notwithstanding, the neo-traditional party-state subordinates modern tendencies to its higher priorities.[11] The result, according to Jowitt, is that the USSR, like many Third World states, or like the Ottoman Empire, will bounce between ineffectual and limited efforts to reform itself and likely backlashes that will put the marketizing elements (both political and economic) back in their place. Neither marketization nor democratization, from this perspective, can go very far, given Jowitt's conception of what is politically possible in a system and society dominated by a Leninist party-state.

Jowitt, like Brzezinski and Lowenthal, who reach analo-gous conclusions but by a different path, shares the counsels of alarm, in part because he adheres to a relatively undifferentiated image of establishment interests. He treats the party apparatus as relatively monolithic with respect to *status* orientations, united in its commitment to maintaining the leading, dominant role of the apparatus, with functional differentiation not a strong enough component to neutralize this deeper basis for unity. He does per-ceive within the apparatus a more consequential split between the ascetics and the corrupted (from which he derives the political base for predictions of an alternation between periods of entrench-ment of corruption and campaigns against it). He differentiates little between the interests of the top leadership and the interests of the bulk of Soviet officialdom, for he sees the level of leadership autonomy as quite low, treating the leaders as highly constrained by the requirements of accountability to elite constituencies. This view of the establishment is consistent with Jowitt's emphasis on the Leninist character of the party-state and, more importantly, with his view of Leninism as a monolithic ideology. For Jowitt, the ideological tradition can justify heroic projects, party interventionism, and anti-corruption campaigns as ways of breaking through stagnation. But it cannot justify a breakout that seeks to institutionalize the rule of law, market coordination, or public opposition to the "leading role of the party." Hence, Jowitt's could be called a tightly-bounded cyclical view of the Soviet future (in contrast, say, to those who envisage the real possibility of a Hitler-like fascist backlash against the turmoil of Gorbachev's "Weimar Russia".[12]

To some extent, the relationship between Jowitt's image of the establishment and his predictions for the future is a product of his theory or philosophy of history. Jowitt is very impressed by the power of *identity* concerns in pre-modern systems, and therefore views the party apparatus as an obstacle to reform as obdurate and resilient as a medieval aristocracy.

In sum, whether based upon a developmental theory of Soviet history or an empirical image of attitudes within Soviet officialdom today, counsels of despair are supported by a relatively *monolithic* image of the Soviet establishment, the Soviet ideological heritage, and the relationship between the two.

Facilitators of Radical Reform

In contrast, those who are optimistic about the chances for successful reform in the USSR tend to buttress their case with a more differentiated image of establishment interests and attitudes. According to this perspective, there are reformists as well as conservatives, radicals as well as reactionaries, technocrats as well as traditional mobilizers, cosmopolitans as well as parochials, ascetics as well as "aristocratizers," regionalists as well as centralists, anti-corruption fighters as well as the corrupted within the party and state apparatuses.[13] In many officials, several of these orientations probably coexist, sometimes in ways that are mutually reinforcing (e.g. reformist plus cosmopolitan plus anti-corruption), sometimes in ways that conflict. These differences are not all based simply on functional differentiation; they go deeper, and suggest the existence within the party of a political base searching for a fundamental redefinition of the meaning of the "leading role of the party" in the contemporary era. That is, they challenge the image of a party that is monolithic regarding the definition of its *status*, not just role, in the country. What's more, generalizations about the distribution of these "types," while based on scanty data, nonetheless distinguish convincingly between the interests of the central leadership or central party apparatus in Moscow and the interests of many regional elites. The *relative autonomy of the leadership* from its political base, and the all-union, "national interest" perspective its job requires, combine to make for a greater proclivity for transformative thrusts at the top than in the middle of the party-state. Of course, under Brezhnev the conservatives controlled the top leadership. But because of the distinctive vantage point and political needs of the central leadership, there is more likely to be a permanent reformist wing at the center than in the periphery. When circumstances permit or dictate (in particular, when a systemic crisis hits), that wing can come to power, as happened under Khrushchev and again under Gorbachev. None of this is accounted for when we think solely in terms of entrenched bureaucrats defending their "interests" or even their "status."

Counsels of hope also derive from a belief that the political structure of the party-state makes for a manipulable political order. This is so in two respects. First, the advantages of centralization make it easier for a Gorbachev to transform the bureacracy from above, by mobilizing supporters through the patron-client machinery at his disposal. Second, the nominally legislative arenas of the system (the soviets and the party committees [as opposed to the executive bureaus]), though subordinated to the executive structures for seventy years, are available for resuscitation as an alternative arena for political accountability—as, indeed, Gorbachev has done with his resurrection of the local and supreme soviets as new arenas of public power. This also provides Gorbachev an alternative arena within which to mobilize political leverage against entrenched and unreconstructed bureaucrats.

Counsels of hope also are based upon an image of the

ideology that is more differentiated than that propounded by counselors of alarm. While acknowledging that some aspects of the ideological tradition provide powerful support for conservatism and for an aversion to markets (be they political or economic), optimists point out that others provide compelling force for reform. For one thing, Soviet elite political culture displays an aversion to stagnation, and a need for a sense of progress, drama, optimism, and a mission. This helps to foster, and then to legitimize, transformative leadership. What's more, some form of "socialist democracy" or "market socialism" would not have to be legitimized from scratch. As Stephen Cohen has argued, the ideological heritage is substantively dualistic.[14] Lenin's last writings and the New Economic Policy (NEP) of the 1920s can be cited as precedents to justify both political and economic marketization. This is not to say that the aspects of the ideological heritage are equally weighted in Lenin's work, much less in Soviet history. But the actual weights are less important in political life than the fact that both are *available* for purposes of political justification, in a socio-economic context that today can make them compelling. Similarly, the formal ideology of the regime has always maintained the fiction that the soviets and the party committees were the "real" repositories of people's power in the Soviet Union, and that the executive bureaus were chosen by, and accountable to, the legislative arenas. The availability of that formal ideology helps to justify the resuscitation of those latent parliamentary arenas, which is precisely what Gorbachev has been doing during 1988-1989. Thus, a transformative leader in the Soviet context does not have to invent and will an ideological justification; he needs only to argue that the regime must live up to its claims. That does not ensure success against entrenched interests but it certainly makes things easier than they would otherwise be. Thus, a differentiated image of the ideological tradition buttresses a differentiated image of establishment interests and attitudes to provide bases for hope.

Official attitudes are also conditioned by a process of elite and specialist *learning*—a process that has been going on for almost forty years. Brezhnev's longevity contributed to the eventual reform process by thoroughly discrediting conservatism, which is now touted as synonymous with stagnation (*zastoi*). Although officials and specialists certainly vary greatly in their priorities, and in the price they are willing to pay for reform, radicals within the upper reaches of the political establishment have been able to seize the initiative by playing upon the widespread sense of there being no alternative to reform. The *idea* of reform, then, has been legitimized, even though battles rage over how far the process should be allowed to go. Moreover, thirty years of experimentation with more modest reform efforts, both in the USSR, Eastern Europe, and now China have afforded Soviet social scientists and journalists, and their political sponsors, a deeper understanding of the nature of systemic interdependencies, of the limits on the capacity of the unreformed system to perform, of the inevitability of corruption and stagnation in the absence of far-reaching reform, and of the potential consequences for Soviet international competitiveness of a failure to reform the system. On these scores as well, Khrushchev did not have the benefit of such a mood and mentality, a point that should be borne in mind by those who point to Khrushchev's fate as a harbinger of Gorbachev's failure. Thus, optimistic scenarios are typically based, not only on differentiated images of the party-state, and of its ideological tradition, but also on a political learning model of Soviet politics.

Based upon these concrete images of elite and ideational differentiation, counsels of hope are also often informed by theories of modernization that run counter to the neo-traditional theory advanced by Jowitt. The leading advocate of the "modernizing" conception of recent Soviet developmental history has been Jerry Hough, who argues that educational levels, expertise, tolerance of ambiguity, and political (as opposed to commandist) orientations among Soviet officials have been increasing steadily during the past thirty years.[15] In the absence of a generational shift, they might not have become dominant over the cruder traditional orientations. But the generational shift that is taking place, at both the societal and the establishment levels, is making, and will make, a decisive difference for the future direction of the regime. Gorbachev, then, is no accident. He is a representative of the modern wings within the party apparatus. The result will be a more relaxed authoritarian regime, or a partially democratized system, and a significantly marketized economic system that is more fully integrated into the world economy.

Treating the USSR as an embryonic modern system, Hough envisages the growing ascendancy of modern over traditional premises in decision-making (indeed, his work hardly ever discusses corruption). Because Hough does not view either the establishment or the ideology as relatively monolithic, and because he is impressed by generational differences in orientation among Soviet officials, he rejects the image of a political institutional and political cultural heritage that is even inclined to, much less able to, "decisively subordinate" modern to neo-traditional orientations. Thus Hough, in contrast to Jowitt and other pessimists, treats interests as highly subjective and variable over time and as due to circumstances. He downplays issues of identity and privilege and treats the party apparatus as an institution that can change its traditional orientations as a result of generational change and learning.

Not surprisingly, Hough, in contrast to Jowitt, also emphasizes leadership autonomy within the establishment. He posits that the leadership is not captured by constituencies. He further posits that the leadership has a high capacity to ensure enactment and implementation of reformist policies. This is why Hough has, throughout the 1980s, emphasized the centrality of the patron-client system in Soviet politics, and the large scope of Gorbachev's power consolidation. He embraces the image of a highly manipulable political order.

Optimists typically also differ from pessimists in their view of the *permeability* of the political establishment by societal influences. Brzezinski, Lowenthal, and Jowitt tended to treat the establishment as continually seeking, and gaining, a high level of insulation from autonomously mobilized social forces. In contrast, most counsels of hope are based upon the view that Soviet society has evolved greatly in the past quarter-century *and* that those evolving orientations have infiltrated the political establishment, both through co-optation and through influence. The combination of a learning theory, a theory of generational change, and a theory concerning the impact of social forces on political processes distinguishes the optimists sharply from the pessimists. The pessimists envisage degeneration and decay, analogous to Ottomanization of the USSR.[16] The optimists come closer to propounding some variant of convergence theory, whereby the structuring effect of modernization eventually erodes and then subordinates traditional biases.[17]

Both competing images of social structure and competing images of the political establishment capture important elements of the empirical truth, while differing irreconcilably on some interpretive issues. And in both cases we lack the empirical data to chart the distribution of attitudes and orientations very precisely. Nor do we possess either the data or the validated theory of history to allow us to claim with confidence that one set of orientations is destined to win out over the other set. What we can say with confidence, I believe, is that the diversity of orientations provides opportunities, the realization of which will probably hinge on the quality of reformist leadership strategies employed to effect what Zaslavskaya puts forth as the key to the success of such a strategy: to "mobilize the winners and demobilize the losers."[18]

THE INTERNATIONAL CONTEXT

Obstacles to Radical Reform

The main obstacles to reform in the international arena might be called the constraining impact of global overextension. As proponents of the thesis of imperial decline, such as Paul Kennedy, argue, great powers in modern history have frequently experienced decline and "fall" because their international commitments exceeded their economic capacities—draining their treasuries, distorting their economies, and ultimately their international economic and military competitiveness as well.[19] According to counsels of alarm, then, the Soviet international situation fits this pattern well. Worldwide Soviet foreign policy commitments have become a continuing drain, not only on Soviet resources, but also on the attention-span of Soviet leaders. If the international situation were to worsen, and the arms race to be renewed, it would desperately strain the budget and limit the disposable surplus available for redistribution to the benefit of reform. What's more, global overextension increases the probability that crises will suddenly undermine détente in the East-West relationship, and reinforce the political strength of xenophobic forces at home. Finally, overextension in Eastern Europe can generate crises that, if they do not undermine political stability within the USSR itself, can discredit the cause of reformism in the USSR by allowing the same process to get out of hand in Eastern Europe (see the chapter by J. F. Brown in this volume).

Factors Facilitating Radical Reform

The situation abroad can also be a powerful support for reform, either as justification of the necessity for reform or as an influence on the course of reform. Thus, as a source of justification throughout both Russian and Soviet history, there has existed a strong relationship between modernization strategies and perceived national security imperatives. To cite but one example of recent memory, Stalin justified the tempos of industrialization in 1931 by arguing that the alternative would be to be crushed by foreign predators. Similarly, Gorbachev initially justified perestroika in precisely these terms. He cited the economic and military security implications of technological backwardness, and held out the prospect of the USSR slipping to second-class power status in the absence of reform.

There are other international factors that help a reformist Soviet leader to justify the pain of transformation. One of these is ideological. Soviet elite political culture has viewed the USSR as the founding father of an international movement. This makes Soviet leaders unusually sensitive to ideological humiliation. To the extent that Soviet backwardness is embarrassing to officials and intelligentsia alike, and to the extent that successful reform in other socialist systems (for example, prospectively in Eastern Europe or China) makes the USSR appear backward vis-a-vis others within the movement, it facilitates the efforts of Soviet reformists to legitimize their case. Such embarrassment, when combined with the above-mentioned national security fears, may explain why some party ideologues in the USSR are leading theorists of reform. And beyond ideological embarrassment, dominant tendencies toward marketization and privatization in all the leading industrial countries, as well as in the Third World, undermine the morale and persuasiveness of those in the Soviet establishment who argue that radical reform is not necessary in order to maintain international political, economic, and military competitiveness.

While these aspects of the international environment make it easier to justify reform, other aspects provide impetus at the societal level, or create linkages that add momentum to the reform process. One such factor is the "pull" of Westernization. There has long since been a Westernizing pull at both the elite and societal levels. Stalin enforced insulation bordering on isolation against it. Since Stalin, and especially since the early-1970s, Soviet elite and society have been increasingly penetrated by Western ideas, information, science, cultural fads, and standards of comparison regarding economic well-being. It is no coincidence that reformist Soviet leaders tout the centrality of the "information revolution" in the world today. They are aware that international communications have altered conceptions of sovereignty, and that it is fruitless to try to insulate their country from such communications. The computer and satellite revolutions probably make this a hopeless exercise in any case. The tension between these international influences, on the one hand, and xenophobic proclivities and conservative concerns for political control, on the other hand, was palpable during the Brezhnev era. The dilemma is that continued insulation from the information revolution would not only cripple the reform process, but would further alienate the large urban younger generation and perpetuate Soviet scientific backwardness.

Part of Gorbachev's reform program is a conscious effort to break through obstacles and to allow large-scale penetration. A tremendous expansion of exchange programs, tourism, and other access to the West has taken place. Jamming of Radio Liberty, Voice of America, Deutsche Welle, BBC and Israeli Radio has ceased. Computers may now be imported with ease. Yesterday's dissident behavior is today's mainstream glasnost. Rock 'n' roll has been allowed to flourish above-ground, and to become a model for youth. Soviet scientists are rapidly becoming more fully integrated into the international scientific community. The list could be extended.

The attraction of foreign travel, ideas, fads, forms, science, and goods for wide strata of both society and the elite is undeniable.[20] It will continue to compete vigorously for predominance with xenophobic tendencies. But to the extent that this is a generational phenomenon—and the evidence suggests that it is—

generational change will strengthen the Westernizing biases markedly. That is good news for supporters of reform.

Gorbachev has made it a central feature of his foreign policy program to forge an international environment supportive of his reform program. He has crafted a largely concessionary foreign policy in order to create the kind of placid international environment that would allow him to offset xenophobic moods within the USSR, save money, and harness international forces supportive of reform in his country.[21] As David Holloway in Chapter 7 shows, Gorbachev has also sponsored a series of doctrinal reformulations that amount to a redefinition of the philosophical bases of Soviet ideology. This allows him to justify a concessionary foreign policy and to undertake precisely the kinds of changes at home and abroad that Kennedy urges on great powers seeking to avert decline.

The international economy can also provide a powerful support for reform. Indeed, "opening up the Soviet economy" to the competition and investment of the international economy has been a plank of Gorbachev's reform program and, it is claimed by Hough, a means of creating interdependencies that provide a "push" for further reform of the economy.[22] These are themes as well of the chapters by Herbert Levine and Laura Tyson in the present volume. Thus far, the Soviets have legalized joint ventures that allow majority ownership of Soviet projects by foreign capitalists. They have vigorously sought membership in GATT and are now pondering a push for membership in the International Monetary Fund and the World Bank. There are, of course, many obstacles to such integration of the Soviet Union into the global economy. Tyson points to ways in which the Soviet Union is likely to remain an unattractive focus of foreign investments [though recent events in Germany suggest that political considerations may lead to large Western investments in Eastern Europe anyway]. And Levine points to such problems as ruble inconvertibility and the lack of price reform as a major constraint on such integration. Thus, relatively little progress has been made to date toward the final goal of integration, but important first steps have been taken. The point, however, is that both the prospect and the incremental actualization of such integration are powerful impetuses for further reform, and for the entrenchment of relationships created by reform measures. Presumably, success in such integration would also improve the performance of the Soviet economy.

Thus, the international context of reform can support both images of alarm and images of hope, depending upon the specific features of that context during the reform process. In the midst of an expensive arms race, the reform process is likely to be undermined, offsetting such factors as the pull of Westernization and ideological embarrassment. Much may depend, therefore, on both luck and the quality of leadership in Moscow seeking to guide the transition. Our discussion of international factors highlights what may be the crucial role of leadership strategies in shaping the international environment. Paul Kennedy's book has unfairly been criticized as deterministic and overly pessimistic: as describing a tendency for great powers to decline because of global extension. But Kennedy goes to such lengths to describe the pattern precisely in order to warn Western leaders to change their policies and avoid the fate of previous great powers. Kennedy's depiction of the dilemma fits the Soviet Union even better than it does the United States. And his prescription for avoiding decline reads as if Gorbachev and he have been consulting each other. Whether Gorbachev's strategies will ultimately succeed in reversing decline, however, remains to be seen.

It is instructive to note how the leading American theorists of Soviet development factor the international environment into their explanations and predictions. Thus, Brzezinski, Lowenthal, and Jowitt, the leading counselors of alarm, tend to ignore the international environment as a determining or decisively conditioning factor. Their models are largely self-contained. A relatively monolithic Leninist party-state is simply incapable of reforming itself. The condition of the international environment is not treated as a variable capable of affecting the course of structural change. It may spur rising demands for change from society. But recall that these authors all tend to view the establishment as insulated from society. To the extent that Jowitt treats the international environment in his other work, he emphasizes Soviet leaders' urge to avoid dependency and their self-image as leaders of the world communist movement.[23] But he views each of these as reinforcing conservatism, which squares with his image of Leninist ideology and organization.

Hough, in contrast, while generally optimistic about the prospects for reform being pushed by internal forces, sees the international context as an important ally of the reform process. A proper leadership strategy, he argues, would put an end to Soviet economic protectionism and force Soviet managers to compete on world markets, thereby generating additional external pressures for Soviet internal entrepreneurialism.

Alexander Yanov, another theorist and observer of the Soviet scene,[24] is a Soviet émigré who has devoted himself to pondering and influencing the course of Russian history. His work deserves to be brought into our discussion at this point because it represents a distinct perspective, based on a particular mix of views on the nature of Soviet society, politics, and their relationship to the international environment. Yanov is a counselor of both alarm and hope. His image of Soviet state and society is closer to Jowitt's than to Hough's. He views the system as premodern and is impressed by the fierce continuity throughout Russian and Soviet history, such that efforts at democratization or Westernization have regularly been squelched by extremist backlashes and totalitarian restorations. His image of Brezhnevism was that of a highly polarized political establishment and society, within which, in the absence of major reform, the right-wing Russian chauvinists stood a very good chance of coming to power, liquidating all opposition, and restoring a reign of terror. His analogue for the Soviet system was neither the Western industrial world nor the Third World; it was Weimar Germany.

However, Yanov was more optimistic than Jowitt about the possibility of an alternative winning out, in part because he adhered to a more differentiated image of interests within the establishment and an image of establishment permeability by society. He discerned reformist forces in the "aristocratizing elite" (central officials) and the "new managers" that could combine with modern social forces (skilled workers, new middle class, critical intelligentsia) to create a marketized system. However, because Yanov perceived the neo-Stalinist Right to be so strong at both the elite and societal levels, he considered the reformist alternative to be the lesser probability. But the scales could be tipped, he argued, by the condition of the international environment. An arms race, and the failure of the West to materially assist the reform process, would tip the scales against reform. But a benevolent international environment that sought to integrate the Soviet economy into the international economic order, and that was willing to invest heavily in a reformed Soviet economy, could prove decisive for the victory of reform.

In sum, Yanov's perspective is interestingly more contingent than those of the counselors of both hope and alarm. He believes that radical swings to the left or the right are likely, determined in large part by the leadership strategies employed in Moscow and in the West.

THE DAUNTING TASK OF MARKETIZATION

Even those who embrace images supportive of counsels of hope tend to admit that the process of reform is bound to be a very difficult one. The task of reforming any authoritarian system, and especially an anti-market, monopolistic Leninist system, is intellectually and politically daunting. Neither Soviet nor Western theory can tell Soviet leaders just what mix of market and plan even to aim for in order to effect a workable mix of growth, consumption, national security, and social equity. Economic theory cannot tell them how to avoid rampant inflation during the transition, though Levine's chapter in this volume stresses the need to embrace price reform. Political theory cannot tell them how to weather the political storm that often accompanies runaway inflation. Nor can Soviet or Western theory tell them whether "socialist democracy" (democratic one-party rule and a market economy not based on private property) is an impossible mirage of the leftist imagination (it has never been successfully created) or a viable goal. De Tocqueville can advise Soviet leaders that there is no more dangerous time for an authoritarian regime than when it begins to reform itself and discovers the need to backtrack as released social forces go "too far." Theorists of the history of democracy in Western Europe can advise the Kremlin that a "civic political culture" is required, based on individualism and commercialism, in order to support a market economy and a

democratic polity. These bits of advice, however, only alert Soviet
leaders as to how very far they have to go, and how dangerous to
stability can be the passage. They do not provide guidelines or
strategies for managing the marketization process. Nor do they
indicate whether there are alternatives short of capitalist liberal
democracy that might prove viable.

What's more, the process of transition is typically fraught
with contradictions, and the complexities of the ethnic situation
in the USSR compound the problem for Soviet leaders. Contradictions abound during the early stages of reform, as we can see
in contemporary China, Hungary, and Yugoslavia.[25] Rampant inflation is threatening to tear apart the Yugoslav federation. Rapidly
increasing social inequality has become a serious problem in all
three countries; authorities have been unwilling or unable to accommodate or channel political and/or ethnic demands, which
have escalated rapidly.

In the Soviet Union, other contradictions abound, making
it difficult to chart, much less manage, a transition. The Soviet
underworld is shaking down or otherwise dominating the weak
and vulnerable private service sector, creating the reality, not of
a market economy, but of a racket economy. Glasnost has
mobilized people faster than institutions could be created to regulate political conflict. The destruction of even the pretense of
ideological belief has created a moral-ideological vacuum con-
ducive to social disorder and loss of morale among the elite. The
Baltic states may be on the verge of declaring their independence
from the USSR. These are the conditions under which xenophobic
forces come to the fore with simple solutions. Should the Ukraine
blow up and see its politics dominated by similar demands, a
coalition of party, military, and KGB officials, along with the
National Bolshevik intelligentsia and xenophobic Russians, could
demand such repressive solutions. Under these conditions of political transition, economic marketization could pour fuel on the
fire, given its inevitable dislocations and inflationary tendencies.

In the midst of these and other contradictions, Soviet leaders find themselves lacking a political strategy or theory of transformation. It is not enough to say that the success of reform will
take a long time, or "will be a matter of generations." That statement is based on the tenuous assumption that gains will cumulate

rather than unravel. What critical early thrusts are required to achieve a decisive breakthrough against the obstacles to reform?[26] Through what process can the above contradictions be overcome or attenuated in order to facilitate cumulation of gains? How does one go about combining market and plan, democratization and limits, in ways that will not delegitimize the idea of reform? We do not know—nor, probably, does Gorbachev.

Is there hope? Lapidus' chapter on the nationalities problem in the USSR seems to suggest that there is. Though tackling the most intractable problem facing the Soviets, she nonetheless resists counsels of despair, suggests reasons for not assuming the worst, and proposes strategies for navigating the transition. Ruble draws a comparison with Quebec's "Quiet Revolution" to sustain a generally optimistic view. Bonnell's chapter in this volume alerts us to the proliferation of voluntary associations, and their transformation into politically-focused interest groups under Gorbachev, and argues that their institutionalization is a necessary condition for the successful democratization of the USSR. Levine's chapter on the daunting task of economic reform outlines the measures that Gorbachev must take to effectively decentralize the economy. Tyson's chapter takes a similar approach with respect to foreign economic relations, but views the international economy as more of a "hard" constraint that the Soviets might find very difficult to harness to their ends. Let me now propose still another approach to building a "bias for hope".[27] A broader historical perspective on transitions to democracy, and on the nature of transformative leadership, provides some hopeful insights.

BIAS FOR HOPE: SOME COMPARATIVE INSIGHTS

In his chapter, Blair Ruble draws some lessons from recent literature on transitions to democracy to bolster the case for hope. Let me add some more observations from that literature. Transitions are always messy. Democratization and marketization are never effected smoothly, by design from above. In the absence of real disruptions, both economic and political, a genuine transition to new ordering principles is not likely to occur. An unpredictable interaction tends to take place between elite initiatives and released social forces. Instability may be a temporary way-station to regime re-formation, rather than an end-state that dooms the democratization process. A singular focus on the contradictions inherent in the present situation, therefore, alerts us to the difficulties of transition, but not necessarily to its ultimate fate. Political strategies evolve as the elite learn and policies are adjusted. Hence, even optimists about the fate of reform would be wise to anticipate that perestroika will not proceed in unilinear fashion. Zigs and zags are probably inevitable. But an optimist should anticipate that consolidative zags, if not marked by a reactionary Stalinist restoration, will be followed by still more radical zigs. Optimists might therefore anticipate that the Soviet Union, during the next twenty years, with or without Gorbachev, will experience a *rolling reform*, much like the pattern followed in Hungary from 1968 to the present, rather than the previous pattern of a "treadmill" of minor or cosmetic reforms.[28] The defining characteristic of a rolling reform is that frustration due to half-measures leads, not to a backlash against reform per se (the previous Soviet pattern), but rather to a radicalization of the reform proposals enacted.

The recent literature on transitions to democracy differs from the first generation of such literature in ways relevant to our discussion. The earlier literature, which generalized largely from the West European experience, placed the emphasis on objective conditions, and reached the gloomy conclusion that socio-cultural and historical conditions unique to the Judeo-Christian heritage made possible the transitions to democracy in Western Europe. More recent literature, however, places a greater emphasis on the role of leadership as a crucial intervening variable. That is, there are several roads to democracy that are possible, under varied social conditions. Whether you travel one of those roads, and how far you go in the end, may hinge on the leadership strategies employed. For example, one's ability to restrain the military from intervening in politics when the predictable turmoil of transition takes place may be decisive (and, as David Holloway notes in his chapter in this volume, the Soviet military is cross-pressured and more fully controlled than are most Third World militaries). A second lesson of this literature is that a simple focus on intentionality can be misleading. In Western Europe, for example, circumstances often forced or lured non-democrats into democratic forms of behavior, which they later rationalized by adopting democratic beliefs or values. And democracy was rarely the primary goal of those pushing for it. It was sought as a means to some other end (usually, as Bryce pointed out, to "the wish to be rid of tangible evils").[29] The parallels with the USSR are obvious, and may explain the "greening of Gorbachev," as he has made a virtue of necessity in coping with released social forces demanding further democratization.

As Peter Hauslohner has noted:

> . . . recent cases of 'begun transitions' to democracy elsewhere in the world indicate that sometimes a ruling elite will initiate a process over which it then loses control. Incumbent leaders may institute partial political reforms from above, which become the cause or pretext of actions by other institutions and groups in society —actions which, if they come to threaten the existing political order, are liable to force their rulers to choose between additional changes not originally contemplated, or a strategic, and possibly more dangerous retreat.[30]

The most recent literature on transitions to democracy, by Giuseppe DiPalma, takes this observation one important step further, emphasizing the importance of *stalemate* among sharply conflicting social and political forces as an incubator of democratizing outcomes.[31] In the course of protracted, deep conflict between radical and conservative forces, a stalemate may emerge during which conservatives come to perceive the price of restoring the status quo ante to exceed the price of living with the current turmoil. If this lasts long enough, they may then come to perceive the price of living with turmoil as exceeding the price of forging a historic compromise that exits from the stalemate in a democratizing direction. The importance of the quality of leadership, and of leadership strategies, at such moments may be crucial.

It is sometimes argued that democratization in Western Europe took generations, if not centuries, and that we therefore cannot expect the process of transition to work its way through in the USSR in the foreseeable future (e.g. in the next twenty years). A defensible response to this challenge, however, would be that the idea of democracy is so widespread in the world today, the legitimacy of democracy and markets as effective means of political and economic coordination is also so widespread, and the means of communicating the workings of democratic procedures, market-oriented institutions, and the like so fully developed, that countries seeking to democratize and marketize in the late-twentieth century have an advantage over the early democratizers. "Late democratization" benefits from the international communications revolution and the high levels of global interdependence extant in the world today. Just as late-industrializers temporally telescoped processes of industrialization that had taken much longer among the early-industrializers, so late-democratizers are likely to telescope the process (witness Spain after Franco) and to rely on different mechanisms and strategies for effecting democratic and/or market outcomes.

None of this means that the Soviet Union will necessarily follow the path, or reach the same end-point, achieved by Western Europe or post-Franco Spain. But it does lend perspective to the tortured process through which that country is currently going, and alert us to the probability of some unexpected, and apparently paradoxical, outcomes.

The literature on transformative leadership also provides insights that are pertinent to an inquiry into whether Gorbachev's reforms can succeed. How do we recognize "progress" toward the goal of radical change? In a context of ethnic turmoil and sharp elite conflict, are we to say that appropriate progress is being made? Perhaps so, for both economists discussing marketization and political scientists studying democratic transitions emphasize the positive functions performed by disruption and conflict. If the qualities and strategies of leadership are crucial intervening variables, how then are we to judge whether Gorbachev is exercising high quality leadership? Levine's chapter provides advice to Gorbachev on what needs to be done in the economic area. Not much work has been done on how Gorbachev ought to deal with leadership politics to justify and push radicalization. But it does seem that Gorbachev has been following a populist strategy of encouraging the activation of social forces, both as an end in itself and as a way of raising the price of rolling back perestroika. From the standpoint of DiPalma's theory of stalemate, this is a rational strategy.

We run the danger of evaluating the utility of current policies and programs only in terms of their short-run consequences for the performance of the economy or the democratic accountability of officials. How many times have we heard it said, for example, that the joint ventures law is inadequate, or that cooperatives are relatively few in number, are hemmed in by licensing and supply restraints, and are victims of widespread envy? These observations are quite correct, but they miss a key point. Transformative leadership is not only a matter of attaining tangible short-term results. Progress proceeds in stages. The first stage requires delegitimation of past patterns of political and economic coordination, and legitimation of a substitute pattern. Transformative leadership during this stage is not simply a matter of organizational design; it is more importantly a *process* of transforming *biases.* In that light, it is more important that Gorbachev first concentrate on legitimizing iconoclastic new ideas, such as foreign capitalists owning equity in Soviet firms, or public politics, or multiple-candidate, secret-ballot elections, or a mixed economy. He (or his successors) can worry later about making the amendments required to ensure effective performance of the new laws. Indeed, were a transformative leader to try to gain the optimal legislation from an organizational design standpoint simultaneously with the effort to legitimize the new idea, he would likely fail on both counts. When we consider how many sacred cows Gorbachev has delegitimized in just four and one-half years, and how many new practices he has been trying to legitimize, the "results" of his leadership, especially in the political realm but also in the economic, are breathtaking. But, as Levine points out, what he needs in the economic realm is a positive ideology of perestroika, not just a critique of the old system, to build the requisite support for a new system.

Nor should we be misled by manifestations of political conflict within the establishment over the desirability and feasibility of reformist policies. Of course, conflict is the agency through which anti-reformist policies would be enacted. But we should also bear in mind that some types of conflict may prove functional to the cause of reform. Conflict is a necessary ally of the transformative leader. He needs to invite challenges and dissent in order to clarify to all audiences the choices and the stakes.[32] This has the effect of raising the consciousness of audiences, of involving people psychologically in a process of choice. From this standpoint, the most important consequences of the 19th Party Conference (1988) and the Congress of People's Deputies (1989) were not the shortcomings in their delivery to Gorbachev of purge mechanisms. The main, and perhaps most important, consequence was political-psychological: it was a national catharsis to see leaders on television debating critical choices. This is the kind of transformative leadership that "excites the previously bored and apathetic," and encourages them to take up the opportunities for empowerment they are being offered.[33]

Nor should we be misled by simple counts of the number of officials whose orientation is for or against perestroika. Again, this may portend the coalescence of an oppositional force. But it is also the case that transformative leadership does not require a majority of officials to be active fighters for transformation. Rather, it requires a *critical mass* of dedicated followers placed in strategic positions in key organizations.[34] Their presence has the effect of neutralizing people whose orientations are antithetical, but whose sense of political survival dictates bandwagoning rather than oppositional behavior.

The chapters that follow in this volume provide insight into some of the kinds of problems Gorbachev faces and some of the forces on which he can draw for support as he tackles the daunting task of reforming the Soviet political and economic systems. A major task facing political scientists and economists alike is to specify the content of those leadership strategies that might be appropriate to radically reforming a Leninist system. It is not simply a choice between bringing "the state" back into our analyses or, alternatively, bringing "society" back in. A complex new pattern of interaction is taking place between a highly differentiated state and a highly differentiated society. Under those conditions, the decisive factor may be the quality of leadership (perhaps at the societal level as well). The burden of this introductory chapter has been to specify the nature of the problem, some of the forces working for and against marketization, and the ways in which our images of key empirical realities, as well as our theoretical perspectives, tend to predetermine our answer to the question: can Gorbachev's reforms succeed?

NOTES

1. George Feiffer, "The New God Will Fail: Moscow: Skeptical Voices on Perestroika," *Harpers*, Vol. 277, No. 1661 (October 1988), pp. 43-9.
2. See John Bushnell, "The 'New Soviet Man' Turns Pessimist," in *The Soviet Union Since Stalin*, ed. Stephen Cohen, Alexander Rabinowitch, and Robert Sharlet (Bloomington: Indiana University Press, 1980).
3. See Alexander Yanov, *The Russian Challenge and the Year 2000* (Oxford and New York: Basil Blackwell, 1987).
4. Arend Lijphard, *Democracy in Plural Societies: A Comparative Exploration* (New Haven: Yale University Press, 1977).
5. See also Jerry Hough, *Russia and the West: Gorbachev and the Politics of Reform* (New York: Simon and Schuster, 1988); Martin Walker, *The Waking Giant: Gorbachev's Russia* (New York: Pantheon, 1986); Peter Hauslohner, "Gorbachev's Social Contract," *Soviet Economy*, Vol. 3 (January-March, 1987); Gail Lapidus, *State and Society in the Soviet Union* (Boulder, CO: Westview, 1989); Moshe Lewin, *The Gorbachev Phenomenon* (Berkeley: The University of California Press, 1988); and S. Frederick Starr, "Soviet Union: A Civil Society," *Foreign Policy*, No. 70 (Spring 1988) and "The Road to Reforms" (typescript, 1989).
6. Starr, "Soviet Union: A Civil Society" and "The Road to Reforms."
7. Paul Gregory, "Productivity, Slack and Time Theft in the Soviet Economy," in *Politics, Work, and Daily Life in the USSR: A Survey of Former Soviet Citizens*, ed. James Millar (New York: Cambridge University Press, 1988).
8. See Zbigniew Brzezinski, *The Grand Failure: The Birth and Death of Communism in the Twentieth Century* (New York: Charles Scribner's Sons, 1989).
9. See Zbigniew Brzezinski, "The Soviet System: Transformation or Degeneration," *Problems of Communism* (January-February, 1966); Richard Lowenthal, "The Ruling Party in a Mature Society," in *Social Consequences of Modernization in Communist Societies*, ed. Mark Field (Baltimore: Johns Hopkins University Press, 1976); and Kenneth Jowitt, "Soviet Neo-Traditionalism: The Political Corruption of a Leninist Regime," *Soviet Studies* (July, 1983).
10. Jowitt, "Soviet Neo-Traditionalism."
11. See Victor Zaslavsky, *The Neo-Stalinist State* (Armonk, NY: M.E. Sharpe, Inc., 1982); and Andrew Walder, *Communist Neo-Traditionalism* (Berkeley: University of California Press, 1986).
12. See Yanov, *The Russian Challenge*.
13. See Hough, *Russia and the West*; George Breslauer, "From Brezhnev to Gorbachev: Ends and Means of Soviet Leadership Selection," in *Leadership Change in Communist States*, ed. Raymond Taras (London: Unwin Hyman, 1989); Gavin Helf, "Gorbachev and the New Soviet Prefects: Soviet Regional Politics 1982-1988 in Historical Perspective," in *Analyzing the Gorbachev Era* (Berkeley: Berkeley-Stanford Program in Soviet Studies/Center for Slavic and East European Studies, 1989).

14. Stephen Cohen, *Rethinking the Soviet Experience* (New York: Oxford University Press, 1985).

15. Hough, *Russia and the West,* and *Opening up the Soviet Economy* (Washington D.C.: The Brookings Institution, 1988).

16. See Jowitt, "Soviet Neo-Traditionalism"; Timothy Garton Ash, "The Empire in Decay," *The New York Review of Books* (September 29, 1988).

17. See Lapidus, *State and Society,* and Starr, "The Road to Reforms."

18. T. I. Zaslavskaya, "Ekonomika skvoz' prizmu sotsiologii," *Ekonomika i organizatsiia promyshlennogo proizvodstva,* Vol. 7, No. 3 (1985), pp. 3-22.

19. See Paul Kennedy, *The Rise and Fall of the Great Powers* (New York: Random House, 1987).

20. See Starr, "The Russian Way of Reform."

21. For elaboration see Breslauer, "From Brezhnev to Gorbachev"; see also Holloway's chapter in this volume.

22. Hough, *Opening up the Soviet Economy.*

23. Kenneth Jowitt, *The Leninist Approach to National Dependency* (Berkeley: Institute of International Studies, 1978).

24. Yanov, *The Russian Challenge.*

25. For a brilliant analysis of the economic contradictions of transition, see Ellen Comisso, "Market Failures and Market Socialism: Economic Problems of the Transition," *Eastern European Politics and Societies,* Vol. 2, No. 3 (1989).

26. Gregory Grossman, personal communication.

27. See Albert Hirschman, *A Bias for Hope: Essays on Development and Latin America* (New Haven: Yale University Press, 1971).

28. See Gertrude E. Schroeder, "The Soviet Economy on a Treadmill of 'Reforms'," in *Soviet Economy in a Time of Change,* U.S. Congress, Joint Economic Committee, Vol. 1 (Washington, D.C.: U.S. Government Printing Office, 1979).

29. See Dankwart Rustow, "Transitions to Democracy: Toward a Dynamic Model," *Comparative Politics,* Vol. 2, No. 3 (April, 1970).

30. Peter Hauslohner, "Democratization 'From the Middle Out': Soviet Trade Unions and Perestroika," *The Harriman Institute Forum,* Vol. 1, No. 10 (October, 1988)

31. Giuseppe DiPalma (forthcoming), *To Craft Democracies: Reflections on Democratic Transitions and Beyond.*

32. James MacGregor Burns, *Leadership* (New York: Harper and Row, 1980); Noel M. Tichy and Mary Anne Devanna, *The Transformational Leader* (New York: John Wiley & Sons, 1986); Aaron Wildavsky, *The Nursing Father: Moses as a Political Leader* (University, AL: University of Alabama Press, 1987).

33. Burns, *Leadership.*

34. Burns, *Leadership*; Alvin Gouldner, *Patterns of Industrial Bureaucracy* (New York: The Free Press, 1954); Tichy and Devanna, *The Transformational Leader.*

CONVERSATION

MR. MAC NEIL: Finally tonight a conversation with George Kennan. Often called the foremost scholar and analyst of U.S.-Soviet relations, Mr. Kennan first articulated the American policy of containment to respond to Soviet expansionism after World War II. Mr. Kennan capped a long career in the foreign service with ambassadorial appointments to the Soviet Union and Yugoslavia. He has devoted years since to improving U.S. scholarship of Russian studies. His own contribution to that scholarship includes 18 books, among them 2 Pulitzer Prize winners. I talked with him this afternoon and asked him to reflect as a student of Russian history on the significance of this moment.

MR. KENNAN: I think it's of tremendous significance. I don't mean to underestimate the difficulties that Russia is going to have in the immediate future, but I do think that this is a turning point of the most momentous historical significance. I find it difficult to find any other turning point of modern Russian history that I think is so significant as this one.

MR. MAC NEIL: Why? I mean there have been plenty of turning points.

MR. KENNAN: Plenty of turning points, but by what happened on those streets of Moscow and Leningrad in these last three or four days the Russian people for the first time in their history have turned their back on the manner in which they've been ruled not just in the Soviet period but in centuries before. They have demanded a voice in the designing of their own society, their own future, and they have done so successfully. And I can't think of any precedent for this in Russian history, even 1917 had nothing quite like this. It's the most hopeful turning point that I've ever seen in Russian affairs and I think it's a very basic one. I think the fact that from now on Russia is going to be in its political composition, its political habits, its political way it's run, it is going to be a different Russia than it's ever been before.

MR. MAC NEIL: How do you ▓▓▓▓▓▓▓▓▓▓, how this could happen in this way?

MR. KENNAN: Yes. Part of it, of course, is the communications revolution. Part of it is the fact that you now have a far higher proportion of the people of Russia who are educated people, who do read, who do listen to what comes out over the media, but part of it also is the revulsion after the seven decades of mistreatment that they have had at the hands of a Communist regime and I think you see they did realize in 1917 that the czar's government was not a very good government anymore, that the czar was not an impressive person, in fact, that he was a rather foolish man, and they lost their confidence in that sort of a government. Many of them naively thought this one would be a better one, a Communist one, but there was never a greater disillusionment of any people than that. And I think again as I say that it is partly the revulsion of what they've just been through that gave them the courage and the determination not to accept it anymore.

6

356

MR. MAC NEIL: Many people have worried that after centuries of repressive or paternalistic government that the habits, the psychological habits would be so strong that when things became messy and uncertain as they have been with this perestroika that the temptation to go back to something secure and strong just for stability would be irresistible. Why do you think that hasn't happened?

MR. KENNAN: Well, I've worried about --

MR. MAC NEIL: Excuse me interrupting, but plenty of Soviet people have been telling reporters that on the street, well, we'd rather go back to the strong stuff than put up with this chaos.

MR. KENNAN: That was a little bit -- it could delude you, hearing these things from them, because every time there has come a showdown, at least in the great cities, they have come out in favor of an attempt to have a democratic development. I am not sure how all this proceeds out in the countryside. I think there is much less understanding in large parts of the countryside far from the great cities for what democracy has to offer than there is in Moscow or Leningrad. On the other hand, these places are the center of the political vitality of the country and there's no doubt about it now, that there's no doubt about the way that public opinion, Russian opinion, inclines. There's been test after test of it, but none ever as complete as this and none where the answer was ever made as dramatically evident as it has been in these last days.

MR. MAC NEIL: So do you think that six years of experimenting with glasnost, freedom, has really changed the political psychology of the Soviet people?

MR. KENNAN: Yes. I think it has. And I think we do owe this in very large measure to Gorbachev and that should not be forgotten. He has had his faults, his weaknesses, his blind spots too, but this is his -- has been his great service to Russia. This is partly the result of it. He was the one, after all, who made all this possible by making glasnost possible, by permitting the press to speak again, by permitting people to speak, all this by throwing open the contacts with the outside world. That all is part of the background of what has now happened.

MR. MAC NEIL: It's really ironic in a way, isn't it, that -- I mean, as he admitted in his press conference today was in some ways the author of his own -- of this misfortune by putting so much trust in so many hardliners close to him, and yet, in another way the author of his salvation by having created or permitted some of the freedoms -- freedom of expression -- that saved him.

MR. KENNAN: That's quite true. And I'm sure that he will hear many accusations that he has a measure of responsibility for these events that happened because of his indulgence of these people. After all, he did appoint several of them and the most important ones to the positions they occupied. But one can be too tough on him here. He was well aware that the party and the police still had great power in large parts of the country, perhaps not as I say in the big cities, but way out in the provincial areas, and I think he wanted, if he could, to keep them aboard and not to push them off into a position where this short of thing would occur. He may have gone too far in acting with them, in giving them positions, in talking with them, and he may suffer for it now, but I think we have to realize that it was not easy for him and also because he still clung for a long time to his belief that the party could be made a suitable instrument of change.

MR. MAC NEIL: I don't know whether you heard that part of the press conference, but he reiterated that today, that he would stay in the party and that he thought that those -- that those forces that were in favor of democratic reform could be encouraged and that the party it sought could be reformed and made an instrument of change.

MR. KENNAN: Robin, here too I would not like to be too hard on him. Loyalty is the only absolute human virtue which is always respected. It's better to be loyal in a way to your shabbiest friends than the opposite. And I know that he parts with great difficulty from his belief in the party. It

7

357

was in the party that he grew up. It was there that he got his position, and in a way I respect him for his fidelity to it. But I think he's wrong.

MR. MAC NEIL: But could he miss? If this is the historic turning point you've said, could he miss that turning point and be left behind because of that loyalty?

MR. KENNAN: Yes. Partly because of that. Mind you, I think that his contribution to the development of Russia was largely exhausted before these recent events occurred. He had -- what I mean by that is that he had done pretty much, what was his historic mission, which was to break the hold of the party over all of Russian life and to throw open freedom of speech, and the other things that he did open up. That was an historic contribution and I'm sure that he will be given credit and good perspective of history for what he's done, but he did, as I say, have one of these blind spots. One of them was his belief that the party could be an adequate means of change and another was of course his hope and belief that the -- the country could be kept together, that the empire could be kept together, that the other republicans -- republics could be held in, I think that too was a failure of insight and judgment on his part. The day for that has passed. The day for the great empires is gone. The day in particular for the unilateral -- the unilingual and the uninational empires is gone. But that I mean the ones that embrace a number of nations and a number of languages. The others have gone, the old Turkish empire, the old Austria-Hungarian empire, the British empire; they have all yielded to the forces of modern nationalism and the -- it was clear that the Russian-Soviet empire was going to have to yield to these forces too eventually.

MR. MAC NEIL: Do you think what happened in the last few days accelerates that?

MR. KENNAN: Yes, I do indeed. I do, indeed, I think is going to affect his position because he had hitched his wagon to the star of the central authority in the Soviet Union. Now what has happened in these last few days is going to increase the authority of the individual republics. And by that same token, it is bound to decrease the importance and the scope of power of the central, of central governmental apparatus. And to the extent that that is diminished, so will be diminished his role in Russian affairs, his influence.

MR. MAC NEIL: Some of the new republics, including Boris Yeltsin's Russian Federation, have talked about having their own armies, their own security forces. Since the United States was so anxious to see the Soviet Union stay together so that it would have one military super power to deal with, does this disintegration or de-centralization you're predicting pose security problems for the West? I mean, you have that massive number of nuclear weapons and everything.

MR. KENNAN: So far as the nuclear weapons are concerned, this union treaty which was to have been thrown open for signature by the republics three or four days ago and that incidentally is probably the crucial fact that caused the timing of this effort to overthrow the regime, this union treaty did, it seemed to me, in its provisions take care of the danger that -- of nuclear weapons getting into the wrong hands. As far as that is concerned, I think we can be relieved, and otherwise, I think that we should recognize the inevitability of the decentralization of this state and not put ourselves in opposition to it.

MR. MAC NEIL: You said a moment ago that loyalty is prized often above everything in politicians. But so also in successful politicians is a degree of opportunism. Is Mr. Gorbachev nimble enough and adroit enough and opportunistic enough to seize this moment and revitalize his leadership, or is he really on the wave of the past do you think?

MR. KENNAN: In my opinion he will not be able to do that. I can't really go into all the reasons why not. They're partly ones of personality, partly ones of what has happened. But everyone, as you know, in public life has his hour and his period. You can't expect to have really many more than one. And I think Gorbachev for whom I have high respect, I think that he, as I say, has pretty well exhausted what he had to give to the Russian situation. We're going on now to another generation, to another group of problems. And I doubt that he can expect to exercise a kind of leadership with

8

relation to them that he has exercised in recent years.

MR. MAC NEIL: Where does Mr. Yeltsin fit into that picture?

MR. KENNAN: He comes out, of course, as "the" great personality of the hour in Russia and in the Soviet Union. He too is a man for whom I have respect. He has qualities quite different from those of, of Gorbachev. Gorbachev was not good really with the contact with the people. Yeltsin, just the opposite, and he has, of course, increased his stature in the public eye enormously by his behavior in recent days. He's shown himself to be a courageous and strong man in a difficult situation. And they all appreciate that. But more important than that too is the fact that he was popularly elected and those who elected him are all aware of that and they are reluctant to be deprived of the choice they made when they came to that decision.

MR. MAC NEIL: Finally, as the man often credited with being the author of the policy that the West adopted which succeeded in the containment policy, brought the Soviet Union to change, internal change, what do you think the posture of the United States should be now towards the new realities in the Soviet Union?

MR. KENNAN: I think that it should be the posture that John Quincy Adams outlined in a Fourth of July speech in Washington a great many years ago when he said that America is the guardian of the liberties of all the world -- or she is, no, she is the friend of the liberties of all the world, she is the guardian only of her own. I think we have to give all the encouragement we can to the Russians in this situation, but in doing so, we cannot regard it as one great undivided country. We have to take account of the decentralization which is in progress and we have to address our efforts, our help, our attention partly to the individual republics whose needs vary, vary greatly among them, and not all to the central government.

MR. MAC NEIL: Well, Professor Kennan, thank you very much for joining us.

MR. KENNAN: Thank you.

ACKNOWLEDGMENTS

Moshe Lewin. "From Village to Megacity," in his *The Gorbachev Phenomenon* (Univ. of California Press, 1988), pp. 43–71. Reprinted with the permission of the Regents of the University of California and the University of California Press. Copyright 1988 by The Regents of the University of California. Courtesy of Yale University Sterling Memorial Library.

Seweryn Bialer. "Domestic and International Factors in the Formation of Gorbachev's Reforms," *Journal of International Affairs* 42:2 (Spring, 1989), 283–297. Published by permission of the *Journal of International Affairs* and the Trustees of Columbia University in the City of New York. Courtesy of Yale University Sterling Memorial Library.

Thane Gustafson. "The Crisis of the Soviet System of Power and Mikhail Gorbachev's Political Strategy," in Seweryn Bialer and Michael Mandelbaum, eds., *Gorbachev's Russia and American Foreign Policy* (Westview Press, 1988), 187–229. Reprinted with the permission of Westview Press, Inc. Courtesy of Yale University Cross Campus Library.

Thomas Remington. "A Socialist Pluralism of Opinions: *Glasnost* and Policy-Making Under Gorbachev," *Russian Review* 48:3 (July, 1989), 271–304. Reprinted with the permission of the Ohio State University Press. Courtesy of Yale University Sterling Memorial Library.

Archie Brown. "Political Change in the Soviet Union," *World Policy Journal* 6:3 (Summer, 1989), 469–501. Reprinted with the permission of the *World Policy Journal*. Courtesy of the *World Policy Journal*.

David Remnick. "The Pioneers of Perestroika," *The Washington Post*, National Weekly edition, March 19–25, 1990, 8–9. Reprinted with the permission of the Washington Post Company. Courtesy of the editor.

S. Frederick Starr. "Soviet Union: A Civil Society," *Foreign Policy* 70 (Spring, 1988), 26–41. Reprinted with the permission of the Carnegie Endowment for International Peace. Courtesy of *Foreign Policy*.

Gail W. Lapidus. "State and Society: Towards the Emergence of Civil Society in the Soviet Union," in Seweryn Bialer, ed., *Politics, Society, and Nationality Inside Gorbachev's Russia* (Westview Press, 1989), 121–147. Reprinted with the permission of Westview Press, Inc. Courtesy of Yale University Cross Campus Library.

Victoria E. Bonnell. "Moscow: A View From Below," *Dissent* (Summer, 1989), 311–317. Reprinted with the permission of the Foundation for the Study of Independent Social Ideas, Inc. Courtesy of Yale University Social Science Library.

Vladimir Brovkin. "Revolution from Below: Informal Political Associations in Russia 1988–1989," *Soviet Studies*, (April, 1990), pp. 233–257. Reprinted with the permission of the University of Glasgow. Courtesy of Yale University Sterling Memorial Library.

Yitzhak M. Brudny. "The Heralds of Opposition to *Perestroyka*," *Soviet Economy*, Vol. 5, no. 2 (Spring, 1990), pp. 162–200. Reprinted with the permission of V. H. Winston & Son, Inc. Courtesy of Yale University Social Science Library.

Alexander Dallin. "Soviet History," in Dallin and Bertrand M. Patenaude, eds., *Soviet Scholarship under Gorbachev* (Stanford: Stanford University Press, 1988), 5–13, 20–25. Reprinted with the permission of the Stanford University Press. Courtesy of *Soviet Scholarship under Gorbachev*.

Abraham Brumberg. "Russia After Perestroika," *New York Review of Books* (June 27, 1991), pp. 53–62. Reprinted with the permission of The New York Review of Books. Courtesy of Yale University Sterling Memorial Library Periodicals.

George W. Breslauer. "Thinking about the Soviet Future," in Breslauer, ed., *Can Gorbachev's Reforms Succeed?*" (Berkeley: Center for Slavic and East European Studies, 1990) 1–34. Reprinted with the permission of the Regents of the University of California and the University of California Press. Copyright 1990. Courtesy of the editor.

Robert MacNeil. "Interview with George F. Kennan, Soviet Affairs Scholar," *MacNeil/Lehrer Newshour Show #4144* [transcript] (Thursday, August 22, 1991), pp. 6–9. Reprinted with the permission of MacNeil-Lehrer Productions. Courtesy of MacNeil-Lehrer Productions.